RY  s
d
A l e
racing rules 2009-2012

By Trevor Lewis

Illustrator: Pete Galvin

© Trevor Lewis 2010

First Published RYA 2010

The Royal Yachting Association

RYA House, Ensign Way, Hamble
Southampton SO31 4YA

Tel: 0845 345 0400

Fax: 0845 345 0329

Email: publications@rya.org.uk

Web: www.rya.org.uk

ISBN: 978-1-906-435-189

RYA Order Code: G80

Totally Chlorine Free **Sustainable Forests**

A CIP record of this book is available from the British Library

Note: While all reasonable care has been taken in the preparation of this book, the publisher takes no responsibility for the use of the methods or products or contracts described in the book.

Telephone 0845 345 0400 for a free copy of our Publications Catalogue.

Cover Design: Design House
Typeset: Creativebyte
Illustrator: Pete Galvin
Indexing: Alan Thatcher
Printed in China through World Print
Photo Credits: Pam Lewis, Rick Tomlinson, Richard Langdon/Ocean Images.

Trevor Lewis became deeply interested in the racing rules as a result of losing too many protests when he first took up sailing. Mary Pera asked him to join her RYA Racing Rules Committee, the body that hears appeals, originates submissions for rule changes, and seeks to improve the understanding of the racing rules. He became Vice-Chairman to Mary and, on her death, to John Doerr, whom he then succeeded as its current Chairman.

He was an RYA National Judge from the inception of the scheme, and, while chairing the RYA's Judging and Umpiring Group, he initiated the RYA's examination-based system for National Judge apppointments, for which he regularly helps to run courses for would-be Regional and National Judges.

As an ISAF International Judge, he is regularly involved with protests and requests for redress, from local club racing to International Juries for major events like the Vendée Globe and La Solitaire du Figaro.

Trevor is currently a member of several ISAF bodies, including its Case Book Working Party and the ISAF Q&A Panel, and has been involved with the RYA Case Book from its inception.

He lives near Norwich in the East of England, where he also currently a local District Councillor. Over the years, sailing interests have replaced his nominal 'day job' of financial adviser. The resulting irregular lifestyle is possible only with the uncomplaining support of Pam, without whose encouragement this book would not have seen the light of day.

Contents

Foreword

This book is for competitors, race officials, aspiring race officials and anyone who wishes to increase their racing rules knowledge.

To race in compliance with the rules of race sailing and successfully a competitor needs a good grasp of only about a quarter of the racing rules of sailing. These rules are followed by fourteen appendices occupying more than double the number of pages taken by the rules themselves. Many rules and appendices address themselves to the army of the sport's officials. These are organizing authorities, race committees, measurers and equipment inspectors, race officers, mark teams and scorers, judges and protest committee members. At club level, the officials are usually competitors as well. Outside of local racing, the officials tend to specialise, and must gain recognised national and international qualifications. Competitors on the other hand let their results do the talking.

This book pays homage to the late Mary Pera's much-missed book, in offering a commentary to the rules in their numerical order, that commentary being substantially based on international cases. Those cases are however limited in explaining the basic vocabulary of the sport, especially its defined terms, and I offer my own interpretations of many of those building blocks. I also rely heavily on the non-authoritative but illustrative national cases of several countries.

I write as one having had a heavy involvement in the case books of both the International Sailing Federation (ISAF) and the Royal Yachting Association (RYA). That is not to say that I find them the best way to understand the rules. The hundreds of appeal cases that explain a few-dozen rules are better suited to study on long winter evenings than to a quick fix in the heat of competition. Indeed, why rely on cases as the primary source of interpretation? What many competitors and officials would prefer is an authoritative interpretation of a rule that is as accessible as the rule itself. Certainty is more important than academic debate. Team racing and match racing calls were introduced to fill this vacuum for those parts of the sport, and this book draws on those calls where they are helpful in fleet racing. The book does not discuss rule 42, Propulsion, in any depth, simply because ISAF issues detailed interpretations of that rule. Judges and umpires can and do argue over those calls and interpretations, against a background that the official documents are right even if they are wrong. I believe that an opportunity to extend this way of explaining the rules was missed when, for this rules cycle, the rules at marks and obstructions were substantially revised without any well-publicised official guidance or commentary.

Another weakness of the cases is that they are driven by supply rather than by demand. National authorities publish selected cases when they arise from appeals, references and questions, and seek to have some of them adopted as authoritative international cases. Only exceptionally will a national authority actively request a club or class to ask a question whose answer can then be published, and only exceptionally will ISAF create a case that does not arise from a submission from a national authority.

Having promoted the cause of certainty, I am conscious that I militate against it when debating the meaning of many rules. When I offer what can only be just an opinion, I may well be wrong, or at least some future case may take a different view. The fact is that the published cases themselves are sometimes realised to be less than fully correct in some way. Usually, this can be corrected by editing, but no new rules cycle has yet removed the need for ISAF and national authorities to reflect on the existing wording of cases that address unchanged rules.

For the moment, therefore, there is a strong parallel between national law and the racing rules. Protest and redress imitate legal processes: the resulting cases, both legal and sailing, seek to explain the laws; and then books seek to explain the cases, and to fill in the gaps between them.

If this book is necessary, it is arguably a pity. I hope at least that it is useful. Despite its title, its contents are not necessarily the views of the RYA or of its many other rules experts. Where is it obscure, opinionated or just plain wrong, the fault is mine. Brickbats or bouquets to rules@tlfs.org.uk

Trevor Lewis

Dick Rose writes...

Racing sailboats is distinctly different from most of the sports we played at school in that almost never are there umpires or referees out on our field of play enforcing the rules. Instead, everyone who races a boat has important obligations –

- To learn the rules.
- To comply with the rules.
- To enforce the rules.

When a dispute arises that is not settled on the water by one boat accepting a penalty, we are expected to protest and argue our case under the rules in the resulting protest hearing.

There are a variety of books available to help learn the rules. Some are very basic – just short booklets with diagrams illustrating the most common situations in which boats meet and showing which boat has right of way and which boat must keep clear. Others are more advanced and thorough – covering each Part 2 rule and some other rules with discussion of several situations in which it applies. These books include references to the ISAF Cases and to a particular national authority's appeals. However, to the best of my knowledge, all such books on the market today were printed **before** the ISAF Cases and the national authority appeals were updated to conform to the 2009-2012 edition of the rules.

RYA Racing Rules Explained 2009-2012 by Trevor Lewis is distinctly different from other books on the racing rules. It fills a void that has existed since 2001 when Mary Pera passed away and an up-to-date version her much admired book, *The Yacht Racing Rules, a complete guide*, was no longer available. Trevor's book is now the only book available that has the following useful features:

- It covers each racing rule, from rule 1 through to the last numbered rule, rule 91.
- It includes very thorough coverage of the rule interpretations made in the ISAF Cases, the appeals published by three national authorities – the Royal Yachting Association, US SAILING and the Canadian Yachting Association, and even some of the ISAF Match Racing and Team Racing Calls.
- Its references to cases, appeals and calls are all to the 2009-2012 versions of those interpretations, rather than the 2005-2008 versions.

A serious competitor or judge who wants to be thoroughly prepared for a hearing, whether for a protest, a request for redress or a rule 69 hearing, will be well served by this book.

Many of us who work on the arcane task of writing the racing rules for sailing refer to a person with a deep understanding and interest in the rules as a 'rulie.' I have had the pleasure of working with Trevor for several years. We both are members of the ISAF Case Book Working Party and we have also served on other special working parties tasked with improving particular parts of the rulebook. Trevor stands out among 'rulies' as one who has a special talent for applying the rules when a situation crops up that the rest of the 'rulie' community has never seen before. He thinks outside the box, often producing unique new ways of explaining how a rule works. And he's not shy – he defends his positions with vigour and humour, rather like a bulldog tugging on a favourite toy while wagging his tail.

I am confident that each of you who read this book, no matter how well you knew the racing rules before you began, will gain new and deeper insights into the workings of the rules.

Dick Rose is a member of ISAF Racing Rules Committee, and the Chairman of both the ISAF Racing Rules Working Party and the ISAF Case Book Working Party. Within US Sailing, Dick is a member and the Secretary of its Racing Rules Committee (having been its Chairman for 12 years), Chairman of its Race Administration Committee and a US Sailing Senior Judge.

Introduction

The Racing Rules of Sailing includes two main sections. The first, Parts 1–7, contains rules that affect all competitors. The second, Appendices A–P, provides details of rules, rules that apply to particular kinds of racing, and rules that affect only a small number of competitors or officials.

Revision The racing rules are revised and published every four years by the International Sailing Federation (ISAF), the inter-national authority for the sport. This edition becomes effective on 1 January 2009 except that for an event beginning in 2008 the date may be postponed by the notice of race and sailing instructions.

Marginal markings indicate important changes to Parts 1–7 and the Definitions of the 2005–2008 edition. No changes are contemplated before 2013, but any changes determined to be urgent before then will be announced through national authorities and posted on the ISAF website (www.sailing.org).

ISAF Codes The ISAF Eligibility, Advertising, Anti-Doping and Sailor Classification Codes (Regulations 19, 20, 21 and 22) are referred to in the definition *Rule* but are not included in this book because they can be changed at any time. The most recent versions of the codes are available on the ISAF website; new versions will be announced through national authorities.

Cases and Calls The ISAF publishes interpretations of the racing rules in *The Case Book for 2009–2012* and recognizes them as authoritative interpretations and explanations of the rules. It also publishes *The Call Book for Match Racing for 2009–2012* and *The Call Book for Team Racing for 2009–2012*, and it recognizes them as authoritative only for umpired match or team racing. These publications are available on the ISAF website.

Terminology A term used in the sense stated in the Definitions is printed in italics or, in preambles, in bold italics (for example, *racing* and ***racing***). 'Racing rule' means a rule in *The Racing Rules of Sailing*. 'Boat' means a sailboat and the crew on board. 'Race committee' includes any person or committee performing a race committee function. A 'change' to a *rule* includes an addition to it or deletion of all or part of it. 'National authority' means an ISAF member national authority. Other words and terms are used in the sense ordinarily understood in nautical or general use.

Appendices When the rules of an appendix apply, they take precedence over any conflicting rules in Parts 1–7 and the Definitions. Each appendix is identified by a letter. A reference to a rule in an appendix will contain the letter and the rule number (for example, 'rule A1'). There is no Appendix I or O.

Changes to the Rules The prescriptions of a national authority, class rules or the sailing instructions may change a racing rule only as permitted in rule 86.

Changes to National Authority Prescriptions A national authority may restrict changes to its prescriptions as provided in rule 88.2.

This book examines Parts 1 – 7 of the Racing Rules of Sailing 2009-2012 in their numerical order. There have indeed been urgent changes with effect from 1st January 2010, and those relevant to this book are included and discussed. The definitions are both set out as soon as they become relevant to a rule, and also are printed in their totality. Appendix M, Recommendations for Protest Committees, is discussed in the context of rules to which the appendix refers. Appendix A, Scoring is printed in full. Appendices F, G, J, K, L, N and P, which affect many competitors and race officials, are commented on in passing but not reprinted.

Boats are often identified in the text and the diagrams as *Iris*, *Daffodil*, etc, and such names sometimes replace the actual boat names or designations (usually a plain A or B) in the text of cases that are quoted. The official diagrams of cases have been redrawn for stylistic consistency, and perhaps greater clarity: if in the process they are inadvertently materially different from the originals, it is of course the original diagrams that are authortitative.

The rules and appendices will not change before 2013 unless there is an urgent need. Reference is also made to ISAF Codes, but, as the Introduction to the Racing Rules of Sailing states, these are more likely to change during the currency of the rule cycle.

The primary source of rule interpretation is The ISAF Case Book, whose interpretations and explanations are authoritative for all racing[1]. The ISAF cases are not themselves rules, but, when the facts from a protest are essentially similar to the facts of an ISAF case, the interpretations in that case should be accepted by the protest committee as correct interpretations of the racing rules for that protest[2]. The ISAF Case Book is available on the ISAF website. The ISAF cases are re-edited at the start of the new rules cycle. This book refers to the latest ISAF case book, as published in February 2009. Care should be taken when consulting books published for the latest rules but before the revised case book was released.

Secondary sources are:
- The ISAF Call Books for Match Racing and Team Racing: these are authoritative only for those parts of the sport[3], but are nevertheless clear guides to many of the rules in action, usually at close quarters.
- The case books of national authorities, whose protest committees are well advised to follow their leaders provided that a national case does not inadvertently conflict with an ISAF case. Most national authorities do not publish a case book (the leading authorities that do are the RYA, US Sailing and the Canadian Yachting Association, of which the RYA's are the most extensive, as reflected in this book). Judges are likely to be most aware of their own national cases, and a judge with that detailed knowledge can often find a case that is of assistance to an international jury of which he or she is a member, whether at home or abroad[4]. The case books of other countries are available on the websites of the national authorities concerned. National cases sometimes develop rule interpretation in areas where no suitable ISAF case exists[5], and occasionally the published cases of different authorities are incompatible with each other. When this is detected, it may result in a submission to ISAF of a case or of a rule change to clarify the matter. The national cases are also re-edited at the start of the new rules cycle. This book uses the 2009 texts of the RYA, US Sailing and CYA cases. Once again, care should be taken when consulting books published for the latest rules but before the revised national case books were released.
- The ISAF Racing Rules Question and Answer Panel, whose answers to questions from ISAF race officials and national authorities are published on the ISAF website. The 'Q and As' are poorly indexed. They are not authoritative, but are 'the carefully considered opinions of an experienced panel'[6]. There is a similar process for agreeing and publishing 'rapid response calls' for match and team racing.

The Racing Rules are addressed normally to a boat, which means a sailboat and the crew on board. It is a boat that breaks a rule, and it is the boat that is penalised. Only by exception is a boat's intention directly relevant to a racing rule[7], and only by exception do the intentions, acts and omissions of individual crew members or of an owner not on board have consequences: these will be considered when they arise.

There are limits to which rules can be changed, and strict procedures for doing so[8]. It is now clearer that a change to a rule includes additions, subtractions and deletions.

---

[1] ISAF Regulation 31.3
[2] US 99
[3] ISAF Regulation 31.3
[4] US 99, RYA 2002/13
[5] RYA cases on rule 28, for instance
[6] ISAF Regulations 31.3.6 and 31.3.8.
[7] A boat intending to race, for instance, in the preamble to Part 2. See also Rule 2, Fair Sailing
[8] See rules 86 and 87

Basic Principle

SPORTSMANSHIP AND THE RULES

Competitors in the sport of sailing are governed by a body of *rules* that they are expected to follow and enforce. A fundamental principle of sportsmanship is that when competitors break a *rule* they will promptly take a penalty, which may be to retire.

The Basic Principle is not a rule, as it is not listed in the definition Rule. No protest can be directly brought for breaking it, since a protest is defined as an allegation that a boat has broken a rule. However, the fundamental principle that a boat must take a penalty when a rule is broken creates a direct link to rule 2, Fair Sailing, which requires competition 'in compliance with recognised principles of sportsmanship and fair play', in default of which protests and penalisation are possible. For example, in ISAF 65, it was held that a boat that knows she has broken rule 30.3, Black Flag Rule, is obliged to retire promptly. When she does not do so, and then deliberately hinders another boat in the race, she commits a gross breach of sportsmanship and, therefore, of rule 2.

Sometimes, retirement is specified to be the only penalty a boat can take, since her breach caused injury or serious damage or gained her a significant advantage[1]. When a boat does retire in these circumstances, it may be that she did so not because of any intention to retire, but simply because damage to herself precluded continuing to race. In ISAF 99, there was contact between S and P that resulted in serious damage to both. Both boats retired, and, as is not uncommon, both were disqualified in the resulting protest. On appeal, S was exonerated, since only P was at fault, but P's disqualification was also reversed, since she had promptly retired, albeit involuntarily. When a boat retires as required by rule 44.1, whether out of choice or necessity, she cannot then be penalised further. So the results for both were corrected to DNF[2].

The obligation to take a penalty does not depend on whether another boat in the incident is protesting. In RYA 1990/8, as a result of an incident between two Lasers, a third boat, L, protested P, alleging that P crossed S, causing the latter to bear away vigorously to avoid a hull-to-hull collision. S's bow, she alleged, hit P's mainsheet. In the protest hearing, P's helmsman was specifically asked by the chairman of the protest committee if he had broken a rule, known that he had done so, and yet neither retired nor taken a penalty. His reply was a simple 'Yes'. The protest committee found that there had been no contact, but that S had had to bear away to avoid P. It disqualified P under rule 10. P appealed on the grounds that S, the alleged victim of the alleged infringement, had chosen not to protest. The RYA not only dismissed the appeal but also added a breach of rule 2 to P's crime-sheet, which upgraded the disqualification to one that could not be excluded from her series score.

> L lodged a valid protest. The facts found show that P broke rule 10 and she was correctly disqualified. There is no obligation on a right-of-way boat to protest when another boat has not kept clear. That she did not protest in no way diminishes the fact that the keep-clear boat has broken a rule. Likewise, the intentions of the right-of-way boat have no bearing on the matter…the Basic Principle, Sportsmanship and the Rules says that when a boat knows that she had broken a rule, she must take a penalty, whether or not the right-of-way boat intends to protest. The appellant therefore broke a principle of sportsmanship, and is to be penalised further for breaking rule 2.

Similarly, ISAF 31 says that if a boat knows she is OCS but is not recalled, and does not return, she breaks rule 2 as well as rule 28, and fails to comply with the Basic Principle,

Many competitors, and indeed many judges, may find it difficult to reconcile this hard line with the way the game is sometimes played today.

---

[1] See rule 44.1(b), Penalties at the Time of an Incident: Taking a Penalty
[2] Did Not Finish. See ISAF 107 for a further example

Retiring is not a defined term. When a boat retires after finishing, by advising the race committee, there is a specific scoring abbreviation of RAF[1]. Retiring during a race means ceasing to race, and not crossing the finishing line. This will be scored DNF, whether or not the reason for not finishing is known to the race committee. A protest committee can also deem a boat to have retired. Rule 23.1 says that a boat that is not racing shall not interfere with a boat that is racing. In RYA 1986/6, *Iris* missed out a mark in order to get to and manoeuvre against *Daffodil*, and was held to have broken that rule (and others), as by not sailing the course she had in effect retired, and so was no longer racing.

Is a decision to retire irrevocable? Not necessarily, according to RYA 2001/2. Boat A lodged a protest against boats B and C for sailing the wrong course. Boat B did not believe she had done so, but 'did the sportsmanlike thing' and retired. Boat C did not retire. Within protest time, boat A checked her facts with the race committee, and found that her protest was unjustified. She withdrew her protest against boat C. Was boat B then entitled to 'unretire'?

With the caveat that the rules were silent with regard to 'unretiring', the RYA replied pragmatically to the effect that, when a boat retires for having gained a significant advantage or causing serious damage in the act of touching a mark or breaking a rule of Part 2, that is irrevocable. The decision continued:

> When a boat retires for some other reason, as in this case, and has indicated her retirement either to the race committee or to another boat, she may reverse this decision before the end of protest time or declaration time, whichever is earlier, provided that she has not broken any other rule in the mean time. For instance, retiring during a race, using her engine, and then resuming racing would preclude 'unretirement'. However, if she has no good reason to 'unretire', she breaks rule 2, Fair Sailing, and the protest committee should, if necessary, extend the protest time limit for any boats that did not proceed with a protest against her because of her initial retirement[2].

Retirement is no bar to a boat being protested, nor will it prevent a protest committee awarding a non-excludable disqualification (DNE) when that is the appropriate penalty for the infringement, whether under rule 2, Fair Sailing[3], or when specified in the sailing instructions.

> When a boat realises that she has broken a rule, and when a turn(s) penalty or some other penalty is not available to her, the Basic Principle requires her to retire. Suppose that…the penalty for breaking [that] rule…is DNE. A boat that realises that she has broken such a rule cannot accept a DNE, and no other penalty is available to her, other than retiring. So retire she must.

> When a boat has retired, nothing in rule 60 prevents her from being protested. Rule 63.1 then requires the protest committee to hear all protests. Rule 64.1(a) says that when a protest committee decides that a boat has broken a rule, it shall disqualify her unless some other penalty applies. Normally, retirement precludes penalisation. However, rule 64.1(b) says that rule 64.1(a) does not apply when a boat has taken an applicable penalty such as retirement where the penalty a protest committee must impose is DNE. In this case, the protest committee can and must apply a DNE penalty, regardless of the boat having retired[4].

---

[1] Retired After Finishing - see rule A11

[2] ISAF Q&A 2008-003 is to the same effect. It does not directly address the question of actions that are incompatible with racing, such as a temporary use of an engine, but adds that, when a boat seeks to 'unretire', 'If the race committee did not reinstate her finishing position and she requests redress, the protest committee should consider if the original retirement was her own fault and if her action to rescind the retirement was timely. Especially if the retirement is rescinded after the end of the protest time limit, it may conclude that the race committee has made no error and they may also find that the score of RAF was not 'through no fault of her own' and refuse the request. If the race committee does reinstate the boat and other boats in the fleet request redress then any such request should be refused as there is no error by the race committee.'

[3] See rule 64.1(b)

[4] RYA 2005/5

Part 1 - Fundamental Rules

Rule 1   **SAFETY**

1.1   **Helping Those in Danger**
A boat or competitor shall give all possible help to any person or vessel in danger.

The racing rules are as much about safe navigation as tactical advantage, and it is entirely appropriate that sailing's first Fundamental Rule should concern safety.

Help may be physical. It may also be oral, such as a hail or radio message warning that the recipient is standing into danger[1]. If it is possible that a boat or competitor is in danger, then other boats should assume that this is the case. ISAF 20 says that boat in position to help another boat that **may be** in danger is bound to do so.

The obligation to help is not negated by the fact that a protest committee later decides that there was no danger, or that help was not asked for[2]. Even if another competitor is seen to be giving help, or a race committee vessel is nearby and capable of giving help, that does absolve other boats nearby from at least finding out whether more help is needed[3]. I think however that when a well-crewed race committee RIB on a radio net is already standing by an upturned centreboard boat in difficult conditions, it is reasonable for another competitor to assume that further help would be redundant, and possibly counter-productive.

Time taken in giving help is compensated by redress, often on the initiative of the race committee[4]. However, the receiving of help may not be as blessed as its giving, since only certain categories of help may be received with impunity, as will be seen later[5].

1.2   **Life-Saving Equipment and Personal Flotation Devices**
A boat shall carry adequate life-saving equipment for all persons on board, including one item ready for immediate use, unless her class rules make some other provision. Each competitor is individually responsible for wearing a personal flotation device adequate for the conditions.

As the rule foresees, most class rules are more specific as to what is to be carried and worn, and, the larger the boat, the more likely that adequate life-saving equipment will be more than just personal flotation devices, and will be prescribed in detail in safety regulations that rank as 'other documents that govern the event' by being referred to explicitly in the notice of race and sailing instructions[6].

Separately, rule 40, Personal Flotation Devices, allows the race committee to signal that personal flotation devices are to be worn while racing, and sailing instructions often go further by amending rule 40 to require such devices to be worn also before and after racing. Rule 40 also advises us that wet suits and dry suits are not personal flotation devices.

---

[1] See RYA 1998/1
[2] See also CYA 24
[3] CYA 34 and CYA 39
[4] Rules 60.2(b), Right to Request Redress and 62.1(c), Redress
[5] Rule 41, Outside Help
[6] Definition Rule, Rules J1.1(3), Notice of Race Contents and J2.1(2), Sailing Instruction Contents

Rule 2 — FAIR SAILING

A boat and her owner shall compete in compliance with recognized principles of sportmanship and fair play. A boat may be penalised under this rule only if it is clearly established that these principles have been violated. A disqualification under this rule shall not be excluded fom the boat's series score.

So what are these 'recognised principles'? We have already examined the Basic Principle of sportsmanship, namely that when competitors break a rule they will promptly take a penalty, which may be to retire – and we have already noted that this is not how many competitors behave. The rules themselves weaken this aspiration further, in two ways.

Firstly, consider a boat that has been compelled to break a rule because another boat has broken a rule, and the matter comes to protest. Rule 64.1(a) requires a protest committee to penalise any unexonerated rule infringement by any party to the protest, whether the protestor or protestee, but rule 64.1(c) makes an exception in the case of a boat compelled to break a rule because another boat broke a rule. So if I am forced to touch a mark because another boat did not give me the room I believe was my entitlement, and if the protest committee agrees with my case, I will not be penalised – but it remains the case that I broke a rule, I knew it at the time, and the Basic Principle says I should take a penalty. There is in effect an unwritten rule that a later decision of a protest committee will retrospectively exempt me from the obligation to have taken a penalty. But, despite previous examples, it would be rare for a protest committee, having found that my admitted touching of the mark was not caused by another boat breaking a rule, to invoke rule 2 and upgrade my DSQ to a DNE. Custom and practice is that I can award myself the benefit of the doubt until a protest committee decides otherwise.

Secondly, there are specific cases of rule-breaking where the rules themselves prohibit penalisation. Rule 14 puts a general obligation on all boats to avoid contact with another boat if reasonably possible, but, in the case of a right-of-way boat or one entitled to room or mark-room, penalisation is not possible if there was neither damage nor injury[1]. RYA 2004/3, where L knowingly allowed non-harmful contact to occur, recognises this unresolved tension: 'Nor is L to be penalised under rule 2. It is true that the Basic Principle, Sportsmanship and the Rules, says that when competitors break a rule they will promptly take a penalty, which may be to retire, that she did neither, and that rule 2 states that a boat shall compete in compliance with recognised principles of sportsmanship and fair play. In this case, however, she is not to be penalised under rule 2, as that would defeat the clear intention of rule 14[2].' That may be pragmatically practical, but it is not intellectually rigorous.

Similarly, a boat can break any of rules 10, 11, 12, 13, 15 and 16 with impunity if she is rounding a mark on her proper course within the mark-room to which she is entitled, since rule 18.5(b) says she is immediately exonerated, and her only risk is, under rule 14, of not avoiding an avoidable collision that results in damage or injury. Instant exoneration seems to be a better device than rule 14's non-penalisation.

Rule 23 prohibits certain forms of interference with other boats, but other types of interference are legitimate. Rule 2 was at one time clearer as what is 'fair sailing', namely the use of speed, skill and (except in team racing) individual effort. This is still reflected in the cases.

---

[1] Rule 14(b).

[2] CYA 4 comes to a similar conclusion on similar facts, but says that rule 2 does not apply because 'there is nothing unfair in a right-of-way boat holding her course'. This does not address the Basic Principle issue, and, although rule 2's title is Fair Sailing, a rule's title is not part of that rule – see definition Rule.

Within limits, it is 'fair sailing' to 'match race' another boat down the fleet to worsen her finishing position, even if it also worsens the finishing position of the aggressor - as gloriously demonstrated by Ben Ainslie in winning the Olympic Laser Gold in Sydney. Those limits, as set out in ISAF case 78, are that:

- The boats must on the same leg of the course (including pre-start manoeuvring), since rule 23.2 forbids manoeuvring against a boat on a different leg.
- It must be aimed at improving the series position of the aggressor: the case does not require the outcome to be that the aggressor will get a better series result than the victim, although, if this is not the outcome, a protest committee should be alert to the possibility that it is intended to benefit a third boat with which the aggressor is linked, which is 'team racing', not 'match racing', and clearly 'unfair sailing'; nor does the attempt to sail another boat down the fleet have to be successful in order be legitimate.
- The aggressor must not deliberately break a rule in the process. So she breaks rule 2 by being OCS at the starting signal and not making any attempt to start, in order to be sure of covering her victim up the beat[1]. By implication, an inadvertent rule breach of a rule of Part 2 or of rule 31 by the aggressor does not of itself take interference outside the scope of fair sailing, but the aggressor must still be careful. If she takes the appropriate turn(s) penalty, the cover will end. If she continues the cover without taking a penalty, knowing that even her disqualification in a protest could be discarded at no cost as long as the victim finishes badly, she would still break rule 2 if she knew she had broken a rule – and the sort of competitor who uses the rules to match race another boat is usually one who will know when she has broken a rule. The sting in the tail for her is that the rule 2 disqualification score that will follow is non-discardable, because the rule says so[2].
- The tactic is unlikely to be legal unless employed in the last race of a series, since only then will this be the sole way that the aggressor can outscore the victim.
- It is implicit that a boat can voluntarily suffer a bad race score, yet improve her series score, only when she can afford to discard the score in the race in question.

If *Daffodil* manoeuvres against *Iris* with no objective other than to benefit *Daffodil*'s associate *Thetis* in fleet racing, this is unfair 'team racing'. Since this would be quite acceptable in 'proper' team racing under Appendix D, Team Racing Rules, one might expect to find in Appendix D a statement that the Fair Sailing rule does not apply, or only partly applies. In fact, there is no such statement. Instead, D1.2(b) adds to rule 41, Outside Help, stating that a boat may receive help from a another boat on her team provided electronic communication is not used. By implication, this 'help' is then sportsmanlike and fair. 'Helping' is the essence of team racing. So when unauthorised team racing occurs in fleet racing, it is a specific breach of rule 41 as well as a general breach of rule 2. The fact that it may therefore be a gross breach of rule 41 gives rise to the possibility of action under rule 69.1 as well.

Tricking fellow competitors can break rule 2, as for example a port-tack boat that deliberately hails 'starboard' when she knows that it is she herself that is the one on port tack[3].

Positioning crew and equipment advantageously does not break rule 2 if no other rule is broken. There is no rule that dictates how the helmsman or crew of a leeward boat must sit, and contact with a windward boat does not break rule 2 unless there is deliberate misuse of positioning[4]. On the other hand, deliberate action (in this case reaching out and touching another boat), with no intention other than to cause a breach of rule 11 breaks rule 2[5].

---

[1] ISAF 34: to achieve the same objective by deliberately missing out a mark to get to a victim breaks rule 23.2, and therefore rule 2 as well – see RYA 1986/6.

[2] I think a protest committee should be equally sceptical when the aggressor retires later in the race, claiming that it was only then that she realised she had broken a rule, if conveniently the cover had by then done its job: likewise if she retires after finishing at no harm to her series position seeking to avoid a protest hearing at which rule 2 might be an issue.

[3] ISAF 47: the question in the case presupposes that the hailer is an experienced sailor while the hailed is inexperienced, but the decision does not make this distinction. I suppose that a deliberately incorrect answer to a question from another boat as to which way to leave the next mark would also break rule 2: on the other hand, claims for and oral denials of room at a mark are unlikely to cross the 'unfairness' threshold.

[4] ISAF 74: an example of misuse might be launching outboard on a trapeze in light winds.

[5] ISAF 73: similarly RYA 1988/8, when masts touch after L heels to windward.

RYA 1999/5 puts an interesting gloss on this. Contact between one boat (including her crew) and another is not a prerequisite of a failure to keep clear, as defined. Rather, it is evidence that a boat is already not keeping clear, and many breaches of the rules of Part 2 will not involve contact. So when, racing in larger boats, the crew of L reached out and touched W, this was no more than proof of the closeness of W and therefore that she was already breaking rule 11 – and therefore rule 2 was not broken.

In RYA 1989/13, a spray hood on a cruiser-racer was raised downwind and lowered upwind. This did not break rule 2, since the use of standard designed positions for equipment not restricted by class rules or by the sailing instructions was not a clear-cut violation of the principle of sportsmanship.

That case reminds us that there is a breach of rule 2 only when it is 'clearly established' that the mysterious principles of sportsmanship and fair play have been violated. So any doubt must be resolved in favour of the accused, but it is not clear to what extent the burden of proof is greater under rule 2, compared with any other rule.

Taking advantage of sub-standard sailing instructions or of a sub-standard competitor does not break rule 2. If a race committee intends a mark to be rounded, but its sailing instructions require only that it be passed, a boat that detects this can sometimes validly sail a far shorter race[1]. Anchoring during a race at a position charted as 'Anchoring Prohibited' breaks no rule, rule 2 included, if the prohibition is not activated by the sailing instructions[2].

Rule 2 applies to both a boat and her owner (who may not be aboard while racing), which opens up the possibility of action under this rule against the boat of a non-competing owner when there is deliberate non-compliance with class rules. A DNE under rule 2 may be only the first step. An owner who is a competitor can be the subject of a rule 69.1 hearing, and a non-competing owner can be made the object of a report to the national authority under rule 69.2.

It is not a breach of rule 2 (or any rule) for a right-of-way boat to hold her course even though she has good reason to believe that another boat is about to break a right-of-way rule with respect to her. So in ISAF 27, *Iris* and *Daffodil* were approaching the port-hand windward mark on port tack. *Iris*, clear ahead and to leeward, tacked (predictably, it was claimed) onto the starboard-tack layline for the mark right across the bows of *Daffodil*, which almost immediately hit her and holed her. The protest committee disqualified both boats, *Iris* under rule 15, and *Daffodil* under rule 2, pointing out that she knew that *Iris* was going to tack but did nothing to avoid collision. On appeal, *Daffodil* was reinstated, as she was not required to anticipate that *Iris* would beak any rule.

It is not a breach of rule 2 for protestors to collaborate over lodging a protest: 'Any boat is entitled to protest any other boat, subject to the provisions of rule 60. If any one boat may do so, three may also do so, and they do not break rule 2 simply because they consult before delivering their protests or because they deliver a joint protest[3].'

---

[1] RYA 1985/4, see also under rule 28.1.
[2] RYA 1989/6: the same applies to any local byelaw or regulation if not called up by the sailing instructions.
[3] US 42, concerning a measurement protest

There is a large, and potentially confusing, overlap between rule 2 and rule 69, Allegations of Gross Misconduct.

	RULE 2, FAIR SAILING	RULE 69.1, ALLEGATIONS OF GROSS MISCONDUCT
Who can be the subject of an action by a protest committee?	A boat, and her owner	Only a competitor, i.e., an individual. Non-competitors can be reported to the National Authority and/or to ISAF for possible action under rule 69.2
Who can be penalised under the rule?	Only a boat	A competitor, and, where appropriate, a boat as well.
What conduct can lead to penalisation?	A breach of recognised principles of sportsmanship and fair play	A gross breach of a rule, of good manners or of sportsmanship: or bringing the sport into disrepute
When can the infringement occur?	While competing. It includes competing in a boat previously modified so as not to comply with class rules	At any time, provided it is related to racing or to an event or a club. It may be something that happens on shore as well as afloat
Who can protest / bring an action under this rule?	Another boat, or a protest committee, or a race committee	Only a protest committee, based on what it sees or learns
Does the rule have to be referred to in the documentation for the hearing?	No, A rule 2 penalty may arise from facts found in the hearing of a protest based on other rules	It must be clear in writing that it is a hearing under rule 69.1, and the alleged gross misconduct must be clearly stated. If it is alleged that there has been a gross breach of a rule, that rule must be identified
What is the procedure?	Where there is a protest by another boat or by the race committee, it is adversarial, and the alleger is present throughout the hearing. Where there is a protest by the protest committee itself, it is inquisitorial, and the source of any allegation is present only to give evidence, unless it is one or more members of the protest committee	It is inquisitorial, and the source of any allegation is present only to give evidence, unless it is one or more members of the protest committee
How big is the protest committee?	Technically, one person is enough	Three people are required
Can the boat be legally represented?	Yes, although this would be unusual	Yes, and in serious cases this is often better for both the respondent and the protest committee
Can a penalty under this rule arise from a normal protest hearing where the rule is not actually referred to in the original documentation?	Yes, if the protest committee finds suitable facts	No. A separate hearing specifically under rule 69 is required. This may arise from facts found in a 'normal' protest hearing
Can there be separate hearings under both rules over the same alleged facts?	Yes – indeed, it is normal and often preferable for facts to be established in a 'normal protest' before proceeding to a rule 69 hearing against a person	It would be unusual for a rule 69 hearing to be followed by a rule 2 protest

	RULE 2, FAIR SAILING	RULE 69.1, ALLEGATIONS OF GROSS MISCONDUCT
Is the ability to call a hearing time-limited?	Yes, rule 63.1, Protest Time Limit applies, although an extension for a 'good reason' is possible	No. Rule 63.1 does not apply to the calling of a hearing under rule 69.1, which may be called after the end of an event
What outcome is possible, apart from dismissing the allegation?	Only a non-excludable disqualification (DNE) for the race concerned	Issue a warning: or exclude a competitor from a race, or from the remaining races, or from all the races of the series, plus (optionally): non-discardably disqualify a boat from a race, or from all the remaining races, or from all the races of the series, and also; take other action within its jurisdiction
Does it end there?	Yes, unless it is followed by a rule 69 hearing	Yes, if there is only a warning: No, if there has been a penalty, which must be reported to the National Authority, which can take further action. Penalties imposed by an international jury appointed by ISAF must also be reported to ISAF
What if the alleged infringer does not attend the hearing?	The protest committee can proceed with the hearing under rule 63.3(b), and may then reopen if the party proves to have been unavoidably absent	The protest committee can proceed if no good reason for non-attendance is given, otherwise it must reschedule, failing which it collects evidence and sends the file to the National Authority

In many cases, a protest committee will have the choice of proceeding under one, the other or both of these rules. Although rule 69 has a reputation of being the more severe course of action, the outcome (in the shape of a warning) under rule 69.1 may be less severe than rule 2's penalty, which is nothing more nor less than a non-discardable disqualification. Protest committees will often bear these possible consequences in mind when deciding how to proceed with an allegation that could be dealt with under either rule.

Rule 3   ACCEPTANCE OF THE RULES

By participating in a race conducted under these racing rules, each competitor and boat owner agrees

(a) to be governed by the *rules*;

(b) to accept the penalties imposed and other action taken under the *rules*, subject to the appeal and review procedures provided in them, as the final determination of any matter arising under the *rules*; and

(c) with respect to any such determination, not to resort to any court of law or tribunal.

Rule 3 binds competitors to the racing rules and their processes, and seeks to deter taking issues elsewhere for resolution. Participation creates obligation, as RYA 1999/3 shows. *Shock*'s owner disagreed with a sailing instruction, and wrote to the race committee claiming that it was dangerous, and that he would hold the club liable should damage result. *Shock* then raced, and was disqualified without a hearing by the race committee. The protest committee, refusing redress, decided that the repudiation of the sailing instruction had invalidated *Shock*'s entry. It changed the DSQ to DNS, saying that *Shock* had made herself ineligible to race.

On appeal, *Shock* was reinstated to a finishing position, since, despite anything she had written, her participation signified her acceptance of the rules, which, as defined, includes the sailing instructions.

CYA 24 confirms that a boat cannot pick and choose which rules to comply with. P was disqualified under rule 10 for a collision that dismasted S, and also under rule 1.1 for not giving help. P appealed the rule 1.1 DSQ on the grounds that giving help might have invalidated her insurance (presumably as some sort of admission of liability). This was rejected, since P had bound herself to be governed by all the rules, rule 1.1 included.

Rules 3(b) and (c) purport to exclude the civil courts and civil arbitration from 'determination of any matter arising under the rules'[1]. This means deciding the facts related to an incident, concluding that a rule has or has not been broken, and awarding a resulting penalty under the racing rules. It does not preclude taking legal action to seek compensation for damage arising from an incident.. Rule 68 says that the question for damages arising from a breach of any rule shall be governed by the prescriptions, if any, of the national authority. The RYA prescribes (and other national authorities have similar prescriptions) that any claim for damages arising from an incident while a boat is bound by the Racing Rules of Sailing shall be subject to the jurisdiction of the courts and not considered by a protest committee.

ISAF's aspiration is therefore clear: when there is a collision or some other incident resulting in financial loss, only a protest committee can decide who was right or wrong, subject to any right of appeal; and only the courts or civil arbitration can decide the amount of damages. Normally, this is what happens, and most cases resulting in damage or injury are settled by insurance companies based on the decision of the protest committee, subject to any appeal.

It is not just financial matters that give rise to attempts to go to law to reverse the findings of protest committees and appeal committees. In each of the last two Olympic Games, competitors have resorted (unsuccessfully) to the Court for Arbitration for Sport to seek to overturn decisions of the Olympic jury. Outside of the Olympic Games, the writ of the Court is 'to resolve through the appeals arbitration procedure disputes concerning the decisions of federations, associations or other sports-related bodies, insofar as the statutes or regulations of the said sports-related bodies or a specific agreement so provide.' For non-Olympic sailing, neither the ISAF regulations nor the Racing Rules of Sailing make any other explicit provision for recourse to the court other than on issues related to doping, and so the final arbiter of most racing rules issues is intended to be either a non-appealable international jury or the national authority appeals committee[2].

An interesting legal case related to damages is the 1897 House of Lords sailing-related appeal case *Clarke v Lord Dunraven*[3], an important part of the modern law of contract, confirming as it did that when boats enter a race and agree with the organizing authority to abide by the rules, a legal contract is formed between the owners of the boats, even though no documents pass between them.

In that case, Mr A.B. Clarke's yacht *The Satanita* hit and sank the Earl of Dunraven's *Valkyrie* in pre-start manoeuvres before the start of a race of the 1894 Mudhook Regatta on the Clyde. Clarke admitted responsibility for the accident, but claimed that his liability was limited to £952 by a tonnage-related formula in the Merchant Shipping Act[4], which in theory applied to all collisions at sea. The Earl's case was that the racing rules of the time made the infringer responsible for 'all damages', which the Court of Appeal had assessed at £7,500. The court was conscious that the lower Merchant Shipping Act formula did not sit easily with the actual cost of a lightweight racing yacht. 'You might as well speak of the value of a racehorse by his weight in pounds of flesh', said Lord Chancellor Halsbury.

The decision was that the parties had individually agreed with the organizing authority when entering the regatta to abide by the rules, resulting in a contract between the parties to contract out of applying the Merchant Shipping Act formula. So the Earl could be fully compensated for the loss of his yacht.

---

[1] In this respect, rule 3(c) has reverted to an older, harder line: its temporary predecessor admitted the possibility of a case ending in the courts after the internal processes of the racing rules and any application to the Court of Arbitration for Sport had been exhausted.

[2] For the UK, this is the RYA's Racing Rules Committee

[3] *Clarke v Earl of Dunraven and Mount-Earl, The Satanita, (1897)* AC 59.

[4] Now the Merchant Shipping (Distress Signals and Prevention of Collisions) Regulations 1996, under which the IRPCAS apply to 'UK ships wherever they may be'.

Nothing in that case was in conflict in principle with the current Racing Rules of Sailing, since fault and liability was not disputed. Matters are more complex when a party to a protest seeks to go to law to overturn an unfavourable protest decision as to responsibility for an incident because of the financial consequences. Rule 3 in itself will not prevent a court hearing such a claim, in the United States at least, as in *Charles Jourdain v Endeavour*[1]. This case was written up for the sailing world by Mary Pera (herself a lawyer by training), as: 'An important case which will affect judgements of law courts in all countries, and certainly those whose systems are based on English law. It sets the Racing Rules of Sailing firmly in place, greatly strengthening the earlier decisions of a hundred years ago.' She continues[2]:

> In October 1992 the 72 ft *Charles Jourdain* and the 120 ft ex-J class *Endeavour* were sailing in separate races in the same event in the Mediterranean. *Charles Jourdain* established an overlap from clear astern at least 60 ft to leeward of *Endeavour*. In spite of having room as defined to keep clear, *Endeavour* held her course until her boom hit *Charles Jourdain*'s backstay. Serious damage resulted from their collision. The protest was heard by an international jury, and *Endeavour* was disqualified under rule 11.

> *Charles Jourdain* then took the matter to the courts in an effort to get damages, claiming $15.4 million for neck whiplash and other injuries plus $600,000 for physical damage to the yacht. The case was heard by the US District Court of Maine in September 1994.

> In a worrying decision the court stated: "There is no dispute that the International Regulations for Preventing Collisions at Sea (IRPCAS) provide the rules which govern the behaviour of these particular boats. Although they were both involved in races which were governed by the Racing Rules of Sailing, the rules of a private racing organisation do not and cannot pre-empt the application of IRPCAS which have been adopted by treaty to govern world-wide. Thus we look to IRPCAS for the controlling rules in this case."

> Thus this court ignored the International Jury's findings, and turned to the IRPCAS: *Charles Jourdain* was the overtaking yacht under the IRPCAS and obliged to keep clear, though the court found both yachts at fault (60% *Charles Jourdain* and 40% *Endeavour*).

> All this seemed to lead to the conclusion that we might as well scrap the racing rules, at least at sea; for no insurance company could be expected to insure yachts that obeyed different rules from those that the courts would apply. However, the decision was appealed and heard in the United States Court of Appeals for the First Circuit before three judges, the Chief Judge being Juan R Torruella, who was [3] also an International Judge in sailing, representing Puerto Rico.

> The court's decision, reversing the issue of liability, is of great importance to anyone interested in the legal framework within which our sport takes place.

>> *"The history of the IRPCAS shows that they were enacted because of the need to establish a code of international rules of the road for maritime traffic through out the world. However, nothing in their history indicates that they were meant to regulate voluntary private sports activity in which the participants have waived their application and in which no interference with non-participating maritime traffic is implicated.*

>> *Surprisingly, considering the extent and history of maritime and yachting traditions there is a dearth of applicable jurisprudence…The cases we have found however, are helpful to the extent that they establish the principle that when one voluntarily enters a yacht race for which published sailing instructions set out the conditions of participation, a private contract results between the participants requiring their compliance therewith*[4].

>> *The parties agreed to the Racing Rules of Sailing for determining fault, they agreed to the adjudicating forum and they were appraised (sic) of the procedures. They appeared before the forum, submitted to its jurisdiction, presented evidence and argument and thereafter were served with that body's findings and final decision. Thus both yachts were contractually bound to race by the rules of the road contained in the Racing Rules of Sailing and to resolve issues related to fault according to these rules.*

> (continued on page 18)

---

[1] United States Court of Appeals for the First Circuit 1995
[2] The document is edited and updated to the references and terminology of the current Racing Rules of Sailing
[3] And still is
[4] *Clarke v Dunraven* is cited

Furthermore, the procedures established by the Racing Rules of Sailing meet the requirements of due process; there is appropriate written notification of their allegations, notice is given of the hearing; the parties are allowed to appear and present evidence and witness testimony; They may also cross-examine opposing witnesses and argue orally; and generally, engage in all those accepted activities held so dear by common law lawyers. Finally, a written decision, in which findings of fact are made and fault apportioned, is issued to all interested parties. Equally important, the evidence is heard soon after the events take place by a panel of experts who are fully versed in the niceties of the activity in question. It is hard to find fault with such a process, particularly when it is exactly what the participants agreed to.

Insistence on blind application of IRPCAS to the facts of this case is not only unsupported by any historical imperative in this legislation and contrary to the weight of the sparse relevant authority, it is logically unsound. Such application would turn on its head and render rife with uncertainty the thousands of private yacht races that take place throughout the United States and world-wide in which participants voluntarily agree to be bound by the Racing Rules of Sailing. The decision could even have a serious negative impact on such international races as the America's Cup or the yachting events of the Olympic Games…Under such logic, notwithstanding agreement by Olympic participants to abide by the Racing Rules of Sailing and to have protests decided by International Juries, they could thereafter regurgitate any issues in the courts under the IRPCAS. Such absurdity is difficult to countenance, and cannot have been contemplated by Congress or the treaty negotiating authorities when the IRPCAS were adopted."

Coming to the question of damages, the court quoted RRS 68 and approved of an interpretation in an earlier case: 'The courts are the rightful location of litigation over yacht racing damages unless national racing authorities provide in essence, for private resolution'.

There being no agreement about the determination of the damages, the court decided that *Charles Jourdain* was entitled to claim and prove that the damages caused by *Endeavour* based upon the determination of fault by the International Jury. The outcome of all this should be a firm base for solving future problems[1].

The *Charles Jourdain v Endeavour* case therefore addresses three issues – the competence of the courts to consider matters arising from racing, the rules to be applied by the courts, and the determination of damages.

As for the ability of the courts to interest themselves in boat racing matters, that is a matter for the courts. Rule 3 on its own is no absolute barrier. Outside of damages issues, English courts will intervene in sporting matters, but usually only when natural justice may be been denied, or when the livelihood of a party is affected (for instance, if under rule 69.2 the ISAF eligibility of a professional sailor has been suspended). 'Justice can often be done in domestic tribunals better by a good layman than a bad lawyer[2].' Transatlantic courts are similarly reticent. 'The courts should rightly hesitate before intervening in disciplinary hearings held by private associations…intervention is appropriate only in the most extraordinary of circumstances, where the association has clearly breached its own rules, that breach will imminently result in serious and irreparable harm to the plaintiff and the plaintiff has exhausted all internal remedies. Even then, injunctive relief is limited to correcting the breach of the rules. The court should not intervene in the merits of the underlying dispute[3]'. Likewise, in relation to selection issues, a Canadian judge ruled: '…the bodies which heard the appeals were experienced and knowledgeable in the sport of sailing, and fully aware of the selection process. The appeals bodies determined that the selection criteria had been met… I would be reluctant to substitute my opinion for those who know the sport and knew the nature of the problem[4].'

---

[1] Although it does not affect the principle of the judgement, the same case coming before an International Jury today would be likely to result in the disqualification of both boats, L under rule 14, Avoiding Contact, for not avoiding the contact, and W under rule 14 as well under rule 11. In this respect, the Racing Rules of Sailing have come closer to the IRPCAS, but as concerns obligations when boats meet, they remain different in the matter of 'overtaking'.
[2] Lord Denning, in a Court of Appeal case *Enderby Town Football Club v Football Association Ltd [1971] 1 Ch 591*
[3] *Harding v United States Figure Skating Association* [1994] 851 F Supp 1476, a case of the Federal District Court
[4] *McCaig v Canadian Yachting Association & Canadian Olympic Assocation*, Case 90-01-96624 (1996), regarding Olympic selection for the Mistral class.

In actions for damages, the racing rules and the courts are in harmony. It is a proper matter for litigation, and the amount of damages is the sole prerogative of the courts. However, the liability for those damages in an English court may not follow the spirit of the *Endeavour* case, despite Mary Pera's optimism. In *Meggeson v Burns* it was held the outcome or absence of a protest is immaterial for the purposes of establishing liability for any damage: the protest committee's jurisdiction was confined to determining the outcome of the race, and the court was at liberty to consider quite separately the issue of liability for damage[1]. It is also the case that the basis on which protest committees decide fault is different from the basis on which courts decide damages. Under the racing rules of sailing, a boat either does not break a rule, or she does break a rule, in which case she is either to be penalised or exonerated because a rule says so, and the same judgement is applied separately to any other boat in the incident. The courts on the other hand frequently apportion blame (and therefore damages) – as did the original American court in the *Endeavour* case - and in so doing they may well rely on the IRPCAS as well as or instead of the Racing Rules of Sailing to decide that liability.

The problem is that captured in *Charles Jourdain v Endeavour* – when a court has jurisdiction, how can it not apply the IRPCAS, which have the force of law in the coastal waters of most countries (in the United Kingdom by virtue of the Merchant Shipping Acts)? That case said, as above, that this was not what the framers of the IPRCAS intended. Breaking the IRPCAS is a crime, but, since there is no known case of a criminal prosecution for breaking an IRPCAS rule with respect to another competitor in the race, it must be supposed that pragmatism rules, since to seek to find otherwise would make racing untenable. Perhaps an analogy can be made with the sport of boxing, where participants agree to tolerate actions that, if committed on the streets, would constitute criminal assault, yet where no known law permits this violence.

The IRPCAS cannot be ignored. They apply when a boat racing under the Racing Rules of Sailing meets a boat that is not[2]. The sailing instructions can say that the right-of-way rules of the IRPCAS apply instead of the rules of Part 2 of the Racing Rules of Sailing: and rule 48 makes sound signals and lights compulsory as provided in the IRPCAS when safety requires, which is firm evidence that the framers of the Racing Rules of Sailing intended IRPCAS provisions to apply only in specific circumstances between boats that were racing, and not generally, otherwise rule 48 would not have been necessary[3]. Were there to be a criminal prosecution of a boat that was racing, for breaking the rules of the IRPCAS or harbour byelaws, for instance for an illegal crossing of a traffic separation zone or for obstructing a vessel constrained by her draft, the fact that the sailing boat was racing under the Racing Rules of Sailing would not prevent a prosecution or punishment.

Rule 4   **DECISION TO RACE**
The responsibility for a boat's decision to participate in a race or to continue *racing* is hers alone.

On the face of it, this is a simple self-evident rule, if the paucity of appeal cases is any guidance. In US 39, a boat believed that conditions were too dangerous for racing, did not start, and sought redress against the race committee. Redress was correctly refused, since, under rule 4, only a boat herself is responsible for deciding whether or not to race or to continue racing. If she decides not to race, she cannot claim that her finishing place was worsened by the race committee.

In the background however, there is a tension between this rule and the law of the land, which will become an issue when there is death, injury or damage. In law, an organizing authority and a race committee have a duty of care to competitors, and, when a club is not an incorporated body, that responsibility and liability for any failure can fall on individual volunteers. Suppose it is realised that a boat is in an unsafe condition: should the organizing authority take any action? If its action is merely to draw the competitor's attention to the state of the boat, despite which the boat races with adverse consequences, has the organizing authority made its position better or worse in law? Arguably the latter, since it knew of the problem and did nothing about it.

---

[1] [1972] 1 Lloyds Rep 223
[2] Preamble to Section A of Part 2
[3] RYA 1989/6

What of a dinghy in difficult conditions that keeps capsizing and is obviously getting less and less able to cope? Should the decision as to whether to continue to race be solely that of the competitor, whose judgement is becoming increasingly impaired?

The problem is even more serious when the competitors are children, and clearly less able than an adult to make an informed decision as to whether to continue racing. If all competitors are equally affected by worsening conditions, the race committee should abandon the race under rule 32.1(e) on safety grounds – but an Optimist event, for example, will have children with a wide range of size, strength, skill and judgement. The UK Optimist class addresses these issues with standard major event conditions that include the following:

> 6.5   *The Race Committee may stop a boat launching, or require it to return ashore, if he or she considers the boat, its equipment, helm or crew are not adequate for the likely conditions, or for any other reason. The decision is final and will not be grounds for redress.*
>
> 6.6   *Competitors in difficulty shall obey any instruction given by a patrol boat crew.*

Many other examples exist with other classes and events, and they sit uneasily beside rule 4. Risk assessment and risk mitigation measures are today an essential part of race management, and there is little doubt that a sensible club will prefer to risk losing a rules appeal from a competitor it has prevented from racing or continuing to race, compared with the consequences of fatality, injury or damage that it might have been able to prevent. An RYA guidance note on outside help, to be found on the RYA website, says:

> If the race committee in pursuance of their responsibilities for safety wish to require boats and competitors to comply with their instructions, it will be appropriate to include a sailing instruction similar to the following. This is particularly important for junior classes.
>
> **Boats and Competitors in Difficulty**
> *When the race committee considers that a boat or competitor is in difficulty it may instruct the boat or competitor to accept outside help, retire or sail ashore.*
>
> Some observers may note that such a sailing instruction conflicts with rule 4, Decision to Race. However rule 4 is unlikely to be a legally effective defence following an accident to a young or inexperienced sailor.

So rule 4 may be valuable in enabling redress to be denied under the racing rules to 'non-triers': but as an exemption clause, it is inadequate on its own, witness also the further clauses that the RYA for example recommends to be added to the Notice of Race and entry forms[1], added to which any exemption clause is of limited significance where there has been negligence

Rule 5   **ANTI-DOPING**
A competitor shall comply with the World Anti-Doping Code, the rules of the World Anti-Doping Agency, and ISAF Regulation 21, Anti-Doping Code. An alleged or actual breach of this rule shall be dealt with under Regulation 21. It shall not be grounds for a *protest* and rule 63.1 does not apply.

As the rule says, this is not an issue for a protest committee. As now worded, it removes any need for competitors at club level to seek permission for prescription medication.

---

[1] Addendum A (RYA) to Appendix J of the Racing Rules of Sailing, printed in the RYA version of the racing rules, YR1/09.

Part 2 - When Boats Meet

The rules of Part 2 are defensive, in that they are designed for safe sailing and to avoid collisions. They are also aggressive, in that they will give a tactically-exploitable advantage to one of two boats that are near each other.

There is a logical structure to Part 2.
- The preamble says when Part 2 rules apply, and explains their relationship to the IRPCAS
- Section A, Right of Way, identifies which of two boats that meet has to keep clear. It does not impose any obligation or limitation on the right-of-way boat.
- Section B, General Limitations, places those limitations on right-of-way boats. It does not add to the obligations of a keep-clear boat[1].
- Section C deals with rights and obligations at marks and obstructions.
- Section D covers particular situations where sometimes Section A rules do not apply.

The terms used to create obligations are *keep clear*, give *mark-room* and give *room*, which are, as the italics imply, defined terms, to be examined in detail; and 'avoid', 'avoid contact', 'not cause', 'not prevent' and 'not interfere with', which are not defined and have their ordinary meaning.

Preamble

*The rules of Part 2 apply between boats that are sailing in or near the racing area and intend to **race**, are **racing**, or have been **racing**. However, a boat not racing shall not be penalised for breaking one of these rules, except rule 23.1.*

When a boat sailing under these rules meets a vessel that is not, she shall comply with the International Regulations for Preventing Collisions at Sea (IRPCAS) *or government right-of-way rules. If the sailing instructions so state, the rules of Part 2 are replaced by the right-of-way rules of the* IRPCAS *or by government right-of-way rules.*

Away from the racing area, the rules that apply to boats that meet are the IRPCAS or the equivalent 'government right-of-way rules', which may be harbour, river or reservoir byelaws[2]. When boats are in or near the racing area, and both intend to race, or are racing, or have been racing, as defined[3], the rules of Part 2 apply when they meet.

Suppose that *Iris*, leaving the shore for a distant race area, collides with *Daffodil*, which is returning ashore from the same race area, and suffers damage. Can she protest? A protest is an allegation that a boat has broken a rule. Such a protest would have to be under a rule of the IRPCAS, and the IRPCAS rules are enforceable by protest only when the racing rules say they apply, which they no not at that moment, since neither boat is 'sailing under these rules' (the racing rules in Part 2). So a protest does not appear to be possible. In any case, protesting alone is of limited use: the preamble makes clear that penalisation is not possible, since neither boat is racing.

Can she request redress? If the damage was solely *Daffodil*'s fault and it prevents *Iris* from competing or slows her when she races, this would seem to meet the requirements of rule 62.1(b) – a claim or possibility that a boat's score in a race or series has, through no fault of her own, been made significantly worse by physical damage because of the action of a vessel not racing that was required to keep clear[4]. The same would apply if *Daffodil* had been a vessel totally unconnected with any racing. It is slightly curious that a boat can get redress in a series if wrongly damaged by a non-racing vessel, where she would not be able to do so if she was damaged, while being brought to the event on a trailer, in a road accident that was the other car's fault.

---

[1] As will be seen, rule 14 applies equally to right-of-way boats and keep-clear boats, but the Section A obligation of a boat to keep clear is not added to by the rule 14 obligation to avoid contact if reasonably possible.

[2] See ISAF 109 below. For the avoidance of repetition, future references to the IRPCAS alone can be taken to include government right-of-way rules.

[3] A boat is defined as racing from her preparatory signal until she finishes and clears the finishing line and marks or retires, or until the race committee signals a general recall, postponement or abandonment

[4] While the IPRCAS uses the term 'keep out of the way of' rather than 'keep clear', the word 'vessel' implies a craft that is not governed by the racing rules, and to which the IRPCAS therefore applies.

If there is an incident between boats sailing in or near the racing area that are not racing[1], and each of them either intends to race or has been racing, then a protest is technically possible, but no penalty is possible. Redress remains a possibility. If the racing-area incident is between a boat that is racing and one that has been racing or intends to race, then the boat that is racing can be penalised as if the other boat had been racing, whereas the boat that had been racing or intended to race can only be penalised, under rule 23.1, for interfering with a boat that was racing when it was reasonably possible not to do so. The penalty would apply to the race sailed nearest in time to that of the incident[2].

The interaction of the IRPCAS, government rules and the racing rules is amplified in ISAF 109.

Question 1
What are the 'government rules' to which the preamble to Part 2 and rule 48 refer? How do those rules differ from the *International Regulations for Preventing Collisions at Sea (IRPCAS)*?
Answer 1
The *IRPCAS* apply only 'upon the high seas and in all waters connected therewith navigable by seagoing vessels' (*IRPCAS* rule 1(a)). On a country's harbours, rivers, lakes and other inland waters, governments and other responsible authorities are permitted to establish other rules. Those other rules are the 'government rules' to which the Part 2 preamble and rule 48 refer. Such rules, which may apply nationally on all inland waters or only on specific inland waters, may restate, replace, change or add to the *IRPCAS* (*IRPCAS* rules 1(b) and 1(c)).

Question 2
When the notice of race, sailing instructions and other documents that govern an event do not mention the *IRPCAS* or government rules, do any rules of the *IRPCAS* or government rules apply to a boat racing under *The Racing Rules of Sailing*?
Answer 2
Yes. When safety requires, a boat racing shall sound fog signals and show lights as required by the *IRPCAS* or applicable government rules (rule 48). Also, when a boat sailing under the Part 2 rules meets a vessel that is not, the *IRPCAS* or government right-of-way rules apply between them (Part 2 preamble).

Question 3
May the notice of race, sailing instructions or another document that governs the event make the *IPRCAS* or government right-of-way rules other rules of the *IRPCAS* or government rules applicable?
Answer 3
Yes, in three ways.
  (1) The sailing instructions may state that the right-of-way rules of the *IRPCAS* or government rules replace all of the rules of Part 2 (Part 2 preamble and rule J2.2(38)). This is often done for oceanic races and also for racing at night.
  (2) The sailing instructions may state that a particular rule from the *IRPCAS* or government rules (other than a right-of-way rule) will apply to the event and include the text of that rule (rule J2.2(38))[3].
  (c) The definition Rule includes '(g) any other documents that govern the event.' Such a document may include the text of a particular rule or rules from the *IRPCAS* or government rules (other than a right-of-way rule) that will apply to the event. Rules for crossing shipping lanes are often made available in such a document. To govern an event, a document must be listed in the notice of race (rule J1.1(3)), stating where or how it may be seen, and in the sailing instructions (rule J2.1(2)).

A boat that breaks a rule in the *IRPCAS* or a government rule can always be prosecuted by an authority responsible for its enforcement, but a protest may be made under such a rule only when the rule concerned 'governs the event'.

---

[1] See note 3 on page 21
[2] Rule 64.1(d)
[3] A British example is the Southampton Water Byelaw concerning the moving prohibited zone that is deemed to precede and adjoin a large vessel.

Question 4

If the sailing instructions state that the right-of-way rules of the *IRPCAS* replace the rules of Part 2, which rules of Part 2 are replaced by which rules of the *IRPCAS*?

Answer 4

All the rules of Part 2 are replaced. Part B of the *IRPCAS* contains the *IRPCAS* 'Steering and Sailing Rules', which are, in effect, 'right-of-way rules'. However, Part B of the *IRPCAS* must be read in conjunction with the whole of the *IRPCAS*, particularly Part A. For example, many terms used in Part B are defined in Part A[1].

Question 5

Is it possible to provide for a wider or narrower range of replacements?

Answer 5

A sailing instruction may only replace all the rules of Part 2 with all the right-of-way rules of the *IRPCAS* or government rules. Rule 86.1 states that the sailing instructions shall not change Part 2, which includes its preamble. Therefore, a wider or narrower range of replacements of right-of-way rules that apply between competing boats is not permitted.

RYA 1989/6 is an example of the need for sailing instructions to specify 'other documents that govern the event.' While racing in light winds and an adverse tide, six boats anchored in an area which was marked on a chart as 'Fishing and anchoring prohibited', apparently under an Admiralty Regulation. *Sigmatic* did not anchor, and, believing that the notice on the chart was mandatory and that she had been clearly disadvantaged by not kedging, lodged a protest against them claiming that they had broken rule 2.

The protest committee, in upholding the protest, said that although the sailing instructions did not say that Admiralty Regulations must be complied with, it considered that if the protest were dismissed this decision would indicate that the RYA condoned the disregard of Admiralty Regulations; and that a race committee had no authority to allow boats to anchor in the prohibited area which, by implication, it would be doing by dismissing the protest. The resulting appeal of the six boats was upheld:

Racing is run under the rules, which are defined as the ISAF racing rules and some ISAF regulations, the prescriptions of the national authority, class rules, the notice of race, sailing instructions, class rules and any other documents governing the event. Rules J1.1(3) and J2.1(2) say that the 'other documents governing the event' shall be listed in the notice of race and the sailing instructions 'to the extent that they apply'. That this is the intention of the rules is confirmed by rule 48, Fog Signals and Lights. There would be no need for this rule if compliance with IRPCAS etc. were automatically compulsory.

The coasts are dotted with areas subject to special prohibitions. Many oyster fisheries are protected by laws dating back to the Middle Ages, yet these are cited when there is a case between yachtsmen and fishermen. Some regulations are issued as warnings, but it is not always clear whether this is a warning that an infringer may be prosecuted, or a warning that she may be damaged or lose an anchor. Wreck warnings may apply in areas so deep that they will affect deep draught ships but not racing boats. Firing ranges, sewer outfall works, cable laying, mining grounds, archaeological diving positions, prohibited deep channel areas all combine to form an intricate network of permanent and temporary regulations. Some are shown on some charts, others not.

It would be unreasonable to expect a competitor to comply with all these without explicit warning and sailing instructions. When a race committee considers that it is necessary for such regulations to be complied with, it must either list them in the notice of race, stating where or how they may be seen, and list them again in the sailing instructions; or reprint them in the notice of race and in the sailing instructions.

US 83 is to the same effect:

Government buoys marking a security zone are not obstructions unless they fit the terms of the definition Obstruction. Boats may pass such obstructions on either side unless the sailing instructions prohibit sailing inside the security zone. A boat cannot be penalised under the racing rules for violating government regulations unless the sailings instructions make the regulations a rule governing the event.

---

[1] This raises the question of why boats might want to race under the IRPCAS. It is commonly done for racing at night between specified hours, and when away from the coast in transoceanic races. Its advantage is that any sailing boat encountered, especially at night, is to be treated by the same set of rules. Its disadvantage is that the IRPCAS does not work well for mark-rounding and getting room to tack at the shore. The advantages of using the IRPCAS are less clearcut since 1997 when aggressive luffing disappeared, and collision avoidance became central to the racing rules.

When a boat that is racing meets a large motor vessel, it may not be clear which has to keep out of the way of the other. RYA 2004/2 sensibly says that when a boat that is racing meets a large powered vessel in a fairway or narrow channel, she is to presume and act on the basis that the vessel can safely navigate only within the channel, and therefore has right of way.

A race committee vessel under way has rights and duties under IRPCAS. These cannot be varied by sailing instructions. In RYA 2002/14, a sailing instruction said *'Any committee vessel manoeuvring in the vicinity of the starting area will be deemed to be an obstruction. Committee vessels will manoeuvre without regard to competing boats and it shall be the sole responsibility of competitors to keep clear.'*

Before the starting signal, a small committee vessel was motoring slowly upwind to stand off the outer limit mark to record OCS boats. *Phoenix*, her vision obscured by other boats, did not see the committee vessel until very late. She tacked to try to avoid contact, but contact occurred. She was protested by the race committee and was disqualified under the sailing instruction. Her appeal was upheld:

> The definition Rule includes preambles and so the preamble to Part 2 of the Racing Rules of Sailing (RRS) is a rule of Part 2. The preamble states that the IRPCAS apply between a boat sailing under the racing rules and a vessel that is not. Rules 86.1(a) and (b) say that sailing instructions may not change a rule of Part 2.

> The sailing instruction, in purporting to impose the sole responsibility to keep clear on the competitor, clearly conflicts with IRPCAS rules 6, 7 and 18, and is therefore invalid.

Section A - Right of Way

 *A boat has right of way when another boat is required to **keep clear** of her. However, some rules in Sections B, C and D limit the actions of a right-of-way boat.*

It is obviously necessary for boats that meet to be able to decide quickly which is the keep-clear boat. When no question of tacking arises, there are only two criteria – which tack is each on, and, if they are on the same tack, are they overlapped?

A boat is always either on starboard tack or on port tack, even when she is tacking. Her tack, port or starboard, is defined as corresponding with her windward side, and her windward side is the side that is not her leeward side. Her leeward side is defined as 'the side that is or, when she is head to wind, was away from the wind. However, when sailing by the lee or directly downwind, her *leeward* side is the side on which her mainsail lies. The other side is her *windward* side.'

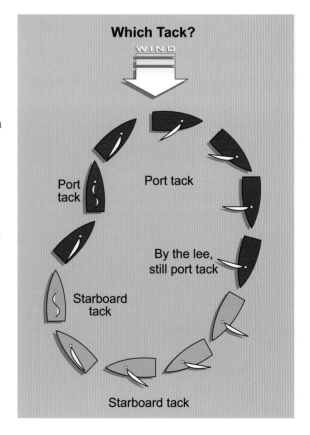

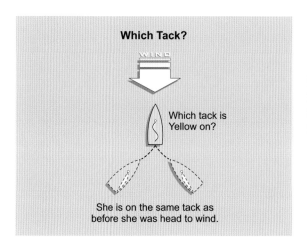

Note that it is not possible to decide the tack of a boat that is head to wind when first encountered. It depends how she became head to wind, as she is on the same tack as she was before she became head to wind.

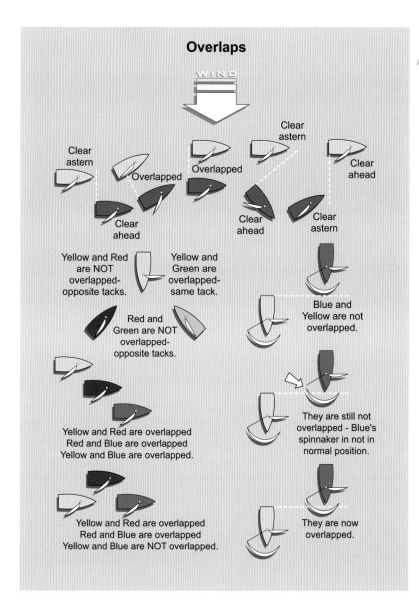

Definition *Clear Astern*
One boat is *clear astern* of another, as defined, when her hull and equipment in normal position are behind a line abeam from the aftermost point of the other boat's hull and equipment in normal position. The other boat is *clear ahead*. They *overlap* when neither is *clear astern*. However, they also *overlap* when a boat between them *overlaps* both. These terms always apply to boats on the same tack. They do not apply to boats on opposite tacks unless rule 18 applies or both boats are sailing more than ninety degrees from the true wind.

If boats are on the same tack, they are either overlapped, or one is clear astern of the other, making the other clear ahead.

If boats are on opposite tacks, they may also be overlapped before or at marks and obstructions. That does not change the applicable right-of-way rule, but permits the separate requirements of rules 18 and 19 to apply to them.

Retractable bowsprits for asymmetric spinnakers (gennakers) are increasing common. When are they 'in normal position'? Match racing call UMP 21 gives a general test: 'Is this how the boat would be normally be sailed, in the absence of other boats?' So an extended bowsprit will be in normal position prior to hoisting the spinnaker or after its removal, as long as it has not been extended prematurely or left in position too long. But its normal position in pre-start manoeuvres and when beating will be retracted.

In match racing, call MR21 says that an observer or a cameraman (presumably perched on the pushpit) does not count for the purposes of overlaps (or contact), whereas a camera, bracket or antenna fixed to the boat is 'equipment in normal position'. A flagstaff counts, the call says, but the flag on it does not. Note that the definition does not include the crew for the purposes of overlaps, presumably because the crew in normal position is unlikely to be ahead of the stem or abaft the transom. The line used to determine overlaps is sometimes called the 'transom line', but it is further outboard when the rudder is transom-hung. In this context, it is implicit that only equipment that is visible above the water line is relevant.

Having established tacks and overlaps, the three main right of way rules can be applied.

ON OPPOSITE TACKS
When boats are in opposite *tacks*, a *port-tack* boat shall *keep clear* of a *starboard-tack* boat.

ON THE SAME TACK, OVERLAPPED
When boats are on the same *tack* and *overlapped*, a *windward* boat shall *keep clear* of a *leeward* boat.

ON THE SAME TACK, NOT OVERLAPPED
When boats are on the same *tack* and not *overlapped*, a boat *clear astern* shall *keep clear* of a boat *clear ahead*.

Common to all of these is defined term *Keep Clear*:

Definition **_Keep Clear_** One boat *keeps clear* of another if the other can sail her course with no need to take avoiding action and, when the boats are *overlapped* on the same *tack*, if the *leeward* boat can change course in both directions without immediately making contact with the *windward* boat.

Only the first part of the definition Keep Clear applies to rules 10 and 12. Under rule 11, the second part of the definition also applies. The definition makes no reference to contact. The point at which a boat has not kept clear will be before there is contact, and so a collision is usually no more than evidence that one boat has already not kept clear of the other. Occasionally, there can be contact, despite which there is no failure to keep clear – for example, when a spinnaker, sheet or halyard unexpectedly flies free from its normal position on a close-hauled clear-ahead boat and touches a boat astern[1]. Similarly, when a boat is unable to avoid contact with a boat that is capsized, recovering from a capsize, is anchored or aground or is trying to help a person or vessel in danger, rule 22 suspends normal rights of way, replacing them with a requirement to avoid 'if possible', which it may not be.

---

[1] ISAF 77

The fact that a boat required to keep clear is unable to do so because she is out of control does not entitle her to exoneration for breaking a rule of Part 2[1]. RYA 1994/4 concerned a failure to give room rather than to keep clear when out of control, but its decision holds good for both situations: 'It may appear harsh to disqualify a boat that is genuinely out of control, but frequently the occurrence is caused by over-canvassing or careless handling, which are avoidable, or by inexperience, which is no justification for exoneration.'

It is common for a right-of-way boat to hail ('Starboard!' under rule 10, 'Up, Up' under rule 11, or – increasingly it seems in dinghy racing – just an 'Oy!' or a whistle, regardless of the situation) when it is possible that the other boat may not keep clear. The rules do not explicitly require a hail, but a hail may be useful evidence in any subsequent protest. Also, if there is contact resulting in injury or damage, and the right-of-way boat could have hailed but did not do so, she is at risk of penalisation under rule 14, Avoiding Contact, for failing to 'act to avoid contact', as to 'act' is not restricted to changing course or speed, but can include hailing[2].

A hail by the keep-clear boat of 'Hold your course!' puts no obligation on the right-of-way boat, which is entitled to change course if she believes it necessary to avoid a collision[3].

It is no defence to a protest for failing to keep clear under a rule of Part 2 that a right-of-way boat behaved unpredictably. At a starboard-hand windward mark, P will expect that S will tack onto the port-tack layline to round the mark. But no rule requires S to do so, and if S, for whatever reason stands on for a collision course with P, P must keep clear[4].

The first part of the definition Keep Clear does not address itself directly to what the keep-clear boat is doing. Instead, it measures its effect on the right-of-way boat (the 'other' in the definition). Let us first consider the simplest case, under rule 12.

If Iris is clear astern of *Daffodil* and closing on her on the same tack, it is assumed that there is a point at which *Daffodil* (the clear-ahead right-of-way boat) will 'need to take avoiding action[5]'. In these circumstances it is usually too late for avoiding action by the boat ahead to be effective, but as the need is there, *Iris* has failed to keep clear before any contact occurred.

Those were the facts in ISAF 30. *Iris* blanketed *Daffodil* in closing on her while both boats were on starboard tack, caused *Daffodil* to gybe involuntarily to port tack just before the collision. At the moment of the contact, *Iris* had become the right-of-way boat under rule 10, but the infringement had already occurred before the gybe, under rule 12. True, *Daffodil* then broke rule 10, but only because *Iris*'s breach of rule 12 caused her to do so, thus leading to exoneration for *Daffodil*.

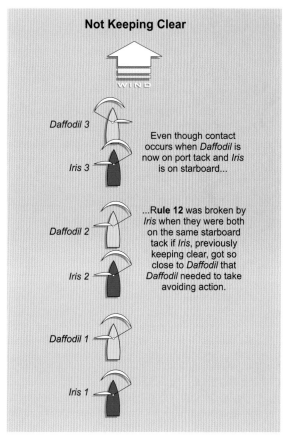

Not Keeping Clear

WIND

Daffodil 3

Iris 3

Even though contact occurs when *Daffodil* is now on port tack and *Iris* is on starboard...

Daffodil 2

Iris 2

...**Rule 12** was broken by *Iris* when they were both on the same starboard tack if *Iris*, previously keeping clear, got so close to *Daffodil* that *Daffodil* needed to take avoiding action.

Daffodil 1

Iris 1

---

[1] ISAF 99

[2] ISAF 107, which also says that a boat that is not keeping a lookout may thereby fail to everything reasonably possible to avoid contact: see below under rule 14. A hail of starboard does not commit a starboard tack to standing on, and she can then tack without breaking a rule: see CYA 6.

[3] US 27 and RYA 1967/5: if such a hail is made, I think it can postpone the point at which, under rule 14, the right-of-way boat must take avoiding action when it is 'clear that the other boat is not keeping clear'.

[4] ISAF 9.

[5] Even though in practice a Thames Barge might not be very concerned about a sportsboat closing rapidly from astern.

For the same reason, if contact does occur between same-tack boats that had previously not been overlapped, it may not matter whether the contact was bow to transom (i.e., with a boat clear ahead) or bow to port or starboard quarter (i.e., just after an overlap has begun from clear astern) if the protest committee is satisfied that the moment of not keeping clear (as opposed to the moment of contact) was while one of them was still clear astern.

If an *Iris* clear astern is sailing a course to pass to leeward of a *Daffodil* clear ahead on the same tack, *Daffodil* breaks no rule if she bears away below a proper course to frustrate this, provided that, as required by rule 16.1, *Daffodil* gives *Iris* room to keep clear. However, if in bearing away *Daffodil* creates a temporary overlap and becomes a windward boat under rule 11, *Daffodil* has no protection under rule 15, because she gave up her right of way because of her own action[1].

The simplicity of rule 12 in action is reflected in a paucity of published cases related to this rule alone. ISAF 77 referred to above, as concerns equipment that unexpectedly flies free, can be contrasted with ISAF 91, where there was, after a leeward mark rounding, contact between a boat clear astern and the spinnaker of the boat ahead that had been flying astern for several seconds from the top of the mast. In this case, it was found that a boat required to keep clear must keep clear of another boat's equipment out of position when the equipment has been out of its normal position long enough for the equipment to have been seen.

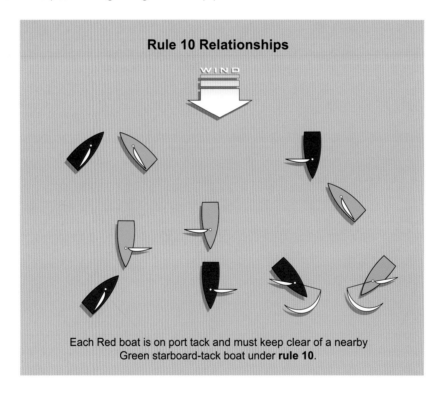

Rule 10 Relationships

WIND

Each Red boat is on port tack and must keep clear of a nearby Green starboard-tack boat under **rule 10**.

Rule 10 is more complex than rule 12 in operation, since it can apply to boats that are approaching each other more rapidly.

---

[1] Because of the abolition of rule 17.2 that applied until 2008, this is now the case offwind as well as on a beat to windward.

It is equally true that contact is not needed in order for a boat to be found not to have kept clear. Can you decide (fig 1) whether P is keeping clear of S[1]?

Is P Keeping Clear?

fig 1

In fact, you do not yet have enough information to apply the test of whether S can sail her course with no need to take avoiding action. What are the wind and wave conditions? What sorts of boats are involved? What are the speeds of the boats, and so how long is there before contact? How quickly can P manoeuvre? Is there eye contact between the helms? Had S hailed 'Starboard' and had there been any reaction by P? Has P just hailed that she will duck?

In the actual facts of ISAF 88, P and S were 7m keelboats, sailing in 12 to 15 knots of wind and minimal sea conditions. S hailed 'Starboard' at three lengths, and again a second or so later, but P did not then respond. Just after the position shown, S luffed believing contact was likely, while P bore away sharply and missed S's stern by less than a metre. On appeal, P was disqualified under rule 10, as S was fully justified in expecting a collision and concluding that only her action would prevent it. So S was unable to sail her course 'with no need to take avoiding action'.

It was while racing close-hauled in dinghies in sight of each other on opposite tacks on a 'dark and stormy night' in a force 7-8 wind in RYA 1986/1 that S hailed 'Starboard' at six lengths. P heard it, but did not bear away until two lengths, at which point S took avoiding action that created contact that might not have occurred had she held her course. P said that she was in control of the situation, but her penalisation was upheld because, in the prevailing conditions, she had not taken avoiding action early enough.

ISAF 50 offers a valuable discussion of keeping clear under rule 10.

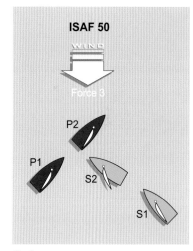

ISAF 50

Force 3

fig 2

On a windward leg in Force 3, P and S, identical 27-foot keelboats, met. P sailed a course to cross ahead of S. S bore away and protested under rule 10, stating that she had to bear away to avoid colliding with P. The protest committee, in dismissing the protest, said 'The need to change course could not be substantiated by the conflicting testimony of the two helmsmen.' S's appeal was upheld:

> Rule 10 protests involving no contact are very common, and protest committees tend to handle them in very different ways. Some place an onus on the port-tack boat to prove conclusively that she would have cleared the starboard-tack boat, even when the latter's evidence is barely worthy of credence. No such onus appears in rule 10. Other protest committees are reluctant to allow any rule 10 protest in the absence of contact, unless the starboard tack boat proves conclusively that contact would have occurred had she not changed course. Both approaches are incorrect.

S's diagram, later endorsed by the protest committee, shows that S bore away to avoid contact. P's diagram, which was not endorsed by the protest committee, shows a near miss if S did not bear away. P did not deny or confirm that S bore away but said that, if she did, it was unnecessary.

A starboard-tack boat in such circumstances need not hold her course so as to prove, by hitting the port-tack boat, that a collision was inevitable. Moreover, if she does so, she will break rule 14. At a protest hearing, S must establish either that contact would have occurred had she held her course, or that there was enough doubt that P could safely cross ahead to create a reasonable apprehension of contact of contact on S's part and that it was unlikely that S would have 'no need to take avoiding action' (see the definition Keep Clear).

---

[1] ISAF 88

In her own defence (fig 2 page 29), P must present adequate evidence to establish either that S did not change course or that P would have safely crossed ahead of S and that S had no need to take avoiding action. When, after considering all the evidence, a protest committee finds that S did not change course or that there was not a genuine and reasonable apprehension of collision on her part, it should dismiss her protest. When however it is satisfied that S did change course, that there was reasonable doubt that P could have crossed ahead, and that S was justified in taking avoiding action by bearing away, then P should be disqualified.

On the facts, as shown in the diagram and the report of the protest committee, the ability of P to cross ahead of S was doubtful at best. The appeal of S is upheld, and P is disqualified[1].

The other side of the coin in the same circumstances is when P and S are dinghies, typically single-handed, and P is not sure whether she will keep clear passing ahead of S. She will often hail 'Can I go?' to S. S, more often than not, will reply in the affirmative, not wishing P to tack ahead of her and then give her same-tack dirty air, assessing that the starboard tack is favoured, and realising that to oblige P to duck might result in P responding in kind if later in the race the positions are reversed. S may need to bear off a little to allow P to cross her. If a third boat were to see this and protest P under rule 10, what should a protest committee decide? If you take 'sail her course' in the definition Keep Clear as meaning 'sail her chosen course', then I think that S is indeed sailing her chosen course, a curved one from which she does not need to deviate further, and so P does not break rule 10[2].

Most rule 10 cases concern windward legs. The rule applies equally when sailing downwind, and it is important for a port-tack running boat to realise how few rights she has.

Yellow (fig 1) running on port tack will have to keep clear of all Blue boats except one that is running on port tack to windward clear astern of her – and a gybe by the other boat will change that.

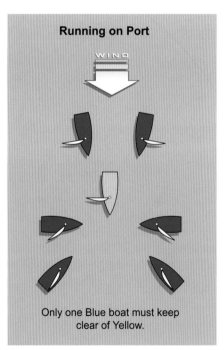

fig 1

---

[1] RYA 1981/9 is to the same effect

[2] Note that a course need not be straight – it is the course made good over the ground, and not the direction in which the boat is pointing (see RYA 1988/8). The definition Mark-Room and rule 18.4, Gybing, show that a proper course (and so, by inference, any course) may be curved. This situation can be distinguished from RYA 1990/8, discussed previously under the Basic Principle, because here there is a consensual arrangement between the boats.

Traditionally, downwind rule 10 situations have been slow-speed affairs, but many modern classes sail downwind at high gybing angles, at great speed, with limited control and needing a good look out to see another boat approaching on the same tack. Rule 10 applies to this situation without modification, but the point at which S (fig 2) can no longer 'sail her course with no need to take avoiding action' may be at a greater separation than in a close-hauled windward situation.

Deep Reaching

At what point can S no longer 'sail her course with no need to take avoiding action'?

fig 2

Rule 11 introduces a new element to keeping clear when boats are overlapped on the same tack (fig 3). The basic test in the first part of the definition Keep Clear, of whether the right-of-way boat can sail her course with no need to take avoiding action, still applies, but will be satisfied by a boat sailing a parallel course only a short distance to windward. So the definition adds that one boat is keeping clear of another, '…when the boats are *overlapped* on the same *tack*, if the *leeward* boat can change course in both directions without immediately making contact with the *windward* boat.'

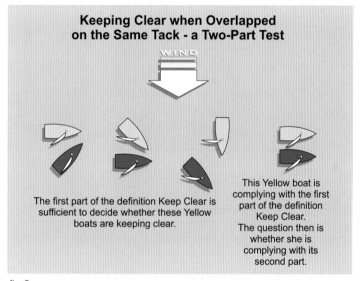

Keeping Clear when Overlapped on the Same Tack - a Two-Part Test

The first part of the definition Keep Clear is sufficient to decide whether these Yellow boats are keeping clear.

This Yellow boat is complying with the first part of the definition Keep Clear. The question then is whether she is complying with its second part.

fig 3

This further test raises three issues. Firstly, what is 'immediately'? Less than a second? More than a second? Secondly, what rate of changing course is to be assumed? We are not told, nor is there yet useful case or call guidance to this relatively new concept. Thirdly, the test is an academic and theoretical one. If L actually changes course and causes contact to prove that W is not keeping clear, it would appear that, while W is breaking rule 11, L is also breaking rule 16.1, Changing Course. She is also breaking rule 14, Avoiding Contact, and will be penalised under that rule too if the collision results in injury or damage. ISAF Q&A 2009-004 considers this, without any clear outcome.

Question

W gets increasingly closer to L. They are overlapped on the same tack. There is no contact. L protests under rule 11. In deciding whether W has kept clear, how is the protest committee to decide whether contact after a hypothetical course change by L is 'immediate'? A very gentle change of course might not result in contact for several seconds. A substantial movement of the helm might result in contact in less than a second.

Answer

The protest committee should consider facts, such as distance between the boats, wind and sea conditions and the manoeuvrability of the boats, to decide if W kept clear. The shorter the time between L's change of course and contact, or the risk thereof, the more likely W did not keep clear at the time of L's change of course.

Ultimately, the assessment is one that has to be made by a protest committee, although a leeward boat upset by the proximity of a windward one can help her cause in the hearing by being heard to call out the distance between the boats. The prosaic truth is that, the closer that W gets, the more likely that she is not keeping clear.

The fact that W believes that L is sailing higher than she is allowed to do does not relieve W of her obligation to keep clear. In ISAF 14, L became overlapped from clear astern and sailed what she believed to be a proper course that was higher than the course W believed to be proper. There was contact, resulting in the penalisation of L that was reversed on appeal, because, when rule 17 applies, different boats can have different proper courses from A to B. W was disqualified, because, when, owing to a difference of opinion on the proper course to be sailed, two boats on the same tack converge, W is bound by rule 11 to keep clear.

This partly obscures the point that W is required to keep clear even if L is undoubtedly sailing above a proper course when rule 17 requires her not to do so. If W can respond, she must, otherwise she breaks rule 11, which she was not compelled to do by L's breach, and so she will not be entitled to exoneration under rule 64.1(c)[1]. Therefore, both boats will be penalised.

Similarly, W will be in a weak position if L, unimpeded by rule 17, luffs harder than W believes rule 16.1 allows. If W tries promptly to keep clear, and fails, she will prove her case. If she does nothing, then she risks the luff being found to be legal, resulting in her penalisation under rule 11. The fact that one boat is breaking a rule does not excuse another boat for breaking a rule unless she is compelled to do so.

A precise and technical definition of keeping clear appears to be of limited significance in big-fleet dinghy starts, where it sometimes seems possible to walk from one end of the line to the other without getting one's feet wet. Boats are close, and often touching, but it rarely results in either a penalty being taken or a protest. But when boats are nearly stationary, and L is not in a tolerant mood, exhorting W to be some distance further away than her current position, W's only way to get clear and yet avoid contact may be to sheet in and squirt forwards – into a OCS position. That is W's problem, and she cannot seek to avoid acting to keep clear in the grounds it will ruin her start.

Rule 11 is not broken if L bears away, no doubt in search of cleaner air, and W does likewise (while remaining clear of her) to frustrate this[2].

 **Rule 13**

WHILE TACKING

After a boat passes head to wind, she shall *keep clear* of other boats until she is on a close-hauled course. During that time rules 10, 11 and 12 do not apply. If two boats are subject to this rule at the same time, the one on the other's port side or the one astern shall *keep clear*.

As the rule says, this is an exception to rules 10,11 and 12. The term 'tacking' in the title is not defined, and it usually means the process of getting from having the sails drawing on one tack to having them drawing on the other tack. Within this general process, a boat loses all rights under rules 10, 11 or 12 when she passes head to wind, and she may regain rights under one of them when she reaches a close-hauled course. That can be a close-hauled course on either tack, so that if she passes head to wind but (as sometimes happens when stalled on a starting line) she does not continue to a close-hauled course on that tack, and instead passes back through head-to-wind, she remains a keep-clear boat until she reaches the close-hauled course on her previous tack.

---

[1] Team race calls C4 and D5
[2] Because of the abolition of rule 17.2 that applied until 2008.

Except when boats are deliberately trying to be between head to wind and close-hauled for some time, as in the starting line situation, the time during which rule 13 is in effect is brief – even a large modern racing keel boat can go from tack to tack in a few seconds, and dinghies are even quicker. The importance of rule 13 is often not so much the tacking boat's loss of any rights once past head to wind, but rather what happens next.

The act of passing head to wind always changes the boat's tack, from port to starboard or *vice versa*. At that moment, she may now become overlapped on the same tack as another boat: she may have ended a previous same-tack overlap; and she may now be on the tack opposite to that of a nearby boat. At that point, these are largely academic issues, since, whatever her new relationship with others, she must keep clear of them for the moment, and the significance of her new tack starts to apply only once she reaches a close-hauled course, when she

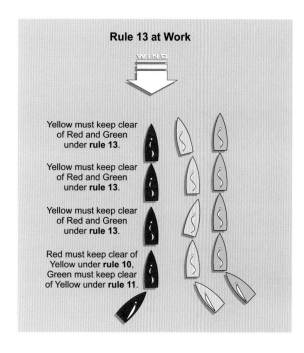

Rule 13 at Work

WIND

Yellow must keep clear of Red and Green under **rule 13**.

Yellow must keep clear of Red and Green under **rule 13**.

Yellow must keep clear of Red and Green under **rule 13**.

Red must keep clear of Yellow under **rule 10**, Green must keep clear of Yellow under **rule 11**.

may now have right of way, or she will be required to continue to keep clear. If she acquires (or reacquires) right of way by tacking from port to starboard, her ability to exploit this will be limited by rule 15, as we shall see, and if she tacks too close to another boat she may not be able give the room that rule requires. If she then continues to bear away past a close-hauled course, rule 16 may be an issue.

Luffing only as far as head to wind does not bring rule 13 into force, even though the boat intends to pass head to wind, In an RYA case that is no longer published[1], *Iris* luffed head to wind, intending to tack, but owing to a jammed winch did not pass head to wind, and fell back onto her starboard-tack course. *Daffodil*, clear astern, bore away to keep clear. *Daffodil* won her protest under rule 13, but this was reversed on appeal. Whatever the reason, *Iris* had remained on starboard tack, and *Daffodil* was required to keep clear under rule 12 – which she did. Rule 13 did not apply, and no rule had been broken.

A boat is head to wind when her bow is facing the wind and the centreline of her hull is parallel to it, irrespective of the position of her sails – for instance, her jib may still be cleated in or held as for the previous tack, either by accident[2], or deliberately, to assist her tacking. Rule 13 stops applying when the boat reaches a close-hauled course, regardless of her movement through the water or the sheeting of her sails[3], and if she bears away past that close-hauled course, it will now be one of rules 10, 11 and 12 that will apply.

Rule 13 has its own built-in exception, when two boats are both subject to this rule at the same time – the one on the other's port side or the one astern shall keep clear. Unless the tacking of the two boats is precisely synchronised, this exception will apply only for the even briefer time while both boats are between head to wind and a close-hauled course. So before either boat luffs, one of rules 10, 11 and 12 will apply between them, then when one of them passes head to wind that boat will lose any right of way, but when the other also passes head to wind that right of way may pass to the boat on the other's starboard side, and then promptly be lost when one of them reaches a close-hauled course while the other is still between head to wind and a close-hauled course, followed by a further change of right of way when both are no longer subject to rule 13 – all in a second or so.

---

[1] Not because it was wrong, but because it was felt to be too obvious!

[2] US 17

[3] ISAF 17

The lack of appeal cases on this indicates that it is more of a quiz question than a real-life problem. And beware if you are the boat 'on the right' that believes herself to be 'in the right'. As an exception to the normal provision of rule 13, you are a right-of-way boat possibly as early as the moment you pass head to wind, but your ability to keep bearing away to a close-hauled course (as with Yellow) may be limited by rule 16.1 and possibly to rule 15 as well. In practice you may have to delay until the other boat has kept clear. So this provision may be of little benefit to you.

Section B - General Limitations

As previously stated, the rules of this section place limitations in effect only on right-of-way boats. They do not add to the obligations of keep-clear boats (rule 14) or do not affect keep-clear boats (rules 15, 16 and 17).

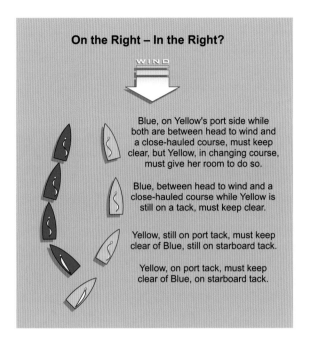

On the Right – In the Right?

WIND

Blue, on Yellow's port side while both are between head to wind and a close-hauled course, must keep clear, but Yellow, in changing course, must give her room to do so.

Blue, between head to wind and a close-hauled course while Yellow is still on a tack, must keep clear.

Yellow, still on port tack, must keep clear of Blue, still on starboard tack.

Yellow, on port tack, must keep clear of Blue, on starboard tack.

Rule 14

AVOIDING CONTACT

A boat shall avoid contact with another boat if reasonably possible. However, a right-of-way boat or one entitled to *room* or *mark-room*

(a) need not act to avoid contact until it is clear that the other boat is not *keeping clear* or giving *room* or *mark-room*, and

(b) shall not be penalised under this rule unless there is contact that causes damage or injury.

Rule 14 is well-intentioned, but flawed in its execution. Its first sentence is a clear statement of ISAF policy, addressed to all boats, whether keep-clear, right-of-way or room-entitled. But as has been seen, a keep-clear boat has to do more than just avoid contact, so it is hard to see how the first sentence makes any difference to her. Technically, when a keep-clear boat is found in a protest not to have done so, and there is contact, the protest committee should add rule 14 to the right-of-way rule that has been broken on the protest form: my experience is that few do, but no harm results. Perhaps rule 14 offers a clearer route to penalisation under rule 2 or rule 69 of reckless sailing.

If the first sentence of rule 14 were to apply unaltered to right-of-way boats, that would create a conflict with rules 10 to 13[1]. It would also create uncertainty, and defeat the excellent safety principle enshrined in the IRPCAS[2], that when one boat has to keep out of the way of another, the other shall keep her course and speed until it is apparent that other boat is not giving way. Indeed, rule 14 is mirrored on the IRPCAS rule, with one exception, namely that minor bumps are inherent in sailboat racing, and so rule 14(b) removes the risk of penalisation from a right-of-way boat or one entitled to room or mark-room that decides not to avoid an avoidable collision when neither damage nor injury results. The risk for that boat is that minor contact may result in major damage, as when a clipped backstay brings the rig down.

This creates the curious concept of a non-punishable infringement. As already discussed, it does not sit easily with the Basic Principle, Sportsmanship and the Rules, which requires a boat that breaks a rule to rotate or retire. It also adds another largely needless step in the completion of protest decisions by protest committees, namely the recording of a breach of rule 14 for which no penalty is to be imposed.

---

1 As was found from experimental rules in 1995, from which the current structure of the rules was developed for 1997.
[2] IRPCAS rule 17

If a keep-clear boat finds it impossible to avoid contact with a right-of-way boat, she has either got into that situation through her own fault, and will break or will have already broken a rule; or it has happened because a right-of-way boat has broken a rule such as rule 16.1, which will entitle the keep-clear boat to exoneration under rule 64.1(c) because it was not possible to keep clear. In either case, rule 14 becomes just another reason for penalizing or not penalizing, in addition to the primary right-of-way evaluation of the situation.

Therefore, the question of what is possible in terms of collision avoidance, and then whether it is 'reasonably' possible, applies to all boats, but is significant only for a 'a right-of-way boat or one entitled to room or mark-room', as reflected in the cases.

Thus, in RYA 1975/4, S and P tried and failed to avoid contact that resulted in damage. P was disqualified under rule 10, but S was found not to have broken rule 14, as her effort to avoid a collision was reasonable for S's inexperienced helmsman, even though she did not act to avoid contact until after it was clear that P was not going to keep clear. This was reversed on appeal, and S was disqualified as well as P:

> The test of whether it was reasonably possible for S to avoid contact is an objective one. The inexperience of helmsman and crew cannot justify a lower standard of care.

Avoidance may be **theoretically** possible, but not **reasonably** possible, on safety grounds. In ISAF 99, in keelboat racing in difficult conditions, P was careering out of control an a broad reach towards S, whose minor changes of direction to try to avoid contact were defeated by P's erratic course. There was contact resulting in damage. The protest committee penalised P under rule 10 and S under rule 14, noting that S could have keep clear earlier by trying harder than she did, and could still have kept clear just before the collision by crash-gybing, albeit at risk of damage to herself. S's appeal was upheld.

> She was not required to act to avoid contact until it was clear that P was not going to keep clear. It was only at that time that rule 14 required her to avoid contact if reasonably possible. The protest committee found that, when it became clear to S that P was not going to keep clear, the only action available to S was to crash-gybe, which risked considerable damage to S. That is equivalent to finding that it was not reasonably possible for S to avoid contact – her disqualification is reversed.

The case also confirms the point previously made[1] that the fact that P was out of control does not justify exonerating her under rule 10. It does not address the academic question of whether it was reasonably possible for P to avoid contact: presumably there must be a point at which conditions make contact avoidance impossible by even a skilled and experienced P.

ISAF 99 says that the right-of-way boat breaks no rule by not taking avoiding action before it is clear that the other boat is not keeping clear, even if it reasonable to expect that she will not keep clear. ISAF 27 makes the same point: 'A boat is not required to anticipate that another boat will break a rule.'

ISAF 99 confirms that the test of whether collision avoidance is possible is to be made when it is clear that the keep-clear boat will not do so. RYA 2002/11 says that if it is possible at that time, the fact that it may soon after become impossible does not exonerate the right-of-way boat. Keelboats were beating in 12 knots, and the protest committee found that at 10 seconds before contact occurred it was clear to S that P would not keep clear in crossing her. S struck P's quarter 130mm from her stern, causing damage, and she was disqualified under rule 14. S admitted that she had not borne away, believing that she would pass close astern of P (note the distinction between avoiding contact and keeping clear), but that this had been frustrated by P's helmsman leaving his position, causing P to change course and changing a near miss into a direct hit. While not accepting that P had changed course, the RYA dismissed the appeal, saying that a boat that elects to pass close astern of a boat crossing ahead of her does so at her own risk if she was able to pass further away[2].

---

[1] RYA 1994/4

[2] See also ISAF 26: 'A right-of-way boat need not act to avoid a collision until it is clear that the other boat is not keeping clear. However, if the right-of-way boat could then have avoided the collision and the collision resulted in damage, she must be penalised under rule 14.'

If a boat does not keep a good lookout, she may fail to do everything reasonably possible to avoid contact, and, if she does not hail if that could have averted a collision, she has not 'acted to avoid contact'. In ISAF 107, before the starting signal, *Ephesian* (S) and *Jupa* (P), both heavy 10m keelboats, collided with damage, head-to-head. Neither was previously aware of the other, and both were penalised, *Ephesian* under rule 14. She appealed, asserting that, in the light conditions, she had limited manoeuvrability, and could not have avoided *Jupa* by changing course or speed. Her appeal was dismissed.

> The requirement of rule 14 to 'avoid contact with another boat if reasonably possible' means that a boat must do everything that can reasonably be expected of her in the prevailing conditions to avoid contact. This includes keeping a good lookout, particularly in a crowded starting line situation. The protest committee had concluded that if either boat had seen each other a collision could have been avoided, even at the last moment, particularly if *Ephesian* had hailed. when it was clear that *Jupa* was not going to keep clear, the moment when she must 'act to avoid contact'. The word 'act' is not restricted to changing course or speed. Hailing was an action that *Ephesian* should have could have taken[1].

It should be noted that rule 5 of the IRPCAS requires all boats to keep 'a proper lookout by sight and hearing'. That rule does not apply directly to boats that are racing, any more than any other IRPCAS rule. The requirement for boats racing to keep a good lookout is not explicit in the racing rules: it is a not-immediately-obvious implication of rule 14, to be found only in the cases. Since this is an important point, and since neither the ISAF casebook nor textbooks like this one are the bedside reading of every competitor, there is a good argument for making it an explicit requirement in the rules, although continued compliance could be inconveniently difficult, not to say impossible, in some modern designs of centreboards with sprit-rigged spinnakers, and in single-handed oceanic racing.

What is damage? ISAF 19 tells us (or, rather, doesn't tell us).

> It is not possible to define 'damage' comprehensively, but one current English dictionary says 'harm . . . impairing the value or usefulness of something.'
> This definition suggests questions to consider.
> Examples are:
> 1. Was the current market value of any part of the boat, or of the boat as a whole, diminished?
> 2. Was any item of the boat or her equipment made less functional?

RYA 2001/3 is rather more helpful. 'Damage includes something that a prudent owner would repair promptly.'

So under either test, a gouge to a newly varnished wooden hull may well be damage, whereas the umpteenth wound to an elderly Topper hull would probably not be. RYA 2001/3 makes a further point: 'Damage includes damage a boat causes to herself.' So the fact that damage is incurred only by the right-of-way boat that fails to avoid avoidable contact will not preclude penalisation under rule 14.

RYA 2008/3 goes further. *Iris* wrongly denied *Daffodil* mark-room, and *Daffodil*, in avoiding *Iris*, crashed into *Thetis*, damaging her. 'In a protest, the right-of-way boat or one entitled to room or mark-room may be penalised under rule 14 even if the damage or injury referred to in 14(b) is incurred only by a third boat that is not a party to the hearing, if it is a consequence of the original breach of a rule of Part 2 by one of the parties.'

The logical consequence of this would seem to be that penalisation under rule 14 is possible if damage is caused to a vessel not racing, or even a jetty or shore installation. Likewise, the injury may be to a person on a vessel not racing, or a spectator on the shore – as long as there is a causal link with the original failure to keep clear.

''Injury' in the racing rules refers only to bodily injury to a person, and 'damage' is limited to physical damage to a boat or her equipment[2].' 'Damage' (or 'injury[3]') to a boat's finishing position or prospects thereof are not applicable to the several occasions when those terms arise in the rules.

---

[1] CYA 71 makes the same point as concerns keeping a good lookout, as does ISAF 26: 'All boats, whether or not holding right of way, should keep a lookout at all times.'
[2] ISAF 110: I wonder whether an injury to the ship's cat, or to the swan in the reeds I have crashed into, might also count.
[3] US 98

A curiosity. A right-of-way boat that realises that she has broken rule 14 may be able to take a two-turns penalty. Her turns will be ineffective if her breach gained her a significant advantage or if injury or serious damage resulted[1]. But if there was damage that was not serious, and no injury, her turns will protect her against penalisation. Likewise, a keep-clear boat that takes a two-turns penalty when there is contact but neither significant advantage, serious injury nor damage will simultaneously exonerate the breaches of rule 14 and the relevant right-of-way rule.

ACQUIRING RIGHT OF WAY

When a boat acquires right of way, she shall initially give the other boat room to keep clear, unless she acquires right of way because of the other boat's actions.

'Rule 15…embodies the principle in the rules that when the right of way suddenly shifts from one boat to another, the boat with the newly acquired right of way must give the other boat space and time to response and thus a fair opportunity to keep clear[2].'

Rule 15 is rule of limitation, in a section entitled General Limitations. Specifically (as with rule 16), it limits the right-of-way boat's ability to sail as she pleases and to manoeuvre against a give-way boat, which is permissible unless a rule says that it is not. (As has been seen, rules 10 to 13 address themselves purely to the keep-clear boat, and do not themselves place any obligation or limitation on the right-of-way boat). It is addressed to the right-of-way boat, and can be broken only by a right-of-way boat. It is usually an issue when a boat has not kept clear and is seeking a good reason for exoneration, namely, under rule 64.1(c), that she was compelled to infringe because of the infringement of the right-of-way boat.

The rule refers to acquiring right of way, not to retaining right of way under a change of rule of Section A.

Blue (fig 1) is keep-clear boat, at position 1 under rule 12, By gybing at position 2, Yellow does not acquire right of way, rather she maintains it under a different rule, and so owes no new room to Blue. Rule 15 does not apply. Blue gains right of way under rule 11 at position 3 by gybing, so she must initially give Yellow room to keep clear. Yellow makes a bad choice by gybing at position 4, and it is now rule 10 under which she must keep clear. Blue does not acquire right of way, since she already had it, and so need not give Yellow room to keep clear. If Yellow is not now keeping clear, there is no exoneration, since Blue's initial duty to give room had ended.

The rule applies only for a short time, as evidenced by the word 'initially'. If the newly obligated give-way boat delays keeping clear, she risks losing the protection of the rule. The right-of-way boat's obligation under rule 15 'is not a continuing one; it protects [the keep-clear boat] only temporarily, and only if she responds promptly after the overlap begins[3].' That time had long since expired when Blue did not keep clear of Yellow in RYA 1990/1 (see fig 1 on page 38).

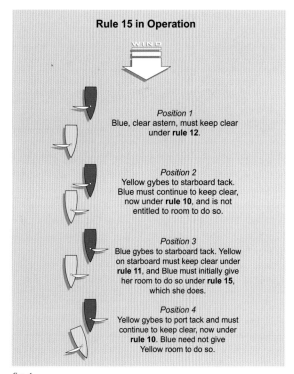

Rule 15 in Operation

WIND

Position 1
Blue, clear astern, must keep clear under **rule 12**.

Position 2
Yellow gybes to starboard tack. Blue must continue to keep clear, now under **rule 10**, and is not entitled to room to do so.

Position 3
Blue gybes to starboard tack. Yellow on starboard must keep clear under **rule 11**, and Blue must initially give her room to do so under **rule 15**, which she does.

Position 4
Yellow gybes to port tack and must continue to keep clear, now under **rule 10**. Blue need not give Yellow room to do so.

fig 1

---

[1] Rule 44.1(b)
[2] ISAF 24
[3] ISAF 24

To quote the case's abstract, 'When a boat is obliged to change course to keep clear of another boat that has acquired right of way, she must act promptly, since a right-of-way boat is required only initially to give her room to do so. After that, rule 15 does not apply'.

Both Room and Keep Clear are defined terms, and the latter has already been discussed in detail.

Definition Room The space a boat needs in the existing conditions while manoeuvring promptly in a seamanlike way.

Room in rules 15 and 16.1 is, to use the term in rule 14, an 'entitlement' of a keep-clear boat that a right-of-way boat must satisfy in certain circumstances.

While the word used is 'space', the obsolete rules term 'time and opportunity' equally well expresses the concept.

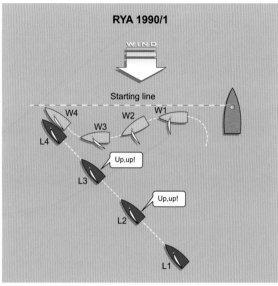

fig 1

Different boats will need different amounts of space, depending on their size and manoeuvrability, and, the worse the conditions, the more the space that will be needed. A boat entitled to room is expected to act promptly, within the transient operation of rule 15, as we have seen, failing which she will have no excuse for then not keeping clear. Whether these requirements have been met is an issue for the protest committee, based on the circumstances and conditions.

If L becomes overlapped to leeward from astern while W is stalled, as on the starting line, the space that she provides may not be the space that W wants to take, namely the open water ahead of W on the course side of the starting line that she will intrude into by sheeting in.

If L becomes overlapped to leeward from astern[1] on the beat, and can then sail higher that W, L will have complied with rule 15 by giving W enough space to tack off, whether or not W wants to. If W does not tack when she can, she will have no defence for being unable to keep clear a short time later.

If L becomes overlapped to leeward from astern on a reach, then L will have complied with rule 15 by giving W enough space to luff.

In all these cases, if the keep-clear boat acts promptly to keep clear as required, but there is contact, then sufficient room has not been given – provided that contact was not caused by the keep-clear boat doing more than was needed just to keep clear[2]. However, room will have been given if a port-tack boat alters course in one direction and there is contact with the starboard tack boat, if there would not have been contact had she altered course in the other direction – she must 'promptly manoeuvre in a way which offers a reasonable expectation that she will keep clear[3].'

So some elements of Room are variables, dependant on the circumstances. One however is not, namely the 'seamanlike' standard, which has three implications. Firstly, the give-way boat that is required to manoeuvre must be capable of the 'boat handling that can reasonably be expected from a competent, but not expert, crew of the appropriate number for the boat[4]'. If room meeting this description has been given, a boat that through less-than-competent boat handling fails to keep clear cannot invoke rule 15 (or rule 16.1) as a defence.

---

[1] L must not sail above her proper course, however, see rule 17, but on a beat L's own close-hauled course will always be 'proper', and it will prevail over W's proper course if she cannot sail so high or is sailing to a different less-windward mark.
[2] ISAF 24
[3] RYA 2008/6
[4] ISAF 103

Secondly, it is a yardstick of the space afforded by the right-of-way boat. Room will not have been given if 'a keep-clear boat, despite having taken avoiding action promptly, cannot keep clear in a seamanlike way[1].' So 'When a boat becomes overlapped to leeward from clear astern, the other boat must act promptly to keep clear. When she cannot do so in a seamanlike way, she has not been given sufficient room[2].' In US 78, *Iris* tacked from port to starboard. *Daffodil* tacked in response, but *Thetis* did not have room to respond.

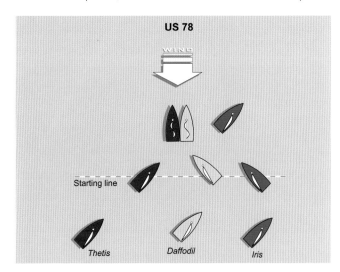

In the absence of *Thetis*, *Iris*'s tack to a right-of-way position may have complied with rule 15. But *Iris* was found to have caused *Daffodil* to collide with *Thetis*, and so to have been compelled to manoeuvre in an unseamanlike way. *Daffodil* was exonerated for breaking rule 15 with respect to *Thetis* because *Iris* broke rule 15 with respect to *Daffodil*.

Thirdly, it is a maximum as well as a minimum standard. The inference to be drawn from ISAF 24 is that if a newly-obligated keep-clear boat is able to keep clear, but only by crash-tacking, crash-gybing or by some other unseamanlike manoeuvre, then room to act in a seamanlike way will not have been given.

In summary, the phrase 'in a seamanlike way' applies to both boats. The right of way boat must provide enough room so that the other boat 'need not make extraordinary or abnormal manoeuvres to keep clear of her', while the other boat 'is not entitled to complain of insufficiency of room if she fails to execute with reasonable efficiency the handling of her helm, sheets and sails[3].'

Rule 15 limits a right-of-way boat in three ways. Firstly, it may deter her from acquiring right of way.

Blue must realise that if she tacks, she will acquire right-of-way, but that will be so close to Yellow that Yellow can never have the room to keep clear to which she is entitled, even if Blue tries to give her room. So Blue must not tack.

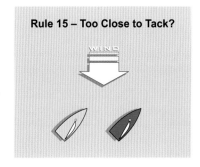

Rule 15 – Too Close to Tack?

Secondly, it has the passive effect of delaying the moment at which it is legitimate for a right-of-way boat to start to manoeuvre against another boat. Referring back to fig 1 on page 37, Blue acquires right of way under rule 10 at position 3 by gybing, which naturally brings her onto a collision course with Yellow, which must now keep clear. Blue must refrain from anything more aggressive until Yellow has had time to keep clear by gybing.

Thirdly, it can require further action by the right of way boat.

---

[1] ISAF 60, a rule 16.1 case, but the same principle applies to rule 15 situations.
[2] ISAF 24
[3] Derived from ISAF 21, which discusses mark-room, but which is equally valid for rules 15 and 16.

Blue is not seeking to manoeuvre against Yellow, but merely finds starboard tack preferable, possibly after a slight wind shift. If Blue were to hold close-hauled course at position 2, Yellow would have to keep clear, but might not have room to do so. Blue can comply with rule 15 at position 2 by bearing away further to pass astern of Yellow[1]. The problem for Blue is that at position 2 (particularly if they are a little closer, or conditions are bad) Yellow may not realise Blue's intention to duck, and so Yellow starts to tack to try to comply with rule 10, which may increase rather than reduce the chance of a collision if Blue is continuing to bear away. I believe that this is a risk that Blue has to accept, and Blue may be required to duck even deeper in order to give Yellow room to keep clear. If Blue is unable to give that additional room, I believe she breaks rule 15. Blue would be well advised to hail 'Hold your course!' to Yellow, but, as we have seen, that is not binding on Yellow, which must make her own assessment of the situation.

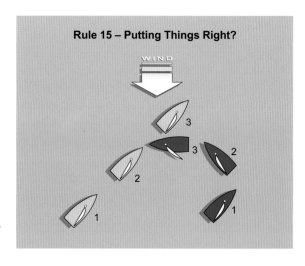

Rule 15 – Putting Things Right?

This is a situation where there is surprisingly little help from published cases, but is consistent with team racing call D3.

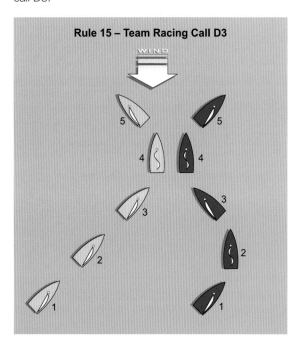

Rule 15 – Team Racing Call D3

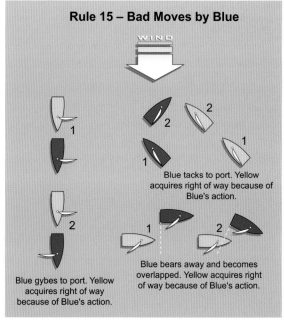

Rule 15 – Bad Moves by Blue

Blue tacks to port. Yellow acquires right of way because of Blue's action.

Blue gybes to port. Yellow acquires right of way because of Blue's action.

Blue bears away and becomes overlapped. Yellow acquires right of way because of Blue's action.

The call states that a boat acquiring right of way may comply with rule 15 by altering course herself. At position 3 Blue acquires right of way through her own actions and must initially give Yellow room to keep clear. By tacking back onto port, she gives Yellow that room. (However, if Yellow had to take avoiding action before Blue completed her tack, Blue broke rule 13. If Yellow had to tack in an unseamanlike way to keep clear, Blue broke rule 15. The call also says that Blue breaks rule 15 if at position 4 the boats are so close that there is a risk of contact.)

---

[1] As we will see under rule 16.1, RYA 2001/5 holds that 'When a right-of-way boat changes course and deprives a give-way boat of room to keep clear, she will have complied with rule 16.1 by making a further change of course that will give the other boat room to keep clear.' Given that the obligation under rules 15 and 16.1 is in either case to give room, I believe that the same principle can apply to rule 15 situations, namely that a further change of course can comply with the rule's requirements.

Another example is where, on a starting line, a boat clear astern moving in towards the starting line becomes overlapped to leeward on a boat ahead that is slow or stationary. That overlap might be established so close to the windward boat's quarter that she cannot keep clear. But if the leeward boat immediately bears away to give room before the windward boat needed to take action, then rule 15's requirements will have been met.

As the rule says, it applies when a boat acquires right-of-way through her own actions. If right of way is foolishly yielded by the other boat, rule 15 does not apply, and that is the other boat's problem. The right-of-way boat's responsibility is limited to collision avoidance under rule 14, beginning when it is clear that the other boat is not keeping clear. Here are some examples, in each of which Blue gives up right of way to Yellow, which is not required to give Blue room to keep clear:

Rule 15 does not say so itself, but breaches of it are automatically exonerated if they occur when a right-of-way boat is rounding a mark on her proper course and taking mark-room to which she is entitled, or when tacking to avoid an obstruction after hailing for room to do so, under rule 20, Room to Tack at an Obstruction[1]. It can still apply when the right of way under rule 19, Giving Room at an Obstruction, changes as between two boats passing an obstruction, for instance if boats are passing to leeward of an obstruction, and *Daffodil*, previously astern of *Iris*, becomes overlapped to leeward of her and so obtains right-of-way under rule 11.

CHANGING COURSE

Rule 16

16.1 When a right-of-way boat changes course, she shall give the other boat *room* to *keep clear*.

16.2 In addition, when after the starting signal a *port-tack* boat is *keeping clear* by sailing to pass astern of a *starboard-tack* boat, the *starboard-tack* boat shall not change course if as a result the *port-tack* boat would immediately need to change course to continue *keeping clear*.

Rule 16 was (together with rule 14) at the heart of the 1997 'rules revolution'. Racing became far less of a contact sport, and complicated luffing rules were replaced with the few apparently simple words of what is now rule 16.1, which was found to be satisfactory except in one situation, which required the later decision to add rule 16.2: this addition was controversial at the time, and remains so, many judges believing it then and now to have been unnecessary.

Unlike the transient rule 15, rule 16 applies at all times: but, as with rule 15, there is automatic exoneration when a right-of-way boat is rounding a mark on her proper course and taking mark-room to which she is entitled, or when tacking to avoid an obstruction after hailing for room to do so, under rule 20, Room to Tack at an Obstruction.

The main elements have already been examined in detail, 'room' under rule 15 and 'keep clear' under rules 10 to 13.

Those defined terms can be expanded to make rule 16.1 read as if it said:
When a right-of-way boat changes course, she shall give the other boat the space the other boat needs in the existing conditions while manoeuvring promptly in a seamanlike way, so that
- the right-of-way boat can sail her course with no need to take avoiding action and so that
- when the boats are overlapped on the same tack, the leeward right-of-way boat can change course in both directions without immediately making contact with the windward boat.

---

[1] Rules 18.5(b) and 20.2.

So a right-of-way boat is entitled to have a 'safety zone' around her, and any course change by the right-of-way boat must not deprive herself of that safety zone if the other boat acts as required.

What is 'changing course'? First, what is a course? It is the course made good over the ground, and not the direction in which the boat is pointing[1]. Secondly, 'what is the meaning of 'change course'? Is it a change of course for a boat to sail in an arc of a circle? If she does not move her helm, is she none the less changing course? 'Yes, a boat changes course when she sails the arc of a circle or any other course where she changes direction, whether or not she moves her helm. This includes a change from moving forwards to moving backwards, or vice versa. To change course means to change the direction in which the boat is heading or moving[2]'.

As with rule 15, the use of the word 'give' implies that fleeting technical breaches of rule 16.1's requirements can be corrected by further action. 'A right-of-way boat changing course may comply with rule 16.1 by changing course further and thus giving the other boat room to keep clear[3].' So in RYA 2001/5, S's course would take her astern of P, but S was lifted and P was headed by a windshift, resulting in a potential collision that P could not avoid in a seamanlike way. S then bore away to a non-collision course, an action that met the requirements of rule 16.1.

When S changed course, she was required by rule 16.1 to give P room to keep clear. She did this by bearing away. When a right of way boat changes course and deprives a give-way boat of room to keep clear, she will have complied with rule 16.1 by making a further change, to a course that will give the other boat room to keep clear.

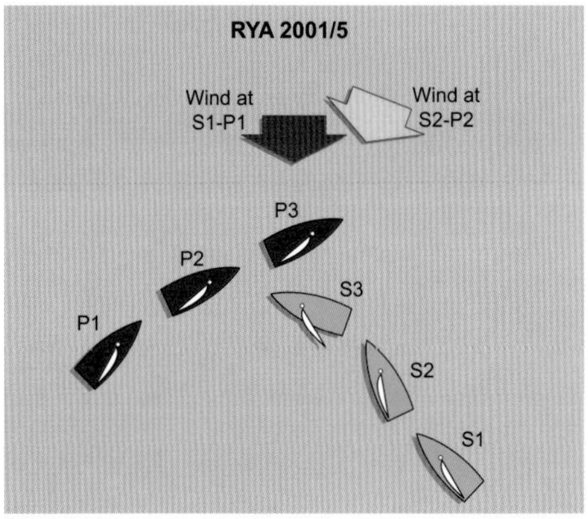

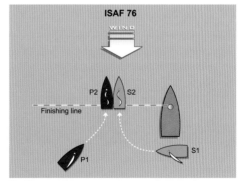

fig 1

If the room given in which to keep clear takes the keep-clear boat across the starting line before the starting signal, no rule is broken by the right-of-way boat, but if the keep-clear boat tries to avoid this happening by not responding to the right-of-way boat's change of course, the keep-clear boat will break a rule (rule 11 when she is being luffed)[4].

Rule 16.1 addresses itself only to the right-of-way boat, not the keep-clear boat. It is legitimate to manoeuvre against a keep-clear boat before the starting signal to drive her away from the starting line, provided that room is given when required. The best tactic for a give-way boat that cannot shake off the other boat may be to keep clear overlapped as close as possible to the right-of-way boat, and on the same tack, restricting the scope for being manoeuvred against. (However, if this pins her out from the starting line, there has to come a moment when she must break free if she is not to lose the start[5].)

The fact that a change of course by the right-of-way boat may be totally predictable does not disapply rule 16.1, as ISAF 76 (fig 2) shows.

No part of rule 18 applies, because of rule 18.1(a), as the boats are on a beat to windward, so breaches of rule 16.1 cannot be exonerated. If the boats hold their S1-P1 courses, P will keep clear ahead of S. P will expect that S, which presumably has overstood, will want to luff to finish, but S in doing so must comply with rule 16.1, even if S is sailing a proper course[6].

fig 2

---

[1] RYA1988/8, as concerns a what is a 'proper course', but the same interpretation would seem sensible for a course simple.
[2] US 33. In the light of RYA 1988/8, if 'heading' is different from 'moving' then 'moving' prevails. See also UMP 35.
[3] TR Call B4. MR Call UMP 11: when the give-way boat is stalled in the water, for whatever reason, or only moving slowly, she may need additional room.
[4] ISAF 13
[5] ISAF 52
[6] The case makes this point about a proper course, but I do not think the outcome would be different if S's course were not a proper course

In this case, S, in luffing after passing the stern of the committee boat, did not give P enough room to keep clear, and so S broke rule 16.1. P broke rule 10, but was compelled to do so because S broke rule 16.1, and so S is to be exonerated under rule 64.1(c). So a keep-clear boat is not required to anticipate a right-of-way boat's alteration of course[1].

When a right-of-way boat alters course to comply with rule 14, she will be exonerated if in the process she breaks rule 16.1, whether with regard to the boat she is avoiding[2], or with regard for a third boat that she affects in the process of avoiding contact with the second boat[3]. However, if the right-of-way boat luffs (or bears away) to avoid contact, breaking rule 16.1 in the process, and if rule 14 could have been complied with by instead bearing away (or by luffing), then exoneration is not possible, because the right-of-way boat was not compelled to break rule 16.1[4].

A right-of-way boat may change course in such a way that a keep-clear boat is newly obliged to take action to keep clear, until a further alteration of course would deprive the give-way boat of room to do so[5].

The room to which a keep-clear boat is entitled may be greater if she has a spinnaker set. If while she is flying it the only way she can respond to a course-change by the right-of-way boat is to bear away, and if she does so promptly but unsuccessfully, she has not been given sufficient room[6]. If she is luffed to the point where her spinnaker ceases to draw, she is entitled to room to drop it, but she must do so promptly, and she cannot complain if, having not dropped her spinnaker when she needed to do it, she is forced further to windward and possibly onto the opposite tack. This applies regardless of whether L has a spinnaker set[7].

When a leeward of three or more boats luffs, she must give room (i.e., time to respond) to all of those other boats, each of which must respond promptly to the luff of the boat to leeward of her[8].

In RYA 2003/1, rule 18 has stopped applying by position 4, and C's luff must comply with rule 16.1, so as give both B and A room to keep clear. If C's luff complies with rule 16.1 but B's ability to respond is curtailed because A does not respond (or responds only belatedly or less quickly than would be seamanlike), then A breaks rule 11, and B would be exonerated under rule 64.1(c) in any protest against her for breaking rule 11.

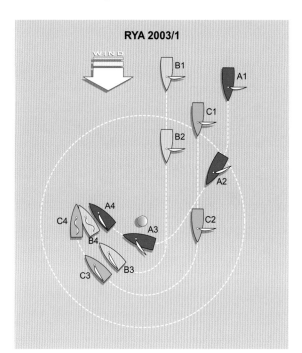

RYA 2003/1

---

[1] RYA 1993/5 makes a similar point, namely that the fact that a boat on the course side of the starting line before her starting signal can be expected to try to return, but if she is a right-of-way boat that bears away before her starting signal, her bear-way must comply with rule 16.1. The application or otherwise of rules 15 and 16 at marks and obstructions is considered under rules 18, 19 and 20.

[2] ISAF 88, RYA 2002/5
[3] US 12
[4] CYA 55
[5] RYA 1991/1
[6] RYA 2002/2
[7] UMP 33
[8] RYA 2003/1: the same principle applies if S bears away towards a number of overlapped Ps.

Match and team race calls provide further illumination.

Team racing call A3 says that Yellow luffs and Blue responds promptly. Yellow continues to luff and Blue cannot avoid contact despite luffing further. In positions 1 and 2, Blue is keeping clear because she is sufficiently far from Yellow that Yellow is able to change course in both directions without immediately making contact. At position 3, after Yellow's first change of course, Blue still has room to keep clear. Blue must, promptly and in a seamanlike way, do whatever she can to establish sufficient distance between her and A so that she is keeping clear. If Blue does this she is protected by rule 16.1.

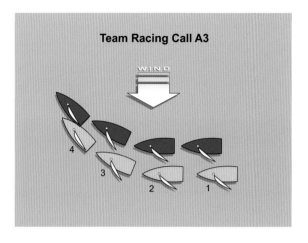

Between positions 3 and 4, Yellow continues to change course, and Blue is no longer able to keep clear. Yellow breaks rule 16.1. The principle is that when a leeward boat continues to luff, and the windward boat responds promptly and in a seamanlike way – her entitlement under the definition Room – the leeward boat will ultimately have to stop luffing when the boats are so close that any further luff by the leeward boat will result in the windward boat being unable to keep clear. If at that moment the leeward boat stops luffing, and the windward boat continues to respond to keep clear, neither boat breaks a rule.

Q&A 2 of UMP 5 is interesting[1].

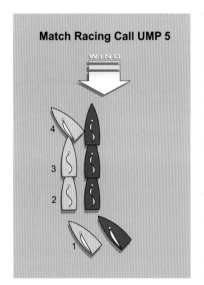

Yellow luffs, Blue luffs and avoids contact. After a time, Yellow bears away and there is contact. Which boat infringed? The answer given is that it will be either Blue or Yellow that has broken a rule, depending on the distance between them. If Yellow's change of course immediately results in contact with Blue, Blue was not keeping clear and broke rule 11. If there was more distance between them, and Yellow bears away hard giving Blue no room to keep clear, then Yellow breaks rule 16.1. The distinction between the two situations is whether the contact is 'immediate', an important concept in the definition Keep Clear regarding boats overlapped on the same tack.

Where Blue was so close as not to be keeping clear, the call does not consider the issue of Yellow's bearing away. Why does rule 16.1 not limit her bearing away? Has she not broken that rule, at the same time as Blue broke rule 11? Yellow was not compelled to bear away, and she could arguably have done so slowly enough for Blue to keep clear, in compliance with the words of rule 16.1. Match racing's tendency is towards deciding that in an incident only one of two boats will have broken a rule. In this case, it looks possible that both broke rules.

If on a windward leg P bears away onto a keep-clear course to duck S, but S frustrates this by luffing so that P no long has room to pass astern, S breaks rule 16.1[2]. On the other hand, if S changes course and then P's subsequent change of course is unsuccessful in keeping her clear, S will not have broken rule 16.1 if P could have kept clear by changing course in the opposite direction[3].

It is not seamanlike to be compelled to touch a mark, so that if a right-of-way boat changes course and the give-way boat, in responding promptly, cannot avoid touching a mark, room was not given[4].

---

[1] See also UMP 4, which is to the same effect as Q&A 2 of UMP 5, and team racing call A5.
[2] UMP 16
[3] RYA 2008/6
[4] UMP 29. There is no fleet-racing case that says so, but it seems a sensible principle.

Rule 16.2

The reason for this rule is to deter a risky manoeuvre. P and S are on a beat to windward, and S will cross P. But S needs to finish more than a place ahead of P to have a better series performance, and so wishes either to sail P down the fleet, or provoke an infringement by P, resulting in time lost taking a penalty. S therefore bears away towards P, forcing P to bear away. S continues to bear away, and P ends up sailing downwind. The 'dial-down' complies with rule 16.1 if S is at all times giving P room to respond. The problem is that S will be carrying out this aggression from a position of limited visibility for P, and if P does not see what is happening, there is a risk of a head-on collision resulting in serious damage or injury. If P is in fact alert and responds, other competitors could be surprised if the aggression continues. P, forced to run on port tack through a fleet of beating boats, will have to keep clear of all of them.

This tactic originated in match racing, where it was stopped by different means, and the fear was that it would spread to fleet racing.

It is additional to rule 16.1, which continues to apply. It starts to apply after the starting signal, even though the boats concerned may not yet have started. It will apply only when P is sailing to pass astern of S. This may be both on a beat to windward, and when boats are running on opposite tacks. On a beat to windward, this may be when the established closed-hauled courses of P and S would have taken S clear ahead of P.

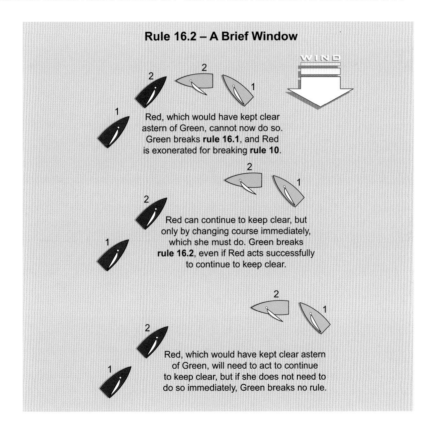

Rule 16.2 – A Brief Window

Red, which would have kept clear astern of Green, cannot now do so. Green breaks **rule 16.1**, and Red is exonerated for breaking **rule 10**.

Red can continue to keep clear, but only by changing course immediately, which she must do. Green breaks **rule 16.2**, even if Red acts successfully to continue to keep clear.

Red, which would have kept clear astern of Green, will need to act to continue to keep clear, but if she does not need to do so immediately, Green breaks no rule.

Rule 16.2 operates only in a brief window, between the time that a course change by S will give P ample time to react and the time when a course change by S will break rule 16.1[1]. The test is whether P will need to change course immediately in order to continue keeping clear. So it will not apply, and no rule has been broken, if the course change P needs to make, when manoeuvring in a seamanlike way in the prevailing conditions, is less than immediate.

---

[1] However, if S breaks rule 16.2, and then continues to bear away towards P, she may now also break rule 16.1 as well. P is not required to anticipate that S will do this, and is required to react only to what S is doing at the time, not what S may do subsequently. See ISAF 92.

Upwind, rule 16.2 will also apply when S and P were on a collision course, but P has borne away below a close-hauled course to duck S, only for S to alter course towards her; or when P is sailing to pass astern of S, and S luffs in order to tack. Again, the rule is transient. If S luffs early enough, there will be no immediate new need for P to act to act to keep clear[1]. If S luffs too late, it is rule 13 that she may break. But the rule 16.2 window is also there[2].

Downwind, it can apply when P is aiming to pass astern of S, which is not sailing straight down wind, but which bears away to a down-wind course, possibly to inconvenience P, possibly in preparation for a gybe. This is an issue for gennaker-rigged boats making big gybes downwind.

The rule can also be an issue for such boats if P is close-hauled and S, deep-reaching to windward of P on a reciprocal course, bears away towards her to gybe.

The rule was and is controversial, firstly because there was little evidence that the 'dial-down' tactic had spread to fleet racing, or was likely to do so, and secondly because an infringement is difficult to prove, given the short time between breaking rule 16.1 and not breaking rule 16.1 in which it operates. A boat length of separation one way or the other will move a rule 16.2 infringement to a rule 16.1 infringement or to no infringement at all.

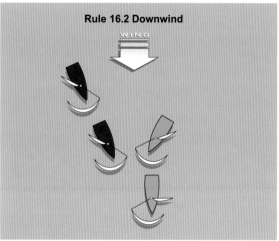

fig 1

Rule 17

ON THE SAME TACK; PROPER COURSE

If a boat *clear astern* becomes *overlapped* within two of her hull lengths to *leeward* of a boat on the same *tack*, she shall not sail above her *proper course* while they remain on the same *tack* and *overlapped* within that distance, unless in doing so she promptly sails astern of the other boat. This rule does not apply if the *overlap* begins while the *windward* boat is required by rule 13 to *keep clear*.

The rule deters 'undertaking' and then luffing, when conditions make this possible. This can be on all points of sailing. We now meet the concept of a proper course.

 Definiton *Proper course* A course a boat would sail to *finish* as soon as possible in the absence of the other boats referred to in the rule using the term. A boat has no *proper course* before her starting signal.

When lecturing about the racing rules, I often remark that if people think the concept of a proper course applies to a situation, they are likely to be wrong. No rule requires a boat to sail a proper course. In rule 17, a boat must sometimes not sail above (i.e., to windward of) a proper course. It does not prevent her from sailing below a proper course. Otherwise, the term is relevant only under rule 18.1(b) to determine whether rule 18 applies between boats on opposite tacks: under rule 18.4 to determine how far an inside overlapped right-of-way boat can sail past a mark without gybing: under rule 18.5 to determine whether exoneration applies for breaking a rule of Section A or rules 15 or 16; under rule 23.2, to decide if a boat is to be penalised for interfering with a boat on another leg; and under the definition Mark-Room, to identify the room to which a boat may entitled at a mark. It is a yardstick rather than an obligation.

---

[1] ISAF 6
[2] My experience is that this way of breaking rule 16.2 is little understood.

A boat on her own can sail any inefficient course she chooses. When rule 17 or some other rule using the term Proper Course applies because another boat is near, there can a range of courses that could be taken, and a boat may be limited to the one which is most likely to result in the soonest possible finish. This does not have to be proved by events. 'Which of two different courses is the faster one…cannot be determined in advance and is not necessarily proven by one boat or the other reaching the next mark ahead[1]'. It will be a proper course, if there were other options, if there was a good reason at the time for selecting it.

A proper course as determined at any particular spot is not affected by the course previously sailed by a boat, even though it may not have been fully efficient until the issue arises. It is gauged solely from the point where it is relevant under a rule. So it is possible that a proper course for a boat below the layline to fetch a course mark or a finishing mark may be above close-hauled[2]. A proper course is the course made good over the ground, not the direction in which a boat is pointing, so a straight-line course made good to a mark may be a proper course for a boat even if, because of the current, she never points at it[3].

So when L and W are on the same leg heading for the same mark, L may have a number of courses options at any particular moment. If L's overlap began from clear astern within two hull lengths, L must not sail to windward of the most windward one that can be shown to be her proper course. If the protest committee accepts this, it makes no difference if W believes that own proper course was lower. All W can do is to keep clear and protest if L was subject to rule 17. If W were not to keep clear because she believed that L's proper course was lower, and she (W) did not respond to L sailing higher, L might be penalised in a subsequent protest for sailing above a proper course when required not to, but W would also be penalised under rule 11 for not keeping clear, as she chose to infringe and was not compelled to do so.

The same will apply if L and W are sailing on different legs of the course, and W finds herself conducted far to windward of where she wants to be. She may have to fall back, or tack and gybe to resume her intended course. L may in the process be interfering with a boat on a different leg, which is prohibited by rule 23.2, but the rule itself makes an exception when L is sailing a proper course.

A boat can be sailing a proper course one moment, and then sailing above a proper course the next, without any change of course.

When rule 17 applies to the situation in fig 2 because Yellow's overlap was begun from clear astern, 'Yellow must gybe at the time she would have borne away to gybe if she had been sailing with no other boat nearby. If she clearly delays beyond that time she will break rule 17 by sailing above her proper course[4].' Yellow therefore goes from compliance with rule 17 to breach of it in a short period, and without changing course.

A proper course for L is explicitly one she would sail from that point in the absence of W, which is the only 'other boat referred to in the rule using the term'. (There may however be other boats nearby whose course and speed will affect what is a proper course for L.)

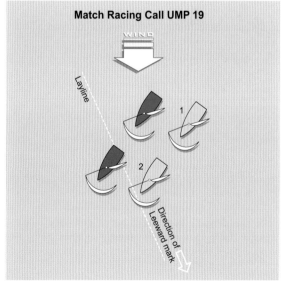

Match Racing Call UMP 19

WIND

Layline

Direction of Leeward mark

fig 2

---

[1] ISAF 14
[2] RYA 1975/6, US 70
[3] As stated in a former US case that applied to the now-withdrawn rule 17.2 rather than to current rule 17
[4] UMP 19

So in UMP 17 (fig 1), Yellow, which had established her overlap from clear astern, would have tacked onto the layline for the windward mark had Blue not been there, and so she is not sailing above a proper course by luffing, even the presence of Blue prevents her from tacking for the mark. Blue breaks rule 11, since Yellow cannot hold her course without risk of contact[1].

Match Racing Call UMP 17

WIND

Layline

fig 1

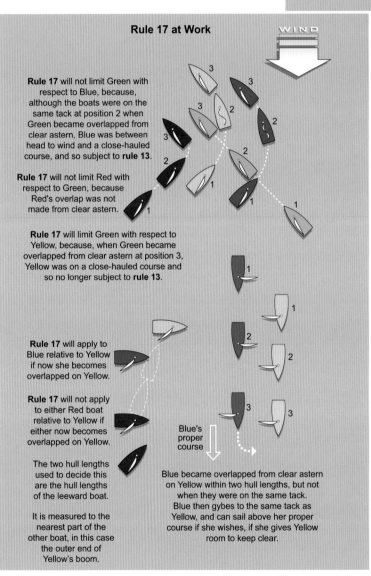

Rule 17 at Work

WIND

Rule 17 will not limit Green with respect to Blue, because, although the boats were on the same tack at position 2 when Green became overlapped from clear astern, Blue was between head to wind and a close-hauled course, and so subject to **rule 13**.

Rule 17 will not limit Red with respect to Green, because Red's overlap was not made from clear astern.

Rule 17 will limit Green with respect to Yellow, because, when Green became overlapped from clear astern at position 3, Yellow was on a close-hauled course and so no longer subject to **rule 13**.

Rule 17 will apply to Blue relative to Yellow if now she becomes overlapped on Yellow.

Rule 17 will not apply to either Red boat relative to Yellow if either now becomes overlapped on Yellow.

The two hull lengths used to decide this are the hull lengths of the leeward boat.

It is measured to the nearest part of the other boat, in this case the outer end of Yellow's boom.

Blue's proper course

Blue became overlapped from clear astern on Yellow within two hull lengths, but not when they were on the same tack. Blue then gybes to the same tack as Yellow, and can sail above her proper course if she wishes, if she gives Yellow room to keep clear.

fig 2

---

[1] The call goes on 'What…if due to shifty winds and/or rough seas it is not clear whether the boats are overstanding the mark?' The answer given is that 'It is not yet clear that her only proper course is on the other tack. Yellow breaks rule 17.1 by sailing above her proper course (close-hauled).' While it is accepted that there will only be a starboard-tack proper course after the layline is reached, nevertheless earlier in the beat while the boats are within the laylines, there may be a proper course for a boat on either tack. This is not supported by any case. ISAF 14 and US 13 say that boats close to each other may have different proper courses. Some say that there can only be one proper course for a boat at any moment (even if it is later proved not to have been the fastest way to the finish). My view as concerns a boat on a beat is that she may have a proper course on either tack on many occasions. The implication of this is that if she is a leeward boat to which rule 17 applies, she may nevertheless luff to head to wind provided that she gives the windward boat room to do likewise, since the presence of the windward boat is not a factor that is relevant to the definition Proper Course. That must be so if she has a proper course on either tack. It does not matter if the proximity of the windward boat will prevent the leeward boat from tacking. If L does legally luff, W may not be expecting it, and W may then fail to keep clear. If the luff is legal, then L does not have to avail herself of the get-out clause in rule 17 of falling back astern of W, possibly then to tack.

For rule 17 to apply to boats that are overlapped on the same tack

- The boats must be overlapped **on the same tack** when the overlap begins. (Boats can be overlapped on opposite tacks when they are both sailing more than ninety degrees from the true wind, see the definition Overlap, but rule 17 will not apply.)
- L must become overlapped from clear astern, and within two of L's hull lengths of W: so an overlap that begins when L is more than two of her hull lengths from W does not then stop L from sailing above a proper course either at that time or if they then come within that distance.
- The overlap must not be an 'instantaneous' one that begins when L tacks to a leeward overlap from the opposite tack, since there was never a time when she was clear astern on the same tack.
- The starting signal must have been made (whether before or after the overlap begins)[1].
- W was not subject to rule 13 when the overlap was created, even if she was now on the same tack as L. If the overlap was created when W became a same-tack boat on passing head to wind during a tack, and became overlapped before becoming close-hauled, there is no proper course limitation on L whether before or after W becomes close-hauled. This is to deter boats like W from 'slam-dunking' too close to leeward boats.

When rule 17 applies, it may continue to apply for some time while the overlap lasts and neither changes tack, during which the boats may change course to pass an obstruction, pass the windward mark onto a reach or run, pass the second mark of a trapezoid outer loop, or pass the leeward mark and luff to a close-hauled course.

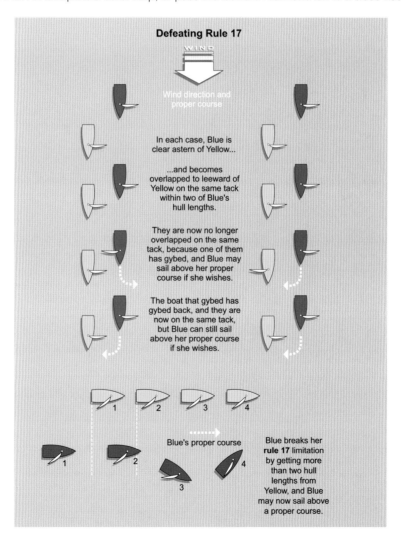

Defeating Rule 17

Wind direction and proper course

In each case, Blue is clear astern of Yellow...

...and becomes overlapped to leeward of Yellow on the same tack within two of Blue's hull lengths.

They are now no longer overlapped on the same tack, because one of them has gybed, and Blue may sail above her proper course if she wishes.

The boat that gybed has gybed back, and they are now on the same tack, but Blue can still sail above her proper course if she wishes.

Blue's proper course

Blue breaks her **rule 17** limitation by getting more than two hull lengths from Yellow, and Blue may now sail above a proper course.

---

[1] C4. Team racing and match racing umpires have to be alert to how a pre-start overlaps was established, since it may some time after that before an issue arises. Likewise, as concerns overlapped boats approaching an upwind or downwind layline.

There are several ways that a rule 17 limitation will end:

- If L gybes to the opposite tack, the limitation ends, and does not begin again if W then gybes back while overlapped, since the overlap was not made from clear astern
- If W gybes to the opposite tack, the limitation ends, and does not begin again if W then gybes back while overlapped, since the overlap was not made from clear astern: in this and the previous example, the boats, if both sailing more than ninety degrees from the true wind, will remain overlapped, as defined, but not on the same tack
- The limitation ends if L becomes either clear astern or clear ahead (not illustrated)
- The limitation ends the gap opens to more than two of L's hull lengths, and does not begin again if the gap then closes to less than two of L's hull lengths

Although I have never seen it result in a protest, it seems possible for L to break rule 17.1 by temporarily losing the grip on the tiller or by being overpowered by a gust, resulting in a luff which, although immediately corrected and occurring far enough from W not to trouble her, would seem to be sailing above a proper course. On a beat, a conscientious competitor might avoid the need to take a penalty by taking advantage of the facility to sail astern of the other boat (and possibly then tack), which will legitimise her having sailed above her proper course.

Section C - At Marks and Obstructions

How did you learn the racing rules? Many of us start to pick it up by crewing, and we get to understand osmotically what the rules permit and forbid, even though we could hardly quote a rule or its number to save our lives – just in the same way that we all consider ourselves to be excellent armchair football referees and cricket umpires without detailed knowledge of chapter and verse. It is usually only when a protest or other dispute arises that we find ourselves groping in the rule book for something that that we are sure to be the case, though we can't quite put our finger on it.

Most sailors get to know the rules concerning marks and obstructions in this way, even though the words of the rules concerned might as well be written in a foreign language when first studied.

So the news that the rules about passing marks and avoiding obstructions have been totally rewritten will be tempered by the fact that what was required, permitted or prohibited in 2008 and earlier will have changed little in 2009 onwards. So why rewrite the rules of Section C? Mainly, on top-level insistence within ISAF, to make these rules simpler and easier to understand when read, but with as few as possible game-changes on the water. Other objectives were:
- To make clear, whenever two boats meet, whether a section C rule applies between them, and, if so, how
- To discourage contact by encouraging orderly behaviour and discouraging last-minute claims

You will be the judge of whether we have a better rule book as a result. If the objectives have not been achieved, it will not have been for lack of trying. I was a privileged observer of the work of the US Sailing / RYA team of rules experts who tackled this task over many months, involving thousands of emails, several drafts and many teleconferences, a process that was not possible for the previous major revision exercise in 1995 and 1996 for the 1997 rules. The main principles of the team were that, as far as possible,
- The new Section C rules should not 'switch off' either the basic right-of-way rules in section A (rules 10 to 13) or the general limitations in section B (rules 14 to 17).
- The new rules should eliminate ambiguities
- The new rules should minimise exceptions, reduce the risk of contact, avoid late claims and be clearer as to when they apply.

This resulted in the following structure:

- Two Section C rules have become three, with passing marks and passing obstructions divided into separate rules, the third rule being tacking at obstructions as before.
- Rule 18, which applies sometimes at most marks, but only at marks, is designed to cope with tactical exploitation.
- Rule 19, which applies at most obstructions, is simpler, reflecting the fact that it is a safety rule rather than a tactical rule. In particular, the concept of the 'zone' is no longer relevant at obstructions, mainly because it was rarely applied in practice, and so the rule has been adapted to be consistent with what actually happens on the water.
- Related to this, the definition Obstruction is changed, so that a vessel under way is never a **continuing** obstruction. The term 'continuing obstruction', and the part of rule 19 relating to it, applies only to static objects and features.
- Rule 20, for hailing for room to tack at an obstruction, remains a safety-based rule.
- All three rules are essentially room-based. As far as possible, they do not change rights of way. Instead they limit some of the Section A rights of a right-of-way boat, and sometimes they exonerate breaches of some of her Section B obligations. The vehicle for limiting rights is, as previously, the duty to give room. Sometimes, a keep-clear boat has not only to keep clear but also give extra space in the form of room. The room that has to be given at marks is a little more specific than at obstructions, and has its own definition of Mark-Room. Sometimes, breaches of Section A rules are exonerated.
- Without dwelling too much on the past, it was never satisfactory to have a rule that began to apply when boats were 'about to round', particularly when an ISAF case said that the distance from the mark when this happened would vary depending on wind and sea conditions. The effect of that concept remains, but by the use of different words.
- The two-length zone becomes a three-length zone, at which no rights of way change, but where mark-room requirements and exonerations may start to apply. No zone, whether of two lengths or three lengths, now applies at an obstruction.
- Terminologically, the word 'rounding' hardly appears in Section C. It is more appropriate for the string test in rule 28, Sailing the Course. Instead, marks and obstructions are 'passed'.

Beyond this overview, there is little point making a detailed comparison between the finer points of the old and the new. If the reader has a good grasp of the old rules, the differences in the new ones will be self-apparent. And there is little point in reinforcing the understanding of old rules. Let the new order speak for itself.

The rules of Section C apply only when boats are near each other. If a boat is on her own, she can leave the mark as close or as far as she pleases, and in a seamanlike or an unseamanlike way. Her only obligations are to leave it on its required side, under rule 28, Sailing the Course, and not to touch it, under rule 31, Touching a Mark. On her own, she can pass an obstruction on either side, and in any way she wants. When she needs to tack at an obstruction in the absence of other boats, she may do so as near from it or as far from it as she chooses.

Section C - At Marks and Obstructions

Preamble *Section C rules do not apply at a starting **mark** surrounded by navigable water or at its anchor line from the time boats are approaching them to **start** until they have passed them. When rule 20 applies, rules 18 and 19 do not.*

The foothills of Section C and of rule 18 itself involve identifying when Section C in general and rule 18 in particular do **not** apply.

In summary:-
- No part of Section C applies at a starting mark surrounded by navigable water or at its anchor line from the time boats are approaching them to start until they have passed them. Otherwise -
- Rule 18, Mark-Room may apply between boats at a mark, including a mark that is also an obstruction, unless it is a continuing obstruction
- Rule 19, Room to Pass an Obstruction, may apply between boats approaching an obstruction to pass it, including a mark that is a continuing obstruction
- Rule 20, Room to Tack at an Obstruction, will apply at an obstruction (and rules 18 and 19 will not) when safety requires a boat sailing close-hauled or above to make a substantial course change to avoid it and she hails another boat on the same tack for room to tack to avoid it, unless the obstruction is a mark that the hailed boat is fetching

Added to this:
- When no rule of Section C applies to boats at a mark or obstruction, the rules of Section A and B will apply without limitation or enhancement
- When a rule of Section C does apply to boats at a mark or obstruction, the rules of Section A and B will also apply[1], but may be limited or enhanced by an obligation to give room (mark-room at marks), and may attract exoneration when broken in taking or giving mark-room.

The first issue in Section C's preamble is what is a starting mark. So what is a mark?

Definition Mark An object the sailing instructions require a boat to leave on a specified side, and a race committee boat surrounded by navigable water from which the starting or finishing line extends. An anchor line or an object attached temporarily or accidentally to a *mark* is not part of it.

A mark can range from a pole to a continent (leave Africa to port). More usually, it is a fixed object, or a floating object either laid for the event, or selected from what is already in place. The whole of the committee boat, if surrounded by navigable water, ranks as a mark when the starting or finishing line extends from (usually) a mast or staff thereon. It follows that a committee boat that is not surrounded by navigable water (whether because it is too shallow, or if the committee boat is too close to or tied to the bank) is not a mark – it may therefore be an obstruction, as we shall see. A committee boat or a continent will both be big enough to rank as obstructions, but rule 19.1 says that if the obstruction is a mark, then rule 19 does not apply to it (and so, by implication, rule 18 does) unless it is a continuing obstruction[2].

It is perfectly proper for sailing instructions to identify points or lines that boat shall / shall not sail to N / E / S / W of, but a dot or line on a chart is (I think) not a mark, as there is no physical object.

Marks are significant in three areas of the rules – here in Section C of Part 2, as concerns how boats are to behave when passing them: in rule 28, as concerns leaving them on the boat's correct side; and in rule 31 as concerns (not) touching them.

---

[1] Other than rule 19.2(c), which may override rules 10 or 11

[2] I think that bits of Africa might need to be treated as a continuing obstruction from time to time, but that does not stop it being a mark for the purposes of rule 18 at other times. However, by the last sentence of the Section C preamble, when it is necessary to hail for room to tack away from Cape Point, it is rule 20 that applies.

On a starting line, a buoy identified in the sailing instructions as the other end of the line from the committee boat is a starting mark (usually called the pin end, and usually at the port end of the line with reference to the course to the first rounding mark). A buoy may also be laid as an outer limit mark on a line formed by a shore transit. This is also a starting mark. The status of other limit marks will depend on the sailing instructions. An 'inner limit mark' is frequently laid to keep boats away from the committee boat when starting. If the sailing instructions say that the inner limit mark is to be left, when starting, on the same side as the committee boat it protects, this clearly establishes a required side for the buoy concerned, and it is therefore a starting mark. If however the sailing instruction merely says that boats shall not cross a line from the buoy to the committee boat nearby at some moment, it is not clear that the buoy ranks as a mark, even if it is so described in the sailing instruction – to be a mark, it must have a required side for a boat.

A starting mark is not to be touched from a boat's preparatory signal until she starts, and a starting limit mark just on the course side of the starting line is not to be touched while a boat is on the first leg of the course[1]. A starting mark shall be left on the required side when approaching the starting line from the pre-start side to start[2], and it is during the same period that Section C rules do not apply if the starting mark (including any anchor line) is surrounded by navigable water[3]. This is what used to be known as the 'anti-barging' rule, with the intention of deterring fan starts, where the virtuous boat's close-hauled starboard-tack approach to start close to the committee boat is spoilt by other boats reaching around the stern of the committee boat. The idea is that the bargers have no right to room.

So what counts as approaching a starting mark…to start' when it is surrounded by navigable water?

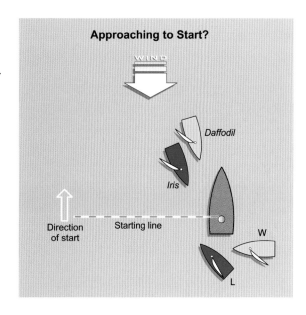

Approaching to Start?

WIND

Daffodil

Iris

Direction of start | Starting line

W

L

Call UMP 13 says that a boat cannot be approaching a mark to start until approaching to pass the mark on the required side. So, including if they are returning to start after individual recalls, *Iris* must give room to *Daffodil* under rule 19.2(b), whenever this occurs.

If L meets W three minutes before the starting signal, L is likely to be doing trial starts, and is not yet on 'final approaches'. At this point, W is entitled to room under rule 19.2(b) to pass what is merely an obstruction if it is a large object such as a committee boat. Rule 18 does not apply, as it does not yet have a required side for her[4]. If however they meet like this a few seconds before the starting signal, then L is clearly approaching the starting mark to start. The section C preamble switches out all W's rights to room at the committee boat, both as a mark (as rule 18 does not apply) and as an obstruction (as rule 19 does not apply). If W takes the room to which she is not entitled, she breaks rule 11 if L needs to take avoiding action. W must hope that L does indeed bear away and does not risk damage and penalisation under rule 14, but that does not change the fact that W has infringed[5].

Suppose that this happens 30 seconds or more before the starting signal, and L, while wishing to squeeze out W, wants in fact to sail down the starting line for some time, to start in mid-line or indeed at the pin end?

---

[1] Rule 31.1
[2] Rule 28.2
[3] A mark's anchor line is not, by definition part of the mark, and so may be touched with impunity, but if touching the mark results in the mark being drawn into contact with the boat, then rule 31 is broken: US 10.
[4] Rule 28.2
[5] My experience is that this is a weakness of the rule. In the protest room, W will often claim that either the room was always there, or that L bore away to avoid being OCS, and W took advantage of the gap she left. To be sure of proving her case, L can allow contact to happen, but puts herself at risk under rule 14 if there is avoidable damage.

UMP 13 addresses this question, but, tantalizingly, fails to answer it. While admitting of the possibility that, on a typically short match racing starting line, the boats may be approaching the pin mark at the far end, it does not say whether, if this is the case, L must give room to W at the committee boat. L may be approaching the **starting line** to start under rule 28.2, but is she approaching the **starting mark** in the shape of the committee boat to start under Section C? There would seem to be good sense in having a correspondence between rule 28.2 and the preamble to Section C (so that rights to room are extinguished while the starting mark has a required side for a boat), but it is not clear from the call that this is the case[1].

The preamble switches out the Section C rules until the starting mark and its anchor line have been passed.

PW is free to tack – but PL has no Section C rights. She is not entitled to hail for room to room to tack - rule 20 does not apply, because the first sentence of the Section C preamble says so (and, in the process, makes the second sentence of the preamble inapplicable). As will be seen, rule 18 gives boats changing course at a mark a 'get-out-of-gaol-free' card for breaking rule 16, amongst others. But as there is no Section C applicability here, rule 18 does not apply, and so a boat can be penalised for breaking rule 16.

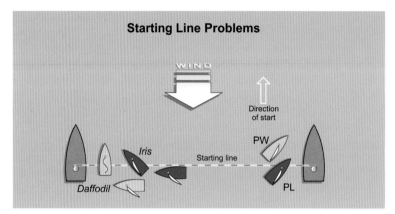

Starting Line Problems

fig 1

When rule 18 does not apply while passing a starting mark, it is as if the mark were not there. *Daffodil* is reaching down the pre-course side starting line towards a committee vessel forming the other end of the line, to start, and is early. Her only way not to be OCS and not to hit the committee boat may be a violent luff at the starting signal, to shoot the mark, a manoeuvre that could break rule 16.1 with respect to *Iris*, without the benefit of exoneration under rule 18.5[2]. However, if *Daffodil* can luff in compliance with rule 16.1, *Iris* must keep clear in the normal way under rule 11.

---

[1] RYA 2008/1 is also helpful concerning rule 28.2 and unhelpful concerning the preamble to Section C. (When the preamble talks of boats approaching 'them', the 'them' is not both or all of the starting marks, but a mark and its anchor line.)
[2] As previously discussed, *Daffodil* is not required to anticipate that *Iris* will act in this way, however predictable, and needs only to keep a lookout and react to what *Iris* actually does. The same applies to Blue and Yellow at the other end of the starting line. That is, of course, subject to the danger of breaking rule 14.

MARK-ROOM

18.1 When Rule 18 Applies

Rule 18 applies between boats when they are required to leave a *mark* on the same side and at least one of them is in the *zone*. However, it does not apply

(a) between boats on opposite *tacks* on a beat to windward,

(b) between boats on opposite *tacks* when the *proper course* at the *mark* for one but not both of them is to tack,

(c) between a boat approaching a *mark* and one leaving it, or

(d) if the mark is a continuing *obstruction*, in which case rule 19 applies.

It is boats that have sides, port or starboard. While a mark might have a side, that is not a meaningful concept in the racing rules. For rule 18 to apply between boats, they must both be required to leave it on the same side. So it will **not** apply if the mark

• is the next mark of the course for only one of two boats approaching it.

• is required to be left to port by *Iris* and to starboard by *Daffodil*, and they approach head-on while each passing it as required[1].

• is required to be left to port by *Iris* and to starboard by *Daffodil*, but one of them, whether through confusion or for safety, elects to pass it on the same side as the other.

In such cases, the rules of Sections A and B, including rule 16, apply without either limitation or the possibility of exoneration, as if the mark were not there, although if the 'mark' is large enough it may rank as an obstruction, in which case rule 19 would apply.

Conversely, rule 18 can apply even if boats are approaching from what appear to be different directions, as happened in ISAF 12, where Yellow over-corrected and Blue under-corrected for a strong current. Blue appealed her disqualification for not giving mark-room to Yellow on the grounds that it was illogical to regard boats on such diverging courses as overlapped, that Yellow could easily have passed astern of Blue, and that this was stretching the application of the terms 'inside' and 'outside'. Her appeal was dismissed: for mark-room entitlement, it is irrelevant that boats are on widely differing courses, provided that an overlap exists between them when the first of them reaches the zone[2].

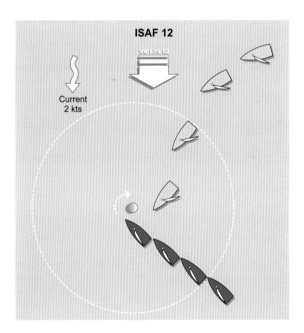

[1] ISAF 26
[2] For an even more extreme example, see RYA 2004/8

It is the entry of any part of a boat's hull into the *zone* that makes rule 18 apply.

 Definition *Zone* The area around a *mark* within a distance of three hull lengths of the boat nearer to it. A boat is in the *zone* when any part of her hull is in the *zone*.

The hull is the yardstick both for the size of the zone, and its being entered. A sprit, a transom-hung rudder and an overhanging bumkin for a mizzen mast[1] will be relevant only for the making, maintaining and breaking of an overlap. It is the hull of the boat nearer the mark that is relevant. A very long boat may come within three of her hull-lengths of the zone before a very short boat clear ahead of her, but the zone is defined in this case with reference to the short boat's hull, as the latter is nearer the mark.

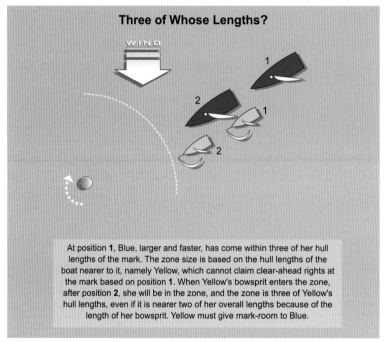

Three of Whose Lengths?

At position **1**, Blue, larger and faster, has come within three of her hull lengths of the mark. The zone size is based on the hull lengths of the boat nearer to it, namely Yellow, which cannot claim clear-ahead rights at the mark based on position **1**. When Yellow's bowsprit enters the zone, after position **2**, she will be in the zone, and the zone is three of Yellow's hull lengths, even if it is nearer two of her overall lengths because of the length of her bowsprit. Yellow must give mark-room to Blue.

fig 1

Why (fig 1) three lengths now[2]? Mainly because of increased boat speeds, especially at leeward marks and gates being approached on opposite tacks nearly at right angles by boats setting asymmetric spinnakers – the additional distance will increase the time for giving room, when required.

But there are still specified mark-leaving situations where rule 18 does not (yet) apply.

Rule 18.1(b) extends this principle to situations where both boats are not on a beat, such as the mark at the top of a trapezoidal course's outer loop, to which one boat is beating but the other is reaching.

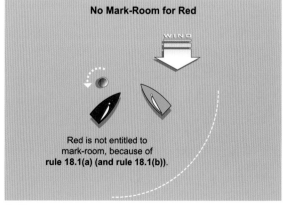

No Mark-Room for Red

Red is not entitled to mark-room, because of **rule 18.1(a) (and rule 18.1(b))**.

fig 2

---

[1] See rule 50.3(a).

[2] Two lengths or four lengths can be specified in some situations, see rule 86.1(b), and it will be two hull lengths without the option for match racing (Appendix C) and team racing (Appendix D), and four hull lengths without the option for radio-controlled boats (Appendix E).

Under rule 18.1(c), both boats may be in the zone, but the gap between them is too great for them for the rule to apply. Yellow will have entered the zone clear ahead of Blue, but it is only rule 10 that applies.

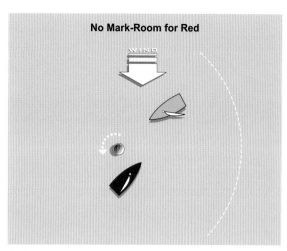

No Mark-Room for Red

fig 3

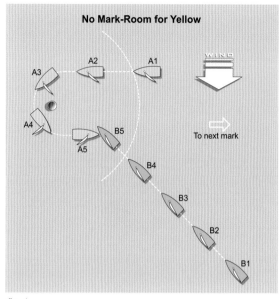

No Mark-Room for Yellow

To next mark

fig 4

If one or both boats were in the zone, and a shortage of wind and an excess of current makes her or them drift out of the zone, rule 18 no longer applies, and will not apply again until one of them re-enters the zone[1].

Normally, when a mark is also an obstruction, rule 19.1 says that it is rule 18 and not rule 19 that applies, but that it is rule 19 that applies when the mark is a **continuing** obstruction, which is echoed by rule 18.1(d). Typically a mark that is also a continuing obstruction will be an island or structure that the sailing instructions say must be left on a specified side. As discussed earlier concerning a continent, the question of whether it is rule 19.2(c) (when passing a continuing obstruction) or rule 20 (when needing room to tack off it) that applies will depend on what the boats are doing at the time, and its status can switch between those rules[2]. What makes an obstruction a continuing one? When it will 'take some time' for the boats to pass it[3], and when it is close enough for questions of room to arise. So when boats are required (fig 5) to leave on one side a breakwater that is a 'continuous structure from the shore to its outer

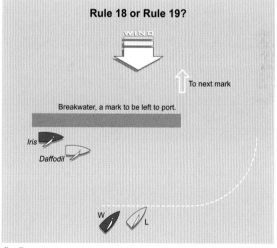

Rule 18 or Rule 19?

To next mark

Breakwater, a mark to be left to port.

Iris

Daffodil

W   L

fig 5

end', it will be a mark to which rule 18 applies if the boats are 'concerned only with the outer end' passing it in a few seconds[4], as for W and L, but it will be continuing obstruction under rule 19.2(c) when boats like *Iris* and *Daffodil* are running alongside much of its length – and the two rules treat establishing overlaps differently. Note that the zone (which in this case is not circular) is relevant only for W and L, and it is irrelevant for *Iris* and *Daffodil*.

[1] ISAF 15
[2] If Africa is the mark, and *Iris* wants room to tack at Cape Point when *Daffodil* can lay it, rule 20.3 says there is no right to hail for room.
[3] ISAF 16, which no longer applies because of a rule change.
[4] ISAF 33

Having whittled away situations where rule 18 does not apply, we can at last consider situations where it does.

18.2

Giving Mark-Room

(a) When boats are *overlapped* the outside boat shall give the inside boat *mark-room*, unless rule 18.2(b) applies.

(b) If boats are *overlapped* when the first of them reaches the *zone*, the outside boat at that moment shall thereafter give the inside boat *mark-room*. If a boat is *clear ahead* when she reaches the *zone*, the boat *clear astern* at that moment shall thereafter give her *mark-room*.

(c) When a boat is required to give *mark-room* by rule 18.2(b), she shall continue to do so even if later an *overlap* is broken or a new *overlap* begins. However, if the boat entitled to *mark-room* passes head to wind or leaves the *zone*, rule 18.2(b) ceases to apply.

(d) If there is reasonable doubt that a boat obtained or broke an *overlap* in time, it shall be presumed that she did not.

(e) If a boat obtained an inside *overlap* from *clear astern* and, from the time the *overlap* began, the outside boat has been unable to give *mark-room*, she is not required to give it.

Rule 18 (as well as rules 19 and 20) is an 'overlay' on the basic Section A right-of-way rules (10 to 13) and the Section B limitations on right-of-way boats (14 to 17). The apparent simplification has been achieved firstly by not referring to those underlying obligations. Instead, when reading Section C rules, you need to remember that a port-tack boat must still keep clear of a starboard-tack boat, a windward boat must still keep clear of a leeward boat, a boat clear astern must still keep clear of a boat clear ahead, and a boat that is tacking and is subject to rule 13 must keep clear of a boat that is not.

There is no longer any reference to primacy when there are conflicts between Section C rules and Section A and B rules: that is because, technically, there are no such explicit conflicts[1].

As well as not changing those Section A responsibilities, rule 18 uses the concept of 'room' in a way different from some of the Section B rules (14 to 17). Right-of-way boats at marks and obstructions sometimes have to give more room (or a different sort of room) compared with the room they have to give in open water. Sometimes, they need not give as much room[2], which will require a keep-clear boat to do more in order to keep clear. Sometimes, keep-clear boats have to keep further away from right-of-way boats than required in open water, and that further distance is also 'room', a concept that does not apply to keep-clear boats in open water. The vehicle for this is a new species of room, namely Mark-Room, which is:

Definition **_Mark-Room_** *Room* for a boat to sail to the *mark*, and then *room* to sail her *proper course* while at the *mark*. However, *mark-room* does not include *room* to tack unless the boat is *overlapped* to *windward* and on the inside of the boat required to give *mark-room*.

This does not replace the definition Room, indeed the italicised use of *room* on three occasions within the definition Mark-Room shows that the basic definition is built into Mark-Room, but it is now more precisely explained in the context of marks (but not obstructions), as future examples will show.

ISAF 21 looks at some of the elements of the room that is part of mark-room.

> The term 'existing conditions' deserves some consideration. For example, the inside one of two dinghies approaching a mark on a placid lake in light air will need relatively little space beyond that required for her hull and properly trimmed sails. At the other extreme, when two keel boats, on open water with steep seas, are approaching a mark that is being tossed about widely and unpredictably, the inside boat may need a full hull length of space or even more to ensure safety.

> The phrase 'in a seamanlike way' applies to both boats. First, it addresses the outside boat, saying that she must provide enough space so that the inside boat need not make extraordinary or abnormal manoeuvres to sail her proper course while at the mark. It also addresses the inside boat. She is not entitled to complain of insufficient space if she fails to execute with reasonable efficiency the handling of her helm, sheets and sails while sailing her proper course.

There will frequently be times when a boat taking mark-room to which she is entitled will not have kept clear, or will not have given the room required under rules 15 or 16 to the other boat if the other boat has not given her enough mark-room. The old rule disapplied Section A and B rules when they conflicted with rule 18 rights at a mark or obstruction, and disapplied rule 16 when a boat was altering course to round a mark. The new rule, seeking never explicitly to disapply other rules when possible, instead offers instant exoneration in rule 18.5 for breaking them in taking mark-room when so entitled.

When rule 18.2(a) applies

Although rule 18.2(a) reads as if it were a general principle, it will in practice apply far less often than rule 18.2(b). That is because it is rule 18.2(b) that applies when the zone is relevant, in addition to which, at a windward mark, rule 18.3 will often apply instead of either rule 18.2(a) or (b) (see page 60).

---

[1] Apart from a semi-exception at continuing obstructions.
[2] Technically, they are exonerated if they do not give open-water room in some situations

Rule 18 did not apply until Blue tacked, because of rule 18.1(a) (fig 1) – until then, the boats were on opposite tacks on a beat to windward. Once Blue went through head to wind, the boats became overlapped on the same tack, at which point rule 18 started to apply, and by now it is too late to consider the zone, so rule 18.2(b) need not be considered. Rule 18.2(a) applies. Blue must give Yellow mark-room, and Yellow must keep clear of Blue within that mark-room, under rule 11.

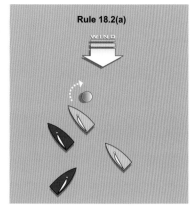

fig 1

If Blue tacks to a clear-ahead position inside the zone, it is only rule 12 that applies at that moment, with Yellow being required to keep clear. Rule 18.2(a) has nothing to say about clear ahead – clear astern situations.

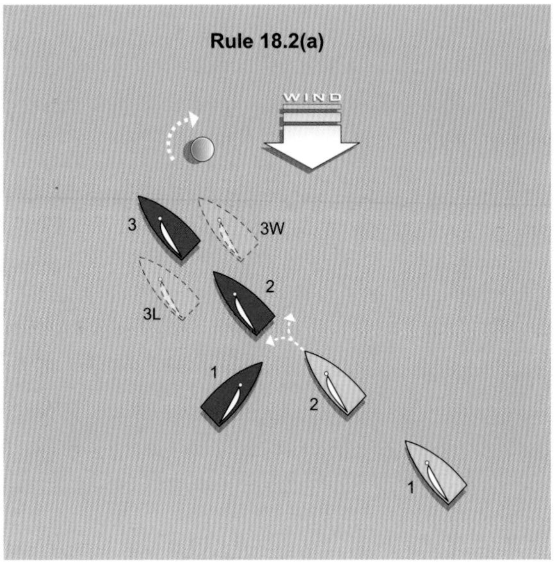

Rule 18.2(a) (fig 2) then applies if an overlap begins. If, travelling faster, Yellow becomes overlapped inside Blue, rule 18.2(a) applies, and Yellow is entitled to mark-room if Blue can give it. If however she becomes overlapped outside Blue, it is she that must give mark-room to Blue, under the same rule. In either case, mark-room includes room for the inside windward boat to tack because the definition Mark-Room says so.

However, if the overlap is then broken before the first of them is at the mark, rule 18.2(a) will cease to apply.

A tack by either boat will switch off rule 18.2(a), although it can begin to apply again if, after tacking, the boats become overlapped. If there was no overlap before the boats' final tack for the mark, but there was one afterwards, then rule 18.2(a) will being to apply for the first time on the mark's windward side, in addition to rule 11[1].

fig 2

The fact that an obligation to give mark-room under rule 18.2(a) is transient, applying only as long as the overlap continues, is shown in ISAF 2 (fig 3).

Yellow approached the mark very wide, possibly because of other boats (not shown) inside her and rounding ahead of her. As a result, it was Blue, clear astern of her, which entered the zone first. In theory, having one boat in the zone made rule 18 potentially applicable. However, it could only be either rule 18.2(a) or 18.2(b) that applied at that point. As they were not overlapped, it could not be rule 18.2(a). Since rule 18.2(b) applies to non-overlapped boats only when it is the boat that is clear ahead that reaches the zone first, it was not rule 18.2(b) either. So, although the diagram shows the zone, it was never in fact relevant.

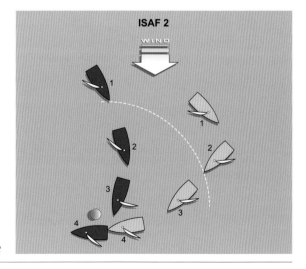

fig 3

[1] As in position 4 in fig 4.

Yellow gybed, still outside the zone. Rule 18.2(a) now applied as they became overlapped, as that term applies to boats on opposite tacks when rule 18 applies. For a brief period, Yellow was required to give mark-room to Blue, which was required to keep clear under rule 10, and then under rule 11 after she gybed, and they were far enough apart for no issue to arise over this. Blue then broke the overlap, and so rule 18.2(a) stopped applying. As rule 18.2(b) could not apply either, no part of rule 18 was in force when Yellow, travelling faster, sailed into Blue's stern, without there being injury or damage.

Blue had become right-of-way boat under rule 12. In so doing, she had to comply with rule 15, since, with all of rule 18 now out of action, the exoneration in rule 18.5 was not open to her. Rule 14 applies whether or not rule 18 applies. On the basis that Yellow could have taken avoiding action in a seamanlike way, by bearing away, but did not do so, while Blue could not avoid the contact, Blue did not break rule 14 or rule 15, while Yellow broke rules 12 and 14. Yellow would be penalised for breaking the former, but not the latter given the absence of injury or damage[1].

Thus it is possible for there to be an incident at a mark without rule 18 applying at the time of a collision, and only in a transient way under rule 18.2(a) before then.

Mark-room has two elements; room for a boat to sail to the mark, and then room to sail her proper course while at the mark. If rule 18.2(a) applies, then the obligation may be one or the other, or both, depending on when the overlap began, and how long it lasted.

When a boat is taking mark-room to which she is entitled under rule 18.2(a) at a windward mark, no rule will exonerate the other boat if she was able to give that room but did not do so. At a starboard-hand windward mark where S is reaching in, having overstood, P is not allowed to go into a tack to leeward of S and so close to S and to the mark that mark-room cannot be given to S. P must judge her tack to enable herself to comply with rule 18.2(a) a few seconds later[2]. Rule 18.2(e) does not exonerate failure to give room to an inside boat when the overlap was created by tacking rather than from clear astern.

Rule 18.2(a) may begin to apply after rule 18.2(b) has stopped applying.

Blue entered the zone clear ahead of Yellow, and is entitled to mark-room under the second sentence of rule 18.2(b). Mark-room explicitly excludes room for a boat clear ahead to tack, and so Blue has to wait until Yellow tacks before herself tacking. When Yellow passes head to wind, the boats are now on opposite tacks, and Blue's proper course is to tack when she can. Rule 18.1(b) switches off rule 18 (rule 18.2(b) included) at that moment. When Blue tacks, the boats become overlapped on the same tack again with Yellow inside, and, since rule 18.2(b) no longer applies, rule 18.2(a) does apply. Blue must keep clear under rule 11. Blue must also give Yellow mark-room at the mark, which may involve being a little further to windward to create space for Yellow's bear-away, and if Yellow's subsequent bear-away is sufficiently forceful to break rule 16.1, rule 18.5(b) will exonerate her.

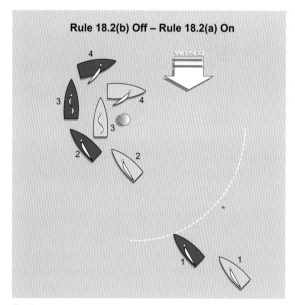

Rule 18.2(b) Off – Rule 18.2(a) On

fig 4

---

[1] Compared with the official case diagram, I have interpolated position 3, and inverted the diagram for (I hope) better comprehension
[2] See fig 39

Rule 18.2(b) when boats are overlapped when the first of them reaches the zone

While rule 18.2(a) may be transient, rule 18.2(b), when it applies, will create a mark-room obligation from the moment that a boat enters the zone, and both elements of mark-room will apply. The obligation to continue to give mark-room will not be affected by breaking or re-establishing the overlap, as stated in rule 18.2(c), provided that no boat entitled to mark-rrom passes head to wind (or leaves the zone).

Rule 18.2(e) will excuse a failure to give mark-room only in the limited circumstances in that rule – a late inside overlap from clear astern. This has two major implications.

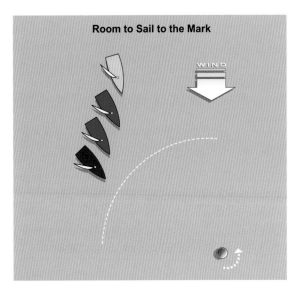

Room to Sail to the Mark

Firstly, all these boats are overlapped on each other, either directly or by virtue of the Blue boats being overlapped between Red and Yellow that would otherwise be clear ahead and clear astern, because of the definition Overlap. Each inside boat is required to keep clear of the boat outside her under rule 11. If the overlaps have existed for some time, Red will have to give mark-room, on entering the zone, to all the boats inside her, Yellow included, with no excuse for not doing so. She must therefore take action before entering the zone to enable herself to do so, as must the Blue boats. To leave it until zone entry would be leaving it too late. Yellow is entitled to room to sail to the mark – in other words, directly to the mark – and the boats outside her will break rule 18.2(b) if they do not do so, even if they are belated able to give her mark-room when she is actually at the mark.

The Blue boats are also entitled to room to sail 'to the mark'. In their case, it is physically impossible for that room to be room to be next to the mark because of the boats inside each of them, and so room to sail to the mark must be room to sail as close to the mark as is consistent with also enabling room to be given to any further room-entitled inside boats.

However, if Yellow has only just become overlapped to windward of the other boats, and if, starting from that moment, they physically cannot give her mark-room, they do not have to try to do the impossible.

Secondly, an outside boat that tries to shake off an inside overlap before mark entry must consider the consequences of failure. Blue may find that she has used her right of way to put herself in a position where it is not possible to give immediate room to inside-overlapped keep-clear Yellow to sail 'to the mark' at zone entry, even if she can later give room 'at the mark'. Neither rule 18.2(e) nor any rule exempts her from giving that room.

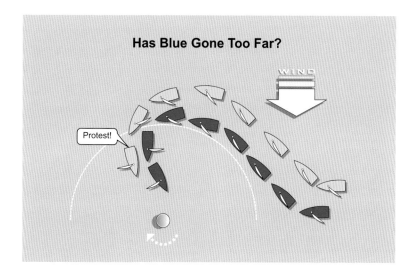

Has Blue Gone Too Far?

If however, she does succeed in breaking the overlap before zone entry, she will benefit from the clear-ahead rights in the second sentence of rule 18.2(b).

Rule 18.2(e) does not apply to <u>outside</u> overlaps from clear astern. If a boat becomes overlapped from clear astern outside another or others close to the zone, then even if she is now the right-of-way boat under rule 10 or 11, nothing removes the requirement to give room immediately under rule 15 and then mark-room at the zone to those now inside her, a fact she should take into account in establishing the overlap.

If it is the inside boat that reaches the zone first, the outside boat's obligation to give mark-room begins at that moment, being at a time before the outside boat has reached the zone. If it is the outside boat that reaches the zone first, her obligation to give mark-room starts at that moment, which means that the inside boat's mark-room entitlement starts outside the zone.

Let us consider mark-room for overlapped boats in more depth, when it is a give-way boat that is entitled to it.

First, it is '*room* to sail to the mark'. We know that *room* is the space a boat needs in the existing conditions while manoeuvring promptly in a seamanlike way. The 'prompt seamanlike manouevring' will be applicable to the inside boat if the outside right-of-way boat, possibly having tried unsuccessfully to shake off the overlap before entering the zone, will now have to turn promptly for the mark to give the mark-room, to which the inside boat must respond. The space that then has to be given will then be conditions-dependent. The room to be given is room 'to sail to the mark'. That room does not have to start to be given until the first boat enters the zone, but it must be given promptly, to enable the inside boat to change if necessary to a course taking her directly to the mark (or as close to it as the presence of other room-entitled boats permits). Without the entitlement for room to sail 'to the mark', an outside right-of-way boat could continue to manoeuvre against the inside boat as long as room was then given at the mark - if the overlap had not been shaken off inside the zone.

The course 'to the mark' is not one aimed directly at the mark, but to a position alongside the mark, so there is a smooth transition between the course to the mark and the proper course around it.

Although mark-room 'at the mark' is room to sail her proper course, room to sail 'to the mark' is only room for seamanlike sailing, which if straight downwind may not be the inside boat's best speed, especially if she is gennaker-rigged.

In effect, from the moment that one of two overlapped boats enters the zone, and an outside boat has promptly made any necessary course change to give room to sail to the mark, there is then a 'corridor' to the mark that is always safe for the inside boat to be on, and onto which the outside boat cannot trespass to so as to interfere with the progress of the inside boat. If the inside boat chooses to venture away from the corridor, it is the rules of Section A that will apply. If the inside boat has right of way (under rule 10 or 11), she is safe to do so, but if as here she is a keep-clear boat, she is not.

When one of a pair of boats overlapped on the same tack enters the zone so as to create a rule 18.2(b) obligation on the outside leeward boat, the room to sail to the mark may be directly down wind. However, the last thing that many modern designs of boats want to do is to sail directly down wind, and the zone may be large enough for several gybes to be fitted in.

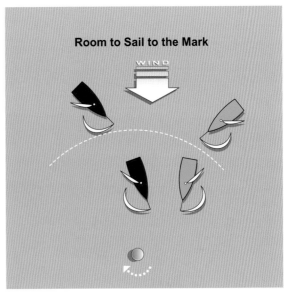

Room to Sail to the Mark

fig 1

Consider, a leeward mark to be rounded to port. Yellow has an inside overlap, and is entitled to bear away to a downwind course to the mark, but if she does so and then holds it, she will lose places with reference to boats that do not. If she holds her course until she can gybe for a close approach to the mark, Blue can follow her, but cannot pin her out beyond the 'corridor' because of the obligation to give room for Yellow to sail to the mark in the corridor. So when Yellow bears away to gybe, Blue must do likewise, and Yellow can now sail a course of her choice in order to round, provided she does not gybe too late[1]. Blue's duty to give room to sail to the mark is now academic, because Blue must keep clear under rule 11.

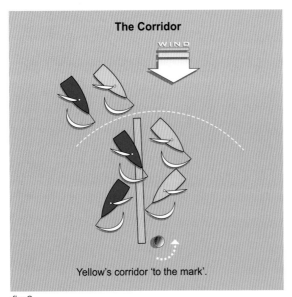

The Corridor

Yellow's corridor 'to the mark'.

fig 2

If in fact Yellow does start to bear away for the mark at zone entry, Blue must respond so as to give Yellow room to sail to the mark. Blue's best option is not to sail downwind, but to gybe to maintain speed. Yellow can now either gybe herself, and pin Blue out until Yellow must gybe for the mark: or alternatively luff again and hold the same tack for a few more seconds, when she can gybe for the mark. She will then meet Blue again on opposite tacks, which may discomfort Blue if this happens before the point at which Yellow must gybe again. But if Yellow sticks to the corridor, Blue may well get ahead of her – see fig 4 page 65.

If the leeward mark is to be rounded to starboard, there is less advantage in provoking a manoeuvre that will result in splitting tacks, only for Yellow to rejoin Blue on opposite tacks, since Yellow will then be on port. But if Yellow stands on, and tempts Blue to follow her, Yellow can once again determine the right moment to gybe and to oblige Blue to give her room to sail to the mark, in the process of which Yellow will become the leeward right-of-way boat, entitled to force Blue out wide until the convenient moment for Yellow's gybe for the mark.

---

[1] See below under rule 18.4

As has been seen, when sailing to the mark, keeping clear is a heavier burden than giving room when a boat is required to do both. At the mark, the reverse may be true. When boats are overlapped at the windward mark's zone, and remain overlapped at the mark, the leeward boat will bear away round the mark, and the windward boat must give her room to do so on her proper course. Since the leeward boat's stern will swing in bearing away, the requirement on the windward boat to give mark-room may mean that she has to be a little more to windward of the leeward boat than the distance needed just for keeping clear if the mark had not been there[1]. Giving room may also be a greater obligation than keeping clear when the proper course of the inside boat is to gybe.

Once the inside boat is 'at' the mark, then for as long as she remains as such, her entitlement changes to room to sail her proper course at the mark. Since a *proper course* is defined as one that she might sail in the absence of the boat required to give her mark-room, she might at a leeward mark wish to start rounding as wide as possible

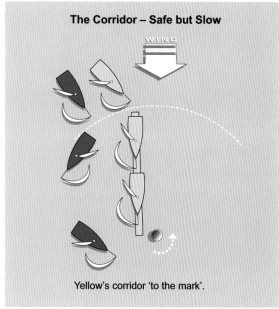

The Corridor – Safe but Slow

WIND

Yellow's corridor 'to the mark'.

fig 3

so as to exit tight on the mark, but the scope for this is limited by her having to start her rounding relatively close to the mark, if she has been shepherded to that spot in sailing 'to the mark'. Her scope to round advantageously on her proper course increases substantially if she can begin to do so from a more favourable position, having been given more than the minimum room while sailing to the mark.

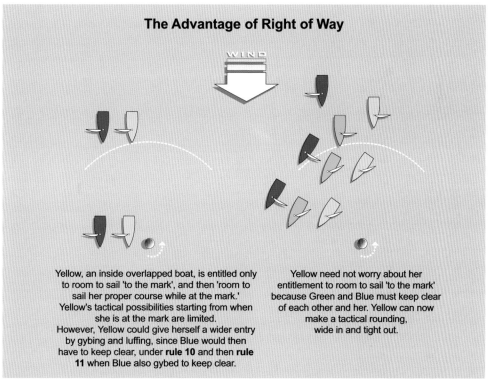

The Advantage of Right of Way

WIND

Yellow, an inside overlapped boat, is entitled only to room to sail 'to the mark', and then 'room to sail her proper course while at the mark.' Yellow's tactical possibilities starting from when she is at the mark are limited. However, Yellow could give herself a wider entry by gybing and luffing, since Blue would then have to keep clear, under **rule 10** and then **rule 11** when Blue also gybed to keep clear.

Yellow need not worry about her entitlement to room to sail 'to the mark' because Green and Blue must keep clear of each other and her. Yellow can now make a tactical rounding, wide in and tight out.

fig 4

---

[1] See diagram under rule 18.2(a)

The situation is different if the inside boat has right of way, whether from the outset, or by gybing after the zone is entered. The outside boat must give mark-room, but that is usually academic, since she must also keep clear, as nothing in rule 18.2 changes rules 10 or 11, and she must respond when possible to the actions of the right-of-way boat. The inside boat with right of way can sail beyond the space representing mark-room, limited only by rules 16.1, and by rule 18.4, under which this situation will be analysed further.

When an inside windward boat's proper course is to tack as part of passing the mark, mark-room includes the room to do that. This will be obvious at a windward mark, or when the course is from reach to reach. At a leeward mark, the proper course of an inside windward boat may be to tack as part of the rounding manoeuvre, and if she chooses to tack as part of her rounding, the outside boat must give her the room to do so. When she does so, the act of passing head to wind then switches off rule 18.2(b), as stated in rule 18.2(c), but the inside boat will have clear water to continue her tack. Just as at a windward mark, the situation of a **clear-ahead** boat entitled to room under rule 18.2(b) is more fragile than that of an **inside overlapped** boat when she tacks while leaving the mark. The boat with clear-ahead mark rights loses her rule 18.2(b) protection the moment she passes head to wind, and will immediately become the keep-clear boat under rule 13. If it is a starboard-hand leeward mark, she will continue to have to keep clear once close-hauled, under rule 10. If it is a port-hand leeward mark, she will gain rule 10 right of way when she is close-hauled, but must give the other boat room to keep clear under rule 15.

Many of these issues are summarised in a reply to a question to an RYA advisory team specially set up to deal with questions from competitors about the new Section C.

Room to sail to the mark includes room for inside overlapped keep-clear boat to change course promptly towards the mark the moment one of them enters the zone. It is then room to sail to point at the mark where the proper course of an inside boat or a boat clear ahead will be to change course to round the mark - the point where she is now 'at the mark'. When no other boat is involved, that will be to a point close to the mark consistent with a seamanlike rounding. When three boats are overlapped at zone entry, that point will be further from the mark, to allow the middle boat to give mark-room to the inside boat. Current, high winds, and other external factors can affect the point of transition.

It should be noted that:

(a)   the room an inside boat or one clear ahead at the zone is entitled to is not room to sail a proper course to the mark - consider a port-tack boat overlapped on a converging course inside a starboard-tack boat at a starboard-hand leeward mark. While the inside boat's proper course may be to hold her course before gybing, the room to which she is entitled is only to sail directly to the mark.

(b)   nothing in rule 18 changes the primary right-of-way rules 10 to 13. Therefore, when a boat required to keep clear must also give mark-room, she must do both: so, for an outside keep-clear boat, keeping clear is a greater obligation than giving room, and no rule requires the right-of-way boat to stay within the room to which she is entitled..

When the proper course of a boat entitled to mark-room is to change course to round the mark, she will be "at the mark". The word "at" should be interpreted in its natural sense. The room required must also take into account any obligations to keep clear of or give room to another boat. The requirement to give mark-room ends when mark-room is no longer needed.

Rule 18.2, if not overlapped at the zone.
Previously, the boat clear ahead on entering the zone acquired or retained right of way until the mark was passed, regardless of changes of tack by gybing after zone entry and during rounding. This *carte blanche* has been restricted slightly by the rule changing to a 'room' rule. When all that boats want to do is to sail straight for the mark, when their speeds are similar and when there is a moderate gap between them at the zone, the new rule makes little difference – no issue arose before, and none does now.

The simplest case is at a port-hand windward mark. Boats will be approaching the mark on the same tack on the starboard-tack layline, and Yellow clear ahead will have right of way under rule 12. While Yellow remains ahead, Blue clear astern has to keep clear under that rule, to which her obligation to give mark-room adds nothing. If, travelling faster, she is able to gain a windward overlap, she remains the keep-clear boat, now under rule 11, and once again, until the mark is reached, her keep-clear obligation is more significant than her give-room obligation (especially if the leeward boat luffs): but then while rounding the mark the now-windward boat has both to keep clear and, if more, give room.

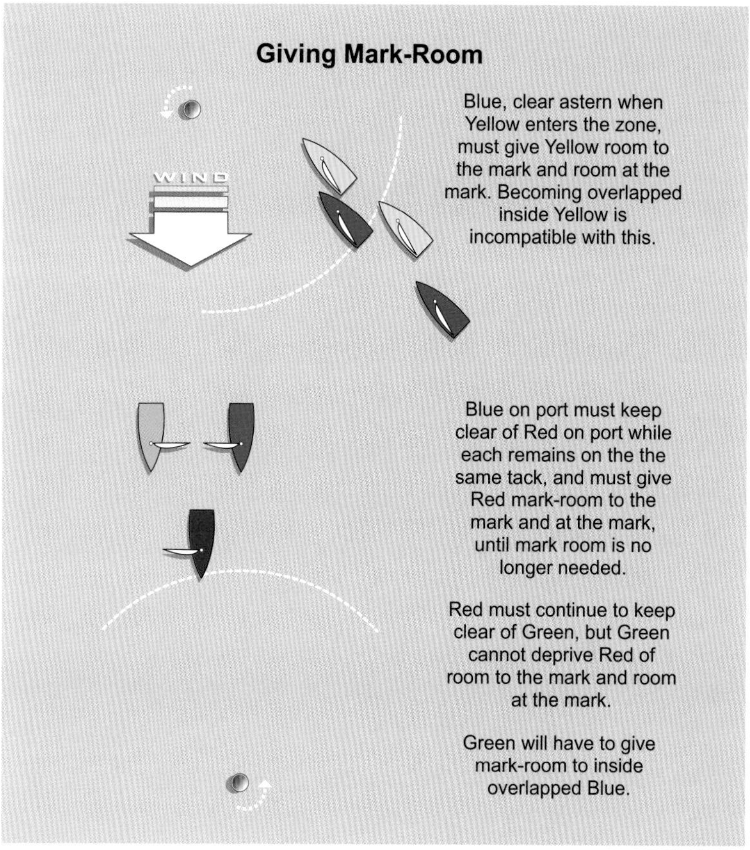

If instead Blue becomes overlapped to leeward of Yellow, as in fig 1, she becomes right-of-way boat under rule 11, which technically requires the Yellow windward boat to keep clear. However, Blue's duty is to continue to give mark-room

Giving Mark-Room

Blue, clear astern when Yellow enters the zone, must give Yellow room to the mark and room at the mark. Becoming overlapped inside Yellow is incompatible with this.

Blue on port must keep clear of Red on port while each remains on the the same tack, and must give Red mark-room to the mark and at the mark, until mark room is no longer needed.

Red must continue to keep clear of Green, but Green cannot deprive Red of room to the mark and room at the mark.

Green will have to give mark-room to inside overlapped Blue.

fig 1

continues. She cannot force the Yellow boat above the 'course to the mark', and at the mark she must not be inside the windward boat, since she would be occupying the space that would represent the windward boat's proper course in the absence of the leeward boat. If Blue does either of those things, and Yellow does not keep clear, rule 18.5 exonerates Yellow. So effectively the leeward boat must either immediately fall back astern again, or bear away and miss the mark, if she is not to break the second sentence of rule 18.2(b) and the first sentence of rule 18.2 (c). The same is true when sailing to a gybe mark or reaching to mark 2 of a trapezoid course. It will also be the case when the leeward mark is approached on the same tack and the boat that entered the zone ahead can round close to the mark.

One feature of modern sports boats, skiffs and catamarans is their high speed under spinnaker and their rapid deceleration when it is recovered. Yellow enters the zone of a leeward mark clear ahead of Blue. Neither will need to gybe before rounding it. Both are travelling fast under spinnaker. Yellow removes her spinnaker early, and slows rapidly. Blue, still carrying her spinnaker, must keep clear, which she can do only by passing one side or the other of Yellow. If she chooses to go outside, she will have little difficulty complying with rule 18.2(c). If she becomes overlapped inside Yellow, and removes her own spinnaker, she may find herself in an impossible position – required to continue to give mark-room by rule 18.2(c), but unable to do so. However, if she blasts past Yellow, to get clear ahead of her, not removing the spinnaker until at the mark, and not obstructing Yellow, now astern, in any way, I believe she has given the required mark-room – nothing stopped Yellow from sailing to the mark, and then sailing her proper course while at the mark.

Here is the plainest leeward mark situation.

Yellow was clear astern when Blue entered the zone, and must give mark-room. She cannot enforce her starboard-tack rights. The 'corridor' concept applies. While in the corridor, Blue is always entitled to room to sail to the mark. If she steps out of the corridor, the situation depends on the underlying Section A rule that applies. This is a small game change, since previously to enter the zone clear ahead on port tack created a right of way over the starboard-tack boat clear astern. Now, the boat clear astern retains her rule 10 right-of-way as long as the boat ahead does not gybe, but it cannot be exploited while the boat ahead remains in the corridor.

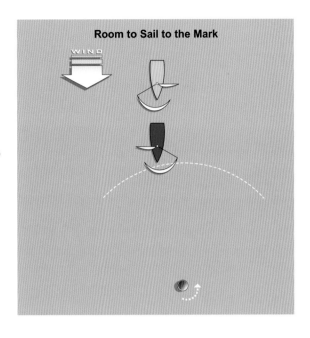

Room to Sail to the Mark

Tacking at a Windward Mark

A boat's entitlement to room to tack at a mark depends on whether she is overlapped to windward of and inside the boat from which she needs mark-room. If she is overlapped in that way, she is entitled to room to tack, otherwise, she is not, as stated in the definition Mark-Room. So when a boat's tack at a mark would otherwise break rule 13, and she is clear ahead of the boat from which she is entitled to room, her only safe course of action is to luff and slow to induce the other boat into an outside overlap in order to keep clear, at which point she will be entitled to room to tack, as discussed under rule 18.2(a).

At a starboard-hand windward mark being approached on starboard tack, a boat clear ahead that tacks loses her clear-ahead status the moment she passed through head to wind, and is now the give-way boat under rule 13 and then 10. She has no protection under rule 15, since her own actions caused her loss of rights. It is for this reason that windward marks are best set to be rounded to port in fleet racing, to avoid incidents, but to starboard in match racing and team racing, to provoke incidents. When a boat tacks from clear ahead on port to starboard at a port-hand windward mark, her period of risk relative to a port-tack boat astern of her is the short time during which she is subject to rule 13 and then, once on a close-hauled course, the time needed to comply with rule 15.

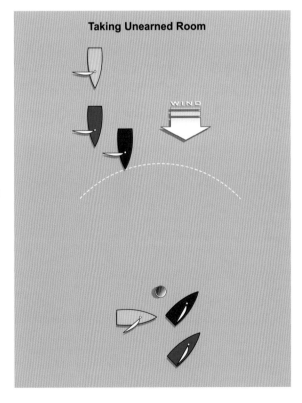

Taking Unearned Room

Taking Room to Which a Boat is not Entitled

Yellow was clear astern of Blue when Blue entered the zone, and required to give mark-room under the second sentence of rule 18.2(b). Because of Red, Blue left a gap, and Yellow used it. Yellow became overlapped inside Blue, but acquired no rights under rule 18.2(a) because rule 18.2(b) continued to apply. Has Yellow failed to comply with the requirement to give mark-room to Blue? No – because Blue's proper course at the mark had to take account of Red inside her, and nothing Yellow did interfered with that[1].

---

[1] ISAF 63: 'When a boat voluntarily or unintentionally makes room available for another that has not rights to such room, the other boat may take advantage, at her own risk, of the room.'

When does the obligation to give mark-room end?

Rule 18.2(c) states two moments when rule 18.2(b) stops applying, firstly if a boat entitled to mark-room (and therefore either clear ahead at the zone or overlapped inside) passes head to wind, and secondly if the boat entitled to mark-room leaves the zone.

The wording of rule 18.2(c) has been the subject of an urgent change from Jan 1st 2009. Rule 18.2(b) cannot now be switched off by a change of tack by the boat required to give mark room. Blue is required to give the Yellow boats mark-room by rule 18,2(b) when they enter the zone clear ahead of her. If Blue is sailing faster than them, she cannot now defeat rule 18.2(b) by herself briefly changing tack and then claiming mark-room for her late overlap under rule 18.2(a). Rule 18.2(b) now continues to apply.

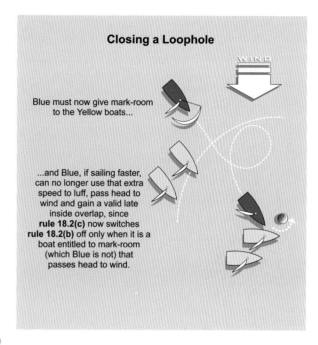

Closing a Loophole

Blue must now give mark-room to the Yellow boats...

...and Blue, if sailing faster, can no longer use that extra speed to luff, pass head to wind and gain a valid late inside overlap, since **rule 18.2(c)** now switches **rule 18.2(b)** off only when it is a boat entitled to mark-room (which Blue is not) that passes head to wind.

This change affects only leeward marks. If Yellow enters the zone of a windward mark on the same tack as Blue, and one if them is either clear ahead or overlapped inside the other at the zone, then a change of tack by either boat will still switch off rule 18.2(b), not because of rule 18.2(c) but because rule 18.1(a) or (b) will now disapply all of rule 18 once they are on opposite tacks. (If the other boat then passes head to wind, this may now bring rule 18.2(a) into effect, as discussed under that rule, if the boats are then overlapped on the same tack again.)

Unfortunately, the commonest way that an obligation to give mark-room ends is not stated, and it is the common-sense criterion (rather than anything in the rules) that mark-room will no longer needed. That may mean that the inside boat or the boat clear ahead has passed the mark. It may also mean that the outside boat or the boat clear astern is so far from the room-entitled boat that it would never be possible for mark-room not to be available to the room-entitled boat. In that case, the obligation to give mark-room may have ended before either boat reached the mark, indeed it may never have begun. This has to be inferred from the rule. It was not made explicit because there was no easy generalisation that could made. The obligation to give mark-room will end when the first of any of the written and unwritten 'terminal events' happens. Without this insight, it would be possible to assume that the main criterion was the written one of a boat being entitled to mark-room leaving the zone. In fact, that is the least likely of all the criteria to apply, since it will be the first to happen only when in a light wind and an adverse current a boat drifts back out of the zone without having sailed her proper course round the mark.

Doubt over an overlap

RYA 1992/9 explains the application of rule 18.2(d) to a protest committee.

> When the protest committee is unsure about the facts, it is normally the protestee that gets the benefit of any doubt. However, rule 18.2(d) states that, in the special case of reasonable doubt that a boat obtained or broke an overlap in time, it shall be presumed that she did not, a presumption that may favour either protestee or protestor.

There is a rare divergence between RYA 1992/9 and a US Sailing case on this topic. US 92 says '"Doubt" refers both to doubts by boats involved in or observing an incident and to doubt by the protest committee.' There was an exchange of hails on approaching the zone, one boat claiming an overlap, and the other claiming there was none. This was '…evidence that there was doubt as to whether the boat had obtained an overlap in time, and therefore it should have been presumed that she had not.' This is questionable on two grounds. First, if all it takes to switch the onus of proof is a hail, far fewer overlaps will found to have begun. Secondly, RYA 2002/15 claims that the rule 'is addressed to the protest committee. It does not change rights and obligations on the water…the protest committee was incorrect to say that a dispute at the time of the incident as to whether an overlap had been established meant the automatic operation of the rule. Disagreements of this nature are commonplace, with each boat firmly believing herself to be in the right. Rule 18.2(d) puts no additional obligations on a boat when her claim is denied [by the other boat]. The rule is an aid to the protest committee when evidence given by all parties at the hearing is inconclusive.' In addition to the merits of these competing arguments, it should be noted that a version of US 92 was submitted to ISAF for adoption as an ISAF case, but was not accepted.

No hail is required to establish or deny any right under rules 18 and 19. A hail is just an opinion expressed at the time, evidence of which will assist any subsequent protest. The more precise the hail, the more difficult it will be to dispute the facts later. A good sequence of hails approaching a mark's zone might be 'Four lengths – overlapped…three lengths – overlapped, room please…two lengths - still overlapped, I need more room[1].'

The fact that an overlap can be asserted to exist over a period of time will help offset the difficulty of judging distances, as coaches often prove to their charges with a 'boat-park shuffle' of boats on trailers. The person at the helm of a boat that is claiming a small overlap when the boat ahead enters the zone will be nearly five lengths from the mark at the actual moment of mark entry.

Tacking When Approaching a Mark

If two boats were approaching a mark on opposite tacks and one of them changes tack, and as a result is subject to rule 13 in the zone when the other is fetching the mark, rule 18.2 does not thereafter apply. The boat that changed tack

(a) shall not cause the other boat to sail above close-hauled to avoid her or prevent the other boat from passing the mark on the required side, and

(b) shall give mark-room if the other boat becomes overlapped inside her.

If this rule applies, it will spring into life the instant the tacking boat passes head to wind: before then, no part of rule 18 applied, because of rule 18.1(a), or, if the non-tacking boat is sailing below close-hauled having been above the layline, because of rule 18.1(b). The rule's intention is to promote orderly windward mark rounding and to deter port-tackers (assuming the mark to be a port-hand one) from tacking on the mark to spoil the day of boats that tacked on the starboard-tack layline further from the mark. With the change from a two-length zone to a three-length one, the rule now applies even further from the mark.

The rule does not change any rule of Sections A and B, which still apply as if the mark were not there. So rule 13 applies to the tacking boat, and her tack must be complete far enough from the non-tacker to comply with rule 15 if she acquires right-of-way[2]. If she breaks either of these rules, the question of considering whether rule 18.3 has also been broken is less important. If the tacking boat tacks to a leeward overlap or to a clear-ahead position, the non-tacking boat must keep clear once she is required to do so by rules 11 or 12, and rule 14 still applies, even if the boat that tacks is breaking rule 18.3: since a boat that is breaking only rule 18.3 can usually be avoided by the non-tacking boat, the rule 18.3 breach will not compel any breach of rules 11, 12 or 14, and so the non-tacking boat will not be entitled to exoneration under rule 64.1(c).

---

[1] My experience from observing afloat at a recent event in Italy is that a hail of 'Aqua' serves both for room hails and 'Starboard' hails. Elsewhere, 'Oy, oy, oy" is a common all-purpose hail.

[2] She will not do so at a mark to be left to port if she crosses ahead and the other boat becomes overlapped to leeward before the tacking boat reaches a close-hauled starboard-tack course – a 'slam-dunk'. The tacking boat will have been the keep-clear boat at all times, under rules 10, 13 and then 11.

Rule 18.3 adds to the tacking boat's Section A and B obligations. She may comply with rule 13 and 15, but can still break the additional requirements of rule 18.3.

The first trigger for rule 18.3 is when the tacking boat is between head to wind and close-hauled on the opposite tack (and therefore subject to rule 13) in the zone. Her luff may have begun either inside or outside the zone. Her passing head to wind may have happened inside or outside the zone. She may in fact not have completed her tack at the moment she breaks rule 18.3, for instance if she passes head to wind and then continues in a 'rule 13 condition' in order to shoot the mark with her momentum, delaying bearing away to a close-hauled course until she is able to pass the mark.

The second trigger is that the non-tacking boat is fetching the mark, as defined:

Definition **_Fetching_** A boat is fetching a *mark* when she is in a position to pass to windward of it and leave it on the required side without changing *tack*.

Therefore, the non-tacking boat can be below the layline, as long as she can shoot the mark.

When Blue, the tacking boat, passes head to wind, she will now be on the same tack as Yellow, which is fetching the mark, and they will be overlapped, now or shortly. Yellow is not required to give mark-room, because rule 18.3 says that rule 18.2 does not apply. The test for breaking rule 18.3 is what Yellow has to do to comply with rule 14 while Blue is subject to rule 13, and what Yellow has to do to comply with rule 11 or 12 if the tack is completed. If Yellow has to luff above close-hauled[1], or bears away and cannot leave the mark on its required side[2], the tack was made too close to Yellow. So the message to a boat contemplating tacking on or near the windward mark is not to do it unless it can be completed without interfering with the approach and rounding of the non-tacking boat.

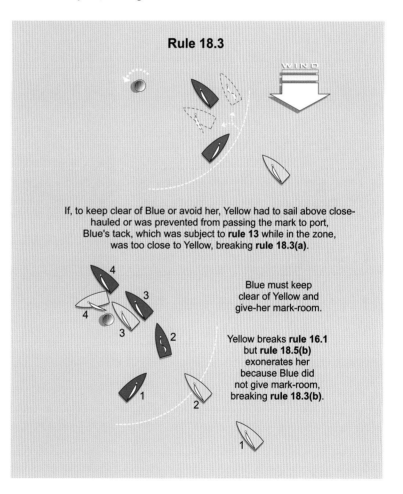

Rule 18.3

If, to keep clear of Blue or avoid her, Yellow had to sail above close-hauled or was prevented from passing the mark to port, Blue's tack, which was subject to **rule 13** while in the zone, was too close to Yellow, breaking **rule 18.3(a)**.

Blue must keep clear of Yellow and give her mark-room.

Yellow breaks **rule 16.1** but **rule 18.5(b)** exonerates her because Blue did not give mark-room, breaking **rule 18.3(b)**.

---

[1] Judges observing the rounding will be looking for a flapping jib.
[2] See RYA 1974/8

If the tacking boat can cross the non-tacker before tacking, and the non-tacker then gets an inside overlap from clear astern, the now-windward boat must give mark-room. At first sight, this does not seem necessary, because the windward boat has to keep clear in any case. However, rule 18.3 makes rule 18.2 non-applicable, and the right to mark-room has to be restored to the non-tacking boat by rule 18.3(b) in order for her to regain the protection of rule 18.5(b), Exoneration, which frees her from any rule 16.1 constraints in bearing away while rounding it. However, there are constraints on the non-tacking boat. Exoneration for breaking rule 16.1 under rule 18.5(b) applies only to a breach occurring while rounding the mark. The same applies to any breach of rule 15. So there is no automatic exoneration if the non-tacking boat, although fetching the mark, needs to luff to pass it – her luff must comply with rules 15 and 16.1, as ISAF 93 (fig 1) makes clear.

Blue tacks in the zone to a track far enough ahead and to windward of Yellow for Yellow to have mark-room at the mark, but Yellow, becoming overlapped to leeward, then luffs more than she needs just to pass the mark. Yellow breaks rules 15 and 16.1, by denying Blue room to keep clear, and Bue is exonerated, not at the time of the incident by rule 18.5, no part of which applies to her, but by the protest committee in any later protest, under rule 64.1(c), as there was no seamanlike way that she could have kept clear, once required to do so. Since Blue complied with rule 18.3, the situation was then as if it had happened away from any mark. L may also have broken rule 17, whose application is unaffected by any part of rule 18, if her premature luff took her above a proper course at that point.

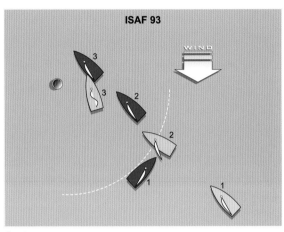

fig 1

While it will often be the case that the 'non-tacking' boat will have been on the mark's layline for some time, that is not a necessary condition for the application of rule 18.3 – the boat that is fetching the mark may herself have only just tacked for the mark. The following example shows several aspects of rule 18 at work at a windward mark.

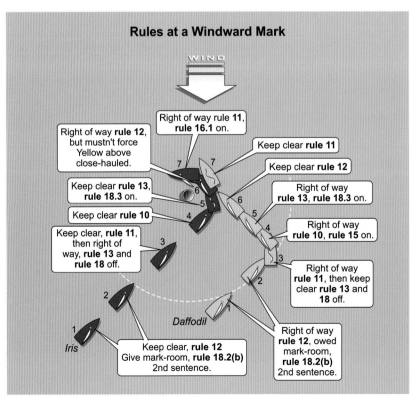

fig 2

A port-tack approach is favoured. *Daffodil* has right of way under rule 12, and, as the first to enter the zone, is entitled to mark-room from *Iris* under the second sentence of rule 18.2(b) (not that at this moment it represents any increased burden). *Daffodil* tacks for the mark in the zone, her right to mark-room ends because of the second sentence of rule 18.2(c), and rule 18 itself stops applying because of rule 18.1(b) because they are now on opposite tacks, and *Iris* has yet to tack for the mark. *Daffodil* was keep-clear boat under rule 13 from head to wind to a close-hauled course. She becomes right-of-way boat again under rule 10 when on a close-hauled course. *Iris* now has room to keep clear, starting from that moment, so *Daffodil*'s reacquisition of right of way complied with rule 15.

Iris delays her tack until she too can lay the mark. Her tack complied with rule 15, since *Daffodil* is able to act promptly to keep clear in a seamanlike way. However, since *Iris* was subject to rule 13 while *Daffodil* was fetching the mark (even though only in the last few seconds), rule 18.3 applies, and *Iris* breaks it, since *Daffodil*'s luff to keep clear, as required, took her above a close-hauled course. When they became overlapped, *Daffodil* was then required to continue keeping clear, now under rule 11.

Iris, although holding right of way under that rule, and although rounding on her proper course, did not have any entitlement to inside-overlapped mark-room under rule 18.2(b), because rule 18.3 switches off rule 18.2 'thereafter'. Therefore there was no exoneration under rule 18.5(b) if *Iris* broke rule 16.1, since rule 18.5 will exonerate only a boat taking mark-room to which she is entitled.

Rule 18.3 issues in general, and this one in particular, are likely to be more common as a result of the increase in the zone size.

Gybing

When an inside *overlapped* right-of-way boat must gybe at a *mark* to sail her *proper course*, until she gybes she shall sail no farther from the *mark* than needed to sail that course. Rule 18.4 does not apply at a gate *mark*.

A boat that has right of way at zone entry, either as an inside overlapped boat under rule 10 or 11, or if clear ahead under rule 12, has considerable scope, as has been seen, for not remaining in the mark-room 'corridor'. When they are overlapped, rule 18.4 is often regarded as simply placing a obligation on the inside boat not to delay her gybe. This is partly true, but only indirectly. Although the title of the rule is 'Gybing', the direct relevance of gybing is that the rule applies only when an inside overlapped right-of-way boat must gybe at a mark to sail her proper course. This most commonly occurs at a leeward mark, but it will also apply at a bear-away mark where the course is from reach to reach[1]. Once these conditions are satisfied, the requirement of rule 18.4 is, until she gybes, not to sail farther from the mark than needed to sail a proper course. This is explained in the leading case ISAF 75.

S is an inside overlapped boat holding right of way under rule 10. P must keep clear, and must also give mark-room to S under the first sentence of rule 18.2(b) because they are overlapped - the definition Overlap says that the term can apply to boats on opposite tacks that are both sailing more than ninety degrees from the true wind.

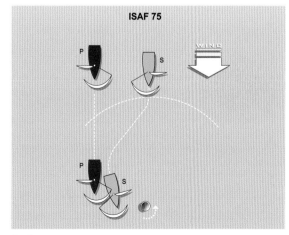

fig 3

---

[1] CYA 12, CYA 50

The mark-room that P was required to give S was the space S needed in the existing conditions to sail promptly to the mark in a seamanlike way. That space was a direct corridor from S1 to a position close to and alongside the mark on the required side. P gave S that room. However, because S had right of way she was not required to remain within that corridor; she was permitted to sail any course provided that she complied with rules 16.1 and 18.4.

S luffed gradually through approximately 45 degrees while sailing about three lengths forward, and P made no effort to keep clear. Shortly before position 2, S needed to act to avoid P. At that moment P broke rule 10. When S luffed after position 1, if P had acted promptly there was space for her to have manoeuvred in a seamanlike way to keep clear of S. Therefore S did not break rule 16.1.

When S gybed just after position 2, she had not sailed farther from the mark than needed to sail her proper course. Indeed, in the absence of P (the boat 'referred to' in the definition Proper Course), S's proper course might well have been to sail even farther from the mark and higher than she did, so as to make a smoother, faster rounding and to avoid interference with her wind by being backwinded or blanketed by other boats ahead.

S therefore did not break rule 18.4. Note the words 'S's proper course might well have been to sail even farther from the mark and higher than she did'. ISAF 86, showing an inside overlapped right-of-way boat sailing much further from the mark than S in ISAF 75, is withdrawn after 2009, but not because it was doubtful in any way. It no longer appears simply because it added nothing to ISAF 75 other than offering an example of the distance the inside boat might legitimately sail from the mark before gybing. That maximum distance from the mark that the inside boat may sail will depend on the size and type of the boats and on the weather conditions.

What happens when and after an inside right-of-way boat gybes? This is rarely analysed. Here, Yellow is making that even-wider approach that rule 75 says she is allowed.

Blue, at zone entry, must give mark-room to Yellow, namely room to sail to the mark; and (which is more relevant at that moment) Blue must keep clear of Yellow under rule 11. Yellow's luff must comply with rule 16.1, since there is no exoneration under rule 18.5(b). That rule refers to exoneration for a boat breaking rule 16 while rounding the mark on her proper course, but that is only for a boat taking mark-room to which she is entitled, and Yellow is sailing above her mark-room corridor. Yellow's course is one she would sail in the absence of Blue, and so it is a proper course, in compliance with rule 18.4. If Yellow had previously become overlapped from clear astern so as to be carrying a rule 17 limitation, it would still apply, but she does not break that rule, for the same reason. Yellow does not sail above a proper course, since she gybes at the point that will give her the optimum rounding. When Yellow bears away into a gybe, Yellow is now calling on her entitlement to room to sail to the mark. In effect, the original 'corridor'

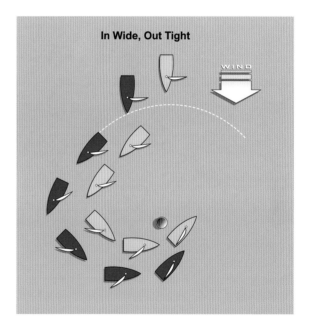

In Wide, Out Tight

to the mark has been replaced by a new one, and it includes room for Yellow to gybe. After gybing, Yellow becomes an inside overlapped windward boat. She is not yet at the mark. She must keep clear of Blue. Blue must give Yellow room to sail to the mark, so there is a period after the gybe and before being at the mark when S no longer has a proper course entitlement, only the right to sail to the mark. Finally, in the last two positions shown, Yellow is at the mark, and now has a proper-course entitlement, but it means little at this point.

CYA 12 says that a boat that delays her gybe when not set up to do so at the right moment because an injury to the crew breaks rule 18.4[1], and CYA 50 says that a boat that elects to luff and tack rather than gybe, carrying a windward boat with her for a while, breaks rule 18.4[2].

If an inside overlapped right-of-way boat does sail above or beyond her proper course before she gybes, the outside boat must still keep clear if she is given room to do so. In strong winds, a wipe-out by the inside boat might make that impossible, but if the manoeuvre is controlled, then the fact that the inside boat is breaking rule 18.4 does not necessarily compel the outside boat to break a rule, in which case in a protest both boats would be disqualified.

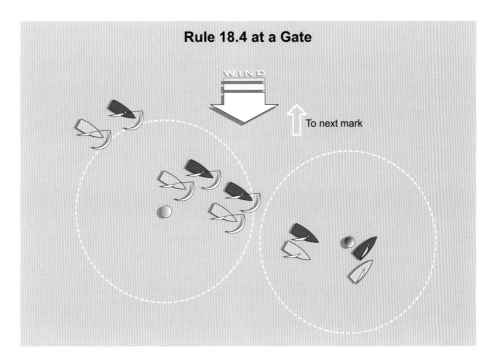

Rule 18.4 does not apply at a gate, so this rule does not require Yellow to gybe when passing the left-hand mark, since she has chosen the right-hand mark. However, if she had obtained her leeward overlap so as to make rule 17 apply, she must not sail above a proper course, and her only proper course at this badly-laid gate may be to gybe at the left-hand mark.

Although the marks are shown with non-overlapping zones, it does not appear to raise issues if the zones intersected by having the marks laid somewhat less than six hull lengths apart (as well as being properly aligned!). At the first mark, Blue must keep clear, and give Yellow mark-room. The mark-room obligation ends before the first zone is left, and a new one then begins when Blue enters the second mark's zone, now requiring Blue to give mark-room to Yellow. It would require the distance between the marks to be narrowed to four lengths or less for mark-room conflicts to arise. Blue must keep clear of Yellow under all times, under rule 11. When overlapped boats are approaching a gate from a more windward direction, it is the right-of-way boat that has the choice of which mark to round, and intersecting zones do not hinder that choice.

---

[1] In my opinion, that case is questionable. What course would she sail to finish most quickly in the absence of the windward boat?
[2] But if the rig is danger while gybing in strong winds, you can argue that tacking IS the proper course, and it is not the case that L MUST gybe to sail it. L is not entitled to room to tack round: W must keep clear of L only until she passes head to wind, and L's luff must comply with rule 16.1. But is rule 18.4 actually broken, particularly as L never gybes at all?

18.5 **Exoneration**

When a boat is taking *mark-room* to which she is entitled, she shall be exonerated

(a) if, as a result of the other boat failing to give her *mark-room*, she breaks a rule of Section A, or

(b) if, by rounding the *mark* on her *proper course*, she breaks a rule of Section A or rule 15 or 16.

The rationale of Section C is that it does not explicitly to disapply any rule of Section A or B. In practice, conflicts will occur between rights and obligations under Sections A and B and mark-room entitlements under Section C. Belated exoneration under rule 64.1(c) is insufficient, since that rule applies only when a boat is **compelled** to break a rule. That will not be so when, at a leeward mark, an inside windward boat does not keep clear of the right-of-way leeward boat that was not giving her room when sailing to the mark. The inside boat could luff the wrong side of the mark to keep clear, and indeed win a later protest, which would be little consolation if she loses places in getting back and rounding. If instead she holds her course to the mark and there is contact between her and the leeward right-of-way boat, rule 64.1(c) alone would not exonerate her for breaking rule 11, since she was not compelled to infringe. In addition, exoneration under rule 64.1(c) can be granted only by a protest committee.

Rule 18.5 therefore grants immediate exoneration in such circumstances - for breaking a Section A when taking mark-room to which she is entitled, either because the other boat has not given her that room, or if she breaks that rule while rounding the mark on her proper course. In addition, she may break rule 15 or 16 with impunity when rounding a mark on her proper course within the room to which she is entitled.

Here are examples of rules of Section A being broken by Yellow, but with exoneration by rule 18.5(a), and Blue breaks rule 18.2(a).

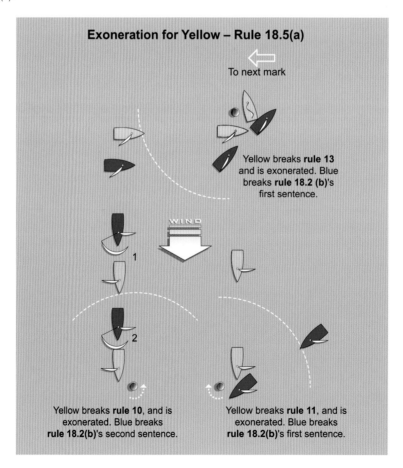

Exoneration for Yellow – Rule 18.5(a)

To next mark

Yellow breaks **rule 13** and is exonerated. Blue breaks **rule 18.2 (b)**'s first sentence.

WIND

1

2

Yellow breaks **rule 10**, and is exonerated. Blue breaks **rule 18.2(b)**'s second sentence.

Yellow breaks **rule 11**, and is exonerated. Blue breaks **rule 18.2(b)**'s first sentence.

The rule 13 example also qualifies for exoneration under rule 18.5(b), as she is rounding when denied mark-room. That example makes a further point. Yellow lost mark-room entitlement when she passed head to wind, because rule 18.2(c) says so, and because in any case rule 18.1(a) stopped rule 18 applying. Blue's failure to give mark-room happened before Yellow passed head to wind, since Yellow's mark-room entitlement included, by definition, room as an inside windward boat to tack.

Here is a situation where rule 18.5(b) alone provides exoneration.

Exoneration under rule 18.5(b) for breaking rule 16 (in particular rule 16.1) reflects the fact that right-of-way boats must be expected to make rapid changes of course at a mark, and keep-clear boats must handle themselves with this in mind. But for exoneration for breaking rule 16 to apply, the boat must be 'at' the mark and rounding it on her proper course, for which she entitled to room. If an inside leeward boat in the zone and only half-way to the mark decides to luff for an initially wide rounding, that may be her proper course, but she is not yet 'at' the mark, and therefore is not entitled to luff harder than rule 16.1 allows[1].

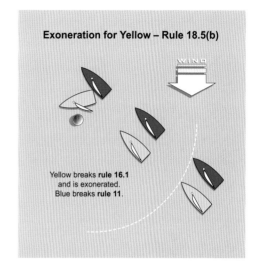

Exoneration for Yellow – Rule 18.5(b)

Yellow breaks **rule 16.1** and is exonerated. Blue breaks **rule 11**.

Rule 19 ROOM TO PASS AN OBSTRUCTION

The differences between rules 18 and 19 can be summarised as follows:

Rule 18, MARK-ROOM	RULE 19, ROOM TO PASS AN OBSTRUCTION
Applies when the mark is an obstruction, unless it is a continuing obstruction	Does not apply when an obstruction is also a mark, unless it is continuing obstruction
The mark must be required to be passed on the boats' same sides	There is no required side, and the obstruction can be passed on either side when it is possible to do so, as the right-of-way boat chooses, except if the obstruction is a continuing obstruction that is also a mark
It is *mark-room*, as defined, that must be given	It is *room*, as defined, that must be given
Does not apply between opposite-tack boats at a windward mark	Does not apply between opposite-tack boats unless both are sailing more than ninety degrees from the wind
The rule starts to apply at zone entry , three of the nearer boat's hull lengths from the mark	There is no zone. The rule applies at the obstruction
Rights at the mark are often determined at zone entry	Rights at the obstruction are not finally decided until the obstruction is being passed
The rule deals with clear-ahead and overlapped situations	The rule deals only with overlapped situations at 'ordinary' obstructions, and only with clear-ahead situations at continuing obstructions
There may be no penalty for breaking rules 15 and 16	Rules 15 and 16 always apply
Marks have a fixed location (except for a boat displaying flag M)	A boat racing or a vessel under way may be an obstruction
Marks are identified in the sailing instructions	Obstructions are self-evident, except in the case of an area defined in the sailing instructions as an obstruction

[1] See ISAF 75, as discussed under rule 18.4

An obstruction is defined as:

Definition **_Obstruction_** An object that a boat could not pass without changing course substantially, if she were sailing directly towards it and one of her hull lengths from it. An object that can be safely passed on only one side and an area so designated by the sailing instructions are also _obstructions_. However, a boat racing is not an _obstruction_ to other boats unless they are required to _keep clear_ of her, or, if rule 22 applies, avoid her. A vessel under way, including a boat racing, is never a continuing _obstruction_.

At its simplest, an obstruction is a stationary object or feature, like a boat on moorings.

An obstruction may be an 'area', such as a zone bounded by defined buoys, but only when the sailing instructions say so, or one whose extremities, even if not buoyed, are given chart positions in the sailing instructions, or are identified with reference to a charted zone[1]. 'Government buoys marking a security zone are not obstructions except insofar as an individual buoy is large enough to be an obstruction in its own right. Boats may pass such obstructions on either side unless the sailing instructions prohibit sailing inside the security zone. A boat cannot be penalised under the racing rules for violating government regulations related to a prohibited zone unless the sailing instructions make the regulations a 'rule governing the event[2].'

A starting line before the starting signal is not an obstruction, and a boat finding herself being legitimately luffed to an OCS position cannot ask for room to stop this happening. Likewise, I believe that when sailing instruction say that boats shall not cross a line from the committee boat to a buoy near her and approximately on the starting line, that line is not an obstruction. Nor is a given line of latitude or longitude that boats must not cross. These last two examples are valid sailing instructions, and a boat can be penalised as a result for breaking them. The difference between a line and something that ranks as an obstruction is that rules 19 and 20 give the right to room at obstructions, but not at lines; and crossing a line may break a sailing instruction, but touching an obstruction breaks no rule unless the obstruction is also a mark or (sometimes) another boat racing or some other vessel.

A right-of-way boat may be an obstruction, as when boats are overhauling a clear-ahead boat from astern, or when two port tack boats sailing close-hauled meet a starboard close-hauled boat. In each case, Green is an obstruction to Yellow and Blue.

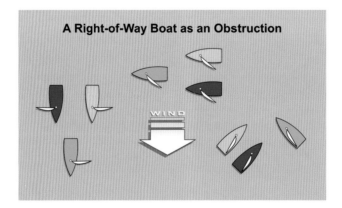

A Right-of-Way Boat as an Obstruction

---

[1] RYA 1989/6
[2] US 83

A boat is an obstruction to other boats that are required to keep clear of her only as long as they are required to do so. In fig 61, the boats are on port tack, and *Thetis* is an obstruction to *Iris* and *Daffodil*, as she is clear ahead. *Iris* and *Daffodil* gybe to starboard tack, and *Thetis* must now keep clear. Iris and *Daffodil* must each initially give *Thetis* room to do so under rule 15. However, a change to the definition Obstruction from 1st January 2010 means that *Thetis* ceased being an obstruction to them the moment Iris and *Daffodil* gybed, and not during the following few seconds while rule 15 applied. If during this time *Iris* and *Daffodil* were closing on *Thetis*, *Iris* is not entitled to room from right-of-way *Daffodil* to pass between Thetis and *Daffodil* in the process of giving *Thetis* her rule 15 room, because *Thetis* is not an obstruction, and so rule 19 does not apply. So *Iris* may have to overtake *Thetis* to windward to give her that room.

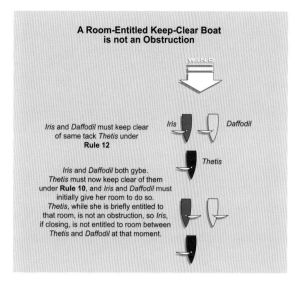

A Room-Entitled Keep-Clear Boat is not an Obstruction

Iris and *Daffodil* must keep clear of same tack *Thetis* under **Rule 12**

Iris and *Daffodil* both gybe. *Thetis* must now keep clear of them under **Rule 10**, and *Iris* and *Daffodil* must initially give her room to do so. *Thetis*, while she is briefly entitled to that room, is not an obstruction, so *Iris*, if closing, is not entitled to room between *Thetis* and *Daffodil* at that moment.

When two boats meet a boat they must avoid under rule 22, she is an obstruction. That rule lists a capsized boat, a boat that has not regained control after capsizing, a boat that is anchored or aground, or one that is trying to help a person or vessel in danger.

What happens when two right-of-way boats meet a keep-clear boat that is not keeping clear? She is not an obstruction. Both right-of-way boats are required to avoid contact, by rule 14, and, if in so doing one of them breaks a rule of Section A in respect to the other, it will have been an infringement compelled by the keep-clear boat's infringement, resulting in exoneration under rule 64.1(c)[1].

An area defined in the sailing instructions as an obstruction, and an object that can be safely passed on one side only, are automatically obstructions. A right-of-way boat, a boat entitled to room or mark-room, and a boat that has to be avoided will rank as an obstruction only if it meets the general test in the first line of the definition, namely that a substantial course change would be needed at one hull length from it. This general test determines whether an object not specifically listed is large enough to be an obstruction. Applied strictly, it can raise questions.

Daffodil is sailing as close to windward of *Iris* as is compatible with keeping clear. The anchored boat is not an issue for *Iris*. *Daffodil* could avoid it with a slight bear-away in the absence of *Iris*. Since the definition Obstruction refers to a substantial course change, is the anchored boat an obstruction giving rise to an entitlement to room? Yes, because the definition poses a hypothetical test, related to whether a substantial course change is needed at one length when a boat is sailing directly towards it. If *Daffodil* were sailing directly towards the anchored boat (I think one must assume towards its middle), a substantial course change would be needed. Therefore, it is an obstruction giving rise to the right to room even if in practice it requires only a small course change.

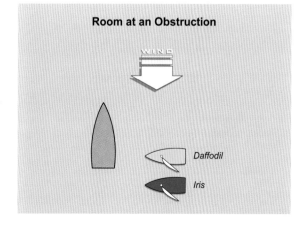

Room at an Obstruction

Daffodil

Iris

The fact that *Iris*, in the absence of *Daffodil*, would not need to take avoiding action does not make rule 19 any less applicable. It is enough that *Daffodil* could not avoid the obstruction[2].

---

[1] ISAF 10, RYA 1989/12
[2] ISAF 11

A race committee boat forming one end of a starting or finishing line is usually large enough to be an obstruction, but sometimes it is rule 18 that applies to boats approaching it, sometimes rule 19, and sometimes neither. The sailing instructions may state that the committee boat is a starting or finishing mark, but when they do not do so and the committee boat is surrounded by navigable water, the definition Mark does it for them, because the starting or finishing line projects from a specified mast on the boat.

When the committee boat is surrounded by navigable water:-
- It is an obstruction where room must be given under rule 19 until boats are approaching it to start
- When boats are approaching it (and its anchor line) to start until they have passed, it neither rule 18 nor 19 applies, and so there is no right to room or mark-room at it
- If boats are required by the sailing instructions to sail through what was the starting line during the race, often at the end of a lap, this becomes a gate, of which the committee boat is one mark, at which rule 18 applies
- If boats are not required to sail through the starting line during the race, but happen to do so or cannot avoid doing so, then the committee boat is an obstruction at which rule 19 applies
- If boats are prohibited from sailing through what will be the finishing line before finishing, then I do not think that the committee boat is a rule 18 mark, since the whole line including committee boat and pin buoy can be left to either side: instead, it can be a rule 19 obstruction
- When the committee boat forms one end of the finishing line, it is a mark to which rule 18 applies, and where there may be mark-room entitlements, as discussed under rule 18.

When the committee boat is not surrounded by navigable water, then it is no longer automatically a mark, because the definition Mark says so, despite the fact that the starting or finishing line projects from it. Rights to room will be decided at all times by rule 19. That includes when approaching the starting line to start, because the preamble to Section C switches off the rules of Section C then only when it is a mark that is being approached. Room will have to be given to an inside overlapped boat that is 'barging'.

A committee boat may also be a starting or finishing mark because the sailing instructions say so (see rule L9.4). When the water around it ceases to be navigable on a falling tide, or if it was never navigable at all, then it remains a mark when it has a required side at the start or finish of the race, and during the race if applicable. When it is being approached to start, the preamble to Section C will still not operate, because, although it is a mark, it is not surrounded by navigable water. So which rule of Section C applies – rule 18 or rule 19? The first sentence of rule 19.1 (see below) tell us that it is rule 18 that applies, because it is a mark with a required side, and it is mark-room rather than ordinary room that may have to be given, including mark-room inside overlapped boat that is 'barging'. However, the committee boat now has a zone which will deprive a boat getting a late inside overlap from any entitlement to mark-room.

One boat racing may be an obstruction to another boat racing, but that in itself has no relevance in the rules. Although the general test for an obstruction refers to its effect on one boat only, the fact that an object (including another boat racing) may be an obstruction is significant only when it is being approached by two boats. Rule 19's purpose is to secure safe navigation between two or more boats that approach an obstruction, by requiring one to give room to the other, so as to allow the other to avoid the obstruction. My experience is that protestors completing a protest form over an incident involving only two boats will sometimes get distracted into issues relating to obstructions when it is in fact a simple Part 2 of Section A rule matter.

When Rule 19 Applies

Rule 19 applies between boats at an *obstruction* except when it is also a *mark* the boats are required to leave on the same side. However, at a continuing *obstruction*, rule 19 always applies and rule 18 does not.

If due to lack of communication a large navigation buoy is chosen as a port-hand mark by one club, and as a starboard-hand mark by another, then, as between a boat from one club that meets a boat from the other at the buoy, it is not rule 18 that applies between them, because of rule 18.1 and rule 19.1. However, it may not be rule 19 either. If it a windward mark, and boats meet it on its windward side on opposite tacks and are not both sailing more than 90° off the wind, they are not overlapped, as defined, rule 19 cannot apply, and so rule 10 will apply. If the large buoy is a leeward mark, and opposite tack boats meet head-on on its leeward side, they are now overlapped, but it is not possible to say whether either boat is outside or inside, and so I think rule 19.2(b) cannot apply, and the situation has to be resolved by rule 10.

On the other hand, as previously stated, an island that the sailing instructions say is to be left to port is a mark, but rights to pass it are determined by rule 19 when it is a continuing obstruction.

19.2(a)&(b) **Giving Room at an Obstruction**
(a) A right-of-way boat may choose to pass an *obstruction* on either side.
(b) When boats are *overlapped*, the outside boat shall give the inside boat *room* between her and the *obstruction*, unless she has been unable to do so from the time the *overlap* began.

For rule 19.2(b) to apply, the boats must be overlapped. That term will always apply to same-tack boats. The definition Overlap makes the term apply to opposite tack boats as well when rule 18 applies, and, in the case of an obstruction, when boats are both sailing more than ninety degrees from the true wind. So boats sailing directly towards each other reaching on opposite tacks along the river bank or shore are not overlapped, and rule 19.2(b) does not apply: this is purely a rule 10 situation. If rule 19.2(b) does not apply as between boats that are reaching towards each other, then clearly it does apply either if one or both is close-hauled, as in ISAF 43.

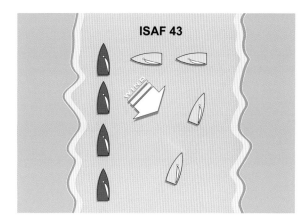

Both boats are passing an obstruction (which happens to be a continuing obstruction, although that is not directly relevant to the situation). But they are on opposite tacks, and neither is sailing more than ninety degrees from the true wind. So Blue is not entitled to room from Yellow under rule 19.2(b): it is rule 10 that governs, and Blue, on port tack, should have taken earlier action to bear away to keep clear of Yellow.

When boats are overlapped on the same tack at an obstruction, then it may still not be possible for rule 19 to decide an entitlement to room, as RYA 1962/8 shows.

The case says that S was an obstruction to PW and PL. PL, holding right of way over PW under rule 11, exercised her entitlement under rule 19.2(a) by choosing to pass the obstruction on her starboard side[1]. 'However, rule 19.2(b) did not create any entitlement to room for either boat. The situations at a mark under rule 18 and at an obstruction under rule 19 are different. When a mark is being approached on the same tack by boats on widely differing courses, an obligation will apply from zone entry onwards for the one that will be outside at the mark to give room to the other, with the mark on the same required side for both – see ISAF case 12. Under rule 19, there is no zone, and the obstruction may be left to port or to starboard, as decided by the right-of-way boat. Room then has to be given at the obstruction by an outside boat. Although PW and PL were overlapped, the terms 'outside' and 'inside' are not capable of applying at an obstruction to boats approaching each other at such a divergent angle.'

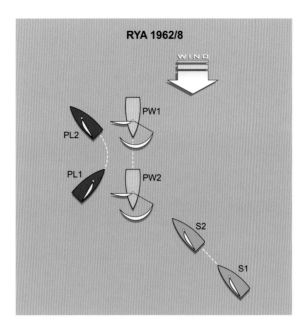

When the obstruction can be passed on either side, it is the right-of-way boat (starboard, leeward or clear ahead) that decides which side she wants to pass it. This may still leave the other boat the option as whether to pass on the same side or on the other side. If the other boat decides to pass on the same side as the right-of-way boat, or if she has no choice in the matter, and if they are overlapped, the other boat is entitled to room.

ISAF 41 explains[2].

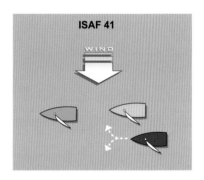

Question 1
Does rule 19 apply between Yellow and Blue as they overtake and begin to pass Green? If so, which parts of it apply and when do they apply?
Answer 1
…rule 12 requires both Blue and Yellow to keep clear of Green. Therefore, Green is an obstruction to both Blue and Yellow. However, Green is not a continuing obstruction, as the last sentence of the definition Obstruction makes clear. As Blue and Yellow overtake A, Blue[3] may choose to pass Green on either side (see rule 19.2(a)). When either Blue or Yellow begins to pass Green, provided that they are still overlapped, rule 19.2(b) will apply.

If Blue chooses to pass Green to leeward, rule 19.2(b) will require her to give room to Yellow, as inside boat, to do likewise if Yellow steers a course to do so. However, Yellow is not required to take the room provided, and may pass A to windward, keeping clear of her under rule 12 and then rule 11.

If Blue chooses to pass to windward of Green, then rule 19.2(b) requires Yellow to give Blue room to pass Green and rule 11 requires Yellow to keep clear of Blue. Rule 12, and later rule 11, require Blue to keep clear of Green.

Question 2
Does Yellow have to hail for room to pass to leeward of Green? If not, would Blue risk disqualification by not giving room?
Answer 2
Yellow is not required to hail for room, although that is a prudent thing to do to avoid misunderstandings. Rule 19.2(b) requires Blue to give room to Yellow if they both pass to leeward of the obstruction, whether or not Yellow hails for room.

---

[1] In rules 18 and 19, the 'side' is always the side of the boat to which that word applies, and not any side that a mark or obstruction may either happen to have or that is quite validly made relevant by a sailing instruction, such as 'leave channel marks on the channel side', or '(do not) pass to the north of xx'.
[2] Colours are substituted for initials, and the diagram is reorientated
[3] The right-of-way boat under rule 11

The right to room is subject to the outside boat's ability to give it, relative to the time the overlap began. If the overlap begins close to the obstruction, the right-of-way boat may not be able to give room: if so, she does not have to. Suppose that an obstruction can be passed on either side. If a boat just clear ahead and sailing a course to windward of a boat clear astern chooses to pass an obstruction to leeward, and bears away to do so, her course change may make the other boat overlapped to leeward, and therefore now the right-of-way boat. The right to choose which side to pass the obstruction passes to the leeward boat. If the leeward boat now decides that she wishes to pass to windward of the obstruction, she may do so provided that the other boat can now luff to give her room to do so[1].

In all rule 19 situations, but in this one in particular, a late course change by a right of way boat must comply with rule 16, and, if the overlap has begun within two hull lengths measured by the leeward boat's hull, rule 17 will preclude a windward passage if that is not her proper course.

A boat is entitled to room even if it was needed only because she created the overlap, for instance by tacking to a leeward overlap[2].

When the obstruction to the boat needing room is a right-of-way boat approaching rapidly, the boat that has to give that room will normally be presumed to be aware of the situation and to know that she has to give room, even if there is no hail for room, and even if the boat needing room does not try to take the room[3].

Because the outside boat is deemed to be aware of all that is happening inside and ahead of her, and to act when needed without being hailed to do so, this is more difficult for the outside boat when there are three overlapped boats approaching an obstruction, and even more difficult when the obstruction is then a right-of-way boat in motion. The definition Overlap says that each of the boats is overlapped on the other, even if, in the absence of the middle boat, the inside boat and the outside boat would not be overlapped, as long as the outside boat is overlapped on one side of the middle boat, and the inside boat is overlapped on the middle boat's other side.

This fact rarely becomes an issue, since most situations can be resolved by looking at the obligations of the outside and middle boats and the middle and inside boats separately. However, the link between the outside and the inside boat suggests that an outside boat of three or more must act, if she can, in anticipation of the room that will be needed by the inside boat, and is not entitled to wait until a middle boat starts to give room.

Note that the inside boat is not herself an obstruction to the middle and outside boats, following the change to the definition Obstruction on 1 Jan 2010. So why must the outside boat make room? Because they are all at the 'real' obstruction – an object or a boat holding right-of-way over them - and the outside boat's duty is to give the inside boat room at that obstruction, which she can do only by giving the middle boat room to do likewise.

There will be more time for compliance with rule 19(b) when the right-of-way boat that is the obstruction is travelling in the same direction of the boats between which room must be given.

---

[1] ISAF Q&A 2009-21
[2] ISAF 33
[3] ISAF 49, a case published to illuminate protest hearing procedural issues, but which supports these points, partly implicitly. I have again reorientated the ISAF diagram, which I think gives it a new perspective

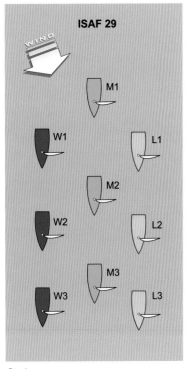

fig 1

This is analysed in ISAF 29.

Rule 11 required W to keep clear of L throughout the incident. While M was clear astern of L, rule 12 required her to keep clear of L, and after she became overlapped with L rule 11 required her to keep clear L. As fig 1 shows, both M and W met these requirements.

Because both W and M were required to keep clear of L throughout the incident, L was an obstruction to W and M during that time (see the penultimate sentence of the definition Obstruction). When M became overlapped with W, rule 19.2(b) began to apply between them… It required W to give M room between her and the obstruction, unless she was unable to do so from the time the overlap began. As the facts clearly show, W was able to give M that room when the overlap began and continued to do so at all times until the boats finished. Therefore, W complied with rule 19.2(b) … M broke no rule.

Suppose that L and W had been closer together, so that there was initially not room for M to sail through the gap. Once, this would have been a 'continuing obstruction' issue, as now addressed in rule 19.2(c), and M would not have any rights if she became overlapped between W and L. Now, it is a rule 19.2(b) situation[1]. All of the decision quoted from ISAF 29 applies, with the addition that M would have initially to give room for W to keep clear under rule 15, and W would need to luff slightly to keep clear under rule 11 and give room to M under rule 19.2, both of which she which she was able to do[2]. In addition, in each case, rule 17 will also apply to M, to prevent her from sailing above her proper course, although if she did so, W would have to keep clear and then protest.

In all these three-boat examples, rule 19 applies because there is one boat that is an obstruction by virtue of her right of way over two other boats that are 'at' the obstruction. Even when boats abeam of each other are on opposite tacks, rule 19 is capable of applying, since the definition Overlap says that the term applies to boats sailing more than ninety degrees from the true wind.

Note that, although the title of rule 19 is Room to Pass an Obstruction, the word 'pass' is relevant only to the choice given to the right-of-way boat under rule 19.2(a) or when rule 19.2(c) applies. As stated in ISAF 29, rule 19.2(b) does not apply until boats are overlapped 'at' an obstruction, and as discussed above under ISAF 41, that overlap may change the identity of an obstruction.

It follows that, as between three boats, it does not matter whether two caught one, or one caught two. For rule 19.2(b), all that is relevant is the relationship between them, frozen at the point at which they are all overlapped on each other. Taking all eight permutations of tacks that can apply, the question in each case is whether there is a boat that has both the other boats on one side of her and is an obstruction to both of them. If so, the boat on the other side of the trio will be an outside boat at an obstruction, and required to give room. In the first in fig 68 two cases, this is not so, and any port-tack boat must keep clear of an adjacent starboard tack boat, however she got into this position[3].

---

[1] Because L was a boat under way, L was not a continuing obstruction to them (see the last sentence of the definition Obstruction) and so rule 19.2(c) did not apply.
[2] RYA 1977/7
[3] ISAF 23

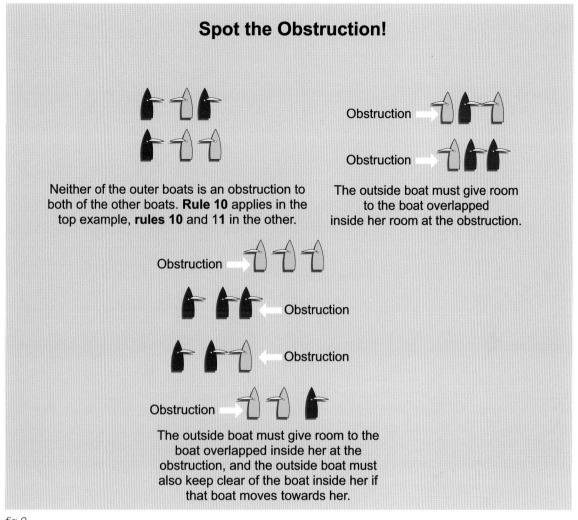

Spot the Obstruction!

Obstruction →

Obstruction →

Neither of the outer boats is an obstruction to both of the other boats. **Rule 10** applies in the top example, **rules 10** and **11** in the other.

The outside boat must give room to the boat overlapped inside her room at the obstruction.

Obstruction →

← Obstruction

← Obstruction

Obstruction →

The outside boat must give room to the boat overlapped inside her at the obstruction, and the outside boat must also keep clear of the boat inside her if that boat moves towards her.

fig 2

Of the remaining six situations, in four of them the obligation of the outside boat to give room does not add to the fact that the outside boat is also required by rule 11 to keep clear of the inside (or middle) boat, which may luff away from the obstruction, subject (in three cases) to any rule 17 limitation that may have been created if she became overlapped on the boat outside her from clear astern on the same tack. The obstruction is also entitled to move towards the boats outside her, in which case they too must change course to continue to keep clear.

That leaves two situations where the keep-clear (or middle) boat is entitled only to room from the outside boat holding right of way over her to keep clear of the right-of-way starboard tack that is an obstruction to both of them. If the boat that is the obstruction decides to luff, her change of course must allow the outside boat to be able to give any further room to the middle boat to continue to keep clear, including room for the middle boat to gybe. If the middle boat gybes, the outside boat now has to keep clear as well as give room.

It does not matter, as between a boat required to give room and one entitled to room, whether they are level or one is advanced on the other, as long as they are overlapped. When the overlap ends, rule 19.2(b) stops applying.

When the boat needing room and the boat to give that room are overlapped on a close-hauled course and are approaching an obstruction, it will often be the case that the leeward boat that would have to give that room is also affected by the obstruction, giving her the right to hail for room to tack. If the leeward boat hails for room to tack, and the windward boat hails for room to bear away, or does not hail at all, it is the hail for room to tack that prevails, since it must always be responded to. The preamble to Part C says that when rule 20 applies, rule 19 does not, as will be discussed under rule 20[1].

19.2(c)

Giving Room at an Obstruction

While boats are passing a continuing *obstruction*, if a boat that was *clear astern* and required to *keep clear* becomes *overlapped* between the other boat and the *obstruction* and, at the moment the *overlap* begins, there is not *room* for her to pass between them, she is not entitled to *room* under rule 19.2(b). While the boats remain *overlapped*, she shall *keep clear* and rules 10 and 11 do not apply.

This rule has the effect of deterring a keep-clear boat from becoming overlapped between the boat ahead and a continuing obstruction, which, as defined, will not be another moving vessel, and especially not another boat that is racing. It is, however, worded so as to apply only to a boat that dares to become overlapped in this situation.

What is a 'continuing' obstruction.? It can be a physical feature, such as the shore or a river bank. It can be a vessel that is NOT under way, such as an anchored or moored commercial vessel. The fact that the obstruction is of some length is relevant only if the boats are sailing close to it for some time[2]. But for how long? Given that rule 19.2(c) situations usually occur when the boat ahead is sailing only a little more slowly than the boat astern, and given also that the rule requires both boats to be passing the continuing obstruction, I think that the answer is self-referential – is there time for a boat to go from clear astern to overlapped, during which both boats are always passing an obstruction? That suggests an obstruction of at least three boat-lengths, and usually more, as in the breakwater discussed under rule 18[3].

Both boats must be passing the continuing obstruction for rule 19.2(c) to apply, so that an overlap beginning when most of the boat ahead has started to pass the obstruction, but none of the boat astern has, will be governed by rule 19.2(b) while the continuing obstruction is still being passed. The right of way will not change, and there is more opportunity for an inside boat with (or gaining) right of way to manoeuvre against the outside boat.

Rule 19.2(c) offers no comfort to a port-tack boat clear ahead of a starboard-tack boat – the port tack boat must either keep clear, or gybe to starboard to limit the options of the boat astern. The rule is a limitation only for a boat clear astern **and required to keep clear**, namely a same-tack situation (rule 12), or a port-tack boat astern of a starboard-tack boat (rule 10). Indeed, it is important to see rule 19.2(c) as a limitation to a boat's rights under rule 19.2(b) rather than an opportunity, given the greater rights of a boat clear astern with right of way, which will be entitled to room if she becomes overlapped between the boat ahead and the obstruction, but where in any case her Section A rights are undimmed. Under 19.2(c), the boat astern and required to keep clear has no rights if she becomes overlapped between the boat ahead and the obstruction, unless the space between them is sufficiently wide.

---

[1] ISAF 3
[2] ISAF 33
[3] See fig 3 page 58

If the conditions for rule 19.2(c) to be applicable have been met, and the boat astern wants to become overlapped between the boat ahead and the continuing obstruction, the question is whether, at the moment an overlap would begin, there is room as defined for her to pass between them. Curiously, there does not appear to be any case that says so, but it is generally accepted (correctly, I believe) that the gap must be assumed not to narrow for the foreseeable future, even if, in practice it will narrow if the boat ahead holds her course. Another way of looking at it is to pretend that the boat ahead is stationary at the moment the overlap is established, and ask whether the boat astern could sail through the gap.

If the gap is wide enough, the keep-clear boat astern is entitled to become overlapped inside the boat ahead. If they are on the same tack, a leeward overlap from astern will now require the windward boat to keep clear under rule 11 as well as giving room under rule 19.2(b), but the leeward boat will be limited to a proper course by rule 17. If that is not relevant, the inside right-of-way boat can drive the outside boat further from the obstruction. If the inside overlap from astern is to windward of the outside boat, the outside boat's only obligation is to give room under rule 19.2(b), and the outside boat can therefore shepherd the inside boat along the obstruction even if her next objective is somewhere to leeward of that course. This will be so when the boats are on the same tack, or the when a port-tack boat astern becomes overlapped between a starboard tack boat and the continuing obstruction.

These obligations will continue while the boats continue to pass the obstruction without gybing, with the inside boat being allowed more room only when there are projections from the obstruction, such as a jetty or a shallow patch[1]. If either gybes, this may change rights, and any same-tack rule 17 limitation will end.

Room at a Continuing Obstruction

No room to pass between, so no room entitlement for the boat astern, which must keep clear in any inside overlap.

Green is entitled to room from Blue, but no more, while they are overlapped at the continuing obstruction. Green must keep clear.

Room to pass between, so the keep-clear boat astern is entitled to room when overlapped.

WIND

Green is not a keep-clear boat, so not **rule 19.2(c)**, Red must keep clear under **rule 10**.

Yellow must not only give room to Red but also keep clear. Red can luff only if she has a proper course on the other bank.

If the gap is not wide enough, the act of the boat astern becoming overlapped inside the boat ahead turns her (the inside boat) into a keep-clear boat with no entitlement to room from the boat that was ahead, which retains her right-of-way status, even if she is now a windward boat, since rule 11 is disapplied. The outside boat can close the gap, whether by luffing or bearing away, limited only by the risk of damage or injury resulting from any collision, and the inside boat would be advised to fall astern, so that the break of overlap would reset the situation to what it had been before the unsuccessful intervention. This is the only situation under Section C where a Section A right of way is explicitly overridden.

[1] RYA 1968/11

Rule 19.2(c) is relevant only occasionally in most types of racing, but is a semi-permanent concern on the sort of river where I learned to sail, fringed with reeds and navigable right up to them. Bermudan-rigged boats will often be caught up by traditional gaff- and gunter-rig boats with overhanging booms that are nearly as long as the boats themselves. I am sailing a Bermudan within 4 metres of the leeward bank, with one of these antiques roaring up from astern several knots faster, boomed out and goose-winged, occupying 8 metres of river width. She removes the whisker pole, gybes the jib, hauls in the main towards the centreline, uses her momentum to shoot through the small gap, possibly with the end of her boom sweeping though some of the pliant and insubstantial reeds, and is ahead of me, goose-winged and away in a few seconds, with no risk of contact. Was there room for her to do it? Yes, I suppose, since she did it 'in a seamanlike way in the prevailing conditions', which are light to moderate winds and flat water. Elsewhere and in other conditions, it would be more difficult for a gap of that size to be deemed to be sufficient for an entitlement to room.

The entitlement to room will end at a continuing obstruction in the same way as at any obstruction, because it is the same rule 19.2(b) that grants the right to room. That will be when the room is no longer needed, because the obstruction has ended, or because a gybe has ended a rule 17 proper course limitation on what had been an inside leeward boat, which is now able to drive the outside boat further from the obstruction.

Three-boat situations – interaction between rules 18 and 19

As has been seen, when three boats meet, rule 19 will apply when one of them is an obstruction, as defined, to the other two, which more often than not will be the case. When there was only one rule for marks and obstructions, the obstruction element when three or more boats met at a mark tended to be ignored, and only the mark-room issues were considered. Now that the mark rule and the obstruction rule have been separated, the obstruction issues are now exposed, and have caused a considerable degree of head-scratching and concern.

Obligations at marks under rule 18 are often decided by the situation when the zone is entered. However, there is no zone at a rule 19 obstruction, and the definition Obstruction said that a boat entitled to room or mark-room could be an obstruction to other boats. No rule says explicitly that rule 19 will <u>not</u> apply in three-boat situations to which rule 18 applies. The effect of this was belated realised to be that a boat clear astern of two or more others at zone entry might nevertheless become entitled to rule 19 room if she established a late overlap inside or between the boats ahead that were entitled to rule 18 mark-room from her. True, she broke the second sentence of rule 18.2(b) in the process, but that did not entitle one of the boats ahead to deny rule 19 room to her if it could be given.

As a result, it was felt that the only legal option for a boat ahead at the zone was to give room to the interloper, and then protest her under rule 18.2(b).

This was a significant, complicated and unintended game-change, which has now been addressed with a rule change with effect from 1st January 2010. The solution adopted was to remove boats entitled mark-room from the definition Obstruction. If a boat entitled to mark-room can no longer be classified as an obstruction to other boats, then rule 19, which applies only at obstructions, cannot now apply. The obligations of the boats at marks in three-boat situations are therefore decided only by the rules of Sections A and B of Part 2, and by rule 18.

Since this has the effect of making the rules say what most people thought they said (or ought to say), the change will have little impact in practice. The urgent amendment removed boats entitled to 'room' as well as 'mark-room' from the definition Obstruction. That does not appear to be any loss when considering three-boat situations away from a mark, under rule 19. Nor does it impact on the operation of the other 'obstruction' rule, rule 20 as discussed on page 89.

Rule 20 **ROOM TO TACK AT AN OBSTRUCTION**

20.1 **Hailing and Responding**

When approaching an *obstruction*, a boat sailing close-hauled or above may hail for *room* to tack and avoid another boat on the same *tack*. After a boat hails,

(a) she shall give the hailed boat time to respond;

(b) the hailed boat shall respond either by tacking as soon as possible, or by immediately replying 'You tack' and then giving the hailing boat *room* to tack and avoid her; and

(c) when the hailed boat responds, the hailing boat shall tack as soon as possible.

20.2 **Exoneration**

When a boat is taking *room* to which she is entitled under rule 20.1(b), she shall be exonerated if she breaks a rule of Section A or rule 15 or 16.

20.3 **When Not to Hail**

A boat shall not hail unless safety requires her to make a substantial course change to avoid the *obstruction*. Also, she shall not hail if the *obstruction* is a *mark* that the hailed boat is *fetching*.

When approaching an *obstruction*...

What may be an obstruction, as defined, is discussed under rule 19, noting that rule 20 does not apply at a starting mark and its anchor line being approached to start until they are passed, because of the preamble to Section C (which also disapplies rules 18 and 19); and noting also that rule 20.3 contains a further mark-related exception. The preamble to Section C says that when rule 20 applies, rule 19 does not.

Therefore, when a windward boat would like to bear away behind an obstruction, even if she hails for room, her right to room to duck will be negated by a hail for room to tack by the leeward boat, as this brings rule 20 into effect and disapplies rule 19[1]. So when a leeward boat or a boat clear ahead is on collision course with an obstruction she can avoid either by tacking or ducking, the choice as to which to do is hers[2].

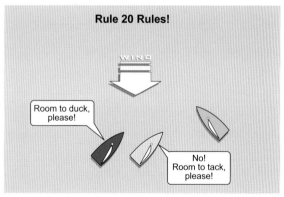

fig 1

Note that the starboard tack boat in fig 1 is an obstruction because the definition Obstruction says that a right-of-way boat is an obstruction to boat required to keep clear of her, and Green holds right of way under rule 10. If this were the mirror-image situation with Blue and Yellow on starboard tack approaching a close-hauled port tack boat that was not keeping clear under rule 10, then Yellow is not entitled to hail for room to tack.

---

[1] ISAF 3, US 24

[2] RYA 1974/5: 'When a close-hauled port-tack boat needs to make a substantial change of course to avoid an obstruction in the form of a close-hauled starboard-tack boat, she is entitled to hail another boat on the same tack as her, to windward or clear astern, for room to tack, even though she has an alternative means of escape by bearing away.'

However, if she does hail, Blue must respond as required by the rule, and Blue can then protest Yellow under rule 20.3. Alternatively, Yellow might tack without hailing, giving rise to a protest under rule 13 or rule 10. In either case, the protest committee will find that Yellow broke a rule, but may well conclude that in acting to comply with rule 14, Avoiding Contact, Yellow was compelled to break a rule because the port-tack boat was breaking rule 10, in which case Yellow would be exonerated under rule 64.1(c)[1].

...a boat sailing close-hauled or above may hail for *room* to tack and avoid another boat on the same tack.

A boat will often be above (i.e., to windward of) close-hauled when 'fiddling' along the bank of a river and catching the occasional favourable shifted gust to enable her to keep moving, a subject discussed later. The hailed boat will either be overlapped to windward or astern and on a more windward course. Rule 20 does not apply to close-hauled boats on opposite tacks, as was pointed out to the port-tack boat in both ISAF 43 and RYA 1984/11. So P in fig 1 is not entitled to hail S for room to tack. Instead, P was required to alter course in time to keep clear of S by bearing away and passing astern of her.

The room that a boat can hail for is not just room to tack, but also room to avoid the other boat, the mechanism for which is discussed below. The 'avoidance' is more relevant when tacking off the 'left bank', as the hailing boat will be tacking onto port tack. At the 'right bank', the hailing boat will be tacking onto starboard tack, and so may be in less need of the rule, indeed she may be able to tack without any need to hail at all.

Although rule 20 is primarily a safety rule, it is often used tactically. A boat ahead that needs to tack will sometimes luff and delay her hail until she can be sure of making the boat astern tack with her: whereas the boat astern will make a tactical choice as to whether, when hailed, it is better to tack as well, or to duck and hold the same tack longer.

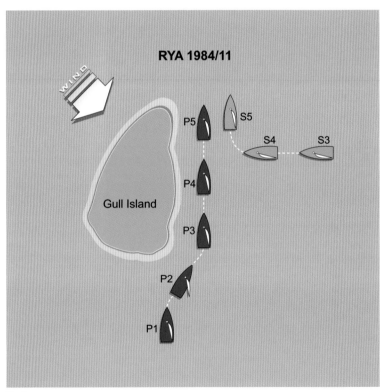

fig 1

After a boat hails...she shall give the hailed boat time to respond...

A boat must hail in good time for the other boat to respond, and must not hail and tack at the time[2]. 'When a hailing boat observes no response to her hail, adequate notice of intent to tack requires a second, more vigorous hail[3].' A hail for room to tack will often come as no surprise, but 'a windward boat is not required to anticipate a leeward boat's actions with respect to a converging right-of-way boat[4].' 'It is implicit in rule 20.1 that a boat's hail for room to tack must be capable of being heard by the hailed boat. Although the hailed boat is not required to take any action before the hail is given, she must be on the alert for it, and, when it is made, must respond promptly to it[5].'

---

[1] RYA 1989/12
[2] US 45
[3] ISAF 54
[4] US 45
[5] RYA 1988/3: the problem remains that, on big boats in bad weather, a hail may not be heard. A submission to ISAF to require the hail to be accompanied by the hand signals used in match racing was not successful.

Thus in ISAF 54, A and B, close-hauled on starboard tack, were approaching the shore, with A a hull length ahead and one length-and-a-half to leeward. A hailed for room to tack but B did not hear the hail. After waiting for a short interval, during which time there was no response from B, A tacked onto port. Then, in spite of bearing away as rapidly as possible with her sheets free, A hit B's leeward side. A protested B under rule 20.1(b) and B protested A under rule 10.

When A appealed her disqualification, it was held that when the hailed boat fails to respond in any way, as with B in this case, the hailing boat should hail again, more loudly. A did not do so. Also, A gave B little or no time to respond, thereby depriving her of the choice of actions provided in rule 20.1(b), and also risking contact with her. A broke rule 20.1(a), and also rule 14 because clearly she could have avoided contact with B by complying with rule 20.1(a). By failing to keep clear of B she also broke rule 10. But although A's disqualification was upheld, B was not out of the woods. At the hearing, B had acknowledged that she was aware of the position of A before A tacked, but B's helmsman and crew had not observed A during the thirty seconds before the collision. So B also contributed to causing the collision. Rule 14 required her, as well as A, to avoid contact 'if reasonably possible'. This requirement meant that a boat must do everything that can reasonably be expected of her in the circumstances to avoid contact. That included keeping a lookout, especially when two boats approached an obstruction together. B's failure to observe A for a 30-second period was in this case a clear breach of rule 14, and B was disqualified as well.

Giving the hailed boat time to respond is more complex in three-boat situations approaching an obstruction, all on starboard tack. ISAF 113 says that when the boat astern of or windward of two others can hear the leeward boat's hail, she must respond and not wait for the intervening boat's hail. Suppose however, that, with all boats on starboard tack approaching a 'left-hand' bank, the first boat to hail is ahead as well as to leeward of the second boat, which in turn is ahead and to leeward of the third boat, which is out of earshot of the first boat but hears the hail from the middle boat. Respond she must - but was the middle boat's hail valid?

As will be seen under rule 20.3, a boat shall not hail unless safety requires her to make a substantial course change to avoid an obstruction. The shore is not yet an obstruction to the middle boat, which in any case, unless she tacked, would collide with the tacked first boat before reaching the shore. Nor is the tacked first boat, now on port tack, an obstruction to the two other boats, even though rule 20 entitles her to room, because a give-way boat entitled to room no longer qualifies as an obstruction as defined – perhaps an unintended consequence of the 2010 change to the definition Obstruction. However, for there not to be a right for all related boats to be hailed about is unthinkable, and passing the hail from boat to boat is a well-established procedure.

After a boat hails…the hailed boat shall respond either by tacking as soon as possible…

The hailed boat has no right to ignore the hail because she disputes its validity. The hailing boat may be well away from the shallow water, but there may be some flotsam in the water that the hailed boat cannot see. If the hailed boat disagrees with the hail, the protest room is the place to resolve the matter. Late-detected flotsam might result in a boat hailing and tacking without giving the hailed boat time to respond, but I think that she must still hail when she tacks. If there is then a coming together, no rule seems to excuse the hailing boat for not doing the impossible by hailing earlier, and so the hailing boat might be advised to take a two-turns penalty.

When a hail is properly made, the hailing boat is 'entitled to expect that the [hailed boat] would respond and give her room to tack' and is 'not obliged to anticipate [the hailed boat's] failure to comply with rule 20.1(b)[1].' However, if the hailed boat does not tack, the hailing boat is not automatically to be exonerated, for instance for then colliding with a right-of-way boat that is the obstruction. Rule 64.1(c) will get her off the hook only if she could not then avoid breaking a rule (usually rule 10). If when there was no response to her hail she could keep clear of the obstruction by ducking, but she did not do so, then she is not entitled to exoneration[2].

The tack must be started as soon as possible, and finished as soon as possible. A boat that responds to a hail but tacks so slowly that she delays completion of the tack beyond a reasonable time is not responding as soon as possible after the hail.

---

[1] ISAF 3
[2] US 2

In RYA 1982/6 (fig 1), the two boats were tacking in a light wind against the current, taking full advantage of the slacker current by the bank. L and W were overlapped on port tack when L neared the bank and hailed for room to tack. There was approximately a one-second delay between the hail and L beginning her manoeuvre. W also began her manoeuvre at the same time. Both boats began tacking, W only slowly, and there was contact between them when L had tacked to a close-hauled course on starboard tack, while W had just passed beyond head to wind.

The protest committee disqualified W for breaking rule 20.1(b). W appealed, saying that she had started to tack instantly and completed her tack in about ten seconds which she asserted was not too long a period for a Merlin Rocket in light winds; she claimed that L should have kept clear while she (W) tacked.

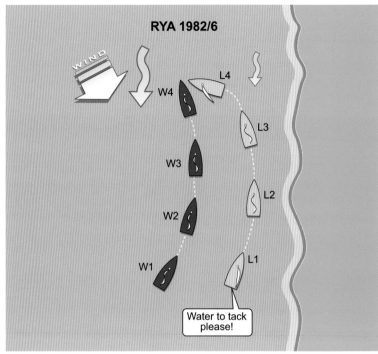

fig 1

Her appeal was dismissed. 'W was still in the process of tacking nine to ten seconds after the hail, when L had already completed her tack. W did not comply with the requirement of rule 20.1(b) to tack as soon as possible after the hail. Her own evidence that she luffed 'gradually and progressively' does not accord with the requirement of the rule. She also broke rule 13[1].'

...or by immediately replying 'You tack' and then by giving the hailing boat *room* to tack and avoid her...

This usually happens when the hailed boat judges that she can stand nearer into the obstruction (usually the shore in this case) than the hailing boat, and so will bear away if necessary behind the tacking hailing boat to continue further on the same tack.

However, if a hail is made at such a distance ahead or to leeward that the hailed boat judges that the hail was not justified, the hailed boat can, at her own risk, reply 'You tack' and then stand on. If the hailing boat then has the space she 'needs in the prevailing conditions while manoeuvring promptly in a seamanlike way[2]' to tack, and also then to avoid, the hailed boat, the hailed boat will have complied with the rule. This will be demonstrated if the hailing boat is able either to pass safely astern of the hailed boat, or if she has room first to tack back towards the obstruction and then, if necessary, time to hail again for room to tack and give the hailed boat time to respond (this time usually by tacking).

---

[1] L avoidably broke rule 14, but injury or damage was not an issue in the case. L was taking room to which she was entitled. She had been the right-of-way boat throughout, under rule 11 and then rule 13; so although she would also have been entitled to exoneration for any breach of rule 15, that never happened.
[2] Definition, Room

...and, when the hailed boat responds, the hailing boat shall tack as soon as possible.

If she does not tack as soon as possible, she not only breaks rule 20.1(c) but also demonstrates by sailing on for some distance that her hail was premature, contrary to rule 20.3.

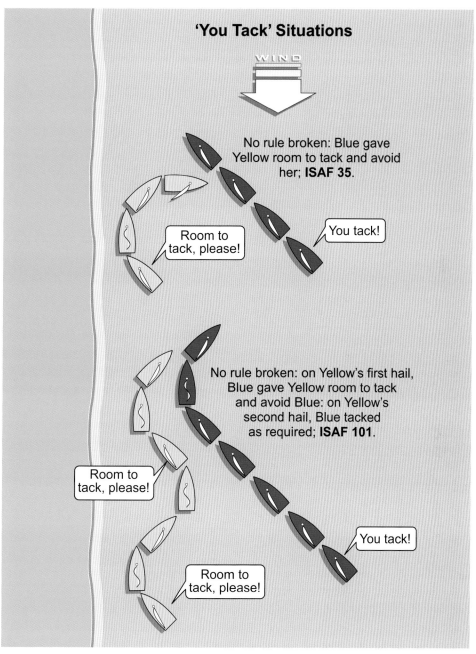

fig 2

In RYA 1973/5, W and L were sailing parallel courses, close-hauled on port tack, under a hull-length apart, approaching the shore. L hailed for room to tack and W tacked immediately. L maintained her original course for about a further three hull-lengths before tacking some 8 seconds after W. W protested L under rule 20.1(c) in that she failed, W having tacked, to tack as soon as possible.

The protest committee dismissed the protest, considering that in view of the conditions prevailing and the experience of the helmsman, the time taken by L complied with rule 20.1(c) .W appealed, stating that L was the more experienced helmsman of the two and that there had been no reason why she should not have tacked earlier. Her appeal was upheld, and L was disqualified.

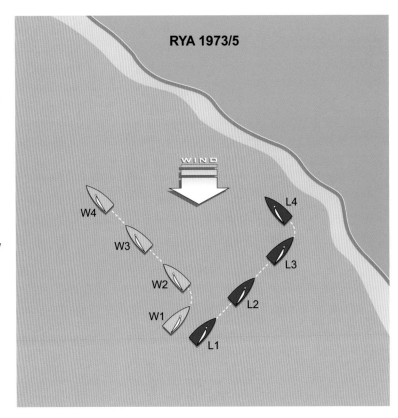

In hailing when safety did not require her to do, as evidenced by her being able to delay her tack, L broke rule 20.3. Rule 20.1(c) requires the hailing boat to tack immediately she has room to do so. L sailed on for at least three boat lengths after W had tacked, which broke rule 20.1(c).

When a boat is taking *room* to which she is entitled under rule 20.1(b), she shall be exonerated if she breaks a rule of section A or rule 15 or 16 (rule 20.2).

When a boat on starboard tack hails for room to tack at the 'left bank' and the reply is 'You tack', she may for a few seconds be on port tack under the bows of the hailed boat which is still on starboard. The hailing boat must be excused this technical breach of rule 10, and it is for the hailed boat to give room so that the hailed boat does not need to act to keep clear. The same applies if the boat that replied 'You tack' has misjudged her ability to give room, resulting in the hailing boat breaking rule 13 with respect to her.

The rule 16 exoneration is similar. Consider two boats overlapped on a beat in open water close to each other, and the leeward one suddenly luffs. She may break rule 16.1 if she does not give the windward boat room to keep clear. Move this situation to the shore, and add to the facts that the leeward boat has called for room to tack, and the windward boat, misjudging the situation, has replied 'You tack'. Both boats are required to give room, the leeward boat under rule 16, and the windward boat under rule 20.1(b). Rule 20.2 tells the leeward boat that she can break rule 16.1 with impunity.

When a boat on port tack hails for room to tack at the 'right bank', and the reply is 'You tack', her tack to starboard might in other circumstances have broken rule 15. Again, she is doing only what the rule requires, and must be forgiven. By replying 'You tack', the hailed boat accepts full responsibility for there being room, and (in this case) for keeping clear.

While some, possibly all, of these exonerations would be available from a protest committee under rule 64.1(c) were there no rule 20.2, it does no harm for the situation to be totally clear within rule 20 itself, especially given its focus on safety and the need for clarity as to which boat must do what.

A boat shall not hail unless safety requires her to make a substantial course change to avoid the _obstruction_ (rule 20.3).

It is safety rather than tactical considerations that should govern the hail. It is generally accepted that the risk of grounding is a safety issue, even if there is little or no possibility of damage. I referred earlier to river racing, where the only thing worse than 'fiddling' along the leeward bank and catching the odd favourable gust would be to tack into the lee of the vegetation on the windward bank. But a boat sailing this way and slowing for lack of suitable wind may realise that a boat doing the same astern has got a better puff, and momentum will carry her through to windward, in the process depriving the boat that was ahead of what little wind is available for several seconds. It is not unknown for the boat ahead to hail for room to tack as soon as the other boat has got too close for a 'You tack' reply. Both will then head for the wind shadow, but the hailing boat may be able tack back at just the right moment to avoid the dead area into which the other boat cannot avoid sailing.

In truth, there may not have been any need to make a substantial course change, and, even if there were it was not safety-driven. At the worst, the boat ahead would just have slowed and possibly stopped, a situation easily retrieved in light winds, albeit a tactical disaster. I have never known a protest over this, perhaps because any protestor would want to retain the option to do exactly the same when the boot is on the other foot.

RYA 1973/5, discussed on page 94, makes the point that the substantial course change must be needed to be made shortly after the hail, not some time later. US 15 notes that when a boat is clear ahead of the one she might hail, she might be able to pass to leeward of the obstruction with only a small course change, in which case she is not entitled to hail for room to tack. (The same might be true of a brief 'shoot' above close-hauled to pass to windward of an obstruction she can 'fetch' (see below), as long as the obstruction is not a moving right-of-way close-hauled starboard-tack boat, as that would not be keeping clear.) Indeed, if the boat ahead or to leeward can pass to leeward of the obstruction without any need to alter course, her hail for room to tack will be clearly improper[1]. She must bear away to give room unless or until the other boat decides to tack off.

As stated, a boat that thinks that another boat's hail for room to tack is improper has no choice other than either to tack, or reply 'You tack' and give room. If she wishes then to protest, it will be under rule 20.3.

Also, she shall not hail if the _obstruction_ is a _mark_ that the hailed boat is _fetching_.

Definition _Fetching_ A boat is _fetching_ a _mark_ when she is in a position to pass to windward of it and leave it on the required side without changing _tack_.

A boat may therefore be below the layline for the mark, yet able to shoot it by sailing above a close-hauled course and pass it to windward of it without tacking. When another boat that would elsewhere be able to hail her legitimately for room to tack does so when she is fetching the mark, she must respond by tacking or responding 'You Tack' and giving room, but she may now protest. In this way, safety is assured. On the other hand, a boat that makes an improper hail for room to tack will avoid penalisation by taking a two-turns penalty, unless significant advantage or unfair sailing is an issue.

When the mark is the committee boat well before boats are approaching it to start, and two boats are approaching it during pre-start manoeuvres, a hail for room to tack does not break rule 20.3, even if the hailed boat does not need to tack, since the definition Fetch is careful to include the fact that it applies only when the hailed boat can leave the mark on its required side. The committee boat does not have a required side before it is being approached to start, and so rule 20.3 does not apply.

---

[1] ISAF 11

However, when boats are starting close-hauled and one of them finds she needs room to tack to avoid a committee boat surrounded by navigable water, the preamble to Section C says that no rule of Section C applies[1]. Nevertheless, her hail will compel the other boat to tack, and the issue can then be resolved by taking a penalty, or in front of a protest committee.

When the mark is the committee boat with a mast from which the **finishing** line projects, and boats are approaching it close-hauled, the reference point for rule 20.3 is the windward end of the committee boat and not the point at which the line exits the committee boat.

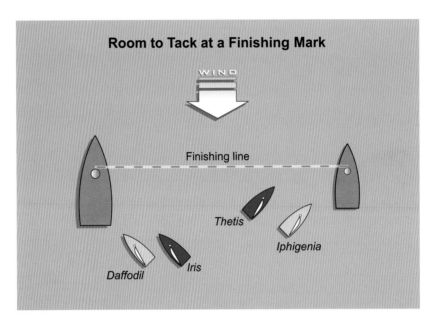

So *Daffodil* is entitled to hail *Iris*, because *Iris* cannot fetch the mark either. *Iphigenia* on the other hand is not entitled to hail *Thetis*, because *Thetis* can fetch the mark, and the fact that she will not fetch it until after finishing is not relevant[2]. (In addition, the definition Fetching speaks only of being able to pass the mark, and makes no reference to its anchor chain, which is, by definition, not part of the mark. Presumably, if a boat cannot avoid hitting the anchor chain, she cannot be said to be able to pass to windward of the mark itself.)

Section D - Other Rules

When rule 21 or 22 applies between two boats, Section A rules do not.

STARTING ERRORS; TAKING PENALTIES; MOVING ASTERN

A boat sailing towards the pre-start side of the starting line or one of its extensions after her starting signal to *start* or to comply with rule 30.1 shall *keep clear* of a boat not doing so until she is completely on the pre-start side.

---

[1] It is perhaps a pity that that statement should be so far in the rule book from the rule affected
[2] ISAF Q&A 07-003

When a boat is OCS at her starting signal, she initially retains all her rights. However, when she turns back (whether after three seconds or three minutes) towards the starting line or towards one of its extensions she must keep clear of all boats not so doing from the moment that her course is 'towards the prestart side of the starting line or one it its extensions.' Any starting line in open water will have an extension whether or not rule 30.1 is in force, and it will be towards an extension that that a boat will be sailing before she can be said to be sailing towards the starting line. I think that this rule applies at an open-water starting line very soon after her course is below a parallel of the starting line. Where the starting line is from bank to bank of a river, I think she has to turn further before the rule applies. The preamble to section D says that Section A rules no longer apply. Therefore, Section B rules still apply, but other boats that have instantly gained right of way over her need not be concerned by rule 15, since they did so because of the OCS boat's action of starting to sail towards the pre-start line or one of its extensions. When two or more boats meet while both are returning, they retain their Section A rights and obligations as between themselves, and any non-OCS boat they meet is a potential rule 19 obstruction[1]. So when rule 21 applies, a starboard-tack boat that is returning has to keep clear of a port-tack boat that is not.

Once the starting line or one of its extensions has been completely crossed, the returning boat may have regained right of way over boats that have not yet started. If so, rule 15 requires her to give them initial room to keep clear, as she has gained right of way through her own actions.

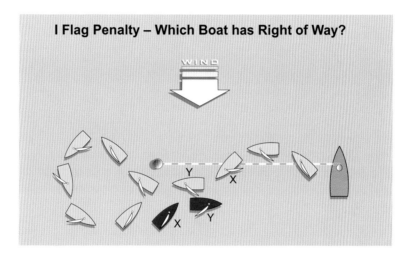

I Flag Penalty – Which Boat has Right of Way?

When an OCS boat in an I flag start is returning as above[2], it is unclear whether the boat temporarily regains the potential to be a right-of-way boat after her crossing back over the extension from the pre-course side (in which case she will presumably lose it again when she then turns back for the extension), or whether she remains a keep-clear boat at all times (and in particular at positions X and Y before finally clearing back across the extension. The rule was never written with this option in mind.

 **21.2**   A boat taking a penalty shall *keep clear* of one that is not.

The process of getting well clear of all other boats under rule 44.2 is not part of the penalty, and so a boat getting clear retains her rights until she goes into her turn or turns.

Two boats taking a turn(s) penalty near each other are bound by the full panoply of Section A and B rules as between themselves.

---

[1] And if they are tacking back after being OCS at a running start, rule 20 might also apply between them
[2] Held by ISAF Q&A 07-004 to be a valid compliance with rule 30.1

21.3 A boat moving astern by backing a sail shall *keep clear* of one that is not.

Match racing call UMP 2 points out that a boat remains a keep-clear boat when she is still moving astern through the water after stopping backing the sail, when it was the backing of the sail that caused the moving astern; and, when there is current, it is the motion relative to the current and not over the ground that is relevant.

If one boat were head to wind, and moving astern by backing a sail, to windward of and towards another boat doing the same, the windward of the two boats whose sails are pinned on the same side would still be clear ahead, as defined, and therefore right of way boat under rule 12[1]. However, all the boat astern needs do to counter this is to stop moving astern, at which point she resumes right of way under rule 21.3.

When one boat with her mainsail pinned to one side is sailing backwards towards another boat with her mainsail pinned on the other side, rule 10 must apply between them – but which is the starboard-tack boat? When a boat on starboard tack goes head to wind, she is still on starboard tack. However, the definition Leeward and Windwind goes on to say that her leeward side (which indirectly determines the tack she is on) is the side of which her mainsail lies when she is sailing directly downwind. If a boat making a sternboard is 'sailing directly downwind', then if the same boat now pins the sail out on her starboard side, that now seems to make it her leeward side, putting her on port tack[2].

Rule 22 **CAPSIZED, ANCHORED OR AGROUND; RESCUING**
If possible, a boat shall avoid a boat that is capsized or has not regained control after capsizing, is anchored or aground, or is trying to help a person or vessel in danger. A boat is capsized when her masthead is in the water.

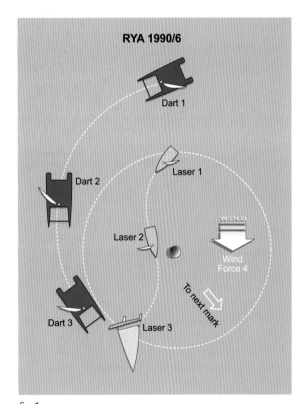

RYA 1990/6

fig 1

The requirement is to avoid, not to keep clear, and, a miss is as good as a mile when avoidance is concerned, which is certainly not the case with keeping clear. The preamble to Section D says that the rules of Section A do not apply, but that means that the rules of Section B and C may still do. Unlike most other rules, rule 22 begins 'If possible...', and sometimes avoidance will not be possible. These points are illustrated in RYA 1990/6 (fig 1).

The two boats approached a port-hand gybe mark on a starboard-tack reach in a stiff breeze. When she entered the zone, the Laser was clear ahead of the Dart, which was steering a course further from the mark than the Laser's, and which then became overlapped outside the Laser. The Laser gybed on to port tack within one boat-length of the mark to assume her new course.

Immediately the Laser had gybed, the Dart began her gybe more than three hull lengths from the mark and at around two hull lengths from the Laser[3]. On taking her new course, the Laser, ahead and to windward of the Dart, lost control. She gybed involuntarily, skewed to starboard and then capsized on to her port side so that she lay at right angles to the new course and across the bows of the Dart.

---

[1] UMP 38, which also points out somewhat obscurely that rule 21.3 situations are not confined to windward-leeward relationships
[2] See the definition Tack, Starboard or Port
[3] Hull lengths of the Laser, which is also the boat whose length is significant as concerns the zone size

A collision took place about 2-3 seconds after the capsize in which the Laser suffered damage. The protest committee disqualified the Dart under rule 18.2(b) for not giving the Laser sufficient room to pass and gybe, considering the wind conditions and speed differences. The Dart's appeal was upheld, she was reinstated and the Laser was disqualified.

The second sentence of rule 18.2(b) required the Dart to give mark-room to the Laser, which was clear ahead at the zone, and she did so. That obligation ended when, shortly after position 2, the Laser no longer needed room to sail a proper course while at the mark. When the Laser then involuntarily altered course and gybed, she became the right-of-way boat under rule 10. She did not give the Dart room to keep clear, and broke rule 16.1 before her capsize and before the collision, for which she was penalised.

Once the Laser had capsized, rule 22 began to apply, requiring the Dart to avoid the capsized Laser, if possible. Given the brief interval between the capsize and the collision, avoidance was not possible. Because rule 22 applied, the rules of Section A such as rule 10 did not – as stated in the the preamble to Section D.

The Dart did not therefore break rule 22. She did break rule 10, but was exonerated under rule 64.1(c) because she was compelled to break that rule when the Laser broke rule 16.1.

Rule 22 grants a quasi-right of way (or perhaps non-way!) to boats once they have capsized, and to boats that are anchored, aground or trying to give help. The preamble to Section D disapplies Section A rules when rule 22 applies.

Rule 22 does not offer any exoneration for a boat that broke a rule while getting into trouble just because the other boat is now required to avoid her, if possible – and rule 22 applies only to the situations referred to in the rule. When a right-of-way boat breaks rules 15 or 16.1 while out of control, no exoneration applies[1], and that would not be affected by a subsequent capsize. The same is true when a keep-clear boat breaks a rule of part 2 because she is out of control[2]. Nor does a keep-clear boat get any protection because damage limits her ability to manoeuvre. When in CYA 61 a port-tack boat's broken diamond stay prevented her from gybing to keep clear, the protection of rule 22 was held not to be relevant when she failed to keep clear. 'P's wisdom in preserving her mast in this case left her subject to protest for breaking rule 10.' Apart from the protection given by rule 14, possibly by rule 16.1[3], and in some cases by rule 22, the racing rules, like nature, are not kind to wounded animals.

The rule states that a boat is capsized when her masthead is in the water, but the obligation to avoid her continues not just until it is out of the water but until control has been regained. I think this means that all the crew are back on board, and the boat is able to manoeuvre sufficiently to comply with Section A rules.

Rule 23 **INTERFERING WITH ANOTHER BOAT**

23.1 If reasonably possible, a boat not *racing* shall not interfere with a boat that is *racing*.

23.2 Except when sailing her *proper course*, a boat shall not interfere with a boat taking a penalty or sailing on another leg.

---

[1] RYA 1990/6, RYA 1994/4
[2] ISAF 99
[3] The room to keep clear to which a keep-clear boat is entitled is the space that she needs in the 'existing conditions', and a restricted ability to manoeuvre could be an 'existing condition'

A boat is defined to be racing from her preparatory signal until she finishes and clears the finishing line and marks or retires, or until the race committee signals a general recall, postponement and abandonment. In the exhilaration of finishing on crossing the finishing line, boats can sometimes forget that they are still racing until they have cleared the finishing line and its marks, and are still liable to disqualification for breaking a rule of Part 2. Even after they are no longer racing, the rules of Part 2 will govern their navigation until they have left the racing area, even though no penalty for breaking all-but-one rule of Part 2 is possible. The exception is rule 23, which applies when a boat that is not racing but has not yet left the racing area interferes with a boat that is racing, which includes a boat that has finished, but not yet cleared the finishing line and marks.

In US 16, *Iris* luffed and tacked onto port in the act of crossing the biased finishing line, and shortly afterwards was struck by *Daffodil* on starboard tack, resulting in damage.

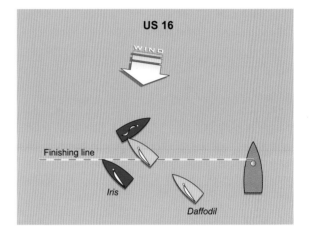

Daffodil's protest under rule 13 was dismissed because *Iris* had cleared the finishing line and marks, and the protest committee decided that, as she was no longer racing, *Iris* was not subject to disqualification. *Daffodil* appealed, with mixed results. *Iris* broke rule 13 (or possibly 10), but, as she was no longer racing, she could not penalised for that. However, she interfered with *Daffodil* which was still racing, and so was to be disqualified under rule 23.1. *Daffodil* herself, since she was still racing, could be penalised for breaking a rule of Part 2, even if the other boat in the incident were not racing. In this case, *Daffodil* could have avoided the contact that resulted in damage, and so was also to be disqualified, under rule 14[1].

At a finishing line, rule 23.1 normally operates in a very brief window during which one boat has cleared the finishing line and marks, while the other has not. During that time, and indeed at any time when rule 23.1 applies, the rules of Part 2 will determine who should keep clear of whom, and rule 23.1's main effects will be:
- to allow the penalisation of a boat that did not keep clear as required by a rule of Part 2, but cannot be penalised for that;
- to allow the penalisation of a right-of-way boat for interfering, when no longer racing, even if the other boat that was still racing did not keep clear;
- to allow the penalisation of a right-of-way boat that is still racing for not keeping clear when she is able to do so, even if the other boat was no longer racing and had broken rule 23.1, as in RYA 1996/1.

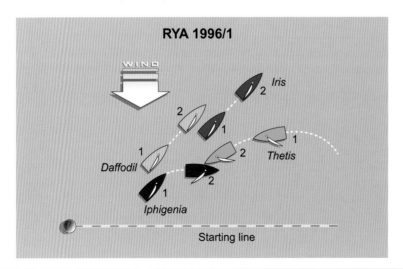

---

[1] CYA 9 is to the same effect.

Thetis's race had been recalled 20 seconds before the incident. *Daffodil*, *Iris* and *Iphigenia* were sailing through the starting area to begin the next lap of their race that had started some time previously. *Thetis* bore sharply away to avoid a collision with *Iris*, avoided *Daffodil*, the next boat behind her but collided with *Iphigenia*, causing damage. *Iphigenia* tried to avoid the collision but in vain. *Iris* sailed a steady course throughout, hailing *Thetis* that there was a general recall and that she (*Iris*) had right of way. The protest committee disqualified *Iris* and *Iphigenia* for breaking rule 10. *Iris*'s appeal was dismissed, and the disqualification of *Iphigenia* was annulled (even though she had not appealed), leading to the possibility of redress.

> The rules of Part 2 applied to all boats, since they were either racing, or had been racing. The preamble to Section D of Part 2 states that when rule 21 or 22 applies between two boats, Section A rules do not. It follows that when rule 23, also a Section D rule, applies, the right-of-way rules in Section A still apply. In addition rule 23.1 does not require a boat that is not racing to 'keep clear'.

> It follows that *Iris*'s obligation under rule 10 was in force and she was required to keep clear. This she failed to do, and was correctly disqualified. Had she tacked or borne away, keeping clear of *Iris*, she could then have protested *Iris* under rule 23.1.

> *Thetis*, trying to fulfil her obligation under rule 23.1, bore away to go astern of Iris, a manoeuvre that finally resulted in a collision causing damage between *Thetis* and *Iphigenia*. This was due to *Iris*'s failure to fulfil her obligation under rule 10, and, whether *Thetis* infringed a part of rule 16, or *Iphigenia* broke rule 10, or both, both boats are exonerated under rule 64.1(c).

Classifiation for the purposes of rule 23.1 as 'not racing' may be a fact, or it may be deemed by the protest committee to have occurred, as in RYA 1986/6, where *Daffodil*, in order to sail *Iris* down the fleet, missed out a mark to get at her. 'When she abandons the attempt to sail the course, she may be considered to have retired, and if she then manoeuvres in the racing area against another boat, she breaks rule 23.1 for interfering with another boat that is racing.'

Because *Daffodil* had missed out a mark, she was still on her previous leg and so not on the same leg of the course as *Iris*. Since *Daffodil* was clearly not sailing a proper course, that also broke rule 23.2, whereas the same manoeuvre, done on the same leg without deliberately breaking a rule, might have been perfectly legal, even when the aggressor was not sailing a proper course[1].

When a boat has left a mark on the wrong side, and is retracing her course round it to correct it, she will still be on the previous leg of the course until, after unwinding, she now properly passes the mark on its required side[2]. While re-rounding, she retains all her rights and obligations under the Part 2 rules. If she complies with those obligations but, while unwinding, nevertheless interferes with a boat that is rounding normally and is a give-way boat or a boat required to give her mark-room, she has done so from a position on another leg, but she does not break rule 23.2, since her proper course at the time is to unwind.

Part 3 - Conduct of a Race

 NOTICE OF RACE, SAILING INSTRUCTIONS AND SIGNALS
The notice of race and sailing instructions shall be made available to each boat before a race begins. The meanings of the visual and sound signals stated in Race Signals shall not be changed except under rule 86.1(b). The meanings of any other signals that may be used shall be stated in the sailing instructions.

This procedural rule has not given rise to any significant issues. The meaning of a postponement signal made ashore is frequently changed, to state a time greater than a minute before a warning signal will be made afloat. The Race Signals do not list race committee signals that are to be found in an Appendix, such as for Windsurfing (Appendix B), Match Racing (Appendix C), Team Racing and for indicating the status of parts of rule 42, Propulsion, under Appendix P. In practice, the requirement of the last sentence of rule 25 is not applied to such signals.

---

[1] See under rule 2
[2] RYA 2001/1

Rule 26

STARTING RACES

Races shall be started by using the following signals. Times shall be taken from the visual signals; the absence of a sound signal shall be disregarded.

Signal	Flag	Sound	Minutes before starting signal
Warning	Class flag	1 sound	5*
Preparatory	P, I, Z, Z with I, or black flag	1 sound	4
One-minute	Preparatory flag removed	1 long sound	1
Starting	Class flag removed	1 sound	0

*or as stated in the sailing instructions

The warning signal for each succeeding class shall be made with or after the starting signal of the preceding class.

The reference in rule 26 to the primacy of the flag for timing purposes and to the non-significance of the absence of a sound is an exception to the general rule, which is that a race signal comprises both the flag and the sound signal – so normally the lack of a sound signal, especially an individual recall under rule 29.1, may give rise to redress[1]. Presumably, the exception in rule 26 is so as to avoid the need to postpone the start sequence after the misfire of a cannon, shotgun or starting pistol. Problems with other signals made at other times have less impact on race management. Is this exception still reasonable when most races are started with horns for the sound signals, and where pistol-launched maroons (popular in continental Europe, and expected to be allowed in the UK under firearms legislation) rarely misfire?

The mistiming (as opposed to the absence) of a sound signal might theoretically give rise to redress, but this is unlikely, as it will be only one of several sound signals in the sequence, and for redress to be due it must affect a boat's score, whether delaying her starting, or resulting in her being OCS, and in circumstances where she could not be expected to see the flags.

Because rule 26 sets out the standard starting system, there is no need to specify its use in the sailing instructions, unless it is changed in some way[2]. A change to the timing of the warning signal relative to the starting signal does not require the sailing instruction to refer to this as a change to rule 26, because the rule contemplates this possibility; but a change to the timing of the preparatory signal to anything other than four minutes before the starting signal needs a statement to the effect that rule 26 is changed, because of rule 86.1(b)[3].

Starting sequences will often not begin at the precise time stated in the sailing instructions, and may be delayed in multi-start events by general recalls. No redress is available to a boat that 'starts' at the advertised time and is scored DNS, not realising that the flag sequence and starting signal were for a previous class with a delayed start[4].

---

[1] ISAF 31
[2] But despite L11.1, I have yet to see a set of sailing instructions where it is not referred to!
[3] L 11.1
[4] CYA 79

 **OTHER RACE COMMITTEE ACTIONS BEFORE THE STARTING SIGNAL**

27.1 No later than the warning signal, the race committee shall signal or otherwise designate the course to be sailed if the sailing instructions have not stated the course, and it may replace one course signal with another and signal that wearing personal flotation devices is required (display flag Y with one sound).

27.2 No later than the preparatory signal, the race committee may move a starting *mark*.

27.3 Before the starting signal, the race committee may for any reason *postpone* (display flag AP, AP over H, or AP over A, with two sounds) or *abandon* the race (display flag N over H, or N over A, with three sounds).

The course to be sailed must be displayed no later than the warning signal, and any later change of what is displayed can give rise to redress if a boat relies on the course she sees displayed at the warning signal[1]. The sailing instructions may allow for course notification or change to be made after the warning signal, but rule 86.1(b) requires the sailing instruction to state that rule 27 is changed[2]. Coastal races often sensibly provide for the course to be changed by radio in mid-race, to get the fleet back to their starting point rather than having to be shortened at a far-away mark.

A signal or action that does not comply with rules 27.1 or 27.2 and which is not then countermanded by postponement will remain valid unless contested in a request for redress. Many competitors would prefer a race officer to reposition a drifting starting line mark after the preparatory signal rather than postpone, and redress would be due to a boat only if she could show that this 'improper' action affected her score, for instance by being early or late at the starting line as a result of a transit taken when the mark was out of position.

Rule 27.3 allows for abandonment as well as postponement before the starting signal, which includes before the warning signal. However, flag N is available before the starting signal only with flags H or A, while the race signal N says that N on its own applies only to races that have started. To send ashore a race that has not yet started, either AP or N, over either H or A, will have the same effect[3], but N over H or A will apply to all races, including those which have started, which simplifies matters when wishing to get everyone ashore after an urgent local weather warning. Perhaps N also conveys a greater degree of seriousness than AP.

 **SAILING THE COURSE**

28.1 A boat shall *start*, leave each *mark* on the required side in the correct order, and *finish*, so that a string representing her track after *starting* and until *finishing* would when drawn taut
(a) pass each *mark* on the required side,
(b) touch each rounding *mark*, and
(c) pass between the *marks* of a gate from the direction of the previous *mark*.
She may correct any errors to comply with this rule. After *finishing* she need not cross the finishing line completely.

 **28.2** A boat may leave on either side a *mark* that does not begin, bound or end the leg she is on. However, she shall leave a starting *mark* on the required side when she is approaching the starting line from its pre-start side to *start*.

---

[1] RYA 1983/7
[2] RYA 1997/2
[3] H keeps open the possibility of further racing that day, A does not.

A boat shall *start*…

Start A boat *starts* when, having been entirely on the pre-start side of the starting line at or after her starting signal, and having complied with rule 30.1 if it applies, any part of her hull, crew or equipment crosses the starting line in the direction of the first *mark*.

When a starting mark is wrongfully shifted by another boat under the nose of a boat approaching it to start, that boat is not exempt from leaving it on the required side, and may have to return in order to start, as defined[1]. It is implicit that a boat must start before she can begin ticking off the course marks, and, if the starting line remains open long enough, a boat that was OCS[2] or left a starting mark on the wrong side may, unknown to herself, have started when her course at the end of the first lap takes her across the starting line in the same direction[3]. Likewise, the fact that a boat is unavoidably OCS because another boat broke a rule and forced her over does not remove the requirement to return and start[4]. However, sailing instructions may absolve an OCS boat from the obligation to start, as for instance on the Round the Island Race around the Isle of Wight, where to return, possible up-wind and up-tide, to an already crowded starting line would be dangerous: therefore a different penalty is imposed where no advantage has been gained[5].

… shall leave each *mark* on the required side in the correct order…

The required side is determined by the string test, as we shall see. It may be possible validly to leave a mark without rounding it, contrary to the intentions of the race committee, but this advantage may be limited by the requirement to leave each mark in the correct order. So if in the following diagram the sailing instructions said that the course included 2(S) 3(S) 4(S) without specifying that 3 was to be rounded, I think that *Iris* would not comply with rule 28.1 were she to leave mark 3 as a 'passing mark' rather than round it by looping it, since she would not have 'left' the marks in the correct order: mark 4 would be left abeam before mark 3 was left abeam[6].

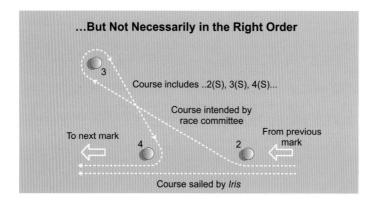

…But Not Necessarily in the Right Order

3

Course includes ..2(S), 3(S), 4(S)...

Course intended by race committee

To next mark

From previous mark

4

2

Course sailed by *Iris*

Sailing instructions can be ambiguous. Sometimes they can be so bizarrely drafted that it is impossible to sail the course as specified. In RYA 1993/1 no boat was able to sail the course in the sailing instructions, but all 'made a reasonable attempt to extract a sailable course from the instructions given', and none sailed further than any other. Redress for all boats affected, in the shape of their scores, was deemed appropriate. In RYA 2006/5, the course was stated twice in the sailing instructions, with one buoy marking the channel edge featuring in one list but not the other, resulting in a protest against boats that had not left it on the required side.

---

[1] ISAF 28: likewise being wrongly forced the wrong side of a mid-course mark does not entitle the victim not to return to leave the mark on its required side, no matter how many places may be lost (RYA 1982/10); but at least, unlike when taking a turn for touching a mark, a boat returning to a mark to round it correctly retains all her Part 2 rights (RYA 1988/9).
[2] A11: Did not start: on the course side of the starting line at her starting signal and failed to start, or broke rule 30.1.
[3] RYA 1982/13: she would still need to sail the required number of laps, and the one just sailed would not count. If she had broken rule 30.1, I Flag Rule, her first 'lap' might also rank as compliance with its requirement!
[4] RYA 2003/6, US 101
[5] 'RRS Appendix A4.2 is changed in that a boat that is OCS will be scored with a time penalty of 5% of the boat's elapsed time rounded to the nearest second, unless the Race Committee decides that the boat has gained a significant advantage in the Race, in which case she will be scored as OCS.'
[6] In RYA 1985/4, as will be seen shortly, the order is only just correct, with D being left abeam of the string only just after C is left abeam.

There is a clear thread in appeal decisions that a boat is given the benefit of the doubt as to which is the correct course when the description of the course is ambiguous and there is no proven advantage either way. (See for example RYA 1993/1: in that case there was no clearly correct course for any boat, while in this appeal there are two equally valid possibilities, but the principle is the same.) Although it is not necessary to decide this case by reference to entitlement to redress, the publication of ambiguous sailing instructions is an improper action, and it was further held in RYA 1989/10 that, 'in cases involving errors by the race committee, it is a good principle that any doubts be resolved in favour of the competitor'. In this case, that doubt should be resolved in favour of the protestees who were at risk of penalisation.

The same principle applied in RYA 2008/2, where the course for (apparently) all starts was shown without any class references at the stern of the committee boat, whereas a course intended for a catamaran class start was displayed with the class symbol on the side of the committee boat. *Danger Mouse* saw the first course and sailed it, did not see the other course intended for her, and was successfully protested by one of the rest of the catamarans that had sailed the course intended for them. Upholding her appeal against disqualification, the RYA said that she had no reason not to believe that the course she saw was not intended for her, and that the display of two equally valid courses was an improper action of the race committee giving rise to entitlement to redress[1].

The sailing instructions must identify the course marks clearly. It breaks no racing rule to leave a permanent navigation buoy on the 'wrong' side if there is no reference it in the sailing instructions[2]. Nor does the fact that after sailing a lap a boat will normally cross the starting line when beginning the next lap mean that boats must pass through that line[3].

… and *finish*…

> **Finish** A boat *finishes* when any part of her hull, or crew or equipment in normal position, crosses the finishing line in the direction of the course from the last *mark*, either for the first time or after taking a penalty under rule 44.2 or, after correcting an error made at the finishing line, under rule 28.1.

It follows that it is not necessary to pass through the finishing line to have validly finished, as rule 28.1 confirms: a dinghy that has overstood a windward finishing line may come reaching into it with the crew trapezing, and she will have finished if the crew in this normal position is the first element to cross the finishing line – if so, she can then bear away and will have finished without any part of her hull having cut the line[4]. There are risks in not passing completely through the finishing line. I write this having just returned from jury duty at a national championship where we refused redress to a boat scored DNF that claimed to have overstood on the last windward leg and reached in to the finishing line, clipping the line on port tack, then bearing away to avoid a starboard-tacker. In this case, we were satisfied that she was seen not to finish (as opposed to not being seen to finish[5]), and the reason was that in the few seconds before she cut what she believed to have been the finishing line, another boat had got hitched to the finishing mark and had towed it (and therefore the finishing line) upwind. There was no improper action or omission by the race committee, it being impossible to reclaim it in the brief time available, and so we could not find any justification for giving redress.

---

[1] When, on appeal, redress is found to be due, the RYA normally returns the case to the protest committee to decide appropriate redress based on the full facts in its possession: average points would be suitable in this case. In CYA 53, where either of two marks might have been the correct one because of improper inaction of the race committee, the Canadian appeals committee preferred to decide redress for itself, which was to 'cancel' the race, which seems a little harsh if there were options to readjust the races scores, depending on the courses sailed.
[2] US 83
[3] RYA 1974/1: if the sailing instructions did require this, the starting line would become a 'gate'.
[4] The punctuation of the definition shows that requirement to be in a normal position applies only to the crew and equipment, as confirmed in ISAF Q&A 2008-002, which however continues: '…does a capsized boat correctly finish if she crosses the finishing line when:
a) all of the crew members are (somehow) on board even though the boat is capsized,
b) some of the crew members are not on board but are very close to the boat and trying to straighten it out , and
c) some of the crew members are not on board because they have become disconnected from the boat and its equipment, but are swimming to reach the capsized boat?
Answer
Yes. It is normal for dinghies to capsize and therefore a capsized dinghy and its crew in the water are in a normal position. It follows that a boat finishes correctly in all of the conditions stated in the question. Also, the boat does not break rule 47.2 while the crew are making all reasonable attempts to recover the boat and get back on board provided they are not making any attempt to progress the position of the boat in the race. If they attempt to 'swim' the boat across the finishing line, they would break both rule 47.2 and rule 42.1, and possibly rule 2.'
[5] CYA 97 makes clear the significant difference between those concepts, as concerns a recalled boat returning to start.

Note that in that example the boat will have 'crossed the finishing line in the direction of the course from the last mark', even though her recent course may have little connection with the location of the last mark. The criterion of the right direction is in effect the string test – the tautened string of her course from the last mark to the finishing line. If in crossing the finishing line the string first hooks round one finishing mark rather than passing between the finishing marks, the line will have been crossed in the wrong direction, but that allows approaches from a wide range of directions to be valid. 'The 'direction of the course' does not refer to a rhumb line from any mark, and its only purpose is to allow a DNF score to be given to a boat that hooks round a finishing line mark and then crosses the finishing line from the wrong direction without then unwinding and finishing as required[1].'

Issues concerning badly-laid finishing lines are to be resolved in favour of the competitor. 'When a finishing line is laid so nearly in line with the last leg that it cannot be determined which is the correct way to cross it in order to finish according to the definition, a boat may cross the line in either direction and her finish is to be recorded accordingly[2].'

Even a clearly non-compliant finish may count when it is induced by an improper sailing instruction, as in ISAF 45, where the race committee, with the best of intentions, specified a hook finish (contrary to the non-changeable definition Finish) that was complied with by *Daffodil* (and others) resulting finishing positions; but not by *Iris* (with others). *Iris* was scored DNF, and asked for redress, which was granted in the form of a score for all the boats in the order the finishing line had been crossed, regardless of in which direction. *Iris* felt that this did not go far enough, since *Daffodil* had retained a finishing position despite having finished contrary to the definition. Her appeal was dismissed, since *Daffodil* was the victim of an improper sailing instruction that was in conflict with the definition Finish[3], and, since no boat gained or lost compared with all having crossed the line in the same direction, it was as fair an arrangement as possible, as required by rule 64.2.

In order for such redress to be given, there must be a non-resolvable contradiction between a sailing instruction and the definition, and a misinterpretation of the definition by the race committee is not sufficient. Thus, in RYA 1980/2 (fig 1), mark D was to be rounded to port after rounding mark A, after which it was a mark of the finishing line when it would be left to port when approached in the direction of the course from mark C, the last mark.

The race was shortened to a line to mark D, which happened to be the full-course finishing line[4], when boats were approaching D from A. *Wings* and others crossed the finishing line directly from A, and were scored DNF, *Wispozora* and others hooked round D and received finishing positions. The decision to dismiss protests and requests for redress by *Wings* and others was overturned on appeal. 'When D became [a] mark of the finishing line, it ceased to be a rounding mark and became [a] mark to be passed in accordance with the definition Finish. Consequently, only the boats that finished by crossing the line in the direction of the course from A, leaving mark D to starboard, finished correctly...When the course is shortened and a course mark becomes a finishing line mark, its required side may change...The protestors are reinstated and the protestees are disqualified.'

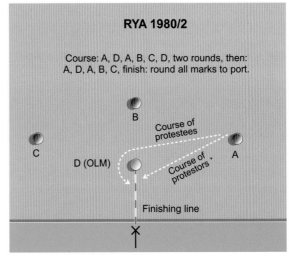

RYA 1980/2

Course: A, D, A, B, C, D, two rounds, then:
A, D, A, B, C, finish: round all marks to port.

B

Course of protestees

C

D (OLM)

Course of protestors

A

Finishing line

fig 1

---

[1] RYA 1985/4
[2] ISAF 82
[3] Both rank as rules, as defined, but a sailing instruction cannot change a definition, see rules 86.1(a) and (b).
[4] It was not the fact that this was the designated finishing line that permitted the course to be shortened to it, as this is not one of the lines permitted for shortening in rule 32.2, nor were boats required to cross that line at the end of each round even if doing so was unavoidable (rule 32.2(b)); but because D was the next rounding mark (rule 32.2(a)).

106 | RYA Racing Rules Explained

In contrast with ISAF 45, nothing that *Wispozora* and the other 'hookers' did was induced by any improper sailing instruction. It was simply that *Wispozora*, the race committee and the protest committee had all not understood the rule. If the race committee had made a sound signal to those it believed to have finished correctly as they crossed the finishing line, this would not prevail over a later decision of a protest committee or of the national authority that found they had not finished[1].

The fact that a boat breaks a rule while finishing does not change the fact that she has finished.

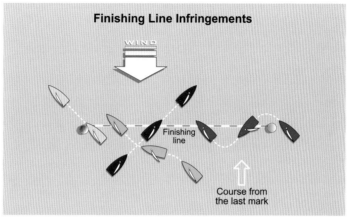

fig 2

Yellow has finished. She touched the finishing mark, and is clearly not taking a penalty, but it will require a protest against her to dislodge her from her finishing position[2].

Blue's string lies on the wrong side of the finishing mark, but she has crossed the finishing line in the direction of the course from the last mark. So she has to be scored as finished, and a protest against her under rule 28.1 is required in order to deprive her of her finishing position[3].

Red clearly broke rule 10 with respect to Green but finishes and is clearly not taking a penalty. So a protest against her is required to deny her her finishing position.

As will be seen later, the fact that all this happens under the eyes of the race committee does not entitle the race committee to do anything other than initially to score a boat in her finishing position.

The String Test

What is this string? Because it is boats that have sides, not marks, it may be easier to think of it as a flat tape with a port side and a starboard side. When the course is affected by the geography, so is the string, suggests RYA 2000/5.

> Question
> Must the string referred to in rule 28.1, when pulled taut, lie in navigable water only?
> Answer
> There is no direct guidance in the rule itself or in ISAF cases. However, it would be curious for a boat's track to be regarded as passing over dry land, and the pragmatic interpretation of rule 28.1 is that the string, when pulled taut, lies in navigable waters only, is caught on headlands, passes to one side of non-navigable shallows or prohibited areas, and follows the course of a river.

---

[1] RYA 1996/4 – likewise if a boat was OCS and did not return, or never entered. A finishing bell or hoot is just a courtesy.
[2] ISAF Q&A 06-003
[3] ibid

To decide differently might sometimes mean that a mark identified by the sailing instructions as a rounding mark would otherwise have to be looped, requiring a boat to cross her own track.

An analogy can be drawn with the separate and different requirement in the definition *Finish* to cross the finishing line in the direction of the course from the last mark. This has the effect of prohibiting 'hook finishes' in open waters, but where the race is on a river it is quite possible that the course of a river can result in the line being approached in the opposite direction from the rhumb line from the last mark. Here too, it is implicit that the direction of the course is constrained by physical geography.

Similar situations can occur with a sea course that finishes within a harbour.

The String Test at Starting Marks

When a boat starts, the port side of her string must be towards the port-end starting mark, and the starboard side of her string must be towards the starboard-end starting mark. In ISAF 90 (fig 1), winds were light at the start and boats drifted back. Pull boat Blue's string taut at the moment she starts, and it will be hooked up with its starboard side away from the starboard-end committee boat, and so rule 28.1 has not been complied with[1]. But pull Yellow's string and, at the moment she starts, her string will be correct with respect to the starting marks. That complies with rule 28.1(a), and because it is on the right side relative to the committee boat, it does not matter that the committee boat is also later on the wrong side of the string, because nothing in the rule prohibits this.

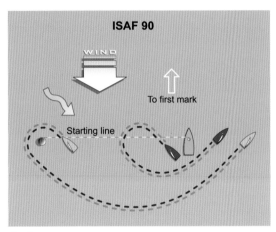

fig 1

The String Test at Course Marks

The string must touch each rounding mark. What is a rounding mark? Firstly, in a truly circular argument, it is a mark that a string will touch. Consider the usual dinghy course, whether windward-leeward, trapezoidal or 'sausage[2] and triangle'. Normally, there is no need to specify that the marks are rounding marks, because they are made to be such by the string test (apart from the unused mark of a gate), and there is no possibility of cutting a corner without breaking rule 28.1[3].

Secondly, it is a mark that the sailing instructions identify as a rounding mark. Sometimes, this label is unnecessary, as with the dinghy courses referred to above. Sometimes, there are unintended consequences, as in RYA 2000/5 (fig 2).

The course set in Poole Harbour included Rebbecks (S)[4], Oscar (P), Bell (S). The race committee had intended that Oscar was to have been a passing or 'boundary' mark, to keep the race away from the starting line being used by other boats, but the sailing instructions also said that all marks were rounding marks, which had the effect opposite to that which was intended.

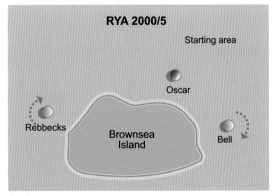

fig 2

---

[1] See also CYA 81

[2] In France, a 'sausage' (windward and leeward legs) is, curiously, called a 'banane', reinforcing the British prejudice that continental Europeans want standards under which bananas must be straight.

[3] Sometimes, such courses specify that, when a committee vessel is stationed at a mark to signal a changed next leg after a windshift, boats shall pass between the mark and the vessel. One reason for this is if there is a very large windshift requiring the next leg and the rest of the course to be reset by up to 180°. Under certain configurations this would allow boats further down the fleet to avoid having to go anywhere near the mark where the leg change is being signalled, and to cut the corner to the subsequent relocated mark. The sailing instruction makes a gate of the mark and vessel, and makes all boats take the same route. See L12.2.

[4] Current name 'Chris Somner'

Question 1

Were boats entitled to interpret the true intentions of the race committee and not loop Oscar?

Answer 1

No. The sailing instructions required marks to be rounded, and therefore the only correct course was to loop Oscar[1]. The fact that the intentions of the race committee were to the contrary does not change this.

Question 2

If a boat decided not to loop Oscar and was successfully protested, could she then seek redress?

Answer 2

For redress to he granted, there must be some improper act or omission by the Race Committee. Requiring Oscar to be looped was not automatically an improper action of the race committee. If some boats elected not to round Oscar, were successfully protested and then sought redress, then a protest committee might rightly regard the setting of such a course as an improper action if it brought the fleet into conflict with other boats in the vicinity of the starting line. If some boats looped Oscar and others chose not to do so for safety reasons, then it is possible that the only equitable redress might be to abandon the race.

The situation is further complicated when all marks are specified to be rounding marks, but it is not clear how this affects a particular mark. RYA 2000/5 continues as follows as concerns a mark specified to be a rounding mark laid close to the rhumb line from the previous mark to the following mark such that, if laid just on one side of that line, the string will glance it, but if laid just on the other side, it will need to be looped.

If, from observations afloat, competitors cannot be expected to be sure on which side of the rhumb line it lies, then a competitor who does not loop it and is protested should be exonerated if in fact it should have been looped.

However, if fixed marks are used and if boats can be expected to have a chart on board, then the charted position will determine whether the mark has to be looped.

The race committee may be damned if it specifies all marks to be rounding marks, but, for coastal racing round existing navigation marks, it may be damned if it doesn't, as RYA1985/4 (fig 3) shows.

The course set by the race committee was A – B – C – D - finish, all marks to port.

The race committee's intention was that D was to be looped. The sailing instructions did not identify D or any mark as a rounding mark. The race committee scored *Deva* DNF, as she had not finished in the direction of the course from D, which it intended to be the last

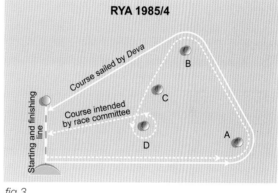

RYA 1985/4

fig 3

mark. The protest committee refused redress because *Deva* had not sailed the course, and referred its decision to the RYA, which reinstated *Deva*.

When a race committee intends that a mark is to be looped, so that a boat returning from that mark will cross her own track, the sailing instructions must either clearly say that the mark is a rounding mark, or must state how a mark shown on a course board is to be identified as a rounding mark.

When a mark is not properly identified as a rounding mark, a boat is entitled sail a course such that the string representing her track, when pulled tight, does not touch the mark, provided that she leaves it on the correct side and in the correct sequence. The identification of a mark as a rounding mark must be unambiguous. For instance, to state that a mark is to be left to port (or starboard) gives a boat the option not to round it[2].

---

[1] A mark is looped when the taut string representing a boat's track to the mark, round it and on to the next mark crosses itself. As CYA 74 points out, this is an unnecessary hazard best avoided if possible. See also RYA 2006/8

[2] As would a sailing instruction that said a mark was to 'left or rounded' on a specified side. Note also that *Deva* DID finish in the direction of the course from last mark, whichever mark it was, since, as discussed, it would cease to be so only if a finishing line mark were 'hooked round'. So the race committee had no business scoring her DNF - it should have protested her.

A decision of this sort can be very frustrating to the virtuous but less-sharp competitors who go all the way to a mark to loop it when in fact it may be treated as a 'passing mark' and never approached. They have not broken rule 28.1, since, if it is a port-hand mark, when they loop it their string will leave it to only port as required (and *vice versa*). Might they be entitled to redress? No, it is assumed, since there was no improper action or omission of the race committee, just low-grade course planning, unless boats were put in harm's way[1].

The string test at a gate mark

As with a rounding mark, a gate can be explicitly identified, as with two leeward marks described in the sailing instructions as '2a-2b (gate)'. It is for the boat to decide which of the two marks to round, and her string will pass between the marks and caught on the chosen mark. The requirement to round is implicit, not explicit. The commonest mistake, which can happen after an incident with other boats or a capsize, is not to comply with the explicit requirement to pass between the gate marks, either by rounding both of them, or passing through after rounding, not before. Blue's string is correct, but the string of both Yellows is incorrect (fig 1).

A gate can also be implicitly created when the sailing instructions require a boat to pass through what was the starting line at the end of each lap, usually for recording purposes. If this happens upwind, there is no requirement for the string to touch any starting mark, just to pass between them[2].

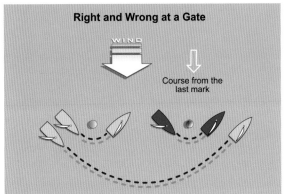

Right and Wrong at a Gate

Course from the last mark

fig 1

The string test at a finishing mark

ISAF 106 shows that what is true at a starting mark, as in ISAF 90, is equally true at a finishing mark.

The case as published relates only to Blue, saying 'When the course requires boats to pass between two marks at a finishing line or at a gate, a boat complies with rule 28.1 if the string representing her track when drawn taut passes between the marks from the direction of the previous mark. She complies with rule 28.1 even if the string also passes one mark of the finishing line or gate on the non-required side.'

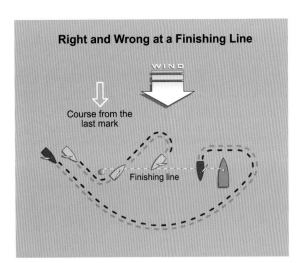

Right and Wrong at a Finishing Line

Course from the last mark

Finishing line

fig 2

Contrast this with Yellow's 'hook finish' (fig 2), which has been added to the case diagram. Even when Yellow turns back to cross the finishing line from the correct direction, and now finishes as defined, without further correction the taut string will never lie as required with the correct side nearer the required mark[3].

She may correct any errors to comply with this rule.

The easiest mistake to make is not fully to correct the error.

---

[1] There is no case that helps, but I believe that a race committee that saw this happen and realised the reason would be entitled to abandon a race under rule 32.1(e) as something affecting the fairness of the competition.

[2] Listing the starting line as part of the course is nothing new, but rule 28.1(c) makes it more clearly legitimate.

[3] ISAF Q&A 06-003, illustrated above

Blue and Yellow (fig 3) have both made the mistake at a gate mark of not passing through it from the direction of the previous mark. Blue corrects her error. Yellow does not – her taut string will not touch either gate mark, but will run directly from the previous mark to the next mark, passing nowhere near the gate.

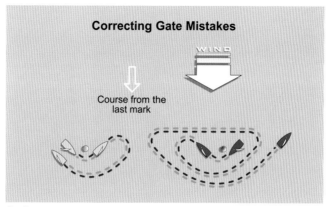

fig 3

Suppose Blue had detected her error only after having passed several further marks. Does she have to sail so as to thread her string back round those marks to get back to the mark where she made an error? No, according to RYA 2001/1.

> She may return directly to the mark concerned. Rule 28.2 says that a boat may leave on either side a mark that does not begin, bound or end the leg she is on. A leg does not end until the mark ending it has been left on the required side. So until a mark is left on the required side, a boat remains on the leg of the course ended by that mark. Any later marks do not begin, bound or end the leg she is on. They may be left on either side. When the string is drawn taut, it will not catch on those later marks, which become relevant only once an error has been corrected, and must now be rounded.

A boat may correct any errors to comply with rule 28.1. The string test is normally applied at the moment a boat finishes, which is when she (or part of her) first crosses the finishing line in the direction of the course from the last mark. The definition Finish leaves open the possibility of correcting an 'error made at the finishing line', namely an inadvertent hook finish.

As in ISAF Q&A 06-003, Yellow (fig 4) has 'hook-finished' at position 1, but a 'hook finish' is no finish. She realises this and wants to correct this mistake made at the finishing line. She must first unwind back round the finishing mark – but in so doing she crosses the finishing line at position 2 in the direction of the course from the last mark. If she does nothing, she has finished, and with 'wrong string'. Without the specific permission to correct her finishing line error, she will have finished with no possibility of getting her string right, and so the definition allows her to rotate again and count her crossing at position 3 to count as her actual finish, from which point her string will pull to a line directly to the last mark.

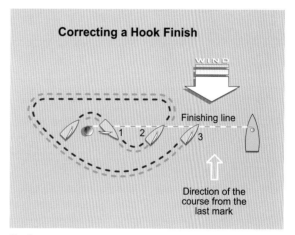

fig 4

The string test when the course is shortened

Depending on which side of the mark the committee vessel stations itself to form the finishing line, the required side for what was a rounding mark may change now that it is a finishing mark. Yellow finishes correctly, Blue does not[1]. For the avoidance of this sort ofconfusion it is preferable for the committee boat to be stationed so as not to change the side on which the mark is to be left.

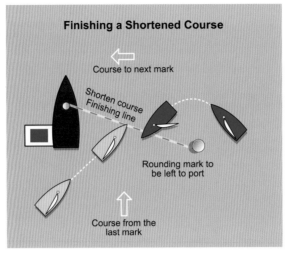

fig 1

When the race is shortened at a gate, a race leader like Blue might pick the wrong line over which to finish. Prompted perhaps by her not receiving a finishing sound signal that is then given to Yellow finishing as required by rule 32.2(c) between the gate marks, Blue may well hook her string round the mark, and then finish as defined, but in breach of rule 28.1. As previously discussed, if she does not avail herself of the possibility to correct an error made at the finishing line by unwinding back round the mark, she has finished, and is to be scored as such, but is then subject to protest by the race committee or another boat under rule 28.1. This is best avoided by stationing the finishing vessel so close to the nearer gate mark that no ambiguity is possible.

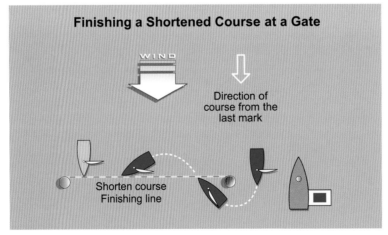

fig 2

---

[1] RYA 1980/2, as previously discussed

In RYA 2001/6 (fig 3), the assumed facts are that the course is 1 – 8 – 7, marks to be left to port, two laps, and boats must cross the starting and finishing line from the committee boat to buoy 5 at the end of each lap. During the first lap, the race committee signals a shortened course when the leading boats are approaching buoy 8.

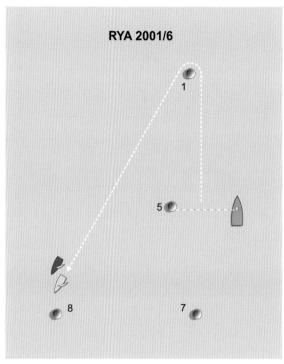

RYA 2001/6

fig 3

Question 1
Which is the finishing line? To buoy 8 (200 metres from the committee boat), in which case is it now to be left to starboard? To buoy 7 (75 metres from the committee boat), in which case is it now to be left to starboard? Or to buoy 5 (30 metres from the committee boat)?
Answer 1
Rule 32.2 refers to shortening 'at' a rounding mark or line. Any of the buoys could be a legitimate place at which to shorten a race, but the committee boat must be considered to be 'at' the closest candidate. The new inishing line was therefore the line from the starting and finishing line from the committee boat to buoy 5, under rule 32.2(b).

Question 2
If the finishing line is to buoy 5, are boats required to continue to sail the prescribed course, thus leaving buoys 8 and 7 to port, before finishing?
Answer 2
Yes, in the absence of a sailing instruction to the contrary[1].

After finishing she need not cross the finishing line completely.
This harmonises with the definition Finish where it says that a boat finishes when any part of her hull, or crew or equipment in normal position, crosses the finishing line in the required direction[2]. The act of finishing may tick all the rule 28.1 boxes, but does not end the boat's rights and responsibilities under Part 2 of the rules, as she is racing, as defined, until she clears the finishing line and marks, and the Part 2 rules will still govern her navigation after she has been racing but is still in the racing area[3].

Rule 28.1, the Race Committee and the Protest Committee
It is understandable that a race committee seeing a boat not sailing the course can be tempted to take summary action and decline to give the boat a finishing place, the commonest ways being to score her DNF or indeed to disqualify her without a hearing. This would be perfectly proper if a sailing instruction empowered the race committee to do this, indeed it is a sensible thing to provide for, as long as a boat has the opportunity to contest a non-finish score via redress.

---

[1] CYA59 suggests otherwise, but it is based on particular sailing instructions, in addition to which it is not clear that the finishing line to which the race was shortened complied with any clause of rule 32.2.
[2] ISAF Q&A 2008-002 would seem to imply that if it happened that a crew member in the water (a normal position, remember), detached from the boat but swimming towards it managed to cut the finishing line with any body part, that boat has finished even if no part of the hull and equipment has cut the line. The implausibility of this interpretation is mitigated only by the improbability of it occurring.
[3] See the preamble to Part 2, When Boats Meet

But when no such power is granted, then no summary steps are available to the race committee. It cannot score her DNF – Did Not Finish – when she did finish, by crossing the finishing line in the direction of the course from the last mark. DNF is reserved for boats that never came near the finishing line because they retired in mid-race – and for boats whose only crossing of the finishing line was a clear 'hook finish'. Nor can it disqualify her without a hearing. Only a protest can result in the removal of the finishing position of a boat that has finished, as defined[1].

But suppose that the race committee nevertheless scores her DNF or 'disqualifies her' and redress is requested. It is not the protest committee's job to make up for the failings of the race committee. So in RYA 2006/8, the race committee's sailing instructions unintentionally required two marks to be looped rather than left as passing marks, and two boats did not loop them. They were recorded as disqualified with a hearing without any provision in the sailing instructions for this, and they asked for redress. No hearing was called, the issue rumbled on, and the race committee then lodged a protest against them ten weeks later.

The protest committee got off to a good start by deciding that the race committee was not allowed to disqualify a boat without a hearing. It then got into a hole and kept digging. The redress it granted was a hearing, in effect of the clearly out-of-time protest. It decided that neither mark was unambiguously designated as a rounding mark, and reinstated the boats into their finishing positions. The race committee appealed, on the grounds that there was no ambiguity. The appeal was dismissed, but not over any question of ambiguity.

> The protest committee was correct to decide that the race committee was not entitled to disqualify the boats without a hearing, nor, had it done so, would it have been entitled to score them DNF, since they both finished, as defined. The protest committee was incorrect to decide that a hearing (in effect, a protest hearing, at which the disqualification of the boats was a possibility) was the appropriate redress. Disqualification can never result from a request for redress alone[2]. Had the protest by the race committee been valid, then that might have resulted in the disqualification of the boats independently of the requests for redress. In fact, the protest was clearly invalid, having been lodged more than two months after the incident, and there was no reason to extend the protest time limit.

> The fact that the race committee had not intended the course to include marks that had to be looped does not relieve a boat of her obligation to loop them[3]. The words used in the sailing instructions clearly made all marks rounding marks for the purposes of the string test in rule 28.1. However, the protest committee was not required to consider the details of the course sailed by the boats. Its correct reason for reinstating them into their finishing positions, in the absence of a valid protest against them, should have been that, unless otherwise specified in the sailing instructions, a race committee has no power to disqualify a boat without a hearing, or (if she finishes, as defined) score her DNF, if it believes she has not sailed the course.

The narrow focus of the role of the protest committee considering a request for redress was established in ISAF 80, when the race committee scored *Iris* DNF because it believed her to have broken rule 28.1 with respect to a course mark, and the protest committee dismissed the resulting request for redress because *Iris* did not sail the course, entirely through her own fault, and not because of an act or omission of the race committee. In upholding her appeal and reinstating her, US Sailing said that a fundamental principle of hearing procedure, whether for protests or requests for redress, is that that a hearing must be limited to the particular 'incident' referred to in a protest or request for redress as required by rule 62.1.

> The race committee acted improperly in scoring *Iris* DNF when she did finish according to the definition Finish. The race committee could have scored *Iris* as DNF only for failing to finish correctly (see rule A5). Since *Iris* crossed the finishing line from the direction of the last mark, she should have been recorded as having finished.

> A fundamental principle of protest committee procedure is that a hearing must be limited to the particular 'incident' alleged in a protest (see rule 61.2(b)) or to the particular incident alleged to be 'an improper action or omission' in a request for redress under rule 62.1(a). Although the incident that was the subject of *Iris*'s request for redress was that she had been incorrectly scored DNF, the protest committee turned to a different incident when it considered whether or not she had failed to sail the course correctly and therefore broken rule 28.1. Since that incident was not the incident alleged in the redress for request, the committee acted improperly.

---

[1] ISAF 80
[2] RYA 1990/7, 2001/12
[3] RYA 2000/5: a boat 'loops' a mark when her track on leaving the mark crosses her track when approaching it

If a race committee believes from its observations that a boat has not sailed the course correctly, it may protest the boat for that breach as permitted by rule 60.2(a). In this case, the race committee did not protest *Iris*. Because *Iris* had not been protested for failing to sail the course correctly, she could not be penalised for that failure.

One of the problems of these decisions is that competitors are even less aware of them than are protest committees, and the request for redress that is submitted following an improper DNF or DSQ will often address itself only to the broader issue of whether rule 28.1 had been broken with regard to a course mark, which then invites the protest committee to consider that as the 'incident'. I believe that, given the clear guidance of the cases, a protest committee should not stray down that path, but should stick to the narrow issues of whether the boat did finish, as defined, and whether the race committee had any power to disqualify her or score her DNF.

Rule 28.1 has thrown up a further problem when one boat wants to protest another for failing to sail the course, for instance by having left a course mark on the wrong side. This is discussed under rule 61.1(a).

It may be that no boat sails the correct course, and yet the race is valid. At a recent event, I was on a RIB on one course when the race officer from another course motored across to me. The sailing instructions specified an 'outer loop' trapezoid course, but all the fleet sailed an 'inner loop' course. Was his intention to take no action correct? I agreed with him. There had been a perfectly fair race. None of the reasons for abandonment in rule 32.1 applied. The last mark of the course was the same for both courses, and all boats had rounded it before finishing. So if the race committee had wanted to act, it would have had to have protested all the fleet. Rule 60.2 says that most race committee protests are optional, not compulsory. No boat would have been able to ask for redress, since there was no improper action of the race committee, and all the fleet was at fault in sailing the wrong course. The only risk was of a valid protest from (presumably) a boat with a poor finishing position hoping to do better if the outcome were after all the abandonment of the race and a resail, a bridge to be crossed if we came to it, which we did not[1].

Rule 28.2 Issues

The first sentence of rule 28.2 puts the string of rule 28.1 and mark-touching under rule 31 on the same footing: if a mark does not begin, bound or end a leg a boat is on, she may leave it on either side, and she may touch it with impunity. Rule 28.2 is something of a nuisance for race officers as concerns limit marks, as its purist approach conflicts with the practicalities of mark-laying.

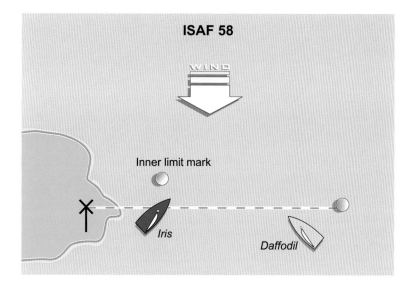

ISAF 58

WIND

Inner limit mark

Iris

Daffodil

---

[1] The situation appears to slip between the cracks of the first and second sentences of rule 35. However, the second sentence of rule 90.3(a) – a rule not directly aimed at this situation and not one I thought about at the time – might be problematical. Perhaps it can be said that a boat that has finished is deemed to have sailed the course until a protest committee decides otherwise.

The finishing line in ISAF 58 (page 115) was from the shore mark to an outer mark, with an inner limit mark that the sailing instructions said was to be left to port, and which was laid to windward of the finishing line. *Iris*'s finishing time was taken when she crossed the finishing line, and *Daffodil* sought redress, claiming that it should have been taken when *Iris* completed the course at the inner limit mark. Redress was refused, and *Daffodil*'s subsequent appeal was then dismissed. Rule 28.2 says that a boat may leave on either side a mark that does not begin, bound or end the leg she is on. 'If a buoy or other object specified in the sailing instructions as a finishing-line limit mark is on the post-finish side of the finishing line, it is not a mark…since the inner limit mark was beyond the finishing line, it did not 'bound' or 'end' the last leg of the course. Only when a limit mark is on, or on the course side of, the finishing line is it a mark, as that term is defined, and only then must a boat leave it on the specified side before, or when, finishing.'

So the race committee was correct to take the time on the crossing of the line, while *Iris* could leave the buoy on the 'wrong' side – it was as if it did not exist[1].

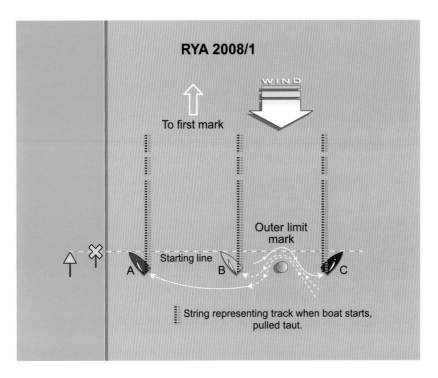

There is a problem with the mirror-image of the post-finish buoy situation, namely a buoy laid as a starting limit mark on the pre-course side of the starting line. A series of RYA cases over many years has established that if such an object is laid more than a boat length below the starting line, it can be ignored. The latest of these is RYA 2008/1. Its principles have not received the support of an ISAF case, some have questioned its logic, but there is no other known authority on the subject.

---

[1] *Daffodil* would in any case be entitled to redress only if she could show that her finishing position had been affected by a an impoper action of the race committee. That is not discussed in the case, but it could only have been relevant if agreeing with *Daffodil*'s interpretation would have resulted in *Daffodil* gaining a place.

Question 1

What marks the point when a boat should be described as 'approaching the starting line...to start', and when does rule 28.2 begin to apply?

Answer 1

A boat is approaching the starting line when she is sailing a course that approaches any part of the starting line. This may be the case even when her heading is away from the starting line, provided that her course at that time does not take her further from all points of the line.

A boat is approaching the starting line 'to start' when her speed and course, and the time remaining before her starting signal, are consistent with crossing the starting line after her starting signal, even if she becomes OCS.

That guidance is, however, more relevant to questions under the preamble to Section C about entitlement to room from another boat while approaching a starting mark than to the issue of sailing the course under rule 28, which focuses on a single boat's position immediately she has started.

When the starting mark concerned forms one end of the starting line, rule 28.2 adds nothing to rule 28.1. The second sentence of rule 28.2 adds a requirement only when the starting mark is a limit mark laid on the pre-course side of the starting line (see Answer 2). Compliance with rule 28.2, like rule 28.1, is tested at the moment after a boat has started. In the diagram, all the boats are approaching the starting line to start at all times, but, as will be seen, boat C does not comply with rule 28.2. Although she had previously left the limit mark on her starboard side while approaching an outer part of the infinitely long starting line, it was not on the starboard side of her track (applying the string test) at the moment after she started.

Question 2

Does the second sentence of rule 28.2, and especially the use of the word 'However', remove the need to apply the 'string test' in rule 28.1 to a starting mark?

Answer 2

No. The string test always applies. An object intended to be a starting limit mark but laid on the pre-start side of the starting line does not begin, bound or end a leg, and without the second sentence of rule 28.2 would have no required side to which the string test could be applied. So the second sentence of rule 28.2 modifies its first sentence, to create a required side at a starting limit mark laid on the pre-start side of the starting line.

Question 3

When does the string test start to apply to a boat at a starting limit mark laid behind the starting line?

Answer 3

The test applies immediately after she starts, as stated in rule 28.1. If a buoy that is intended to be a starting limit mark is laid more than one of her boat-lengths (or, indeed, a little less than one boat-length for a boat starting close hauled) on the pre-start side of the starting line, the string test cannot determine whether it has been left on the required side, as the buoy lies astern of the start of the string. Since the boat cannot fail the string test in these circumstances, she may ignore the object for the purposes of rule 28[1].

Question 4

Is there any action a boat might then take so that she would no longer be described as 'approaching the starting line to start', and therefore rule 28.2 did not apply to her earlier actions?

Answer 4

As is clear from Answer 1, the term 'approaching the starting line... to start' has a broad application. For instance, the fact that a boat is OCS does not necessarily invalidate her previous course as being an approach to start, if an issue under rule 18.1(a) arises, even though she had approached, but did not start as defined.

---

[1] See RYA 2006/1, page 118

As stated in Answer 3, the question is irrelevant at a limit mark laid more than a boat-length on the pre-start side. When a limit mark is laid less than a boat-length on the pre-start side, all that is relevant is the location of the mark relative to the taut string at its starting point – which is the centre of her transom when she starts. If a starting mark lies on the wrong side of the string at that point, she has not complied with rule 28.2.

In the diagram, the boats are shown at their positions just after the starting signal, on a starting line formed by a shore transit, with an outer limit mark. No part of rule 30 applies to the start. The tracks of boats A and B do not appear to lie on the required side of the outer limit mark, which the track of boat C does. However, that is not relevant, since the string test that determines whether a mark has been left on the required side does not begin until they start, and their tracks until then are immaterial. Applying the string test when they start, boats A and B comply with rule 28.2, and boat C does not.

The entitlement to ignore an intended starting mark laid more than a boat length from the starting line on the pre-start side arises from RYA cases based on the use of the word 'wake' rather than 'track' in older versions of rule 28.1, but that does not appear to affect the principle of regarding the track as starting at the boat's transom when she starts. A recent example is RYA 2006/1.

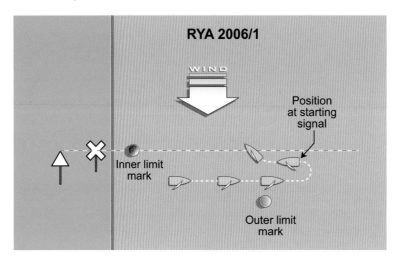

The sailing instructions said that the starting line was a transit with an inner limit mark and an outer limit mark, and that boats were to pass between those marks while approaching the line to start. *Highlander* sailed a course when starting that did not take her between the limit marks when approaching the line to start. The outer limit mark was two boat-lengths to leeward of the starting line. She was protested, was disqualified, and appealed. Her appeal was upheld, and she was reinstated.

The limit marks were starting marks. Rule 28.2 requires a starting mark to be left on the required side when approaching the starting line to start. The effect of the sailing instruction was that the outer limit mark was to be left to starboard at that time. It is the 'string test' in rule 28.1 that decides whether this requirement has been met, and the 'string test' does not begin to apply until after a boat has started. Therefore, the beginning of a boat's track will be at most one boat-length on the pre-start side of the starting line. As a result, the string cannot be said to lie on any side of a starting limit mark when that mark is more than one boat-length on the pre-start side of the starting line.

Rule 29 RECALLS

29.1 **Individual Recall**

When at a boat's starting signal any part of her hull, crew or equipment is on the course side of the starting line or she must comply with rule 30.1, the race committee shall promptly display flag X with one sound. The flag shall be displayed until all such boats are completely on the pre-start side of the starting line or one of its extensions and have complied with rule 30.1 if it applies, but no later than four minutes after the starting signal or one minute before any later starting signal, whichever is earlier. If rule 30.3 applies this rule does not.

This rule is addressed to the race committee: the obligation for a boat to start as defined is in rule 28.1. It can be the source of some confusion when Flag I is the preparatory signal, activating rule 30.1. Suppose a boat was OCS at 50 seconds before the starting signal, returned directly to the pre-course side, and never crossed an extension from the course side to the pre-course side[1]. At the starting signal, the race committee will display flag X, even if all boats were on the pre-course side of the starting line at that moment. Without some further method of hailing or radioing the offending boat being employed, the boat or boats making the sharpest valid start may think that the recall applies to them, and will needlessly return. For this reason, there is a good argument for sailing instructions to change rule 29.1, stating a different recall flag for boats on the pre-course side at the starting signal, but in breach in rule 30.1. (The problem does not occur under rule 30.2, since the penalty is automatic, and with a black-flag start under rule 30.3, rule 29.1 confirms that no recall signal is ever to be used, since an offending boat is disqualified.)

The rule becomes an issue for the protest committee when redress is requested. The commonest reason is that the boat did not return and start, disagrees with her resulting OCS score, and seeks to convince the protest committee that the race committee misidentified her. This is in itself the commonest type of request for redress. International juries and skilled protest committees will be hard to convince. 'A race officer is sighting directly along the line, and concentrating on it at all relevant times, is in by far the best position to make such a judgement[2].' It is common for a notice to this effect to be posted on the official notice board, stating that very high standard of proof will be required for the boat to be reinstated. Once the race officer has satisfied the protest committee that race committee procures, in terms of recording sail or bow numbers both on paper and electronically, are sound, the competitor has an uphill task, and when at a regatta the protest committee has refused OCS redress requests once or twice on the first day, fresh requests are less frequent.

It will often happen that a boat is clearly OCS, and is recalled, but her return is not detected by the race officials. She is scored accordingly, and asks for redress. Here, the odds in favour of the boat are a little better. If she can bring evidence to show that she returned, and the race committee has no evidence to the contrary, she should be reinstated[3]. 'There is a considerable difference between a collective "We did not see any boat come back" from the race committee and a personal "I observed the boat for a period of time after she was identified OCS and she did not come back…" When there is doubt that a race committee has properly fulfilled its obligations and this results in a penalty to a competitor, a protest committee should resolve the matter in favour of the competitor[4].'

Most of the appeal cases revolve around procedural mistakes made by the race committee. Even when a mistake is proved, that does not automatically mean that redress will be given, or that redress will be full reinstatement into the boat's finishing position. ISAF 31 (echoed in ISAF 71) makes an important point, that even when there is a procedural error by the race committee, 'a boat that realises that she was over the line is not entitled to redress, and she must comply with rule 28,1 and, if it applies, rule 30.1. If she fails to do so, she breaks rule 2 and fails to comply with the Basic Principle, Sportsmanship and the Rules.'

The recall signal comprises both flag X and the sound signal[5]. 'When the sound signal is omitted from an individual recall, and a recalled boat in a position to hear a sound signal does not see the visual signal and does not return, she is entitled to redress[6].' However, when the race committee makes two sound signals rather than one with the individual recall, a boat that is unable to see that it is flag X that is flying should not assume it to be a general recall, and if she stops racing on that basis alone, she will be at fault, and therefore debarred from redress. 'She would have lost nothing by continuing to sail her best race until she was able to see the flag on the committee vessel[7].'

---

[1] The situation can also be confusing for the race committee, as will be seen under rule 30.1
[2] RYA 1994/8
[3] *ibid*
[4] CYA 97
[5] RYA 2004/7
[6] ISAF 31
[7] RYA 2004/7

A hail is not a sound signal, and if a recall hail is made but is unheard, the recall flag is not seen, and there is no sound signal, a boat not aware that she is OCS will be entitled to redress[1].

The rule requires the recall signal (whose sound signal should be equally as audible as the starting sound signal)[2] to be made 'promptly', which means 'within a very few seconds of the starting signal. Forty seconds is well beyond the limits of acceptability[3]', and the race committee cannot shelter behind a sailing instruction purporting to place all the responsibility for returning on the competitor. 'When a signal is not made or, as in this case, when the signal is much too late, it places a boat that does not realise that she was slightly over the line at the starting signal at a significant disadvantage...', and the fact she may indeed have been OCS does not count as a fault that would preclude redress. 'The error is entirely the race committee's fault, not that of the disadvantaged boat[4].'

If the protest committee believes that a recalled boat that did not return was wrongly identified as OCS, then reinstatement into her finishing position is the appropriate redress. If the issue is that the boat was OCS, unknown to herself, but the recall was improperly signalled so that she did not return, then the redress is likely to be different. The purpose of redress is neither to punish the race committee nor to reward a boat. Rather, it is to try to put a boat in the position she would have been in had the race committee procedure been proper, as is equitable both to her and to all other competitors. So had the signal been properly made, and had she returned, she would have lost places as a result. Her redress score should therefore be several places worse than her actual finishing position, reflecting the time it would have taken her to return and start[5].

That is particularly true when recall signal aimed at *Daffodil* is removed early. If the protest committee is satisfied that *Daffodil* was OCS, but she did not return, the question is whether she would have returned had it been displayed for the full time required. If not, then the mistiming error did not affect *Daffodil*, and she is not entitled to redress. Even if she can establish a link between the premature lowering of her signal and her not returning, her redress will be limited. In RYA 2006/2, flag X was lowered after a minute, although the boat for which it was intended had not returned, and did not do so.

> A boat is entitled to redress only when she can show that a mistake affected her score. This might be because the boat was not able to see the committee boat during the period flag X was displayed, perhaps because of intervening boats, but would have been able to see it had it been displayed for longer. Alternatively she might be able to convince a protest committee that she had seen flag X, believed it might apply to her, and was on the point of returning when it was lowered. In either situation, the earliest time the error could have affected the boat is the moment flag X was lowered - in this case, about one minute after the starting signal.
>
> If the protest committee is satisfied that the boat would have returned if flag X had been displayed for longer, it should award redress. Appropriate redress would be to reinstate her in the race and add to her finishing time the estimated time for the boat to sail back to the start line and then return to the point at which she turned back which, in this case, is unlikely to be less than two minutes. Reinstating the boat in her actual finishing position will be wrong as it will not be equitable to all boats as required by rule 64.2[6].

29.2 **General Recall**

When at the starting signal the race committee is unable to identify boats that are on the course side of the starting line or to which rule 30 applies, or there has been an error in the starting procedure, the race committee may signal a general recall (display the First Substitute with two sounds). The warning signal for a new start for the recalled class shall be made one minute after the First Substitute is removed (one sound), and the starts for any succeeding classes shall follow the new start.

[1] ISAF 71
[2] RYA 1977/1
[3] ISAF 79
[4] *ibid*
[5] ISAF 31
[6] See also RYA 2000/3

A general recall can be signalled after the starting signal in the following circumstances:
- There are unidentified boats on the course side at the starting signal
- Rule 30.1, 30.2 or 30.3 were in force, and there were unidentified boats on the course side in the minute before the starting signal
- There was an error in the starting procedure.

The first is the norm, the second and third are, in my experience, rare. If the second applies, but the boats have returned at their starting signal, what is to be gained by recalling the start? No virtuous competitor will have been disadvantaged. For starting procedure errors, flag AP before the starting signal and flag N after the starting signal are more commonly used. If there is a gross mistiming with no signals at the starting time, and if rule 30.3, Black Flag Rule applies, then to make a belated starting signal followed by a general recall requires the disqualification of boats who crossed the starting line on what should have been their starting signal, as they are on the course side in the minute before their starting signal. The rule then requires them not to take part in the restart, a situation that no redress can adequately cope with other than possibly for the restarted race to be abandoned. The same would apply to the recall of a rule 30.2 Z flag start. On the other hand, flag AP has no such complications, and in particular, no penalisation.

While the display of flag X is compulsory if one or more OCS boats can be identified ('shall') a general recall is permissive ('may'). Some race officers will use a general recall even if only a few boats cannot be identified, while others will let a start go if no one appeared to gain an unfair advantage from being too early. Like the tide, opinion as to best practice seems to ebb and flow.

Very occasionally, a race officer is able to be sure of who is over by being to identify all the few that are not. The appropriate signal in this case would be an individual recall.

As with all signals other than under rule 26, the signal is both the flag and the sound. So when there were two sounds, but a hail of 'General recall!' rather than a flag, and a boat heard all the sounds and decided to continue racing (with three others), believing that she at least was not OCS, redress of a finishing of a finishing place was deemed appropriate[1].

Rule 30   STARTING PENALTIES

30.1   I Flag Rule

If flag I has been displayed, and any part of a boat's hull, crew or equipment is on the course side of the starting line or one of its extensions during the last minute before her starting signal, she shall thereafter sail from the course side across an extension to the pre-start side before *starting*.

The rule title is changed from 'Round-an-End Rule' because it has been realised that it can be complied with without sailing round an end. Yellow complies because she sails from the course side across an extension – see fig 100. Although the title of a rule is not part of the rule[2], its remaining unchanged would be bizarre. There are some who would have preferred the title to remain, and the rule to revert to words that required a boat to sail round an end, as that is more easily policed, and usually more of a penalty.

---

[1] RYA 1982/7
[2] See definition Rule

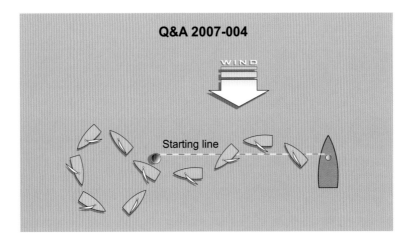

Q&A 2007-004

WIND

Starting line

Rule 30.1 will apply to boat on the course side of the starting line's extensions as well of the starting line itself, and may sometimes trap late arrivals to the starting area who are running down towards it in the last minute, by which time flag I will have been removed as the one-minute signal, and they will not be aware of what has happened[1]. Once again, they will provoke a display of flag X after the starting signal even though they may not be 'interfering with play', which may confuse others. If by good fortune they sail over an extension of the line before starting, they will have complied with rule, but running through the line itself without crossing an extension, even if some time after the starting signal, will result in an OCS score for that race. Race officers sometimes need an eye in the back of their heads to police rule 30.1, and sometimes that eye is Nelsonian.

In large fleets on long starting lines, the I flag can be counter-productive if it encourages bunching at the line ends where taking the penalty will take the shortest time, increasing the probability of a general recall and a move to the black flag.

When the usable part of the starting line is limited by inner or outer limit marks, the gap between those marks and (typically) the committee vessels they protect are not extensions, as the starting line is between the masts on those committee vessels[2].

30.2 **Z Flag Rule**

If flag Z has been displayed, no part of a boat's hull, crew or equipment shall be in the triangle formed by the ends of the starting line and the first *mark* during the last minute before her starting signal. If a boat breaks this rule and is identified, she shall receive, without a hearing, a 20% Scoring Penalty calculated as stated in rule 44.3(c). She shall be penalised even if the race is restarted or resailed, but not if it is *postponed* or *abandoned* before the starting signal. If she is similarly identified during a subsequent attempt to start the same race, she shall receive an additional 20% Scoring Penalty.

The 'penalty zone' for the Z Flag rule (and for the Black Flag rule) is a triangle whose base is the full length of starting line, not just that part of it inside a limit mark. Its apex is the first mark.

---

[1] There is a move afoot to seek to make the one-minute signal the removal of the class flag and to make the starting signal the removal of the preparatory signal, so boats will be able to check in the last minute whether any penalty regime applies to the start
[2] RYA 2004/9

'The ends of the starting line in rules 30.1, 30.2 and 30.3 are those specified in the sailing instructions, and not any limit or distance mark, unless the sailing instructions explicitly change rule 30[1].' So, in a Z flag start, and likewise in a black flag start, both Yellow and Blue are rightly penalised for being in the triangle whose base is masts at each end of the starting line in the last minute, even though they are not in a triangle whose base is that part of the line between limit marks on which they have to start.

Rule 26 offers the combination of flags I and Z as penalty preparatory signals. The effect of the combination is that, if there is no general recall, a boat will have both a bad start after having to cross an extension from windward, and then a place penalty on top – and if there is a general recall, the penalty will apply to the race when it is got away[2]. Because of the different penalty areas for each rule, the Z-flag element will not apply to a boat that is OCS outside the triangle. With this complication in mind, sailing instructions sometimes modify the I flag penalty area to be the same as for the Z and black flag.

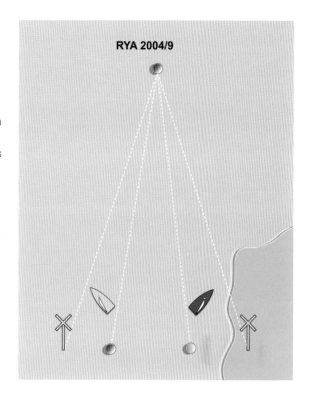

RYA 2004/9

If a boat is detected in the penalty zone of a Z flag start, both when in a start that is then recalled, and again at its restart[3], a second 20% place penalty (ZFP) is incurred, and because of rounding and a maximum value of the penalty[4], the value of the two penalties may not be the same as one 40% place penalty.

The fact that a boat was over the line at her starting signal, resulting in a 20% place penalty, does not relieve her of her obligation to return and start. If she does not do so, she will be scored OCS[5].

When a boat is in the penalty zone in the last minute, and there is a general recall, the fact that the next attempted start of the race is postponed or abandoned before the starting signal does not prevent the penalty being carried forwards to the successful starting of the race. The carry-forward would cease to apply only if the postponement or abandonment had happened in the rest of the one-minute period of the race in which she incurred the penalty[6].

30.3

Black Flag Rule

If a black flag has been displayed, no part of a boat's hull, crew or equipment shall be in the triangle formed by the ends of the starting line and the first *mark* during the last minute before her starting signal. If a boat breaks this rule and is identified, she shall be disqualified without a hearing, even if the race is restarted or resailed, but not if it is *postponed* or *abandoned* before the starting signal. If a general recall is signalled or the race is *abandoned* after the starting signal, the race committee shall display her sail number before the next warning signal for that race, and if the race is restarted or resailed she shall not sail in it. If she does so, her disqualification shall not be excluded in calculating her series score.

---

[1] *ibid*

[2] ISAF 111

[3] See below for the meaning of various terms in rules 30.2 and 30.3. The penalty is carried forwards also when a race is' resailed' after post-start abandonment, and when there is a further general recall or post-start abandonment. Only a pre-starting-signal abandonment or postponement can negate a ZFP or BFD arising from that race, and it will not wipe out a penalty carried forwards from a previous start, which will continue to apply to the race when it is finally started and completed.

[4] See rule 44.3(c) and further guidance under Appendix A: scoring rule 30.2 can be tricky.

[5] Technically, the 20% penalty still applies, but its value cannot make a boat worse than DNF – see rule 44.3(c) – and when scoring under Appendix A the scores in A 4.2 for DNS, OCS and DNF are the same

[6] ISAF 111

If a boat is several hull lengths on the course side of the starting line at the starting signal of a black flag start, she will know then that she is disqualified, and 'she is obliged to retire promptly. When she does not do so and then deliberately hinders another boat in the race, she commits a gross breach of sportsmanship and, therefore, of rule 2, and her helmsman commits a gross breach of sportsmanship[1].' Even if she does not deliberately hinder another boat, the fact that she must know she has broken a rule but does not retire is contrary to the Basic Principle, Sportsmanship and the Rules, and that alone breaks rule 2, as has been seen.

It is common for a sailing instruction to require the race committee to notify BFD boats[2] of their penalty at the first windward mark, at which they must retire from the race. Suppose there is no such sailing instruction, but the race committee tells a BFD boat to leave the race while it is progress – must she comply? If she believes that she did not break rule 30.3, and requests redress after the race, I do not think she breaks a rule by continuing to race, but her position is less certain if she continues to race but does not request redress, and I think a race committee or another boat would be entitled to protest her under rule 2.

When there is a general recall of a black flag start, the race committee displays the sail numbers of BFD boats, which are disqualified and must not take part in the restart. If they do, their penalty becomes a DNE. If a boat believes that she is wrongly identified, can she take part in the restart and request redress? No, she will still be DNE, even if she can show she was wrongly identified, because her infringement relates to ignoring the display of her number, not to being over the line at the wrong time. Her only remedy is not to take part, and to seek redress, which, if given in a series, would normally be based on her results in other races[3]. For this reason, race officers should be cautious about using rule 30.3 in a race that is not part of a series, or, if within a series, is also for a major prize, since no compensation is possible for a misidentified boat, and sailing instructions sometimes set out a mechanism for a BFD boat to take part in the restart by telling the race committee, and then asking for redress afterwards. One such says that if the request is upheld, the BFD is annulled: if the request is refused, the BFD stands; and if the request had no merit or was not in fact lodged, the penalty is upgraded to a DNE.

When the race committee sees a boat breaking rule 30.3 in a start that is recalled, but then fails to display her sail number, so that she competes in the restart, is she then entitled to a finishing place? No, continues ISAF 96.

> The boat should be disqualified as required by the second sentence of rule 30.3. However…she should be scored DSQ and not DNE. If she requests redress claiming that she is entitled to a finishing place because the race committee erred by not displaying her sail number, her request should be denied. While not displaying her sail number is an improper omission by the race committee, it is not the omission that deprived her of her finishing place, but the fact that she had been on the course side of the starting line in the minute before her starting signal. However, if she was scored DNE, redress should be granted to the extent of changing her score to DSQ[4].

That is clear, but the problem sometimes occurs because the number displayed is not the boat's actual sail number, but an allocated bow number in a major event, or only the last few digits of a longer sail number, as with Lasers. Sailing instructions can and should change rule 30.3 to legitimise this, but I think that if that is not done, a boat that does not know for sure that she was over in the last minute is entitled to ignore a faulty number display and restart, and then to seek redress as stated above, However, the principle in ISF 96 would still apply, and the best she can hope for is to revert to the position she would have been in had she not taken part in the restart, namely that her DNE becomes a BFD, so to 'make a point' in this way is only a partial improvement, unless she also wishes to contest that she was over in the last minute.

---

[1] ISAF 65: the last nine words quoted opens up the possibility of a hearing against the competitor under rule 69.1
[2] Black flag disqualification – see rule A11.
[3] ISAF 96
[4] The case uses the abbreviation DSQ. Perhaps it should be BFD, which is the abbreviation recommended by rule A11 for a disqualification under rule 30.3, which is just one type of disqualification, but reserved for the race committee rather than the protest committee. There is no difference in the scoring consequences. BFD in the results will be clearer for the penalised competitor to understand.

The black flag rule has several features in common with the Z flag rule, namely the penalty zone and the durability of the penalty when a race is recalled, postponed or abandoned. In addition, there are two ways to attract a penalty under both rules – to be over the line in the last minute, even if back behind the line at the starting signal; and to be over the line at the starting signal. There are also differences. If a boat is OCS at her starting signal in a Z flag start, she must return and start to avoid an OCS score, though she will still carry the place penalty – but if a boat thinks that she is not over at the start of a black flag race, but is not sure, there is nothing to gain by returning.

Several of the terms in rules 30.2 and 30.3 require clarification. A 2008 submission for an ISAF case suggested the following[1]:

Question

What is a 'restarted race', as referred to in rules 30.2, 30.3 and 36?

Answer

A 'restarted race' is a race

- for which a warning signal was made,
- which was then either postponed before the starting signal or subject to a general recall after the starting signal, and
- for which a fresh starting sequence under rule 26 is begun.

Question

What is a 'resailed race', as referred to in rules 30.2, 30.3 and 36?

Answer

A 'resailed race' is a race

- for which a warning signal was made,
- which was then abandoned, either before or after the starting signal, and
- for which a fresh starting sequence under rule 26 is begun.

Question

If a boat breaks rule 30.2 or 30.3 and the race is later restarted or resailed, does the application of rule 30.2 or 30.3 depend on the reason for restarting or resailing a race?

Answer

Yes. If a race is restarted, the application of rules 30.2 and 30.3 depends on whether (a) the original race was postponed after the warning signal and before the starting signal, or (b) it was subject to a general recall after the starting signal. A boat that breaks one of those rules is not penalised if (a) occurred, but she is if (b) occurred.

If a race is resailed, rules 30.2 and 30.3 again specify different outcomes, depending on whether the original race was abandoned before or after the starting signal. A boat that breaks one of those rules is not penalised if her breach occurred during a starting sequence when abandonment was signaled before the starting signal. However, she is penalised if her breach occurred during the last minute before a start and abandonment was signaled after that start.

 **Rule 31**

TOUCHING A MARK

While *racing*, a boat shall not touch a starting *mark* before *starting*, a *mark* that begins, bounds or ends the leg of the course on which she is sailing, or a finishing *mark* after *finishing*.

Rule 31 applies when a boat touches a course mark she is rounding as required. It ends the leg she was on and begins the next leg. It is not thought to apply if, just after starting on a typical trapezoid course, she touches the leeward mark that has been laid to windward of the starting line. It does not begin or end the leg she is currently on, which is the leg from the starting line to the windward mark. It will not be her next mark until she has rounded the windward mark – indeed, if her course is 'outer loop', it may never be a mark of her course. A mark that is a passing mark to keep boats clear of an area is one that 'bounds' a leg.

---

[1] It was not accepted, but it appears to be correct

A boat must not, while racing, touch a finishing mark before she finishes when the finishing mark will end the leg of the course she is on. Therefore, before she is on the final leg, she can touch a finishing mark, unless it is separately a course mark for her on the leg she is on, such as a mark of a start and finish line that must be passed through at the end of each lap.

A boat must not touch a finishing mark after finishing while she is still racing, which is until, after finishing, she clears the finishing line and marks. So if a boat touches a finishing mark just after cutting the finishing line, she now has to take a turn penalty and return to the pre-finish side of the line and cross the line again. ISAF Q&A 2006-002 explains.

> A boat clears the finishing line and marks when no part of her hull, crew or equipment is on the line and when neither mark is influencing her course. A boat that clears the finishing line close-hauled and continues to sail toward the finishing line pin end mark, where current sets her into the mark, is still racing and has broken 31. A boat that crosses the finishing line, sails away from the line and marks, and then later hits the finishing line mark, does not break rule 31 as she is no longer racing.

ISAF 58, as discussed under rule 28.2, says that a buoy laid as an intended limit mark on the post-course side of the finishing line is not a mark, because it does not end or bound the last leg of the course. Since the 'end or bound' requirement appears in both rule 28.2 and rule 31, it follows that such a 'mark' can also be touched. However that case says that a finishing line limit mark has a required side for a boat when it is laid on the finishing line or its course side, presumably because it bounds the last leg, and therefore it must not be touched.

Consideration of rule 28.2 included discussion of ISAF 58's near-mirror image, a starting limit 'mark' laid on the pre-course side of the starting line. If laid a boat length or more below the starting line, it appears to have no required side, and it cannot be said to start or bound a leg. Logically, it is not actually a mark, and can therefore be touched. However, when a starting limit mark is laid on the pre-course side nearer to starting line, or on the starting line, or on the course side of the starting line, it has a required side and it starts or bounds the first leg. Therefore, it must not be touched while starting.

The rule forbids touching a starting mark before starting. This does not mean that a committee boat (or any starting mark) can be touched immediately after starting, because such marks begin or bound the first leg of the course the boat is now on.

One issue that is sometimes argued but rarely analysed is whether the committee boat and buoys of a starting line can be touched before starting. One view is that, until a boat is approaching the starting line to start, she can touch the committee boat and the starting marks. Why? Because, although rule 31 says that, while racing, a boat shall not touch a starting mark before starting, the definition Mark says that a mark is an object the sailing instructions require a boat to leave on a specified side – and rule 28.2 says that a starting mark does not have a required side for a boat until she is approaching it to start. So in fact, it is argued, those objects are not in fact marks until near the starting signal.

I think most people believe that you must not touch the committee boat and starting marks at any time from the preparatory signal (when a boat is now racing) until the starting signal. The reason is that the definition Mark is to be read as meaning that a mark is an object the sailing instructions require a boat to leave on a specified side at some time in the race. So the leeward 'mark' buoy you meet shortly after starting IS a mark. You can only touch it because it is a mark that does not begin, bound or end the leg you are on, as stated in rule 31. The rule clearly says that a starting mark is not to be touched before starting. The starting marks will acquire a required side when approaching the line to start, and therefore they are always marks, and are not to be touched while racing and before starting. (If one is touched before approaching the line to start, a turn penalty taken promptly as required will rarely interfere with a boat's starting strategy.)

It appears therefore that rules 28 and 31 apply harmoniously to course marks and finishing marks. If you have to leave the mark on a required side, you must not touch it while doing so. The time during which you must not touch a finishing mark is then extended a little beyond the moment when your rule 28 obligation ends. However, there is a period before a boat is approaching the line to start when the mark does not have a required side, yet when it must not be touched, and rules 28 and 31 are not completely synchronised.

Touching a mark includes contact by equipment out of position. 'A boat touches a mark within the meaning of rule 31 when any part of her hull, crew or equipment comes into contact with the mark. The fact that her equipment touches the mark because she has manoeuvring or sail-handling difficulties does not excuse her breach of the rule[1].' Technically, a crew member that has fallen overboard and swims for support to a nearby committee boat or course mark beginning bounding or ending the leg would appear to break rule 31 for the boat.

When a boat touches a mark in an incident with another boat, does not take a penalty and there is a protest (regardless of the identity of the protestor, which might be the other boat, the race committee or the protest committee), she will be exonerated under rule 64.1(c) if the protest committee decides that she was compelled to break rule 31 because the other boat broke a rule[2]. That is also a judgement that the touching boat can form for herself at the time without the need to protest, particularly if the other boat takes a penalty, but it will be subject to review in any protest lodged by anyone else over the same incident.

The mark's anchor line is not part of the mark, and so when a keel or centreboard catches the anchor line, no rule is yet broken, but as US 10 points out, it soon will be if the mark is then drawn onto the hull of the boat. In that case, the line was caught when the boat was five feet away from the mark, but there was current and she had a deep centreboard. In RYA 1989/10, a finishing mark was attached by cordage of a semi-floating variety which was too long when used in shallow areas. The excess was usually tied into a bunch but it became loose. It produced an underwater hazard floating two to three yards to leeward of the mark and, with a flood tide, on the course side of the finishing line. It was not visible to an approaching boat and several boats were caught in this tangle in the act of finishing, were drawn onto the mark and took a one-turn penalty. This affected the finishing position of one of them, *Instant Sunshine*, which requested redress. The protest committee, refusing redress, stated that the mark and ground tackle were the equipment used regularly as a finishing mark in that area and that the length and type of warp was not unreasonable in the circumstances. *Instant Sunshine*'s appeal was upheld, and she was re-instated in her position when she first crossed the finishing line.

> Redress may be given for a race committee's failure to provide suitably equipped marks…Marks are laid for the benefit of competing boats and it is important that ground tackle be arranged to minimise possibility of being fouled by the boats. In cases involving errors by the race committee, it is a good principle that any doubts be resolved in favour of the competitor.

As was seen under rule 28.1, if *Instant Sunshine* had decided not to take a penalty, it would take a protest to dislodge her from her finishing position. If she were protested, a decision to disqualify her would be accompanied by an immediate reinstatement, as being redress for the improper omission of the race committee that had caused her to break rule 31.

---

[1] ISAF 77
[2] ISAF 28

Rule 32

32.1

SHORTENING OR ABANDONING AFTER THE START

After the starting signal, the race committee may shorten the course (display flag S with two sounds) or abandon the race (display flag N, N over H, or N over A, with three sounds), as appropriate,

(a) because of an error in the starting procedure,

(b) because of foul weather,

(c) because of insufficient wind making it unlikely that any boat will *finish* within the time limit,

(d) because a *mark* is missing or out of position, or

(e) for any other reason directly affecting the safety or fairness of the competition,

or may shorten the course so that other scheduled races can be sailed. However, after one boat has sailed the course and *finished* within the time limit, if any, the race committee shall not *abandon* the race without considering the consequences for all boats in the race or series.

Both shortening and abandoning are theoretically possible in the event of one of the circumstances (a) to (e), but it is obviously preferable to shorten rather than abandon when both are possible. Abandonment is not permitted simply so that other scheduled races can be sailed, and it is unlikely that a race would be shortened because of an error in the starting procedure. As the rule says, it will depend on which is appropriate. As discussed under rule 29.2, abandonment for an error in the starting procedure is preferable to a general recall, particularly for a Z flag or black flag start.

In order to shorten or abandon because of insufficiency of wind making it unlikely that any boat will finish within the time limit, first there must be a time limit. 'When there is no time limit and no further races are scheduled to be sailed, as in the race in question, rule 32.1 does not permit a race committee to shorten or abandon a race because of insufficient wind, since the lack of a time limit implies that the race is intended to last until all boats have finished or retired. Nor did any question of the fairness of the competition arise. When the possibility of a prolonged race is contemplated in this way, the competition cannot be regarded as unfair when such circumstances arise[1].'

Abandonment because a mark is missing or out of position is normally not appropriate when a boat has caused one to be shifted only a short distance or temporarily. 'A race committee may abandon under rule 32.1(d) only when the change in the mark's position has directly affected the safety or fairness of the competition[2].'

It is usually via redress hearings that issues arise, either because the race committee did not take action when a boat thought it should, or when it did take action when a boat thought it should not. In RYA 2002/10, the course for a race early in the season was selected from a list of marks in the sailing instructions, headed 'No responsibility is accepted for any error in the indicated positions'. Some of the marks to be used were lifted at the end of the season and laid again each spring by a contractor acting on behalf of the local clubs. Unknown to the race committee, one of the marks had been laid 0.4 nm from its published position. *Fandango* was one of several boats who used GPS to sail to the mark's published position in race in force 4 winds and good visibility, and she lost time locating and rounding the mark as actually laid. She asked for redress.

The protest committee refused redress and referred its decision to the RYA, asking for guidance on the extent to which a race committee was obliged to check the positions of such marks: the extent to which a boat might rely on navigation by GPS alone, given that other boats had detected the error earlier by keeping a good lookout; and whether the caveat in the sailing instructions would always prevail against a redress claim. The decision of the protest committee was confirmed.

---

[1] RYA 1982/17
[2] ISAF 28

As concerns a seasonal mark that is laid by a contractor on behalf of local clubs, a race committee is entitled to expect that the mark was laid in its intended position, and cannot be expected to check the positions of all marks it might use. If it learns of an error, it should advise competitors.

A caveat concerning the accuracy of mark positions in sailing instructions does not relieve the race committee of its responsibilities. When the race committee learns before a race that any mark is out of position, and does not act on that knowledge when it is possible to do so, this may be an improper omission giving rise to the possibility of redress. When a race committee learns during a race that any mark is out of position, it is required to act under rule 34, if possible. If it is not possible, abandonment under rule 32.1(d) may be appropriate if a mark is so far from its intended position that boats cannot be expected to find its actual position, or can do so only at the expense of changes in position too extensive or unquantifiable to be remedied by redress that is fair for all the fleet.

However, a boat that relies solely on GPS for sailing the course in good conditions is not without fault if she is delayed in arriving at a mark that is not in its correct position but is reasonably near it, and she is not entitled to redress.

What looks like a sensible decision to abandon can be made to look foolish by the revived breeze that is frequently summoned by the sound of three guns. In RYA 1999/8, shortening the shore-started three-lap club race was not possible – there was no vessel in which to go to a mark. The time limit was two hours, the first two laps had been sailed in 40 minutes, but the wind then dropped, and some boats went home. With 55 minutes of the time limit left, the race committee signalled an abandonment from a shore mast. This was neither seen nor heard by the remaining competitors, the wind picked up, and the rest of the fleet reached the finishing line in the time limit. The boat that would have won on handicap requested reinstatement of the finishing scores as redress, which was refused. On the decision being referred, the RYA overturned it, as the abandonment was premature, given the time remaining. In effect, with 55 minutes to go, the possibility of a boat finishing within the time limit could not yet be said to be 'unlikely'. Although the case does not say so, the RYA was conscious that it would have had to have been prepared to make the same decision if in fact the wind had not revived. The decision whether finishing within a time limit is unlikely is with reference to the circumstances at the time the decision to abandon is made, and what actually happens is not relevant.

The power to abandon a race after at least one boat has validly finished is rarely used, and the rule is in effect saying 'Are you sure you want to do this?' It includes the possibility of doing so when all boats are ashore, unaffected by any time limit, and when this happens, the announcement can be made by a notice – the flag signals are not needed[1]. If a race committee is contemplating a post-race abandonment for some reason affecting the fairness of the competition, it might be advisable to refer the matter to the protest committee, which might decide to take it into its own hands and consider redress. It too has the option of abandoning as redress, and rule 64.2 also says 'Are you sure?' to the protest committee.

In an unpublished reference of a protest committee decision to the RYA, the race committee of an event in waters controlled by naval authorities was instructed by those authorities to stop a race in progress – the last race of the series - because of an unexpected passage through the course area of a warship. The race committee sent a RIB to the next mark to signal a shortened course, after more than half the race had been sailed. The RIB did not have flag S on board, and so sound signals were made, and all boats had their positions taken and were told to stop racing as they reached the mark. All boats complied, and a finishing order was compiled and posted. The race committee then reviewed its failure to signal the shortening, and decided to abandon the race, and to sail a replacement race. After that extra race, one boat asked for redress in the form of the reinstatement of the published results for the race. The protest committee refused the request, but the RYA reversed this decision.

[1] US 100

It might have been proper to abandon the race at the time that action was required, although the longer the race had been running, the more that shortening – effectively on safety grounds – was the preferable option. Once the decision had been taken to shorten, there was no reason to abandon it. Failure to signal the shortening properly was an omission that might have given rise to redress, but only if it had affected a boat's finishing position, which it had not. If every race committee mistake were to result in abandonment, far fewer races would be valid. The request to reinstate the finishing order was upheld, as the abandonment was improper, and the additional race sailed was not to be scored.

Shortening is a problem in handicap racing. If it is intended that the same time limit will apply to all boats[1], the race officer may have to decide between shortening so that all boats will finish in time, or letting the race run so that some will finish in the time limit and others will not. Whichever is chosen, one end of the fleet or the other may be unhappy. 'It is not improper not to shorten when it is clear that some boats will be out of time. A club may prescribe any time limit it wishes, and many clubs wish to set the same time limit for all boats[2].'

32.2 If the race committee signals a shortened course (displays flag S with two sounds), the finishing line shall be,

(a) at a rounding *mark*, between the *mark* and a staff displaying flag S;

(b) at a line boats are required to cross at the end of each lap, that line;

(c) at a gate, between the gate *marks*.

The shortened course shall be signalled before the first boat crosses the finishing line.

The implications of this rule have already been considered under rule 28.1, and, as discussed above, if the procedure for shortening the race was faulty, but there are no objections in the shape of requests for redress, it will never be an issue. When the finishing line is one that boats would not normally cross during a race, a sailing instruction is needed to use it for shortening course. Likewise, a starting and/or finishing line that boats will normally pass through while racing, but which they are not required to pass through, cannot be used for shortening course without a sailing instruction to that effect. But what when the shortening procedure is questioned?

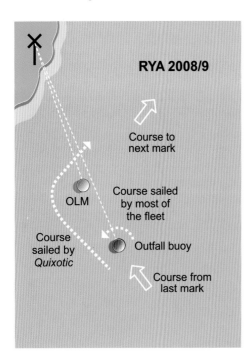

RYA 2008/9

OLM

Course to next mark

Course sailed by most of the fleet

Course sailed by Quixotic

Outfall buoy

Course from last mark

In RYA 2008/9 the next mark of the course for a cruiser handicap race was the outer limit mark (OLM) of the starting and finishing line, to be left to starboard. The OLM was between the shore mark and a red outfall buoy.

The wind had dropped, and, as boats reached the previous mark, the race committee radioed from the shore that the race was to be shortened to the outfall buoy. No member of the race committee was afloat, and flag S was not used. No sailing instruction either required the keeping of a radio watch after the course had originally been announced by VHF, or changed rule 32.2.

Some boats followed this oral instruction, left the outfall buoy to port, and were given a finishing position. *Quixotic*, which was not keeping a radio watch, sailed (with others) to the OLM as her next mark, and rounded it to starboard, passing between it and the shore mark. In the process, she crossed the race committee's intended finishing line, but not (in the race committee's opinion) in the right direction relative to the last mark. *Quixotic* was scored DNF. Having had her request for redress refused, *Quixotic*'s appeal was upheld, and the protest committee was directed to decide suitable redress.

---

[1] See page 132 under rule 35
[2] RYA 1998/2

The race committee did not act in accordance with rule 32, since no flags were displayed, nor was the required sound signal made. Nothing in the sailing instructions validated an oral change to the sailing instructions – see rule 90.2(c).

While the race committee's actions and omissions were therefore sufficiently improper to open the possibility of redress, it should be noted that, for the course set by the race officer, the race could not validly be shortened on a line to the outfall buoy, even if the appropriate signals had been made. Rule 32.2 prescribes three possibilities for shortening:

(a) at a rounding mark: the outfall buoy was never a rounding mark;

(b) at a line boats were required to cross at the end of each lap: there was no required line from the shore to the red outfall buoy;

(c) at a gate: this was not a gate.

The only line that might have been a valid finishing line was from the shore mark to the OLM, because it happened to be the next rounding mark, and could be used for shortening under rule 32.2(a). (Had it not also been a rounding mark, then it too would not meet the requirements of (a), (b) or (c) above despite being a mark of the starting and finishing line.)

Quixotic crossed both the finishing line to the red outfall buoy as actually (but wrongly) used by the race committee to shorten, and also what would have been a valid finishing line to the OLM had the race committee procedures been proper. The race committee claims that she did so in the wrong direction. The shore mark was open of the red outfall buoy by as little as 2° from the previous mark. It was therefore almost end-on to the direction of the course from the last mark, and *Quixotic* is entitled to the benefit of the doubt afforded to her in ISAF Case 82, permitting her to cross it from either direction.

Even if *Quixotic* chose not to keep a radio watch, she was not at fault for the purposes of rule 62.1, since no sailing instruction required her to do so, and she was entitled to expect that any shortening of the course would be done using the flag and sound signals. *Quixotic* would therefore be entitled to a finishing position in a properly finished race.

However, the race was never validly shortened, but that was not the fault of the competitors. The race committee was responsible for this state of affairs, and all boats are entitled to redress. Abandoning what had previously been until the last few yards a perfectly satisfactory race is not an acceptable outcome.

While the rule says that the shortened course shall be signalled before the first boat crosses the finishing line, there may be good reason for sailing instructions for coastal races to state a completely different procedure for finishing and scoring a race, following a radio or text message, based on recorded positions and times (possibly self-taken), at a previous mark when the wind abruptly drops and there is no likelihood of any boat reaching the next mark (for 'normal' shortening) or the finishing line within the time limit.

 CHANGING THE NEXT LEG OF THE COURSE

The race committee may change a leg of the course that begins at a rounding *mark* or at a gate by changing the position of the next *mark* (or the finishing line) and signalling all boats before they begin the leg. The next *mark* need not be in position at that time.

(a) If the direction of the leg will be changed, the signal shall be the display of flag C with repetitive sounds and either
    (1) the new compass bearing or
    (2) a green triangular flag or board for a change to starboard or a red rectangular flag or board for a change to port.
(b) If the length of the leg will be changed, the signal shall be the display of flag C with repetitive sounds and a '–' if the length will be decreased or a '+' if it will be increased.
(c) Subsequent legs may be changed without further signalling to maintain the course shape.

Over the years, this sailing instruction has been augmented to include matters such as rule 33(c) that previously required a sailing instruction. Particularly now that the rule is 'gate-compliant', all that should be needed in sailing instructions is suggested in L12 – yet sailing instructions persist in either repeating some or all of the rule, or (which is worse) needlessly changing rule 33.

This book is not a race management manual, but my experience is that:

- a board is usually more visible than a flag, particularly for the C, and
- the rarely-used '+' and '-' are not always understood, and unless the change in length is considerable, the information is not useful – so race committees should not rush to signal minor leg length changes.

Note the different shapes for the green and red flags or boards, to assist the colour-blind.

CYA 87 shows that when there is a mistake made in the procedure for signalling a change of the next leg (or, indeed, in making any race signal), there must be a causal link between that mistake and a boat's worsened score in order for redress to be granted. Boats of two classes were approaching the leeward mark, and the race committee wanted to signal that all boat should sail to a replacement windward mark on a new bearing. It made the sound signals, displayed the new course, but omitted to display flag C. *Iris* sailed to the old mark and rounded it. There was a protest, and she was disqualified under rule 28.1. Dismissing her appeal, the Canadian Yachting Association noted that the protest committee had found that she realised that the course was being changed despite the defective signalling, and she had admitted that the reason why she had not sailed to the replacement mark was because of a misunderstanding by her of the sailing instructions that led her to believe that the signal applied only to the other class and not to hers.

Rule 34 — MARK MISSING

If a *mark* is missing or out of position, the race committee shall, if possible,

(a) replace it in its correct position or substitute a new one of similar appearance, or

(b) substitute an object displaying flag M and make repetitive sound signals.

Again, a board is preferable to a flag, if only to try to make it clearer that it is this rarely used signal that is being made, and not the much more common rule 33 course change.

Rule 35 — TIME LIMIT AND SCORES

If one boat sails the course as required by rule 28.1 and *finishes* within the time limit, if any, all boats that *finish* shall be scored according to their finishing places unless the race is *abandoned*. If no boat *finishes* within the time limit, the race committee shall *abandon* the race.

When I am asked to check an event's sailing instructions, the first instruction I usually turn to is one that described the time limit. This is because the provision in the rule (that one boat finishing within the time limit makes the race valid for all competitors) is usually negated, but, contrary to rule 86.1(b), the sailing instruction often fails to say that rule 35 is changed. So in RYA 1998/2, referred to above, the bad news for the appellant apparently timed out in a handicap race was that the race officer was not improper in not shortening. The good news, however, was that the time limit sailing instruction made no mention of rule 35 being changed, and as at least one boat had finished within the time limit, the race was valid for all finishers. L15.2 of the Sailing Instructions Guide suggests wording for when the time limit is intended to apply to all boats. Sailing instructions for time limits are sometimes a mixture of the two principles, setting a time limit for the first boat, with the time limit for the other boats being the later of the time limit for the first boat and so many minutes after the finishing time of the first boat.

The rule does not cover all the bases. If no boat finishes within the time limit, the race is clearly abandoned. If one boat sails the course and finishes within the time limit, the race is clearly valid for at least that boat, and for all other finishers unless the sailing instructions change rule 35. That leaves open the possibility that only one boat finishes within the time limit, as defined, approaching the finishing line in the direction of the course from the last mark of the course, but is then found, after a protest, not to have complied with rule 28.1 at an earlier mark, which, as has been seen, is not the same issue. The answer is in rule 90.3, Scoring – the race is not to be scored. However, if the boat is disqualified for breaking some other rule, the race is valid.

RACES TO BE RESTARTED OR RESAILED

If a race is restarted or resailed, a breach of a *rule*, other than rule 30.3, in the original race shall not prohibit a boat from competing or, except under rule 30.2, 30.3 or 69, cause her to be penalised.

The general principle is that, when there has been a general recall (resulting in a restart) or an abandonment (resulting in a resail), most sins are forgiven – with exceptions: when a boat is in the penalty area in the last minute of a black flag start, the whole point of the rule is that she shall carry her BFD and not take part in the restart if there is a general recall or post-start abandonment and resail; nor will those events negate a Z flag penalty, or wipe out misbehaviour warranting a rule 69 hearing or report.

The wording of the rule is unhelpful. It would be clearer if it referred to a general recall rather than a restart, and to an abandonment rather than a resail. Most importantly, it makes no reference to postponements. It is generally believed that a postponement will have the same effect, namely that no penalisation is possible for infringements occurring between the preparatory signal and the AP signal – but this is nowhere written, not is there any appeal case. The reasons I have been offered for this omission are contradictory – either that it is too obvious to need saying, or that it can be inferred from an intricate interpretation of other rules. When a starting-line problem is building up, race officers will often choose to fire off an AP just before the starting signal rather than a general recall a second or so later, and the fact that a starting signal would have be made in one situation but not in the other does not seem to be a good reason for treating previous rule infringements differently – so postponement should be treated in the same way as abandonment or a general recall. The fact is that, at the starting signal, the race has been going for four minutes, at which point there happens to be a requirement to be behind a line, and a few extra rules come into force[1].

An unsuccessful ISAF case submission already referred to in the context of rule 30 addressed rule 36 as well. I believe that it is correct. Here are the questions and answers from it that pertain to rule 36.

Question

What is 'the original race', as referred to in rules 36 and 81?

Answer

'The original race' is the race that is to be restarted, resailed or rescheduled. The term is used only in rules 36 and 81.

Question

What is a 'restarted race', as referred to in rules 30.2, 30 3 and 36?

Answer

A 'restarted race' is a race
- for which a warning signal was made,
- which was then either postponed before the starting signal or subject to a general recall after the starting signal, and
- for which a fresh starting sequence under rule 26 is begun.

Question

What is a 'resailed race', as referred to in rules 30.2, 30.3 and 36?

Answer

A 'resailed race' is a race
- for which a warning signal was made,
- which was then abandoned, either before or after the starting signal, and
- for which a fresh starting sequence under rule 26 is begun.

---

[1] When rule 42, Propulsion is being policed by the 'yellow flag' procedure on the water, Appendix P will apply, and rule P3 is more clearly worded, to put abandonment, postponement and a general recall explicitly on the same footing as concerns the non-carrying forward of penalties, using those actual terms to say so.

Question
Does the application of rule 36 depend on the reason for restarting or resailing a race?
Answer
No. Rule 36 states that, unless rule 30.2, 30.3 or 69 applies, whenever a race is restarted or resailed, a breach of a rule by a boat in the original race shall not result in her being penalised in the restarted or resailed race. When a race is restarted, this is the case regardless of the reason for which the race was restarted. When a race is resailed, this is the case, regardless of the whether the original race was abandoned before or after the starting signal.

When rule 36 applies, the fact that in most instances a boat cannot be penalised over an incident occurring between the preparatory signal and the recall signal does not preclude the holding of a protest hearing. This is most likely to happen after an incident resulting in damage. 'While rule 36 may remove the possibility of a boat being penalised because the race was recalled, a boat is entitled to have her protest heard, since it is only when it is found as a fact in a protest that the other boat broke a rule of Part 2 that redress under rule 62.1(b) can be sought[1].' Even if redress is not sought, the finding of facts will assist an insurance claim[2].

Part 4 - Other Requirements When Racing

Preamble   *Part 4 rules apply only to boats **racing**.*

Rule 40   **PERSONAL FLOTATION DEVICES**
When flag Y is displayed with one sound before or with the warning signal, competitors shall wear personal flotation devices, except briefly while changing or adjusting clothing or personal equipment. Wet suits and dry suits are not personal flotation devices.

This rule has to be activated no later than the warning signal, and cannot be made to apply in mid-race. The operative term is now a 'personal flotation device'. While that may have some minimum specification in legislation and regulations, the device is no longer required to be 'adequate' in this rule. Instead, it is rule 1.2 that puts the responsibility for the adequacy of the personal flotation device on the competitor, depending on the conditions[3].

The rule is a very general one. Class rules (including regulations of the type specified for offshore racing) can be more specific.

The exception in respect of briefly changing or adjusting clothing or personal equipment would appear, euphemistically, to include needing to remove the device in order to take a toilet break[4].

Sailing instructions frequently disapply rule 40, and require instead the wearing of a personal flotation device at all times when racing - or even just 'at all times', which can have the possibly unintended consequence of a boat being disqualified for removing the flotation device more than 'briefly' between races, as in RYA 1969/1:

Assumed Facts
Club byelaws state that personal flotation devices must be worn at all times when afloat. This is repeated in the sailing instructions. A helmsman enters for a race and goes for a short trial spin without wearing a personal flotation device; he puts it on just before the preparatory signal. His boat is protested, and, despite his maintaining that sailing instructions did not become operative until this signal, she is disqualified.

---

[1] RYA 1993/5
[2] The same principle applies when, after there is contact resulting in damage, another boat retires. That retirement is not in itself an admission of fault, in the UK at least, because the RYA prescription to rule 68 says so. The retirement will preclude penalisation for breaking a rule of Part 2, but does not preclude a protest hearing to find what happened and which boat was responsible. The fact the protest is clearly being held for insurance purposes only is no reason for not hearing it, indeed it is a valuable service to competitors.
[3] The RYA prescription to this rule says that 'When a rule requires a personal flotation device to be worn, the device shall comply with the specifications for the personal flotation devices that the boat is required to carry. If more than one specification applies, the personal flotation device worn shall comply with the highest of them.' So in a UK event the crew of a boat required by class rules or regulations to carry devices of, say, 150N buoyancy cannot, when flag Y is displayed, leave them in the locker and put on less cumbersome 50N devices.
[4] Itself a euphemism!

Question

Is her disqualification valid?

Answer

Yes. When a competitor breaks a sailing instruction that is correctly drafted so as to apply when a boat is not racing, that competitor's boat is to be disqualified, under rule 64.1dc), from the race sailed nearest in time to that of the incident[1].

To avoid 'technical knock-outs' of this sort, sailing instructions sometimes restrict the right to protest over flotation matters to the race committee and the protest committee, and/or allow the protest committee to apply a penalty less than disqualification (as is often also done for tallying failures and trashing)[2].

Rule 41

OUTSIDE HELP

A boat shall not receive help from any outside source, except

(a)   help for an ill or injured crew member;

(b)   after a collision, help from the crew of the other boat to get clear;

(c)   help in the form of information freely available to all boats;

(d)   unsolicited information from a disinterested source, which may be another boat in the same race.

Boats should compete using only individual effort, except in team racing. Receiving information or instructions from a coach or parent while racing can break rule 2 as well as rule 41, and could lead to a rule 69 hearing, even if the recipient might find it difficult not to benefit from them.

Just because rule 1.1 requires a boat or competitor to give help to any person or vessel in danger, that does not mean that receiving that help is free of consequences. If none of clauses (a) to (d) applies, as for instance when an uninjured crew member in the water is picked up by a safety vessel, the crew's boat breaks rule 41. Knowledge of this might result in the crew member refusing help, which militates against safe race management. By the time the crew member has deteriorated to a condition ranking as 'ill or injured', the fact that help can now be received without penalty may have become academic[3]. Rule 41 can be changed in sailing instructions, as can be the penalty, to suit local race management standards, and race committees should consider whether they should do so[4].

Help under rule 41(a) for an ill or injured crew member can be both actual treatment and advice give by radio, telephone or email.

After a collision, it is only help 'from the crew' of the other boat that is permitted by rule 41(b). This is in harmony with rule 42.3(g), which says that the other boat is not allowed to use her engine to separate the boats, unless (under rule 42.3(f)) a person or vessel is in danger. If safety requires the use of an engine to separate boats, each will be helping the other. The one that uses her engine will be complying with rule 1.1 in rendering that help, and will not break the propulsion rule because of rule 42.3(f). The other boat has received help, which does not directly seem to be 'from the crew' of the powered boat, and so appears to break rule 41, although she may be able to argue a case for exoneration as being compelled to break the rule if she had no choice in the matter of the use of an engine by the other boat.

Rule 41(b) refers to help from the crew of the other 'boat', rather than 'vessel', and the term 'boat' is usually reserved for boats that are racing. So it may be that outside help in getting disentangled by the crews of a spectator boat, a moored boat or the committee boat breaks rule 41.

---

[1] I think the outcome is the same even if there is no reference to the wearing of personal flotation devices in the club byelaws – the sailing instructions are sufficient, and it is not an issue that will determine whether a competitor will decide to enter, see J1.2(1), so it does not need to appear in the notice of race.

[2] A sailing instruction can be modelled on L16.6.

[3] Perhaps there is 'Catch-22' paradox here. Any person in the water who refuses help is irrational and therefore 'ill' and so is entitled to receive help under rule 41(a).

[4] See the guidance note on Outside Help on the RYA website. It is important to note that rule 41 no longer permits the general receiving of help as required by rule 1.1 (when a person or vessel may be danger), so now there must be help in respect of illness, injury or a collision if it is not to break rule 41.

In this 'information age', the possibilities for receiving information, and therefore breaking rules 41(c) and (d), have rapidly increased. RYA 2005/5 addresses this

> **Question**
>
> Is weather information sent to a mobile phone, to a receiver or to a computer by a weather bureau as part of a dedicated subscription service 'freely available' for the purposes of rule 41(d)? Is the cost of that service relevant? Is information available to all on the internet 'freely available', given that a subscription has to be paid to an internet service provider?
>
> **Answer**
>
> Once a subscription has been paid to a generally available and non-specialised communications service, such as an Internet Service Provider, a telephone service (mobile or terrestrial) or a television licence, any information that is then available to the general public, or is available to all competitors in the event, and that can be accessed readily and at no further cost (other than the cost, if applicable, of a standard rate call or connection) is 'freely available'. The notice of race and sailing instructions may change rule 41 to widen or narrow this.

US 93 offers further clarification. Weather information from public radio stations is "freely available", and the fact that there may be a software or hardware cost to get generally available internet information is not relevant.

> However, if the access to the information, including any equipment or software, is provided for a fee by the same person or entity that provides the information, then the information has a monetary cost and is not "freely available". Examples are satellite radio companies and ocean routing services when they have charged the recipient of the information a subscription fee for accessing their channels or files.

Oceanic races usually override rule 41 to state explicitly what communications resources and outside assistance such as routing are allowed for the event, and what are not.

Inter-boat communication is another matter. When a boat is not in danger, advice that she seeks and receives that will help her to complete the race is outside help, even if it is sought and received on a public radio channel. So in ISAF 100 three large boats were to round a mark near coastal rocks and then sail into a 6-knot current. The wind was light. *Iris* radioed to *Daffodil*, whose skipper was more familiar with the area, asking whether it was safe to anchor in the vicinity of the mark. *Daffodil* replied that it was not safe to anchor. *Vindictive* protested both boats under rule 41, for discussing what tactics were to be used for rounding the mark and sailing the next leg. The protest committee dismissed the protest against *Daffodil*, as breaking no rule, but disqualified *Iris* for receiving outside help. It noted that she was not in danger, as she could have sailed or motored away from the mark in perfect safety at any time, and that the only reasons for anchoring at the mark were to overcome the adverse current and to win the race. *Iris* appealed, on the grounds that she did not believe she had received help, that advice given via a public radio frequency was not outside help, and that a national authority should not condone disqualification for receiving safety information. Her appeal was dismissed

> *Iris* asked for help for tactical racing reasons and received it. It is irrelevant that *Iris*'s question and the information she received were broadcast on a public radio channel. The help *Iris* received did not come within the scope of the exceptions to rule 41, especially not rule 41(d) since she solicited the information. Therefore *Iris* broke rule 41. Even if she needed help because she was in danger, the receipt of such help would have been a breach of rule 41.

Unsolicited information may be help when it comes from an interested source. 'It is obviously impossible to avoid hearing advice given, and a competitor may be fortunate enough, without risk of penalisation under rule 41, to learn from the comments of spectators that his current intentions are not in his best interests. However, when specific advice is given by any person with an interest in the matter, and acted on so as to improve a boat's finishing position, that is information from an interested source, albeit unsolicited, which is clearly outside help that breaks rule 41[1].' Likewise, CYA 76 distinguishes between information sought, as in ISAF 100, and information not sought but gleaned in a general radio conversation: the former breaks rule 41; the latter may not, but the borderline is easy to transgress, as where *Daffodil*, a boat not racing, initiated a general radio conversation with *Iris*, which was racing, and, unasked, described the weather conditions in the area towards which *Iris* was sailing. This was overheard by fellow competitor *Vindictive*, which protested *Daffodil*.

---

[1] RYA 1993/6

Even radio transmissions freely available to all boats are quite capable of breaking rule 41 when advice is given in response to a specific question. Boats engaged in radio conversations while racing do so at their own peril in terms of rule 41. *Daffodil* would have been well advised to tell *Iris* immediately that she could not talk to her during the race.

I believe that the help that can be given and received can be summarised as follows:

TYPE OF HELP	MUST IT BE GIVEN?	DOES RECEIVING HELP OR ACTING ON INFORMATION BREAK RULE 41?
Recovering a competitor from water when separated from boat, when possibly in danger	Yes, for a boat (rule 1.1). A legal rather than a racing rules obligation for the race committee	No, if the competitor is ill or injured (rule 41(a)) Otherwise, Yes.
Recovering a competitor from water when separated from boat, when in no danger	No	Yes, if not ill or injured
Returning a competitor to a boat	No, unless the boat may be in danger without its crew	Yes
Helping to right a capsized boat the competitor cannot right	A moral rather than a racing rules obligation	Yes
Medical information requested by radio or phone		No (rule 41(a))
Assistance from other boat to get clear after a collision		No if the help is manual, from the crew of the other boat (rule 41(b)). But if the other boat uses her engine, it can break rule 42.
Public radio and freely available internet information		No (rule 41(c))
Useful information requested by hail, email, radio or phone	It would be wise for the person being asked to refuse to reply	Yes
Unsought information gleaned or overheard by voice or in email, radio or phone messages		No (rule 41(d))
Flag or radio message from race officer that boat is on the course side of the starting line	Only if the sailing instructions say so	No (rule 41(d))
Telling a boat she has sailed the wrong course	It is inadvisable for the race committee, however well meaning, to do this.	No, if from the race committee or a spectator, even if acted on (rule 41(d). Yes, if from the likes of a coach or parent and acted on. Possibly yes if hailed by another boat in the race in contemplation of a protest and then acted on. Possibly not if intended to be friendly assistance.

TYPE OF HELP	MUST IT BE GIVEN?	DOES RECEIVING HELP OR ACTING ON INFORMATION BREAK RULE 41?
Hail or radio to a boat that she is OCS	No, unless the sailing instructions say the race committee must do so or try to do so.	No, if from the race committee (rule 41(d)) Yes, if from the likes of a coach or parent and acted on. Possibly yes if from another boat in the race in contemplation of a protest and then acted on. Possibly not if intended to be friendly assistance.
Not giving a finishing signal because the boat has 'hook finished' and so not yet finished.	No	No (rule 41(d))
Race committee radio messages warning the fleet of a course change or shortening	No, unless the sailing instructions say the race committee must do so or try to do so.	No (rule 41(d))

PROPULSION

Basic Rule

Except when permitted in rule 42.3 or 45, a boat shall compete by using only the wind and water to increase, maintain or decrease her speed. Her crew may adjust the trim of sails and hull, and perform other acts of seamanship, but shall not otherwise move their bodies to propel the boat.

Prohibited Actions

Without limiting the application of rule 42.1, these actions are prohibited:

(a) pumping: repeated fanning of any sail either by pulling in and releasing the sail or by vertical or athwartships body movement;

(b) rocking: repeated rolling of the boat, induced by

(1) body movement,

(2) repeated adjustment of the sails or centreboard, or

(3) steering;

(c) ooching: sudden forward body movement, stopped abruptly;

(d) sculling: repeated movement of the helm that is either forceful or that propels the boat forward or prevents her from moving astern;

(e) repeated tacks or gybes unrelated to changes in the wind or to tactical considerations.

42.3

Exceptions

(a) A boat may be rolled to facilitate steering.

(b) A boat's crew may move their bodies to exaggerate the rolling that facilitates steering the boat through a tack or a gybe, provided that, just after the tack or gybe is completed, the boat's speed is not greater than it would have been in the absence of the tack or gybe.

(c) Except on a beat to windward, when surfing (rapidly accelerating down the leeward side of a wave) or planing is possible, the boat's crew may pull the sheet and the guy controlling any sail in order to initiate surfing or planing, but only once for each wave or gust of wind.

(d) When a boat is above a close-hauled course and either stationary or moving slowly, she may scull to turn to a close-hauled course.

(e) A boat may reduce speed by repeatedly moving her helm.

(f) Any means of propulsion may be used to help a person or another vessel in danger.

(g) To get clear after grounding or colliding with another boat or object, a boat may use force applied by the crew of either boat and any equipment other than a propulsion engine.

(h) Sailing instructions may, in stated circumstances, permit propulsion using an engine or any other method, provided the boat does not gain a significant advantage in the race.

Note: Interpretations of rule 42 are available at the ISAF website (www.sailing.org) or by mail upon request.

The detailed interpretations of this rule as applicable to dinghies and smaller keelboats, and policed afloat by the protest committee, are issued by ISAF, in both written and video form, and outside the scope of this book. The cases tell us that using a paddle after finishing but before clearing the finishing line and finishing marks breaks rule 42, as the rule applies while a boat is racing, as defined[1]. A boat's momentum gained from the use her engine before her preparatory signal does not break rule 42 if it continues to drive her after that signal, as long as the engine was switched off at the signal[2]. Running an engine while racing, not for battery charging and with no propeller shaft brake fitted, was deemed to break rule 42 when the protest committee was not satisfied that the propeller shaft was not turning[3]. An ISAF case saying that recovering an anchor so as to gather way over the ground breaks the rule has been withdrawn for review, since a case can be made out for the resulting motion to be the near-inevitable result of an act of seamanship.

Use of an engine may be necessary to keep clear and to avoid contact, but it will still break rule 42[4]. Deceleration by putting a foot in the water is generally thought not to be a permissible act of seamanship - but using double rudders in opposition to each other does not break the rule[5]. 'Hitching a ride' on the bow wave and wake of a passing motor vessel, including rudder actions necessary to establish and maintain the ride, is legal[6].

When a crew member gets out of a small boat that has gone aground to try and refloat her, this will normally be an act of seamanship as envisaged in rule 42.1. After going aground, rule 42.3(g) permits the crew to use any available means that exist within the boat, apart from an engine, to get clear[7].

---

[1] RYA 1962/43
[2] ISAF 69
[3] CYA 68: rather harsh, in my opinion
[4] RYA 1988/7.
[5] US 25
[6] ISAF 8
[7] RYA 2007/2

Rule 42 can be changed by class rules, but not by a sailing instruction[1], except now in one respect. Rule 42.3(h) allows the use of an 'engine or any other method[2]', but only in 'stated circumstances' in the sailing instructions. Those circumstances could include permitting the use of an engine:

- when needing to seek shelter or to make repairs
- to cross a shipping channel or traffic separation zone directly or quickly when navigation laws require
- to get to a starting area using the engine after the preparatory signal
- to keep clear of a dangerous or prohibited area

However, there is a catch in this new relaxation of rule 42.1, namely the proviso that the boat must not gain a significant advantage in the race. It may be that ISAF had in mind that a boat was not to take advantage of such a sailing instruction to motor towards the next mark after the need for using the engine had ended, but the rule appears to have been drawn more widely: a boat that makes use of the relaxation is likely to gain a significant advantage over a boat in the same situation that does not use her motor. The RYA, in a guidance note, advises that the sailing instruction might also say that the penalty for gaining a significant advantage could be a discretionary time or place penalty aimed (where the advantage was unavoidable) at equalising matters compared with a boat in the same situation that did not use an engine.

The RYA further believes that rule 42.3(h) must be read together with rule 42.3(g), with the result that using an engine to get clear when aground can never be permitted by a sailing instruction. Even if that is not true, the use of an engine in these circumstances will be the clearest possible case of gaining an advantage, if not using an engine will condemn the boat to a much longer delay before being able to float clear.

Knowingly using illegal means of propulsion will break not only rule 42 but also rule 2, and may result in a rule 69 hearing.

Rule 43 — COMPETITOR CLOTHING AND EQUIPMENT

43.1

(a) Competitors shall not wear or carry clothing or equipment for the purpose of increasing their weight.

(b) Furthermore, a competitor's clothing and equipment shall not weigh more than 8 kilograms, excluding a hiking or trapeze harness and clothing (including footwear) worn only below the knee. Class rules or sailing instructions may specify a lower weight or a higher weight up to 10 kilograms. Class rules may include footwear and other clothing worn below the knee within that weight. A hiking or trapeze harness shall have positive buoyancy and shall not weigh more than 2 kilograms, except that class rules may specify a higher weight up to 4 kilograms. Weights shall be determined as required by Appendix H.

(c) When an equipment inspector or a measurer in charge of weighing clothing and equipment believes a competitor may have broken rule 43.1(a) or 43.1(b) he shall report the matter in writing to the race committee.

43.2 Rule 43.1(b) does not apply to boats required to be equipped with lifelines.

This rule largely became a backwater when the rule was changed to disallow the use of water jackets to increase the upper body mass to assist hiking, and the post-race weighing of clothing and equipment of a sample of competitors, once a standard feature of major dinghy events, is now only occasionally done. The rule gives class rules some limited scope for variation.

In addition, a competitor is not allowed to wear or otherwise attach to the person a beverage container (typically known as a 'camel-back') while racing. An exception, with restrictions, is made for windsurfing[3].

[1] Rule 86.1
[2] So why does not just say 'by any method'?
[3] ISAF 89, B2.1(b)

Rule 43.2 says that there are no detailed clothing weight restrictions on boats required to be equipped with lifelines (the wires or ropes running on stanchions along the edge of the deck). However, the wearing or carrying of clothing and equipment for the purpose of increasing crew weight is always prohibited, via rule 43.1(a), and rule 49 further limits weight exploitation in larger boats.

PENALTIES AT THE TIME OF AN INCIDENT

Taking a Penalty

A boat may take a Two-Turns Penalty when she may have broken a rule of Part 2 while *racing* or a One-Turn Penalty when she may have broken rule 31. Sailing instructions may specify the use of the Scoring Penalty or some other penalty. However,

(a) when a boat may have broken a rule of Part 2 and rule 31 in the same incident she need not take the penalty for breaking rule 31;

(b) if the boat caused injury or serious damage or gained a significant advantage in the race or series by her breach her penalty shall be to retire.

One-Turn and Two-Turns Penalties

After getting well clear of other boats as soon after the incident as possible, a boat takes a One-Turn or Two-Turns Penalty by promptly making the required number of turns in the same direction, each turn including one tack and one gybe. When a boat takes the penalty at or near the finishing line, she shall sail completely to the course side of the line before *finishing*.

Scoring Penalty

(a) A boat takes a Scoring Penalty by displaying a yellow flag at the first reasonable opportunity after the incident.

(b) When a boat has taken a Scoring Penalty, she shall keep the yellow flag displayed until *finishing* and call the race committee's attention to it at the finishing line. At that time she shall also inform the race committee of the identity of the other boat involved in the incident. If this is impracticable, she shall do so at the first reasonable opportunity and within the time limit for *protests*.

(c) The race score for a boat that takes a Scoring Penalty shall be the score she would have received without that penalty, made worse by the number of places stated in the sailing instructions. However, she shall not be scored worse than Did Not Finish. When the sailing instructions do not state the number of places, the number shall be the whole number (rounding 0.5 upward) nearest to 20% of the number of boats entered. The scores of other boats shall not be changed; therefore, two boats may receive the same score.

The penalties that can be taken at the time of an incident are now all grouped together in this rule. A turn(s) penalty is an insurance policy against losing a protest over the incident concerned. Taking a turn(s) penalty is not an admission of fault, in the UK at least[1]. It is something a boat 'may' take when she 'may' have broken a rule.

---

[1] RYA prescription no. 2 to rule 68

So if one boat thinks that another boat has failed to take a penalty as soon as possible after the incident, her protest is not under rule 44[1]. Instead, the protest must relate to the incident for which she was taking the penalty, namely a breach of a specified rule of Part 2[2] or of rule 31[3]. If the protest committee dismisses the protest, finding that port did keep clear of starboard, etc, or that the mark was not touched, then the fact the penalty was not properly taken is irrelevant[4]. The reasonable time for notifying a protest for a rule of Part 2 or of rule 31 begins at the time of the incident. US 46's analysis is interesting, in a case where *Iris* displayed a protest flag five minutes after a racing incident, *Daffodil* took a two-turns penalty 10 minutes later, and *Iris* protested her for not taking her penalty as soon as possible.

> The protest committee was obligated to decide whether *Iris*'s protest was valid before considering its content [see rule 63.5 (Hearings: Validity of the Protest or Request for Redress)]. If the protested incident had been the right-of-way incident, the protest would have been invalid because Iris did not display her protest flag until five minutes after the incident. This was not the "first reasonable opportunity" as required by rule 61.1(a).

> However, *Iris*'s protest of *Daffodil*'s failure to take a proper and timely Two-Turns Penalty met the requirements of rule 61.1(a), since the incident referred to under rule 61.2(b) was *Daffodil*'s failure to take a Two-Turns Penalty when required and *Iris* complied with rule 61.1(a) at that time. *Iris*'s protest was therefore valid.

> However, *Daffodil*'s failure to take a proper and timely Two-Turns Penalty broke no rule. It meant only that she failed to take a penalty, but her failure to take a penalty had no bearing on the protested incident. Since the right-of-way incident was not the incident described in *Iris*'s protest, *Daffodil* could not be penalised for that incident.

Taking a penalty does not mean that the incident cannot be the subject of a protest hearing. Indeed, as above, the protestor's intention may be to prove that the turn(s) did not exonerate the incident, which may be for one or more of a number of reasons, namely that the boat taking the penalty -
- did not get clear of other boats before starting a turn
- did get clear, but not as soon after the incident as possible. Getting clear may take longer than the actual taking of the penalty, particularly for a starting line incident around the time of the starting signal, and positive action is needed, not just waiting until the boats separate after a mark or after starting. Nor is a boat entitled to thinking time after the incident before deciding to take a penalty[5].
- did not keep clear while taking a penalty turn, as required by rule 21.2
- did not take the second of two turns promptly after the first turn
- did not take a second turn in the same direction as the first turn
- took only one turn when two were required
- both touched a mark and broke a rule of part 2, but took only a single turn[6]
- caused injury or serious damage or gained a significant advantage in the race or series: facts related to a request for redress and/or an insurance claim may be sought
- purported to take a penalty for an infringement for which the penalty was not available, such as a breach of rule 2[7], or of rule 42, Propulsion.

In addition, there may be a protest when turns were validly taken for incident resulting in damage that was not serious but which affected the other boat's score in the race or series, resulting in a related request for redress based on the facts from the protest, even though no further penalisation is possible.

---

[1] RYA 1981/7. It is less clear that this principle applies to the taking of a scoring penalty under rule 44.3, where the 'mays' do not explicitly apply, and it is possible that failure to comply with the mechanics of the rule could be protested.
[2] Which however can include breaking the Part 2 rule 20.2 for not keeping clear of other boats while making a penalty turn
[3] *Ibid*: 'When a boat protests, believing that another boat has not taken a penalty as described in rule 44.2, she must establish first that the other boat broke a rule of Part 2 (or rule 31).'
[4] US 46
[5] 'Rule 44 does not provide time for a boat to deliberate whether she has broken a rule. If a boat decides too late that she has broken a rule, the penalty provided by rule 44.4 is not available to her': US 60. Some judges would nevertheless afford her a little thinking time.
[6] The appropriate penalty for an incident involving both infringements is two turns, not three – see rule 44.1(a)
[7] See rule 64.1(b)

'Damage' and 'injury' are considered under rule 14. If there is injury to a person, it will preclude the taking of a two-turns penalty (or a scoring penalty, if available), including by a right-of-way boat that broke rule 14 resulting in contact causing injury. If there is damage, a two-turns penalty is available, including for breaking rule 14, even though rule 14 talks of penalisation being possible for the right-of-way boat in the event of contact resulting in damage. However, rule 44.1 precludes the availability of a two-turns penalty when the damage is serious. What is 'serious'? There is no fixed test. First, there must be damage, as discussed, and it is for the protest committee to decide whether it is serious or not.

In RYA 2001/3, there was a pre-start collision between keelboats *Iris* and *Daffodil*, in respect of which *Daffodil* came off the worse with an exposed core and damaged bulkhead, and did two turns. *Iris* protested, and *Daffodil* was disqualified for breaking a right-of-way rule, causing serious damage and not retiring. The cost of repairs to both boats was substantial, despite which both boats had continued in that race and raced again that day. *Daffodil* appealed on the grounds that the cost of repairs alone did not constitute serious damage if a boat was able to continue racing. Having decided, as previously noted under rule 14, that serious damage under rule 44 includes damage a boat causes to herself, and that *Daffodil* had failed the 'prudent owner' test, the RYA upheld the protest committee's conclusion that the damage was serious, based on both the extent and type of the damage and the cost of repairs to both boats, both in absolute terms and relative to the value of the boats. 'The fact that one or both boats can continue racing does not preclude damage from being serious.' In a later unpublished case the RYA decided that a hole in a boat's side that was expensive to repair relative to the value of the boat was serious damage, even though, in waiting for the result of the appeal for insurance purposes, the boat had campaigned for several months with the hole taped over.

The question of significant advantage is less clear-cut. What is 'significant'? The word also appears in the context of a **dis**advantage when redress is asked for[1], and there most protest committees treat the significance as being self-fulfilling – if a boat feels the need to ask for redress, even if only one place has been lost, that must be significant to her. But it is unlikely that the reverse is always true for an advantage, although the difference between first and second place would probably be significant. The cases do not help, nor do they consider what is an advantage.

Barging though a raft of boats at the leeward mark and getting through from back to front, possibly touching the mark in the process, would clearly be a significant advantage that would negate the validity of a subsequent two-turns penalty, resulting in disqualification in a protest for any breach of a Part 2 rule or of rule 31.

When there is an incident, the act of taking a penalty and then protesting the other boat 'from a position of immunity from penalisation' is not in itself the gaining of an advantage that invalidates the penalty that was taken[2]. Nor is doing the minimum required to carry out a one-turn penalty, even if it does not even delay the boat[3].

The rule does not tell us over whom the advantage is to be measured, nor over what length of time. Suppose that *Iris* does not give room as required to *Daffodil* at a mark. The rest of the fleet is a little way astern, near enough for *Daffodil*, which misses out the mark, to have to come round again and lose places in the process. *Iris* however can take her turns without either gaining or losing places relative to the rest of the fleet. Presumably that invalidates any turns by *Iris*. Or does it? Suppose *Daffodil* is nevertheless able to catch and pass *Iris*. It is unclear whether the advantage need be only temporary - or does it have to be permanent to invalidate the penalty taken?

Is the situation different when, in the above example, *Daffodil* loses places, but so does *Iris* as a result of taking her penalty turns, so that *Daffodil* and *Iris* had approached the mark in 5th and 6th places respectively, but after the incident were 16th and 15th respectively until the finish. *Daffodil* has lost an advantage – but has *Iris* gained one? Is the advantage to be measured before the penalty is taken, or will the penalty be invalid only when, after taking it, the offender is still in an advantageous position? If so, can the offender take the turns sufficiently slowly to negate the advantage, rather like a F1 racing driver escaping a penalty by yielding a place wrongfully gained by cutting a corner?

---

[1] Rule 62.1
[2] RYA 1986/7
[3] ISAF 108, see below

And then what if, as a result of *Iris* not keeping clear of *Daffodil*, *Daffodil* capsizes while taking avoiding action, without contact, nor incurring injury or serious damage, and loses places? Probably, a significant advantage has been gained – but suppose the capsize was more because of poor boat-handling by *Daffodil*?

If it is difficult to apply the 'significant advantage' rule in the race itself, its application to series results, as contemplated by the rule, is no clearer. The lack of appeal cases indicates that this is not an issue that arises in practice, presumably because any advantage initially gained is usually negated by the time taken to turn.

It is clear that, when injury, serious damage or a significant advantage precludes taking a turn(s) penalty, the requirement is to retire. It will often happen that a boat will stop racing, not in compliance with the requirement to do so, but simply because damage to herself precludes her continuing to race. A previously discussed, the Basic Principle, Sportsmanship and the Rules, says retirement is one way to take a penalty, and ISAF 99 tells us that, in incidents involving injury or serious damage, 'When a boat retires as required by rule 44.1, whether out of choice or necessity, she cannot be penalised further'.

The incident will often still come to a protest hearing, if only for facts to be found for insurance purposes, but the RYA's experience from appeal cases is that the message of ISAF 99 is not fully appreciated by protest committees, which will attempt to 'upgrade' the DNF score to DSQ (despite the points value being the same)[1]. On appeal, such DSQs revert to DNF.

My experience when explaining this to parties in a hearing is that it is often either not easily understood, or, if it is understood, that it is seen as the retiring boat 'getting off the hook' in some way. My response is that the protest decision will state the facts, and identify which boat broke which rule(s), which should be sufficient for an insurance company to apportion blame. Once again, a boat that takes a penalty, including by retiring, does not acknowledge a fault, and the fact of her retiring does not preclude her protesting another boat in the same incident, even if she has acknowledged breaking a rule[2].

Although the turns may still be colloquially referred to as '360s' and '720s', rule 44.2 no longer specifies the number of degrees through which a boat must pass, only that that each turn must include a tack and gybe, and that the whole penalty must be taken in the same direction of rotation. The degrees were deleted because it was too difficult to monitor, but the result, as shown in ISAF 108 as concerns a single turn, may not have been what was expected.

The case explains that:

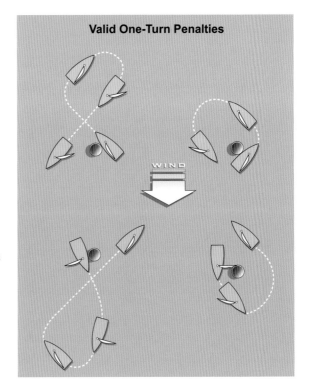

Valid One-Turn Penalties

> In each illustrated situation she takes a One-Turn Penalty that complies with rule 44.2, provided that
> (a) as soon as possible, and before beginning her penalty turn, she sails well clear of any other boats and remains clear of them while making her turn;
> (b) when she begins her penalty turn she is no longer touching the mark; and
> (c) she makes her penalty turn promptly after she is clear of other boats.

---

[1] The standard protest form does not assist, in that the protest has to be upheld, but the invitation to disqualify has then to be declined.
[2] US 56

Rule 44.2 does not require a boat that takes a One-Turn Penalty to complete a full 360° turn, or a turn of any particular number of degrees, and it does not prohibit taking the penalty while making another manoeuvre, such as rounding the mark.

All four illustrated turns comply with rule 28.1. Provided that the string representing the boat's track when drawn taut lies on the mark's required side, the boat would comply with rule 28.1 even if (as not illustrated) a penalty turn resulted in the boat making an extra 360° turn around the mark[1].

The following observations can be added:

- Although the case speaks of first getting clear, in practice, to take the penalty in one of the ways shown, a boat will have to have been already well clear of others when she touches the mark, and far enough away from other for her to remain well clear while turning.
- If she is able to take a penalty while other boats are nearby, doing little or nothing more than she would have done had she not touched the mark, she and other boats nearby must remember that until both the tack and gybe have been completed, she is temporarily a keep-clear boat with respect to boats not taking a penalty. If they had been required to keep clear of her until she started to take the penalty, they have gained right-of-way because of her actions, and so they do not have to give her initial room under rule 15. However, she, on completing her tack-and-gybe turn, will have to give them initial room to keep clear under rule 15 if at that point she regains right of way. While she is taking her penalty, they will break rule 23.2 if, while not sailing their proper courses, they interfere with her
- These options are additional to the full turn that has always qualified as the taking of the penalty, and which is how it is more likely to be taken when other boats are near.
- It is possible to take a penalty without realising it: I have observed a single-handed boat make the lightest of contacts with a leeward mark as in the bottom right example, and almost certainly unknown to the helmsman. She then gybed and tacked as part of her normal mark rounding. Had the incident come to protest, I believe she could not have been penalised for touching the mark, since she had unwittingly taken a penalty for an infringement she was unaware of committing.
- If a two-turns penalty is taken, only one of them can be taken as shown, and the other will have to be a conventional full turn.

It may also be that a one or two-turns penalty taken at the finishing line will validly include the looping of a finishing mark.

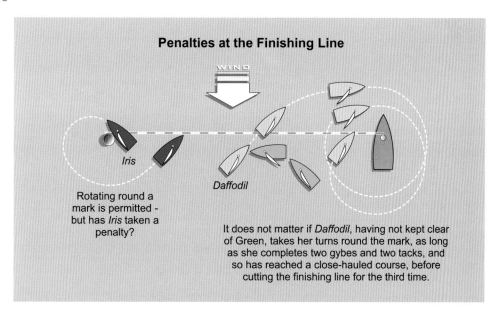

Penalties at the Finishing Line

WIND

Iris

Daffodil

Rotating round a mark is permitted - but has *Iris* taken a penalty?

It does not matter if *Daffodil*, having not kept clear of Green, takes her turns round the mark, as long as she completes two gybes and two tacks, and so has reached a close-hauled course, before cutting the finishing line for the third time.

---

[1] As long as the rule 28.1 string is on the required side of the mark, it does not matter that it is there twice. This applies to a starting mark and a finishing mark as well as to a course mark. Many years ago, the rule 31 penalty required the turn to be taken as a loop around the mark. That was dangerous, and so it became optional rather than compulsory – but I still come across people who do not realise that the rule has changed. If a boat is looping a mark, it is unclear which leg she is on at any particular moment for the purposes of rule 23.2.

In all these cases, the tacking and gybing must be complete before the boat recrosses the finishing line. The race committee will have recorded her as finished at the first crossing, will have noted any turns, and will take her last crossing as her actual finish. If they believe that *Iris* touched the mark and has gybed but did not tack before crossing the finishing line, then they must time her at her first crossing and protest her under rule 31, if they want to make an issue of it[1].

The scoring penalty can be used when the type of boats or the congestion of the waters being raced on make a turn penalty either over-punitive or dangerous. It must be specified in the sailing instructions as being available instead of turning. If it has not been made available, it is not something that a boat can elect to accept as an alternative to turning. Once a yellow flag has been shown, it cannot be revoked. The commonest application of the scoring penalty is its use to calculate a Z-flag penalty under rule 30.2, the mechanics of which are discussed under Appendix A, Scoring.

The fact that, having put up a yellow flag to take a scoring penalty, you cannot then change your mind is a reflection of the nature not only of the scoring penalty but also a turn(s) penalty – as stated at the start of the discussion of this rule, it is an insurance policy, and, as with your car and household insurance, the fact that you did not need to claim on it does not entitle you to a refund of your premium.

In US 86, the situation is posed of *Iris* which in the moment of finishing is (*Iris* believes) compelled to touch a finishing mark by *Daffodil* not giving room. *Iris* protests *Daffodil*, and also, as a precaution, takes a penalty turn, and then crosses the finishing line again. *Iris* wins her protest; *Daffodil* is disqualified under rule 18.2(a). Which of *Iris*'s crossing of the finishing line is to count as her finish? The answer was the second crossing:

> She did not finish until she started to cross the finishing line after taking the penalty…The protest committee cannot ignore or undo the penalty. Although rule 64.1(b) protects a boat from being penalised and provides for her exoneration (i.e., frees her from blame for breaking a rule), it does not provide for cancelling a penalty she has taken voluntarily or for compensating her for distance, time or places lost in taking the penalty.

 **Rule 45**

HAULING OUT; MAKING FAST; ANCHORING
A boat shall be afloat and off moorings at her preparatory signal. Thereafter, she shall not be hauled out or made fast except to bail out, reef sails or make repairs. She may anchor or the crew may stand on the bottom. She shall recover the anchor before continuing in the race unless she is unable to do so.

RYA 1962/4 says that when a boat that is afloat is being held by a person at or after the preparatory signal, the question of whether rule 45 has been broken depends on the reason for so doing and on whether that person is standing in or out of the water.

> If a person is standing in water about six inches deep on a concrete ramp, holding a boat which is afloat, this does not break rule 45. If the person is holding the boat as before, on the same ramp, but standing just out of the water, the boat is made fast, which, at and after the preparatory signal, rule 45 permits only for bailing out, reefing or repairs[2].

In the context of club racing, the requirement to be off moorings at the preparatory does not appear to be a very important one, and the rule could be disapplied in sailing instructions. But for major dinghy events, leading boats will usually be attached to their coach boats between races, and it would be unfair, in difficult conditions, if they were able to remain there longer, getting more rest and being in less danger of capsize or damage than a boat without that support.

---

[1] Team racing call K1 says suggests that the race committee should score the boat 'did not finish'. I believe that it should not be regarded as correct for fleet racing. The boat finished, as defined, the first time she cut the finishing line, since she did not, as a matter of fact, take a penalty so as to make the second crossing the applicable one. See further discussion under rule 28.
[2] If the person holding the boat after the preparatory signal is not one of the crew, this breaks rule 41, Outside Help.

 **PERSON IN CHARGE**

> A boat shall have on board a person in charge designated by the member or organization that entered the boat. See rule 75.

This rule rarely needs conscious compliance. It may apply by implication to a person on whom the sailing instructions impose responsibilities as the 'skipper[1]'. It is otherwise a procedural rule, to establish who is responsible when there is an issue or a protest under rule 78.1, concerning the maintenance of the boat to comply with her class rules and to be duly certified and rated; and who is to certify under rule 78.2 that a valid measurement, rating or insurance certificate that cannot be produced at entry and that it will be produced, on pain of disqualification from the whole event. Rule 46 creates only responsibilities, not rights. By requiring there to be person in charge while racing, this facilitates a link between not keeping a boat in class rules between events, and racing in such a condition. Most rules are not concerned with the identity of individuals, but rule 78 needs to know who might be summoned to a rule 69 hearing in a serious case. Rule 78.1 assumes that the owner will be a person in charge, but that there may be others.

Rule 46 says that the person in charge need not be the person who enters the boat, although in practice they will often be one and the same.

Cases on rule 46 pay more attention to what rule 46 does not say than to what it does say. In particular, the identity of the person steering the boat is irrelevant unless the class rules, notice of race or sailing instructions say otherwise[2]. In a single-handed boat, the issue is meaningless. In a dinghy, there is no reason why the helming cannot be shared by the persons on board. In larger keelboats, the helmsman or helmswoman is just one of the afterguard, it is a duty that is rotated in longer races, and the tactician and owner may have more influence on the conduct of the race. 'It is the boat that is entered in the race and, unless otherwise specifically provided in the class rules, notice of the race or sailing instructions…it is a matter for the owner or other person in charge of her to decide who steers her at any time, provided that rule 46 is not broken[3].'

RYA 1990/2 is to the same effect, and continues with a worked-out example.

Question

A boat belonging to A.B. was entered in a five race series. The sailing instructions said that 'points are attributed to the helmsman, not the boat'. The boat was entered with C.D. listed as helmsman on the entry form. C.D. sailed as helmsman and finished in three races. A.B. sailed as helmsman in two races and did not finish either race. How should this be scored? Was any rule broken?

Answer

No rule was broken at any time, since there is no racing rule that addresses itself to the identity of the person helming a boat. Nor was the sailing instruction broken. The only reasonable interpretation of the sailing instruction is that the points won by a boat in a race will be re-attributed to the helmsman of that boat, in that race. In a series, the winner will be the helmsman with the lowest (or best) attributed total points score. Awards will not be made to boats. So A.B. should score points for DNC in three races, and DNF in two races. C.D. should score finishing points in three races and DNC in two races.

So when a boat has, for example, been helmed by three different people during a series in which points are awarded to the helmsman, the results sheet should then show three different entries, each under the name of one of the people but with the same sail number. The score for any one race is attributed to the appropriate entry in the name of that person, sailing that boat, and the other two entries of boat plus helmsman are scored DNC for that race.

If it is intended to restrict this further, the notice of race and the sailing instructions need to say: 'A competitor shall be in charge of one boat only during the series' or 'Only one set of results per boat shall count for a series result.

---

[1] A term that is not used in the Racing Rules of Sailing
[2] It is common in events that require a high non-professional crew composition to prohibit a 'professional' from helming, either at all or at certain critical times.
[3] ISAF 40. It is not clear how rule 46 could be broken in any meaningful way in this context.

On the other hand, if the identity of the boat is not material, a relaxation clause could be inserted, such as: 'A competitor may accumulate the points he was awarded as a helmsman in the series, irrespective of the boat in which he raced' or: 'A competitor may accumulate the points he was awarded as a helmsman in that class of boat in the series.

When the notice of race or a sailing instruction refers to a 'helmsman', then if another person were allowed steer at any time during the race, there would be two helmsmen during that race. When awards are to a person, not a boat, and it is required to prohibit a temporary helmsman, sailing instructions might state in clarification: 'only one person shall steer the boat throughout the race'. Otherwise, if 'person in charge' is substituted for 'helmsman', others may steer without hindrance to the award of the points to the person in charge.

The identity of the person in change can change during a series – as indeed can other things. In RYA 1997/1, a Sigma 33 named *Serendip* raced in a number of offshore races, gaining points for the year's points prize. She was then chartered for the Fastnet Race in which she entered and sailed under the name *Securon*. Her points in that race were added to the points already won as *Serendip*.

Redcoat sought redress, asserting that *Securon* was in effect a separate boat, whose points should be tabulated separately from those for *Serendip*, and that combining them had boosted *Serendip / Securon*'s series score to the detriment of *Redcoat*'s. Redress was refused, and *Redcoat* appealed. The appeal was dismissed.

The boat's name had been changed, with the approval of the organizing authority, she was entered by a person who was not the owner, and sailed with a different crew. None of these are relevant in the Racing Rules of Sailing, nor were they prohibited by class rules, the notice of race or the sailing instructions.

Had there been any change to the ownership of the boat, to her certificate (which would have been invalidated by change of ownership, under class rules), to her sail number, hull, spars or gear, these would have been matters relevant to the Racing Rules of Sailing or to class rules. But there was none, and she was therefore the same boat.

When a race committee wishes to place limitations on changing the name of a boat or on who may be the person in charge of a boat, it must say so in the notice of race and sailing instructions.

LIMITATIONS ON EQUIPMENT AND CREW

A boat shall use only the equipment on board at her preparatory signal.

No person on board shall intentionally leave, except when ill or injured, or to help a person or vessel in danger, or to swim. A person leaving the boat by accident or to swim shall be back on board before the boat continues in the race.

FOG SIGNALS AND LIGHTS

When safety requires, a boat shall sound fog signals and show lights as required by the *International Regulations for Preventing Collisions at Sea* or applicable government rules.

CREW POSITION

Competitors shall use no device designed to position their bodies outboard, other than hiking straps and stiffeners worn under the thighs.

When lifelines are required by the class rules or the sailing instructions they shall be taut, and competitors shall not position any part of their torsos outside them, except briefly to perform a necessary task. On boats equipped with upper and lower lifelines of wire, a competitor sitting on the deck facing outboard with his waist inside the lower lifeline may have the upper part of his body outside the upper lifeline.

Rules 47 and 48 raise no significant issues. Rule 49.1 prohibits trapezes, but this rule is one that rule 86.1(c) allows class rules to change, which of course they will do for a class so equipped. Class rules are also allowed to change rule 49.2, although for safety reasons it does not seem desirable to be less stringent. ISAF 83 says that repeated sail trimming with a competitor's torso outside the lifelines is not permitted.

In a race for 24-foot sloops the wind is about 15 knots with gusts lasting about three seconds; a choppy sea is striking the boats on the beam. A's spinnaker trimmer is standing on the weather deck holding the sheet, which he is barely able to pull in. His posture changes to compensate for changes in the boat's trim and the load on the sheet. During some of the gusts he is seen to be leaning back with part of his torso outboard of the lifelines.

Questions
1. Is it correct to equate the words 'position any part' in rule 49.2 with a stationary position?
2. Is leaning against the load on a sheet 'to perform a necessary task', for example trimming the sheet?
3. Is the duration of a gust 'brief' in these circumstances?

Answers
It is clear from diagram 6 of Case 36 that the position adopted by A's crew member is capable of breaking rule 49.2. To 'position the torso' does not mean that the torso is stationary; it implies a deliberate act with some duration.

The phrase 'to perform a necessary task' contained within rule 49.2 means that the torso may be positioned outside the lifelines only to perform a task that could not reasonably be carried out from within the lifelines. The use of 'briefly' in the rule makes it clear that the torso must be moved inboard as soon as the task is completed.

The rule is clearly aimed at permitting an otherwise illegal action. Permission does not extend to normal sail trimming even when this would be more effectively achieved by positioning the torso outside the lifelines. Rule 49.2 is for the safety of the crew, and it is unavoidable that it inhibits the gains that might be obtained from optimizing weight distribution of the crew. The action of A's crew member in leaning outboard of the lifelines breaks rule 49.2.

This can be contrasted with US 72, where, in a boat required to be equipped with lifelines, the spinnaker guy was released from the pole 30 seconds from the mark, and a crew member held the guy by hand, leaning out over the lifelines so as maximise the distance between the hull and the guy until the spinnaker had to be lowered, less than 30 seconds later.

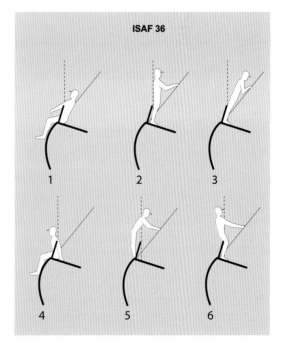

ISAF 36

Without a spinnaker pole, a spinnaker is less efficient and more unstable. As a boat prepares to round a leeward mark, removing the pole is one of the first necessary steps. From that time until the spinnaker is lowered, holding the guy by hand is a less effective but nonetheless useful means of controlling the spinnaker, which remains a 'necessary task' without the pole. The interval of time is normally a brief one, since there is generally no advantage in flying a spinnaker without a pole.

When the boat is not required to be equipped with lifelines, rule 49.2 is not relevant, and holding the sheet of a headsail or a spinnaker outboard is permitted[1].

ISAF 36 explains the second sentence of rule 49.2.

Positions, 1, 2 and 3 do not break the rule; positions 5 and 6 break it. On boats equipped with two wire lifelines, a crew member sitting on deck facing outboard with the waist inside the lower lifeline and the upper part of his body outside the upper lifeline, as shown in position 4, does not break the rule.

[1] ISAF 4

Rule 50 SETTING AND SHEETING SAILS

50.1 **Changing Sails**

When headsails or spinnakers are being changed, a replacing sail may be fully set and trimmed before the replaced sail is lowered. However, only one mainsail and, except when changing, only one spinnaker shall be carried set at a time.

50.2 **Spinnaker Poles, Whisker Poles**

Only one spinnaker pole or whisker pole shall be used at a time except when gybing. When in use, it shall be attached to the foremost mast.

50.3 **Use of Outriggers**

(a) No sail shall be sheeted over or through an outrigger, except as permitted in rule 50.3(b) or 50.3(c). An outrigger is any fitting or other device so placed that it could exert outward pressure on a sheet or sail at a point from which, with the boat upright, a vertical line would fall outside the hull or deck planking. For the purpose of this rule, bulwarks, rails and rubbing strakes are not part of the hull or deck planking and the following are not outriggers: a bowsprit used to secure the tack of a working sail, a bumkin used to sheet the boom of a working sail, or a boom of a boomed headsail that requires no adjustment when tacking.

(b) Any sail may be sheeted to or led above a boom that is regularly used for a working sail and is permanently attached to the mast from which the head of the working sail is set.

(c) A headsail may be sheeted or attached at its clew to a spinnaker pole or whisker pole, provided that a spinnaker is not set.

50.4 **Headsails**

The difference between a headsail and a spinnaker is that the mid-girth of a headsail, measured from the mid-points of its luff and leech, does not exceed 50% of the length of its foot, and no other intermediate girth exceeds a percentage similarly proportional to its distance from the head of the sail. A sail tacked down behind the foremost mast is not a headsail.

The cases focus on outriggers under rule 50.3. The following are not outriggers: a member of the crew or any body part thereof[1]; a jockey pole attached to a spinnaker guy, since a guy is not a sheet[2]; and a paddle used in light airs, without projecting outboard, to support the mid-section of a spinnaker[3].

The RYA has never liked rule 50.4, and prescribes to this rule with its own definition[4].

---

[1] ISAF 4, US 23
[2] ISAF 97
[3] US 31
[4] 'A spinnaker is defined as a sail set forward of the foremost mast with half width (measured as a spinnaker) greater than 75% of foot. Any other sail tacked down forward of the foremost mast is a headsail.'

Part 5 - Protests; Redress, Hearings; Misconduct and Appeals

With 90 main rules, the sport of sailing exceeds the number of rules and laws of cricket (42), rugby union football (28) and association football (17) combined. All those sports are umpired or refereed while the game is in progress, play can stop when the official requires, and there is only one game at a time. Perhaps sailing and golf (34 rules) have more in common, both being primarily self-policing. Golf however can often stop for a ruling, and the competition is effectively one competitor against himself or herself.

In mainstream sailboat fleet racing, the decision-making officials afloat are not involved in inter-boat issues, play cannot stop to resolve a dispute, and in any one race there are multiple rules-related encounters whenever boats meet. Since wrongs in non-umpired forms of sailing can be righted only retrospectively, it is not surprising that a quasi-judicial process of hearings, parties, witnesses and appeals has built up, and this is both one of the glories and one of the weaknesses of the sport. Part 5, which deals purely with the process of standard forms of dispute resolution, has 11 rules covering the same number of pages in the rule book.

The aspiration of sailing is to be self-policing, and penalties available at the time of an incident resolve most matters. When they do not, the speed at which a dispute can be resolved can vary. An umpired decision in match racing or team racing will be made in seconds, arbitration if available may take 15 minutes, a skilled protest committee or international jury will rarely take less than 45 minutes on average for a valid contested hearing, and an inexperienced protest committee might take twice as long. On top of that, an appeal will take months. And what actually happened may never be known for sure until suitable technology is developed[1].

Section A - Protests; Redress; Rule 69 Action

Protests, redress and actions under rule 69 are different things. A protest is defined as an allegation made under rule 61.2 that a boat has broken a rule. Redress is the possible outcome of hearing a claim (or consideration of the possibility) that a boat's score in a race or series has, through no fault of her own, been made worse by one of a list of reasons. A rule 69 action is a disciplinary hearing against a competitor for gross misconduct. Protest hearings concern boats, and while people talk of winning a protest, nothing is gained by the winner other than the satisfaction of the loss by the loser and a score possibly improved by a place. Redress hearings concern boats too, and normally the requester will not be worse off as a result. A competitor and a boat can each be penalised under a rule 69 action. A race committee may make mistakes, but it is not to be penalised for them: rather, compensation is given as redress for the effect of any mistake.

The outcome of a protest hearing can give rise to consideration of redress. But a redress hearing cannot mutate directly into a protest hearing, and a protest hearing cannot mutate directly into a rule 69 action.

Rule 60 goes on to state the options open to a boat, a race committee and a protest committee. An organizing authority (which is the parent of the race committee, see rule 89.2(b)) has no power to protest[2], nor does a class association[3].

---

[1] I write this on my return from an event where, in not particularly trying conditions, the helmsman and crew of a small keelboat being protested under rule 31, and with a good track record of taking penalties, were adamantly and undoubtedly honestly sure their boat had not touched a mark – yet three witnesses, including one from a boat not protesting over the incident, were equally sure that they had. We upheld the protest. The technology that would affordably allow boats to be tracked accurately enough for instant decisions on OCS and possibly even part 2 incidents and mark touching is only just over the 2009 horizon. One day soon, will a boat press a 'protest' button, for a decision to be returned from a judge on shore (or even totally automatically) in seconds?

[2] However, as with a competitor, nothing precludes it from asking a protest committee to consider redress in favour of a boat, or from lodging a report with a protest committee that may lead to the protest committee considering calling a rule 69.1 hearing.

[3] RYA 2001/12. In addition, class rules cannot vary protest procedures for the class, because no rule of Part 5 can be changed by class rules – see rule 86.1(c): as confirmed by ISAF 85, only a sailing instruction can change Part 5 requirements.

Rule 60 RIGHT TO PROTEST; RIGHT TO REQUEST REDRESS OR RULE 69 ACTION

60.1 A boat may

(a) protest another boat, but not for an alleged breach of a rule of Part 2 unless she was involved in or saw the incident; or

(b) request redress.

The corollary of rule 60.1(a) is that a boat can protest in respect of an incident in which she was not involved and did not see if it falls outside of Part 2. Here are some possible examples, where a boat gets to hear after a race about another boat that:

- did not compete in compliance with recognized principles of sportsmanship and fair play, under rule 2 in Part 1[1]
- touched a mark and did not take a penalty (rule 31 in Part 3)
- received outside help contrary to rule 41
- did not comply with her class rules.

The word 'or' at the end of rule 60.1(a) might better be read as an 'and' – a boat can both protest and request redress over the same incident[2], usually on the same protest form, ticking both the 'protest' and 'request for redress' boxes when both types of action are relevant.

Although there is no explicit equivalent of the race committee's rule 60.2(c), there is nothing to stop a boat making a report to the protest committee concerning facts that might lead the protest committee to call a hearing under rule 69.1, as it is entitled to do on the basis of 'a report received from any source'. Boats will sometime try to protest under rule 69.1, which they cannot do, but the protest form containing the alleged facts will be treated as a 'report' for this purpose. Nor is a competitor precluded, when having seen a good deed by another boat that slowed that boat's progress, from telling the race committee or protest committee, with a view to favourable redress for that boat being instituted by the protest committee.

A boat that breaks a rule while racing and is protested but continues to race may protest over a different incident, even though she is disqualified as a protestee before her own protest is heard[3]. She maintains all her rights while racing, pending a hearing of any protest by her or against her[4]. As has been seen under rule 44, a boat that has taken a penalty (including retirement) can protest over the same incident. Her penalty is not to be taken to be an admission of fault. Indeed, it is possible that she openly admits a fault, but protests because the other boat also broke a rule and was not compelled to do so by that fault.

60.2 A race committee may

(a) protest a boat, but not as a result of information arising from a request for redress or an invalid *protest*, or from a report from an *interested party* other than the representative of the boat herself;

(b) request redress for a boat; or

(c) report to the protest committee requesting action under rule 69.1(a).

However, when the race committee receives a report required by rule 43.1(c) or 78.3, it shall protest the boat.

---

[1] Since this is an allegation that could be attached to many breaches of Part 2 rules, it could be a way round rule 60.1(a)'s exclusion of reported breaches of a Part 2 rule, since the protest committee would have to find facts related to the incident which might lead it to dismiss the rule 2 allegation, but nevertheless find facts leading to a conclusion that a Part 2 rule was broken and penalise the offending boat because of rule 64.1(a). Note also, for the purposes of this rule and rule 62.1(b) that rule 2 is not a rule of Part 2 – there is sometimes confusion.

[2] RYA 1999/2

[3] ISAF 1

[4] US 1, CYA 11

Since the operative word is 'may', a race committee is normally under no obligation to protest a boat, even when it knows (or should know) the facts that would justify a protest – so a request for redress for failure by the race committee to enforce its sailing instructions will fail, as there is no improper act or omission[1]. So in ISAF 39, a protest over class rules (a simple issue of the number of crew on board) was found invalid for lack of a red flag. The protestors appealed, on the grounds that the race committee should have brought its own protest.

> To uphold this appeal would amount to a conclusion that a race committee ought to know the class rules of each class, and that it then has an obligation to enforce them when members of the class themselves fail to do so. No such obligation is placed on a race committee and, furthermore, [subject to two exceptions] rule 60.2(a) is clearly discretionary.

The exception is when a written report is received from the event's equipment inspector or measurer concerning excess personal clothing or equipment weights under rule 43.1(c) or, under rule 78.3, concerning compliance with class rules. There is no option other than to protest the boat, which means that in practice a written report under rule 78.3 is, for pre-event inspection, either for a serious deviation possibly showing an intention to cheat, or a last resort when more minor deviations are not corrected. A reported failure of inspection will be protested under rule 78.1.

Rule 60.2(a) lists three sources of information that are not permitted to result in a race committee protest. If the enforcement of a sailing instruction by a race committee requires a protest, then a request seeking redress for enforcement by the race committee of its sailing instruction will fail, not only because the word 'may' makes action optional, but also because this rule makes it impossible. It would seem that it does not matter whether the request for redress is valid or invalid (although it is explicitly stated to matter in the case of information from a protest), and the words 'information arising from a request for redress' suggests something wider than just what is written in the request. This may mean that if information that might lead a race committee to wish to protest is supplied in a request for redress, the race committee is precluding from seeking corroboration from some other witness to bypass the ban on using the information in the request.

The rule also precludes the race committee from protesting 'as a result of information arising from…an invalid protest.' So if *Daffodil* protests *Iris* for touching a mark, and the protest is found to be invalid, the race committee cannot use that information alone, if the protest time limit allows, to lodge its own protest. However, as in the last paragraph, it is unclear whether the race committee can bypass this by making its own enquiries.

An interested party is defined as a person who may gain or lose as a result of a protest committee's decision, or who has a close personal interest in the decision. It is not for the race committee to do a competitor's dirty work, and the crew of boat in the race or series will clearly stand to gain from the penalsation of a fellow competitor if the race committee protests her based on their report. So the boat must lodge her own valid protest[2]. Likewise, a report from a parent or coach cannot be acted on because of the close personal interest, if the outcome of a protest might benefit the boat they are associated with.

Race officials themselves are not interested parties. So even without the final paragraph of rule 60.2, a report from a measurer or inspector who is a member of the race committee does not count a report from an interested party, since the official has nothing to gain or lose as a result of any subsequent protest. Likewise, when the race committee protests, the fact that a member of the protest committee is also a member of the race committee does not make that person an interested party[3].

---

[1] RYA 1999/2
[2] RYA 1990/7
[3] US 18. That would not appear to be best practice, however.

A race committee can protest a boat on the basis of 'information arising from…the representative of the boat herself', despite that person being a clear interested party. So a boat believing herself in danger of being protested by the race committee for touching a mark cannot seek to invalidate such a protest by lodging with the race committee an admission of having indeed touched the mark. That sounds improbable, but consider a race where declarations, with details, are required for taking a turn penalty for touching a mark. Suppose a boat admits in writing to having touched mark 2 and to having done a turn – and the race committee saw a defective turn (too late, or not after having got clear) but did not see the original infringement. As discussed under rule 44, it is not possible to protest just for a defective turn: the protest has to be for the unexonerated touching of the mark. The race committee can now use the admission to support a protest. A question arises, however, over the term '**the** representative'. If it said 'a representative', that would be clear. But the 'the' suggests that the person is already representing the boat for some purpose. That is relevant only to a protest in the course of being heard, under rule 63.3(a)[1]. It is possible that the scope of 60.2(a) may be less extensive than intended by ISAF.

RYA 1969/11 shows the rule at work. The sailing instructions required boats to sign a declaration after finishing to confirm that they had complied with the rules. After a race lasting two days, *Barada* lodged her signed declaration, adding the sentence: 'Except that during the hours 0200 to 0500 we were forced to sail without navigation lights…' The protest committee protested her and found that she had broken rule 48, Fog Signals and Lights. It imposed a 5% time penalty. *Barada* appealed on the grounds that the protest was invalid and that no provision was made in the sailing instructions for that penalty.

Barada's first ground of appeal was dismissed. Her second ground of appeal was upheld, but not to her advantage, as her penalty was changed to disqualification.

> *Barada* admitted in her declaration that she had broken rule 48. This admission entitled the protest committee (or the race committee) to protest her, as permitted by rules 60.2(a) and 60.3(a). Those rules preclude a race committee or a protest committee from protesting based on information from an interested party, and *Barada* was an interested party, as defined, since her report opened her to protest and penalisation. However, those rules make a specific exception for information from the representative of the boat herself. The protest committee's protest was therefore valid.

> The only penalty a protest committee may impose for breaking a rule, unless otherwise stated in the racing rules or in the sailing instructions, is disqualification.

It is good practice for a race committee to seek redress for a boat that goes to help another, especially as the boat giving help may be too modest to ask for it herself. Requesting redress for a boat is also advisable when the race committee realizes that its own act or omission has improperly affected one or more boats, as for instance when a mark drifts a substantial distance and is not replaced promptly enough. While the boats are entitled to ask for redress themselves, the fact that there is also a request from the race committee sends a strong signal to the protest committee as to the desired outcome, which may be a fairer one than as if the race committee had simply abandoned the race.

A race committee cannot bring an action under rule 69.1, but it can not only report what may have happened to the protest committee but also specifically ask the protest committee to act. If there is not already a protest committee in being to consider the matter, the race committee may first have to appoint one, and even if there is already a protest committee at work handling normal protests, the race committee might want to appoint a different committee in order to have members with suitable skills and experience. Nevertheless, it is for the protest committee to decide whether to call a hearing.

---

[1] Rule J1.2(6) refers as well to an 'owner's representative' as one who can lodge an entry form, but that person would not seem to rank automatically as a 'representative of the boat' under rule 60.)

60.3

A protest committee may

(a) protest a boat, but not as a result of information arising from a request for redress or an invalid *protest*, or from a report from an *interested party* other than the representative of the boat herself. However, it may protest a boat

    (1) if it learns of an incident involving her that may have resulted in injury or serious damage, or

    (2) if during the hearing of a valid *protest* it learns that the boat, although not a *party* to the hearing, was involved in the incident and may have broken a *rule*;

(b) call a hearing to consider redress; or

(c) act under rule 69.1(a).

The structure of the rule is complex, with exceptions to exceptions. Here is how it works.

'A protest committee may protest a boat…'

A protest against a boat implies that there will be a hearing. There is no issue in principle over the fact that it may be the same protest committee that will hear the protest it has lodged, putting it in the position of prosecutor (and sometimes chief witness for the prosecution), judge, jury and executioner combined. The boat should be grateful for at least having the opportunity to defend herself. When rule 42 is being policed under Appendix P, a yellow flag is not a protest but a designation of an immediate penalty for which no hearing is required.

The general exceptions to the right to bring a protest as applicable to a race committee also apply to a protest committee, but with relaxations.

'…but not as a result of information arising from a request for redress…'

The request for redress may be valid. For instance, take the protest referred to under rule 28.1, where *Daffodil* was scored DNF. She believed she had finished, having borne away after her bow cut the finishing line to avoid a right-of-way boat. We the protest committee found that the windward finishing line had been moved from where she thought it to be by *Iris* that lassoed and dragged the pin mark upwind. The request was valid (but was refused). But what of *Iris*? No one had protested her. Could we the protest committee now protest her under rule 31 if she had not taken a penalty? No.

When a request for redress is invalid, it may also rank as a report whose information is not available to a protest committee to form the basis of a protest. In RYA 1990/7, an incident occurred between two boats, *Atlantis* and *Caprice*, as a result of which *Atlantis* lodged a protest in which a third boat, *Carina*, was named as witness. There had been no damage. The protest was lodged 15 minutes after the end of protest time, and refused as the protest committee saw no good reason to extend protest time. The next morning, *Carina* lodged a request for redress stating that she had witnessed the incident and alleging that *Caprice* had broken a rule of Part 2. The protest committee extended the time limit, treated the request for redress as a valid protest under rule 60.1(a), and disqualified *Caprice* for breaking a rule of Part 2. *Caprice*'s appeal was upheld.

> *Carina*'s request began: 'Under rules 60.2(a) and 62.1(a) I wish to inform the race committee of an infringement of the rules in race 3'. That amounted merely to a report. It was not a valid request for redress, as it did not include any allegation that the race or protest committee had acted or omitted to act so as to make *Carina*'s score significantly worse. The report came from a competitor, but rule 60.2(a) specifically prohibits a race committee from protesting as the result of a report from a competitor, as does rule 60.3(a) in respect of the protest committee in the absence of a report of injury or serious damage; hence the protest committee, like the race committee, should have taken no action.

> In order to become a party in a valid hearing, *Carina* should have hailed and displayed a protest flag at the time of the incident in accordance with rule 61.1(a), and then lodged a protest within the time limit.

> Rule 61.2 permits the protestor to remedy any defects in the particulars required by that rule, provided that the protest identifies the incident. However, this facility does not extend to a protest committee itself initiating the changing of request for redress into a boat v boat protest, and does not permit the protest committee to protest on the basis of a report from a competitor.

'...or an invalid protest...'

The same principle will apply when a protest by a boat or by the race committee is defective, which will usually be for failure to notify or for not lodging within the time limit.

'...or from a report from an interested party other than the representative of the boat herself...'

Normally, an interested party would be a boat that would stand to gain from the penalisation of another boat, as in the *Carina* case referred to above. However, when a boat's representative makes what is in effect a confession that the boat had broken a rule, the representative is 'a person who may...lose as a result of a protest committee's decision', and is therefore also an interested party. The admission should not allow the boat to escape justice. The *Barada* case, RYA1969/11, discussed above under rule 60.2(a), is equally applicable to rule 60.3(a) – indeed it concerns a protest committee protest.

When neither of the exceptions to rule 60.3 to be discussed below is applicable, the rule embodies the principle in ISAF 80, as discussed under rule 28.1, that a hearing and decision must be limited to a particular incident that has been described in the process. The cases show that the commonest error of protest committees is to believe that they should compensate for the procedural failures of others to ensure that a boat does not evade justice, as in ISAF 80 and in RYA 2006/8, as also already discussed under rule 28.1.

'However, it may protest a boat...if it learns of an incident involving her that may have resulted in injury or serious damage...'

All the foregoing becomes academic if the protest committee learns of a serious incident. Any source, including a request for redress, an invalid protest or a report from an interested party, is permissible. If it gets this information from an invalid protest, and it wishes to protest one of the parties to that protest, it must lodge a fresh protest against her, and she is entitled to new notification of the new hearing, even if she was the protestee in the invalid protest and had been properly notified of the original hearing but had not been present[1].

If a boat is protested under this rule, the protest will not be valid until the protest committee first ascertains that there was indeed injury or serious damage[2].

In RYA 2003/3, there was a series of collisions between a group of small keelboats running in heavy weather, some of which incurred serious damage, and none of which lodged a valid protest[3]. The protest committee decided to protest some of the boats under rule 60.3(a)(1), based on an initial assessment that there had been more than one incident, but no serious damage in the first collision in which it later found that *Iris* (which it had not protested) had not kept clear of *Daffodil*. Boats in the subsequent collisions resulting in serious damage to some were disqualified. In a resulting appeal, the RYA added to its decision some general advice about applying rule 60.3(a)(1).

> When there was an incident that may have resulted in injury or serious damage, rule 60.3(a)(1) states that a protest committee may protest any boat involved. At the time when it is deciding what action to take, it will not have firm facts as to the details of the incident or the precise involvement of each boat. The protest committee is allowed to protest any boat that may have been involved and, when it decides to protest, it should protest all boats that may have been involved. Stating a belief that rule 14 has been broken would be appropriate for this purpose.

> Once the hearing begins, the protest committee must then identify the incident more precisely, and establish that injury or serious damage resulted from it.

---

[1] RYA 2001/15
[2] Rule 63.5
[3] The incident predated rule 61.1(a)(3).

When only two boats are involved, it is not difficult to identify an incident. When more than two boats are involved and there are sequential failures to comply with the rules, the protest committee has to decide whether there is only one, or more than one, incident. The test is that there must be some causal link between the events. If it decides that there was more than one incident, it should proceed only with the protest against boats involved in the incident that resulted in injury or serious damage, and close its hearing against any other boat, as required by rule 63.5.

The protest committee in this case correctly addressed the question as to whether there was only one, or more than one, incident, and decided, before any hearing had been opened, that there was no causal link between any infringement by *Iris* and subsequent infringements. It therefore felt itself precluded from protesting her, whether under rule 60.3(a)(1) or rule 61.1(c). The RYA's decision is that, given several boats in close proximity, *Daffodil* changing course as a result of contact with *Iris*, and then a series of contacts all within a ten-second period, there was a causal link and therefore only one incident.

Once it is established that there was an incident resulting in injury or serious damage, and involving the protestee, a protest under rule 60.3(a)(1) is no different from any other protest. The protest committee must decide the facts and apply the rules to the incident. Any boat involved in the incident and protested may be penalised under the appropriate rule, regardless of whether it was she that caused the injury or serious damage, and the fact that she did not cause injury or serious damage is not of itself a reason for exonerating her.

During the hearing of a protest brought under rule 60.3(a)(1), a protest committee might also realise that it had not initially drawn its net widely enough, and that a further boat was involved that might have broken a rule. It is then entitled under rule 60.3(a)(2) to protest that boat. As that requires a fresh hearing (see rule 61.1(c)), it is obviously preferable if such a boat can be identified earlier and included within the protest under rule 60.3(a)(1) from the outset, if only later to eliminate her.

In this case, *Iris* cannot be penalised by the RYA under rule 71.3 as she was not a party to the protest. The protest committee may not now protest her, as any possible time limit for a protest has long since expired. There is no rule giving the national authority power to return the case to the protest committee and require it to protest *Iris*.

The important points to be teased from this case are:
- When a protest committee wishes to protest under rule 60.3(a)(1) having received a report of an incident that may have resulted in injury or serious damage, it is advised initially to protest all boats that may have been involved. If it then finds that that there was in fact more than one incident, and that serious damage or serious injury did not result from one of the incidents, it should close the hearing relating to that incident.

- If there is a causal link between a series of collisions, they may be regarded as a single incident for the purposes of rule 60.3(a)(1)

- When a protest committee uses rule 60.3(a)(1) to protest a boat, and the boat then is found to have been involved in an incident that resulted in serious damage or serious injury, and to have broken a rule, she is to be penalised under the appropriate rule, even if it were not she that caused the serious damage or serious injury.

- There is no rule giving the national authority power to return a case to the protest committee and require it to protest a boat.

'However, it may protest a boat…if during the hearing of a valid *protest* it learns that the boat, although not a party to the hearing, was involved in the incident and may have broken a rule'
When a protest committee believes that a boat that is not a party to a hearing may have broken a rule, it must first make her a party to a hearing by protesting her. She must be notified and given time to prepare her defence and she has the same rights as any protestee to call and question witnesses. Rule 61.1(c) requires the hearing to be closed, and a fresh hearing to be opened, to include the original parties and any new party, with all protests heard as one hearing.

In RYA 1981/14, when approaching a mark, there was an incident in which *Daffodil* collided with *Iris*, and *Iris*, in turn, collided with *Whitewash*[1]. *Daffodil* protested *Iris* and at the hearing both these boats were exonerated while *Whitewash* was disqualified. The observations of the protest committee read as follows:

> After hearing the statements of all the parties, we the members of the protest committee realised that we had a somewhat embarrassing situation in that the helmsman of *Whitewash*, attending only as a witness, could bear at least some of the blame. We, of course, did not say this to the parties concerned but we did question *Whitewash*'s helmsman very carefully to bring out his side of the question…After considering the facts we concluded that *Whitewash* was at fault…'

Whitewash was disqualified without any further action being taken. Her appeal was upheld.

> It was from the evidence at the hearing of the protest *Daffodil* v *Iris* that the protest committee first had grounds for supposing that *Whitewash*, which was not a party to that hearing, might have broken a rule. If it then wished to proceed against *Whitewash*, rule 60.3(a)(2) gave it power to do so. It was required by rule 61.1(c) to close the hearing of the protest *Daffodil* v *Iris*, and to give notice to *Whitewash* that she was now being protested, identifying in writing the incident, the rule alleged to have been broken and the time and place of the hearing. It had to act in the same manner as if it were a protest made by a competitor, to allow her a reasonable time for the preparation of her defence, as required by rule 63.2.

> This procedure was not complied with and *Whitewash* was disqualified without having been protested, let alone informed that she was alleged to have broken a rule. Thus she had no opportunity to state her case or to call or question witnesses. The protest committee's procedures were flawed, and the reinstatement of *Whitewash* is the only appropriate outcome.

It is important to note that this option for the protest committee to protest applies only in respect of any other boat in the same incident, which is discussed above in RYA 2003/3. If information arises concerning other boats in other incidents, it will be a report from an interested party, and so will not be capable of forming the basis of a fresh protest unless that incident may have resulted in injury or serious damage.

'A protest committee may…call a hearing to consider redress…'
Just as with a race committee, a protest committee that learns from any source that a boat has lost places when giving help as required by rule 1.1 should not wait to be asked for redress by that boat before calling a hearing under rule 62.1(c).

When redress is requested, a protest committee is not entitled to award redress to a boat that is not a party to that hearing based on facts outside the scope of that request. There is a collision resulting in damage between *Iris* and *Daffodil*. Neither is able to continue to race. There is no protest. *Thetis* stops racing to help them, and then asks for redress for the time she has lost in giving help. The protest committee cannot use this hearing consider the cause of the collision with a view to finding fault as between *Iris* and *Daffodil* and to the possibility of awarding redress to the innocent party. A fresh hearing is required[2].

'A protest committee may…act under rule 69.1(a)…'
Only a protest committee can decide to do this. A rule 69.1 hearing has serious implications. While a protest committee should not shirk from calling a hearing when it believes there may have been gross misconduct, it should not use a rule 69.1 hearing as a means of circumventing the validity requirements for a normal protest for a 'non-gross' breach of a rule[3]. Note that a protest committee may have been set up for the sole purpose of considering a report that might lead to a rule 69.1 action.

---

[1] Unlike the fictional names of *Daffodil* and *Iris* that I employ, *Whitewash* was indeed the actual name of the boat.
[2] RYA 2002/9. There is little point in the protest committee protesting either *Iris* or *Daffodil*, since, both having retired, neither can be penalised, but that does not stop consideration of redress for one of them when the process is properly initiated.
[3] RYA 2003/4

PROTEST REQUIREMENTS

There are two compulsory parts to initiating a protest:

- Informing the protestee of an intention to protest (rule 61.1): although the word 'Protest' may be hailed, this is not yet a protest, and no protest may in fact result
- Putting the protest in writing (rule 61.2), normally on a protest form, and delivering it to the race office within the protest time limit(rule 61.3)

Informing the Protestee

(a) A boat intending to protest shall inform the other boat at the first reasonable opportunity. When her *protest* concerns an incident in the racing area that she is involved in or sees, she shall hail 'Protest' and conspicuously display a red flag at the first reasonable opportunity for each. She shall display the flag until she is no longer *racing*. However,

    (1) if the other boat is beyond hailing distance, the protesting boat need not hail but she shall inform the other boat at the first reasonable opportunity;

    (2) if the hull length of the protesting boat is less than 6 metres, she need not display a red flag;

    (3) if the incident results in damage or injury that is obvious to the boats involved and one of them intends to protest, the requirements of this rule do not apply to her, but she shall attempt to inform the other boat within the time limit of rule 61.3.

(b) A race committee or protest committee intending to protest a boat shall inform her as soon as reasonably possible. However, if the *protest* arises from an incident the committee observes in the racing area, it shall inform the boat after the race within the time limit of rule 61.3.

(c) If the protest committee decides to protest a boat under rule 60.3(a)(2), it shall inform her as soon as reasonably possible, close the current hearing, proceed as required by rules 61.2 and 63, and hear the original and the new *protests* together.

Rule 61.1 has been patched and stitched over the years, with the result that its language is a little inconsistent. Some requirements must be carried out 'as soon as reasonably possible', while for others it is 'at the first reasonable opportunity' – which appear to mean the same thing. A boat 'sees', while a race committee or a protest committee 'observes'.

Some requirements must be carried out 'as soon as reasonably possible' / 'at the first reasonable opportunity'. For others it is within the protest time limit.

Sometimes, the informing need only be attempted. Sometimes, it must succeed. Sometimes, it will be deemed to have succeeded.

'A boat intending to protest shall inform the other boat at the first reasonable opportunity...'

This is the general principle, which is amplified and modified by the rest of rule 61.1(a). So when the protest committee is satisfied that hailing and flagging requirements apply and have been met, this principle will be deemed to have been complied with, even if the protestee asserts that she was not aware of the protest against her[1]. As is explained below, only some protests require hailing and flagging, and therefore notification at the first reasonable opportunity is the default requirement for a protest for an incident that the protestee was not involved in, but has heard about, such as a belief that a boat touched a mark[2].

---

[1] 'When rule 61.1(a) applies,...compliance with the requirement in its second sentence to hail, and, if necessary, to flag fulfils the requirement of the first sentence to inform the other boat at the first reasonable opportunity': RYA 2002/7.
[2] See under rule 60.1(a) for other possible examples

'When her *protest* concerns an incident in the racing area that she is involved in or sees...'

An 'incident in the racing area' will include situations when the boats are subject to the racing rules of sailing, but are not yet 'racing', as defined. Although a boat may not be able to be penalised as a result of such a protest, a protest hearing will help find the facts for a related request for redress (and/or insurance claim)[1]. If the boats that are not yet racing are near each other, a 'Protest' hail, and, in some cases, a red flag, will be required at the first reasonable opportunity after the incident – to wait until the preparatory signal will be too late[2].

'...she shall hail 'Protest' and conspicuously display a red flag at the first reasonable opportunity for each. She shall display the flag until she is no longer *racing*.'

When *Vindictive* sees an incident between *Iris* and *Daffodil*, she is perfectly entitled to protest either or both of them[3]. She must comply with protest notification requirements at the time of the incident, and 'cannot justify her own failure to display a protest flag on the grounds that none of the other boats lodged a valid protest[4].' So she must also hail 'Protest' at the time, if within hailing distance, otherwise notify the other boat(s) at the first reasonable opportunity[5].

The actual word 'Protest' (or a derivative such 'protesting' or 'protested') must be used[6]. If this becomes an issue at the start of a protest hearing, then the longer it has taken for that word to emerge after the incident, the more sceptical a protest committee should be. In particular, pointing out to a boat that she has touched a mark, and/or suggesting that she should take a penalty, involves using words that needlessly occupy the first reasonable opportunity for uttering the word 'Protest'. A hail places no obligation on a boat to proceed with a protest. Best advice is therefore to hail 'Protest' first, then think and argue next.

Until 2009, there was disagreement as to when notification had to be made when a boat was seen to leave a course mark on the wrong side. At the mark? Or when the boat finishes with 'wrong string'. RYA and US Sailing cases came to different conclusions. ISAF 112 now resolves the issue[7]. If one boat makes an error in sailing the course, a second boat may inform the first that she intends to protest when the error is made, or at the first reasonable opportunity after the first boat finishes, or at any time in-between.

Assumed Facts
Boat A leaves the first mark of the course on the wrong side. Then, without correcting her error, she sails the remainder of the course correctly and crosses the finishing line from the direction of the last mark. Another boat, B, sees A leave the first mark on the wrong side and decides to protest her.

Question 1
When does A break rule 28.1?
Answer 1
A makes an error when she leaves the first mark on the wrong side. However, rule 28.1 allows her to correct her error at any time before she finishes, but not thereafter. Therefore, A does not break rule 28.1 until she finishes.

Question 2
Does A finish when she crosses the finishing line?
Answer 2
A finishes provided that she crosses the finishing line in accordance with the definition Finish, whether or not a string representing her track complies with rule 28.1.

---

[1] See the preamble to Part 2
[2] RYA 1996/8.
[3] Her written protest will need to identify which boat is believed to have broken which rule.
[4] RYA 1981/7 and 1996/2. Even though one of the other boats may have hailed and flagged, no written protest may result, or it may be too late, or it may be found to be invalid for other reasons. A third boat wishing to ensure that the incident comes before the protest committee must comply with all protest requirements, and if a protest from one of the boats involved is found to be valid, it will be heard jointly with hers.
[5] Rule 61.1(a)(1)
[6] RYA 2002/7
[7] At least, at the time of writing. There are those who still strongly disagree with aspects of it, and it is understood that ISAF will review a number of issues related to rule 28, rule 61 and the definition Finish, with a view to possible rule changes for 2013.

Question 3

When must B inform A of her intention to protest?

Answer 3

Rule 61.1(a) requires a boat intending to protest to inform the other boat 'at the first reasonable opportunity.' Normally this is done by hailing 'Protest' and, when required, displaying a red flag.

Although A does not break rule 28.1 until she finishes (see Answer 1), leaving the mark on the wrong side and continuing to sail the course without correcting her error provides B with a sufficient reason to decide to protest her. In this situation, therefore, B may notify A of her intention to protest when A leaves the mark on the wrong side, or at the first reasonable opportunity after A finishes, or at any time in-between.

It follows that if A is not near B when B finishes, the first reasonable opportunity to inform may not be until the parties meet on shore[1].

When a red protest flag is required to be displayed, it is understandable that it may not be broken out at the same moment as the hail is made, but it must follow very quickly. RYA 1999/1 gives useful clarification, particularly how attentive a protest committee should be over validity formalities.

Question 1

When the rules require a boat to display a protest flag in order for a protest to be valid, should the protest committee expect a competitor to have the protest flag ready to use, or is it reasonable in a larger boat to keep it below or in a locker, and fetch it when needed?

If not, how many seconds does a boat have before the first reasonable opportunity may be said to have passed?

Answer 1

A protest committee should expect a competitor to have a protest flag close at hand. Where it is kept is not important, but if its location delays its display significantly, as it is likely to do if kept below, and there was some other more quickly accessible place where it could have been kept, then it will not have been displayed at the first reasonable opportunity. No particular time for displaying the protest flag can be specified. The longer the time between the incident and the display of the protest flag, the more closely the protest committee should examine the circumstances to see if the first reasonable opportunity had clearly passed[2].

Question 2

Has a protestor acted at the first reasonable opportunity when: the protestor has hailed immediately, and has then waited to see whether the other boat takes a two-turns penalty before displaying a protest flag?

Answer 2

No.

Question 3

Should a protest committee investigate the promptness of the hail and (when applicable) the flag in all cases, or only when the protestee makes an objection?

Answer 3

The purpose of the flag and hail is to do as much as is practical afloat to make the protestee aware of a potential protest. If the protest form claims that the flag and hail were prompt, and when the protestee does not, when asked, dispute this, the objective of the rule has been achieved, and there is no need to investigate further. When the protest form is ambiguous or silent, or when the protestee objects on this point, the protest committee must investigate.

---

[1] RYA 2003/4

[2] So in CYA 88, the retrieval of the flag from below deck was invalidly delayed by five minutes while the crew member sent for the flag first mopped up a water spillage. 'Stowing the protest flag below decks where it is not readily accessible makes it unlikely that the flag can be displayed at the first reasonable opportunity.' And CYA 63 says that a keelboat with a crew of five would have to provide compelling reasons why her protest flag was not displayed within a very few seconds after an incident. Failure to display a protest flag when some member of the crew is not otherwise occupied is a failure to display it 'at the first reasonable opportunity' (US 67), but a boat is not required to give priority to displaying a protest flag at the cost of the crew failing to keep the boat under control or delaying a spinnaker set (US 82).

Question 4
What should a protestor do when he wishes to protest, but is already displaying his own protest flag in respect of a previous incident?
Answer 4
It will be sufficient to hail, a second flag is not required.

What is a protest flag? Many competitors use the 'swallowtail' red flag B, but all it needs to be is a red flag, and, over the years various items have been held not to comply, including a sponge, a glove[1] and a red hat[2]. ISAF 72 addresses the point, albeit in a circular and oblique way.

A flag is used as a signal to communicate the message 'I intend to protest'. Only if the object used as a flag communicates that message, with little or no possibility of causing confusion on the part of those on competing boats, will the object qualify as a flag. A flag must be seen to be primarily a flag.

CYA 63 is more specific, namely that it can be a 'piece of red material, varying in shape but including rectangular, triangular and swallowtail shapes, of a size that is clearly visible, attached at one edge to a staff, spar or rigging[3].' If it not a red flag, a protestee can assert or the protest committee can decide that the protest is not valid, even if the protestor's intention to protest was clear from the hail[4].

It must then be conspicuously displayed. That is a function of its size, and where on the boat it is displayed. The larger the boat, the larger the flag needs to be, up to a point. US 66 says that a 2" x 8" flag on a 40-foot boat is not of sufficient size or of suitable proportions. I have found a protest to be invalid where the dinghy-sized protest flag was flown from the backstay of a 45-foot boat and under a much larger class pennant that obscured it for much of the time. From the jury boat, despite being near for some while, we could not be sure that it communicated the 'I intend to protest' message until we were closer than any competitor could be expected to get while racing.

'However…if the other boat is beyond hailing distance, the protesting boat need not hail, but she shall inform the other boat at the first reasonable opportunity;'
If a protesting boat has any doubt that her hail will have been heard, she should advise the protested boat when their paths next cross (which may be ashore). Protestees are notorious for failing to hear hails (or to see flags). While a hail at the time of the incident may not be required because of this rule, it does not change the requirement to display a protest flag at the time of the incident (if that requirement applies). Why should this be necessary? Because a protest flag is a notice to all boats of an intention to protest, and while it may not have been seen by the protestee at around the time of the incident, it may have been observed by other competitors, who may be requested to witness this if there is any dispute as to validity in the protest hearing.

'If the hull length of the protesting boat is less than 6 metres, she need not display a red flag.'
The thinking behind this relaxation was that it was inconvenient for smaller boats to comply, but it has not stopped some classes (including single-handed dinghies) recommending the retention of the requirement for a protest flag. The difficulty of deciding that a protest is valid when there is only an unheard hail is discussed under rule 63.5, and having to display a protest flag at the time means that a competitor cannot be put under unfair after-race pressure by a parent or coach to lodge a protest, being coerced to claim untruly that a protest hail was made at the time of the incident[5].

Even when the size of boat removes the necessity to show a red flag, some competitors deliberately still display one, to enhance the prospects of a protest being found valid – if there was clearly a flag displayed at the time, it is much more likely that there was a hail, if that is contested.

---

[1] RYA 2001/13
[2] CYA 63
[3] I would also allow as a 'conspicuous display' on single-handed dinghies the method employed when such a thing was needed, namely a flag on string kept under a cap, which is doffed to break it out, after which it hangs behind the body and trails in the wind.
[4] RYA 2001/13
[5] As well, or instead, there is sometimes a requirement in the sailing instructions for an intention to protest to be notified to the race committee boat when finishing.

'If the incident results in damage or injury that is obvious to the boats involved, and one of them intends to protest, the requirements of this rule do not apply to her, but she shall attempt to inform the boat after the race within the time limit of rule 61.3.'

This (together with rule 60.3(a)(1)) removes the bizarre possibility of there having been a major accident, possibly even a sinking, and yet no valid protest, because no one thought to hail or flag at the time. Unlike the notification requirements of other parts of rule 61, this rule recognises that in a serious situation, it may be difficult to inform the other boat, so proof of an attempt to notify is sufficient, provided that the protest committee is satisfied that the damage or injury is obvious to the protested boat as well as to the protesting boat. As in all rules involving injury or damage, injury is bodily injury to a person and damage is limited to physical damage to a boat or her equipment[1]. Damage and injury to feelings do not count, nor does harm to a finishing position. But the damage in rule 61.1(a)(3) need not be serious, it must just be obvious, and I think it must be obvious at the time of the incident, since the rule's purpose is to excuse a failure to hail and flag at the time of the incident.

Even if this reduced requirement is not complied with, the protest committee has rule 60.3(a)(1) in reserve, allowing it to protest when no boats in an incident have protested, although under that rule, the damage need not be obvious, but must be potentially classifiable as serious. Another small difference between these rules is that, in a protest committee protest under rule 60.3(a)(1), the requirement for a protest committee first to satisfy its suspicion that there was injury or serious damage is explicit in rule 63.5, and it does not matter that one of the boats may not be have been aware of the damage at the time of the incident. When a boat protests and seeks the exemption of rule 61.1(a)(3), the protest committee must first satisfy itself that there was injury or damage that was obvious to both protestor and protestee. With both rules, it seems that the injury or damage need not be to the protestor or protestee, but might have been caused to a third boat by a possible infringement by protestor or protestee.

Protests by the race committee or protest committee

L16.4 suggests a sailing instruction to allow the race committee (and protest committee) to notify a competitor of a race (or protest) committee protest as required by rule 61.1(b), by means of a notice on the official notice board. That has to be posted within the protest time limit for an incident observed in the racing area, otherwise as soon as reasonably possible. In particular, there is no need for the same immediate notification that applies to boat-versus-boat protests – as for instance when a boat touches the committee boat at the start, or if a member of the protest committee sees a boat touch a course mark and not take a penalty. Indeed, it can argued that a hail of 'Protest' by the committee member at the time would be invalid on its own if not followed up by a post-race notification, since the latter is what the rule requires when the incident is seen. In RYA 2006/3, the race committee both hailed at the time of the incident, and informed the boat after the race. The boat appealed *inter alia* on the grounds that, when a hail was made, 'the alleged protestor did not identify himself, was some distance away, and there was no reply to my hail to the officer of the day requesting clarification.' Tough, said the RYA. 'The protest was lodged by the race committee. For an incident is sees in the racing area, rule 61.1(b) requires the race committee to inform the protestee after the race, and this was done. To hail at the time of the incident was an additional courtesy.'

Protests by the protest committee arising from information learned in the hearing of a valid protest

As rule 61.1(c) says, this means stopping the hearing in progress, notifying a new protestee and making a fresh start, as explained in RYA 1981/14 (discussed under rule 60.3(a)(2)) and RYA 2001/15 (discussed under rule 63.2).

Protest Contents

A *protest* shall be in writing and identify
(a) the protestor and protestee;
(b) the incident, including where and when it occurred;
(c) any *rule* the protestor believes was broken; and
(d) the name of the protestor's representative.

However, if requirement (b) is met, requirement (a) may be met at any time before the hearing, and requirements (c) and (d) may be met before or during the hearing.

[1] ISAF 110

After a hearing begins, it is too late to correct a misidentification of the protestee. On several occasions, a puzzled protestee has been able to convince my protest committee that she was nowhere near the incident, and that some other boat should have been recorded as the protestee on the protest form. This sometimes arises from an ill-remembered sail number in a big fleet. That protest is invalid, and has to be stopped[1].

There is no requirement in the rules for a pre-printed protest form (whether from ISAF or a national authority) to be used, although such protest forms will help ensure that rule 61.2 is complied with. The modern protest form is two sides of paper, with the front for completion by the protestor or requester, and the back reserved for the protest committee. The space for the description of the incident and any protestor's diagram is deliberately limited – it gives the protest committee, the protestee and any other party a flavour of the issue, which is then explained more fully in the hearing. As the rule states, the information on the protest form can be incomplete, as long as the protest identifies the incident, including when and where it occurred.

US 46, discussed under rule 44.2, sets this out clearly. Similarly, in CYA 101, boats were manoeuvring against each other before the start. They came close, and then came close 20 seconds later. *Daffodil*'s protest form referred to the former, but not to the latter. The protest committee decided that there were two separate incidents, and found that she flagged and hailed in time regarding the second incident but too late for the first. Since there was no timely notification of the intention to protest for the first incident, and no identification of the second incident on the protest form, the protest committee was right to find the protest invalid as regards the first incident, but wrong to proceed to hear (and dismiss) the protest regarding the second incident. Echoing ISAF 80[2], the CYA said that 'when the protest committee considered whether W broke a rule in the second incident, it improperly expanded the hearing beyond the incident that was the subject of L's protest'.

However, as discussed, rule 60.3 does give the protest committee several possibilities of its own protest arising from the information before it, and, as will be seen, a protestor can be penalised in her own protest.

Although the protest form provides space for a protestor's diagram, there is no obligation for a protestor to provide one[3]. I have always regarded a protestor's diagram as part of the description of the incident, indeed I have served on protest committees that have found protests to be valid where the diagram is the only indication of what may have happened – a picture tells a thousand words. Although the rule does require the protest to identify when and where the incident occurred, compliance with this is often perfunctory, but it is not in my opinion an issue over which the protest committee should be unduly concerned as long as the parties are in agreement that there was an incident between them.

Failure by the protestor correctly to identify the rule that may relate to the incident is no reason to find a protest invalid, and it is often the protest committee that completes the requirement to identify any applicable rule when it makes its decision.

In ISAF 22, after a collision near a mark, S protested P, citing rule 18 on her protest form as required by rule 61.2(c). The protest committee declared the protest invalid and refused to proceed with the hearing, because it said the protest should have cited rule 10 rather than rule 18. Had the hearing gone ahead and the parties been questioned, the protest committee said, the protest might have been upheld. S appealed.

---

[1] I was on an international jury that had begun a protest hearing well within the protest time limit, and decided that the protestee had been misidentified. There was time for the protestor to lodge a fresh protest against what she now realised was the correct boat, which she had notified of her intention to protest at the time of the incident. It was found to be valid, and was heard.
[2] Discussed under rule 28.1
[3] RYA 1988/3

Rule 61.2(c) requires the protest to identify any rule the protestor believes was broken. There is no requirement that the rule or rules identified must be the rule or rules that are later determined to have been broken, and it is irrelevant for deciding the validity of the protest that the protestor cited a rule that will very likely not be the applicable rule.

It is the protest committee, after finding the facts, that determines the applicable rule. Rule 64.1(a) states that a disqualification or other penalty shall be imposed whether or not the applicable rule was mentioned in the protest. It is unimportant that the protestor made a mistake in citing the rule. The appeal is upheld to the extent that the protest committee is instructed to hold a new hearing.

I think that it is quite proper for a member of the protest committee to help a protestor identify the possibly applicable rule while completing a protest form, as long as no comment is made or change is suggested regarding the description of the incident. Indeed, one might ask what purpose rule 62.1(c) serves. It has been known, when a protest committee chairman is in a hurry to get a hearing under way while the protestor is still filling in the protest form and thumbing through the rule book in search of the applicable rule, for the chairman to suggest that the research is stopped and 'rule 99' is inserted. It can always be corrected later.

Protest Time Limit

A *protest* by a boat, or by the race committee or protest committee about an incident the committee observes in the racing area, shall be delivered to the race office within the time limit stated in the sailing instructions. If none is stated, the time limit is two hours after the last boat in the race *finishes*. Other race committee or protest committee *protests* shall be delivered to the race office no later than two hours after the committee receives the relevant information. The protest committee shall extend the time if there is good reason to do so.

US 41 gives an example of what should have been a good reason to extend the protest time limit. A boat returned to dock an hour after finishing, her skipper wrote out a protest, and then took two hours of searching before finding a member of the race committee to receive the protest[1].

Occasionally, facts that might justify a protest may not emerge until after the event. In RYA 2005/7, a protestor did not realise that other boats had used sails of a non-permitted material in August's National Championship until he received notice of a related proposal in the following March to change the class rules to allow the material for the first time, and he lodged a protest in May after the Annual General Meeting. The protest committee decided to extend the time limit, but referred its decision so to do to the RYA. In correcting the decision to extend the time limit, the RYA made the following observations.

> It is sometimes unavoidable that the results at the end of an event turn out not to be final. All requests for redress as a result of the publication of the final results must be heard and any subsequent requests for reopening considered. A competitor who has left the site but later finds out his results are not correct is still entitled to have his request for redress heard provided he fulfils the conditions of rule 62.2. Where there is no International Jury, a protest committee's decision may be changed on appeal.

> For protests concerning something that may have happened during racing, however, the RYA considers that a good reason for extending the protest time limit beyond the end of the event will usually be outweighed by the better reason of the need for the results to be as final as possible.

> The requirement to extend the time if there is good reason to do so is to allow for circumstances in which the competitor finds it impossible to submit the protest in time. These reasons might include being very late ashore after being rescued, going to hospital, or poor wind conditions making a return to shore in time very difficult; it does mean however that submitting a protest needs to be done quickly on returning to shore.

---

[1] Similarly, in an unpublished appeal to the RYA, for an event sailed off a Welsh holiday beach, it was proper to extend the time limit for a party who diligently cycled from lodgings to lodgings in search of the race officer.

Regattas need to have closure for new protests involving on-the-water incidents, which includes competing in a boat that does not comply with class rules, and the time limit as described in rule 61.3 should not normally be extended beyond the end of the event.

That does not preclude serious allegations being investigated after the end of an event. Actions under rule 69 have no time limit and can be initiated by a protest committee at any time even after the regatta has finished and the competitors have gone home. An allegation, even in a late and invalid protest, of the knowing use of a better but forbidden sail material would be a good reason for a protest committee to call a hearing under rule 69, but that is a matter for a protest committee to decide.

It should be noted that the default time limit of two hours after the last boat in the race finishes will not be appropriate for an alleged infringement in a race that is not the last of the day if boats do not return to shore between races. If no time limit is stated in the sailing instruction for that sort of event, or if it duplicates the inappropriate wording of the rule, that would be a good reason to extend the time limit.

It can often be difficult for the race committee to comply with the protest time. The race officer will usually be the last off the water, and if notification was not possible while afloat, he or she will have both to notify the competitor of the protest and to write and lodge the protest, all within the protest time limit, on top of other end-of-day duties. A sailing instruction modelled on L16.4 will simplify notification, but a written protest still has to be lodged. The protest committee has the discretion to extend the time limit if there is a good reason to do so, but it has to balance the difficulties of the race committee with the rights of the competitor. My experience is that, when a race committee is not sufficiently versed in the rules so as to realise that it normally cannot disqualify a boat without a hearing, it will be grumpy when this is pointed out, moving rapidly to very upset when it then understands the further hoops through which it must jump to secure the disqualification. But that is no reason for the protest committee to put the race committee in a more privileged position than a competitor.

Rule 62

62.1

REDRESS

A request for redress or a protest committee's decision to consider redress shall be based on a claim or possibility that a boat's score in a race or series has, through no fault of her own, been made significantly worse by

(a) an improper action or omission of the race committee, protest committee or organizing authority, but not by a protest committee decision when the boat was a *party* to the hearing;

(b) injury or physical damage because of the action of a boat that was breaking a rule of Part 2 or of a vessel not *racing* that was required to keep clear;

(c) giving help (except to herself or her crew) in compliance with rule 1.1; or

(d) a boat against which a penalty has been imposed under rule 2 or disciplinary action has been taken under rule 69.1(b).

Most requests for redress concern perceived wrongs by the race committee under rule 62.1(a). 'A boat may not protest a race committee for breaking a rule. However, she may request redress…' says ISAF 44. Despite this, and despite also the clear segregation of protests and requests for redress in the rules, people still talk of 'protesting the race committee'. (I was on the international jury at an event in a part of Europe somewhat more hot-tempered than Great Britain, where several competitors, very upset by what they perceived as a race committee mistake, each struck out the pre-printed 'request for redress' line and tick-box on the protest form, and wrote over it 'Protest the race committee[1].')

---

[1] Perhaps it is not helped by the fact that the body that hears requests for redress is still called the protest committee. Given also its role in rule 69 (under which a hearing is not a protest), perhaps it should be renamed the 'disputes committee' or the 'hearings team'.

So in RYA 1982/3, the starting signal was made one minute early but the race officer judged it advisable to allow the race to continue. Two boats lodged what purported to be protests against the race committee. The facts were not in dispute. Neither of the two boats delayed her start until the correct time. The protest committee, after a hearing, held that no boat's score had been made worse by the admitted error, and decided to let the results stand. The two boats' appeals were dismissed.

> A boat cannot protest the race committee; she can seek redress under rule 62.1(a) and must show that, through no fault of her own, her score was made significantly worse by an error of the race committee. The protest committee was correct to have proceeded on the basis that the 'protests' were in fact requests for redress.

> There was nothing in the appeals to show that the protest committee was wrong to decide that neither boat's score had been made significantly worse by the race officer's mistake in the timing of the starting signal.

What ranks as a 'request for redress'?
It is either a claim made by the boat concerned under rule 60.1(b), or a request on her behalf made by the race committee under rule 60.2(b).

A request for redress does not have to use that term[1], and if it is a letter from a boat complaining that her score was made worse at no fault of her own by one of the grounds in (a) to (d) of rule 62.1, it should be treated as a request for redress.

In RYA 1989/9, *Imperator* was the only entry in her class in the series in July. The starts of several classes were combined. There was a prize for the combined results. *Imperator* finished correctly in her races. The race committee recorded 'No Race' for her series. When *Imperator* received the results the owners wrote immediately complaining that this was incorrect and that *Imperator* was entitled to her points in these races.

The race committee replied that since only one boat had come to the starting line there was a 'no race' situation. After further correspondence *Imperator* lodged a formal request for redress in October. At the hearing the request for redress was found to be invalid and an extension of the time limit was refused on the grounds that there had been unreasonable delay in requesting redress. At the Class meeting in October, *Imperator*'s series was declared invalid and the decision to present no prizes reaffirmed. *Imperator*'s appeal was upheld, including her appeal against the finding of invalidity.

> Although the owners' politely worded letter dated 23rd July did not contain the words "Request for Redress" it in fact met all the requirements for a request for redress, and well within a reasonable time from the receipt of the results. A hearing should have been called at that time. The negative reply to this letter was followed up by another request that something be done, dated 20th August, which mentioned an appeal to the RYA. When the aggrieved competitor finally submitted a request for redress, there was a good reason for the protest committee to extend the time limit, which it was therefore obliged to do.

Indeed, a letter may purport to be something else, and still rank as a valid request for redress: nor is it essential for such a letter to spell out exactly how the boat's score had been adversely, as long as she asserts that it had been. The details are for the hearing. In RYA 2002/1 on a heavy-weather day, the protest committee gave redress to four boats that claimed that they were given insufficient time after being released from the beach to reach the starting area. The redress was the average of the first two races sailed the previous day, when conditions were less onerous.

Another boat, *Really Random*, lodged the usual form (which was and is headed 'Protest Form – also for redress and reopening') on which she had ticked the box marked 'Request by boat …to reopen hearing'. She asked the protest committee to change the redress granted to the four boats to 'a more appropriate basis', as (she asserted) the protest committee had acted incorrectly in some unspecified way in deciding the method of awarding redress in the previous case, and that this had, also in some unspecified way, adversely affected her.

---

[1] As in RYA 1982/3, above

The protest committee, examining the form before starting the hearing, decided that *Really Random* had not been a party to the earlier hearings, and so was not entitled to ask for a reopening. It then decided that the document might rank as a request for redress, but that there was nothing in the form to indicate that *Really Random*'s score in a race or series had been made significantly worse by some improper action of the earlier protest committee – indeed, it was not clear what was the basis for the request.

The protest committee summoned *Really Random*, advised her that her request to reopen was invalid, but that it would consider the form as a request for redress were *Really Random* to modify the form, so as to make clear how the previous decision might be improper and how it had affected *Really Random*'s score. *Really Random* declined to do so, and after some 45 minutes of argument about this between *Really Random* and the protest committee, the hearing was declared closed for invalidity, as the request had failed to indicate which rule or principle had been broken or ignored by the earlier protest committee.

Really Random appealed, seeking either a reopening or a redress hearing. It was upheld, to the extent that the protest committee was to decide the request for redress on the information it had already gleaned, without a further hearing.

> *Really Random* lodged a form asking for the reopening of a hearing to which she was not a party. The protest committee correctly found that she was not entitled to make such a request, since rule 66 applies only to parties to the original hearing. However, having received a written request…the protest committee was required by rule 63.1 to hear the claim as a request for redress.
>
> Having correctly opened a hearing, the first duty was to establish the validity of the claim. The protest committee decided that the content was insufficient to proceed. The protest committee was incorrect in this. The wording on his form indicates that the claimant considered that his boat was adversely affected because the protest committee had acted incorrectly in deciding the method of awarding redress in the previous case. This is sufficient for a request for redress under Rule 62 to be valid, and the protest committee was required to proceed with the hearing of evidence and arguments of *Really Random*.
>
> The questions it asked of *Really Random* when addressing validity were precisely those on which a substantive decision would have been based. In effect, the hearing of the request continued and *Really Random* was given every opportunity to make out her case during the discussions that followed.
>
> The protest committee is therefore now required to decide this as a valid request for redress. Based on what it learned during the hearing and subsequent discussion, it is to find facts, draw conclusions, and either award or refuse redress[1].

So the issue in a request for redress may not be clear until the hearing is started, but once it is clear, the hearing is not to be expanded to consider matters beyond that incident: if there is evidence in the hearing that there is a further incident in respect of which one or more boats might be entitled to redress, either they must ask for redress themselves, or the protest committee must act under rule 60.3(b) to call a hearing to consider redress for them, which is the 'possibility' referred to in rule 62.1.

A request for redress can include a claim of a scoring error – a boat is not recorded as finished, or is recorded in the wrong position, or the calculation of her position on handicap is wrong. It is best if an attempt to resolve this is made between the boat and the race committee outside any hearing, and many events provide 'clearance' forms for this to be attempted, so that only unresolved problems come to the protest committee[2].

What is a 'protest committee's decision to consider redress'?

It can be a hearing called by the protest committee on its own initiative under rule 60.3(b) when there is a 'possibility' of a boat's having been prejudiced in some way. As discussed under that rule, it will often apply when one boat is known to have helped another. It can also arise when *Iris* wins her protest against *Daffodil*, and it is clear from the facts that *Iris*, although not also asking for redress on her protest form, has clearly had her score affected because of resulting injury or physical damage (rule 62.1(b)) or because of unfair sailing that has caused the protest committee to penalise *Daffodil* under rule 2 (rule 62.1(d)). No separate paperwork is required, and there is no time limit, since only a 'request' has to be in writing and lodged in time, and the redress decision will simply be added to the protest form.

---

[1] The protest committee did so, and did not grant redress.
[2] CYA 79: 'No hearing is required to correct an obvious scoring error.'

The significance of 'fault'

The rule makes clear that a boat will be entitled to redress only when she herself was not even the partial cause of the problem – it must be 'at no fault of her own'. This is different from the situation in civil legal cases for negligence, where the negligence of the plaintiff will not prevent the other party being found negligent: rather, this 'contributory negligence' will reduce the amount of damages. In sailing, redress is all or nothing, depending on whether the requester was at fault. In RYA 1999/4, in light airs, *Blue* gave up trying to get the starting area when the race committee began the starting sequence several minutes early. No other boat was affected. The refusal of redress was upheld on appeal.

> A boat that believes she has been adversely affected by a mistake of the race committee, but which chooses not to race or to continue racing although able to do so, is not without fault, since she contributes to her own loss of place, and so is not entitled to redress. The race officer made a mistake, which affected only *Blue*. Any prejudice that might have resulted became irrelevant when, rather than sail the course, *Blue* made no attempt to race and elected to return ashore. For the purposes of rule 62.1, she was not without fault, as it was she that had deprived herself of a score for a finishing position.

In US 86 the question is asked whether a boat whose finishing position is made worse by taking a penalty is then entitled to a better score if she then wins a protest concerning the incident, in the process proving that she had broken no rule. The answer was that she was not, because she was the cause of her own loss of place – in effect, taking a penalty was her choice, and so it was her fault.

A score in the race or series, made significantly worse…

A request for redress will not be valid unless it is also claimed that what happened affected the requester's score. Often, this is implicit, as when an OCS score is contested.

The score is usually in the race concerned. It may also affect the series score as a result. Occasionally, it is only a series score that is affected, as in RYA 1997/1, already discussed under rule 46, where *Redcoat* was not contesting the individual race scores *vis a vis* the boat whose name was changed in mid-series from *Serendip* to *Securon*. The issue was whether it was one and the same boat for the series results (which it was held to be).

When there is, within the overall results for a race, a separate classification or prize for a particular category of competitor or boat (e.g., first woman or first master, or, as in RYA 2002/6, 'first Westerly Class Yacht on handicap), this too will count as a race for redress purposes.

What loss of score is 'significant'? The difference between first and second place is clearly significant. What about the difference between 89th and 90th place? Or 85th and 90th place? Or 9th and 10th place? My experience is that protest committees tend to regard this as self-fulfilling – if a boat is aggrieved enough to ask for redress, the loss of score, however small, is significant for her. It might be different if there were an issue on the last day of a big regatta related to minor places when to hold a hearing would delay the prize-giving. A further point is that it may not be clear until all the evidence is heard whether any loss of score is significant. By that time, there is little point in refusing to grant redress if all other requirements of the rule have been met, since if scoring is done by computer, no time would be gained compared with making a small adjustment to one or more scores.

…by an improper action or omission of the race committee, protest committee or organizing authority, but not by a protest committee decision when the boat was a *party* to the hearing.

The new last sixteen words are to prevent a boat from using the redress route to secure a guaranteed hearing to contest an adverse protest committee decision. The only option for the party is to ask for the hearing to be reopened under the rule intended for this purpose, namely rule 66, alleging that a mistake was made. Under rule 66 the decision to reopen is at the discretion of the protest committee.

It is not clear whether the word 'improper' applies to an omission as well as to an action, but the word 'omission' conveys a sense of impropriety.

Improper actions or omissions by an organizing authority

These might include:

- a defective notice of race that failed to list a requirement that prevented a boat from competing in one or more races of an event until belatedly remedied, such as a requirement to carry non-standard safety equipment.
- A time given in the notice of race for the start time of the first race when this is subsequently brought forwards without giving adequate notice, resulting in the boat arriving too late at the event to sail the first race.
- A purported refusal of an entry, either made after the start of the first race, or without stating the reason[1].

Improper actions or omissions by a protest committee

Rule P4, when it applies, contemplates the possibility of redress arising from a protest committee's 'yellow flag' penalty for breaking rule 42 when it is improper because the race committee signals or class rules have freed boats from some rule 42 restrictions because of the wind strength. Most other protest committee mistakes are made in the context of a hearing, where reopening under rule 66 is the first opportunity for righting wrongs, followed by an appeal. As stated above, the redress route is barred. On appeal, a decision of a protest committee can be found to be incorrect, and it can also be found to be legal but 'improper', as for instance the decision to grant redress against a race committee error in the form of abandoning a number of races when only one or a few of those races was in fact affected[2].

Improper actions or omissions by a race committee

It is these that most often lead to appeals. They will result in redress only if they affect a boat's score. Examples from the cases include:

- Failure to make the sound signal of an individual recall (ISAF 71), or the flag of a general recall (RYA 1982/7) or not making the individual recall signal until 30-40 seconds after the starting signal (RYA 1998/3), or removing flag X prematurely (RYA 2006/2), or not making a recall hail required by the sailing instructions (US 90), or making an additional sound signal in respect of any race signal (RYA 2004/7, CYA 33).
- Laying a finishing line nearly in line with the last leg so that the direction of finishing is unclear (ISAF 82).
- Relaying the starting line too far from its original position to allow a boat to reach it in time (RYA 1969/12).
- Setting a course that is so ambiguous that no boat can sail the course (RYA 1993/1)
- Badly locating a starting cannon so that its shot injures a competitor or damages a boat (RYA 1996/6)
- Knowing that a fixed mark is out of place but not advising competitors of its new position, or replacing it with an object displaying flag M (RYA 2002/10)
- Issuing ambiguous sailing instructions (CYA 73)
- Changing the displayed course after the warning signal (RYA 1983/7)
- Wrongly identifying a boat as OCS, as discussed under rule 29.1
- Abandoning a race when there is no time limit on the race (RYA 1982/17)
- Abandoning a race that cannot be shortened, before it is clear that no boat will finish in the time limit (RYA 1999/8).
- Disqualifying a boat without a hearing or scoring her DNF for leaving a course mark on the wrong side (ISAF 80, RYA 1989/8)
- Allowing excess cordage to stream from a mark, resulting in its being touched (RYA 1989/10)
- Simultaneously displaying two different courses (RYA 2008/2)

Examples where the race committee did nothing improper

- Laying a mark near the bank so that bunched boats could not pass between without colliding, when the water depth precluded the laying of a mark further away (RYA 1985/3).
- A hail during a race to a boat by the race officer that the race committee intended to protest her (RYA 1990/5).
- An oral briefing by the race officer that was misinterpreted by a competitor as changing a rule (RYA 2004/1)
- Failure by the race committee to discover that a rating certificate was invalid (ISAF 68)
- Rescheduling the resail of a race to a date when the boat whose original request for redress had caused it to be abandoned could not take part (RYA 1999/9).

---

[1] See rule 76: however, the redress granted may well be to require the organizing authority to state that reason, in which case the boat will remain excluded from the event, but now knowing why.
[2] ISAF 37

The need for a causal link

The race officer who makes no mistakes has yet to be born, but the fact that there is an improper action or omission of the race committee must not lead to redress unless it is clear that it was that alone that caused a loss of score – and if there was a causal link, the appropriate redress may not restore the boat to her finishing position. The question in RYA 2006/2 was whether an OCS boat that did not return is entitled to redress when the individual recall signal is lowered prematurely – in this case only a minute after the starting signal, and with no valid reason for such an early lowering being applicable.

> A boat is entitled to redress only when she can show that a mistake affected her finishing position. This might be because a boat was not able to see the committee boat during the period flag X was displayed, perhaps because of intervening boats, but would have been able to see it if it had been displayed for longer. Alternatively, she might be able to convince a protest committee that she had seen flag X, believed it might apply to her, and was on the point of returning when it was lowered. In either situation, the earliest time this could have affected the boat is the moment flag X was lowered... If the protest committee is not satisfied that the boat would have turned back if flag X had been displayed for longer, redress should be refused[1].

ISAF 96, discussed under rule 30.3, makes the same point, as concerns a boat whose sail number was not displayed after a recalled Black Flag start, resulting in her taking part in the restart, and being scored DNE.

> While not displaying her sail number is an improper omission by the race committee, it is not the omission that deprived her of her finishing place, but the fact that she had been on the course side of the starting line in the minute before her starting signal.

So her only entitlement was the correction of her score from DNE to BFD, as if her number had been displayed and she had abstained from the restart.

…by injury or physical damage because of the action of a boat that was breaking a rule of Part 2 or of a vessel not *racing* that was required to keep clear.

Redress for injury or physical damage resulting from another boat's breach of a rule of Part 2 will often arise from a protest in which the other boat is penalised for her breach. The word 'physical' is designed to exclude 'damage' to a boat's finishing position that could arise from time lost while avoiding a boat required to keep clear[2], or while recovering from a capsize that did nor result in physical damage. It is therefore the same sort of damage referred to in rule 14(b) and discussed under that rule. Although the rule does not say so, any injury must also be 'physical'. So time lost in recovering the boat's own uninjured crew member from the water following an incident is no ground for redress.

It is not enough that there was injury or physical damage – there must be a causal link with the boat's finishing position. It is quite possible for a boat to be damaged in a collision for which the other boat was responsible, yet be able to continue to race with undiminished speed and unimpaired handling: in which case no redress is possible[3]. It would follow that, despite an injury suffered by a crew member of a well-crewed boat, redress is due only when the boat can show a significantly worsened score resulting from the injury, because the crew member is unable to perform his or her normal duties. If that injured crew member was also overboard, and has to be recovered before the boat continues to race at normal speed, it would seem that redress would be due only to the extent that the time taken to recover the injured person was longer than if there had been no injury.

The injury or damage does not need to have been inflicted directly by the boat that was at fault. Once again, it is a question of a causal link. That will be present if *Daffodil*'s breach of a rule of Part 2 results in *Iris* damaging herself in an unseamanlike manoeuvre to avoid contact, or if, in avoiding *Daffodil* she hits a navigation buoy and damages herself. Likewise, if innocent *Iris*, in avoiding contact with the delinquent *Daffodil*, unavoidably collides with *Thetis*, which was not otherwise involved in the incident, resulting in damage to *Thetis* alone, then *Thetis* is entitled to redress for a worsened score.

---

[1] But what redress to give when it is due? See further information from this case under rule 64.2
[2] ISAF 110
[3] ISAF 110

The boat that has broken a rule of Part 2 may have done so before or after a race as well as during it, because Part 2 rules may apply at those times, as stated in the preamble to Part 2, even if the boat cannot be penalised because the infringement occurred before or after she was racing. The fact that a boat has taken a penalty involving non-serious damage in respect of an incident does prevent a protest committee finding that she broke a rule, and redress will be due if that damage impaired the requester's finishing position.

A 'vessel not *racing* that was required to keep clear' could be a fellow competitor approaching or having left the racing area, in breach of the IRPCAS or local navigation rules, and that could be proved in a protest hearing. It could also be a motor or sailing vessel that breaches a rule of the IRPCAS and causes injury or physical damage in the process. No related protest hearing would be possible. The breach of an IRPCAS rule could happen before, during or after racing. Arguably, a boat having just left port to journey 50 miles to an event but immediately damaged and delayed by another vessel, so missing one or more races, would be entitled to redress.

…by giving help (except to herself or her crew) in compliance with rule 1.1

In ISAF 20, a protest committee refused redress to *Iris* which had helped *Daffodil* when she capsized and got her mast stuck in the mud, since *Daffodil*'s helmsman was an experienced sailor, the wind was light, the rising tide would have freed the boat, *Daffodil* did not ask for help, and there was in fact no danger. This was reversed on a appeal. 'A boat in a position to help another that may be in danger is bound to do so. It is not relevant that a protest committee later decides that there was, in fact, no danger, or that help was not requested.'

The words in brackets in the rule confirm that no redress is available to a boat that takes time to tend to or send ashore a crew member injured in an accident on board.

…by a boat against which a penalty has been imposed under rule 2 or disciplinary action has been taken under rule 69.1(b).

Loss of places resulting from 'normal' incidents are the 'rub of the green' unless injury or physical damage is involved under rule 62.1(b). So when boat is not given room at a mark and loses several places as a result, she may win her protest against the other boat, but she cannot normally regain those places. The exceptions are when it is injury or physical damage that results in her worsened score, under rule 62.1(b) – and here under rule 62.1(d), when the other boat has acted in bad faith. So in ISAF 34, *Daffodil* sailed *Iris* down the course without herself attempting either to start or finish, making *Iris*'s race and series position sufficiently low to allow *Daffodil* to take the series. This was a breach of rule 2, Fair Sailing, it would have been grounds for a rule 69.1 hearing, and *Iris* was entitled to redress.

My experience is that this rule is sometimes misread. It refers explicitly to a breach of 'rule 2', and not to 'a breach of a rule of Part 2'. Rule 2, Fair Sailing, is a rule of Part 1, and redress entitlements under rule 62.1(b) for Part 2 breaches (rules 10 to 23) require there also to be injury or physical damage. But when rule 62.1(d) applies, there need be neither injury nor physical damage.

As concerns rule 69, the 'disciplinary action' is not just the fact that a hearing was called. The reference to rule 69.1(b) means that it has been decided that there was gross misconduct. When a penalty was imposed under rule 69.1(b)(2), that is 'disciplinary action', but it is unclear from the rule whether a warning under rule 69.1(b)(1) meets this description. The RYA Racing Rules Committee believes that it does. Another curiosity is that it refers to 'a boat against which…disciplinary action has been taken…'. The primary recipient of a penalty under rule 69.1(b)(2) is a competitor, and, only when appropriate, a boat. Consider a crew member of a keelboat who, totally on his own initiative, sabotages another boat before or between races, as a result of which the boat is either unable to sail or sails more slowly (the bucket tied to the rudder post). The rule 69 book is thrown at the malefactor, but it is decided that it is not appropriate to penalise the boat on which he sails. It would appear that no redress is then possible, since there was no disciplinary action against a boat, nor did rule 2, Fair Sailing, apply.

Again, there must be a causal link between the gross misconduct and the worsened finishing score. So if there is a Part 2 incident in which the right-of-way boat has lost several places, redress for those places lost will not be due if the other boat has also been the subject of a rule 69.1 hearing and penalty for bad language or abuse in the course of the incident.

62.2
The request shall be in writing and be delivered to the race office no later than the protest time limit or two hours after the incident, whichever is later. The protest committee shall extend the time if there is good reason to do so. No red flag is required.

It is often the case that the facts giving rise to a request for redress may not be known until after the protest time limit has passed. A typical example is the belated publication of the results of the race or series, in which a boat finds herself wrongly scored or wrongly penalised. Sometimes, this may be some while after the end of the event. The protest committee is no longer present at the regatta site, and time is no longer of the essence. There is good reason for the new or reconvened protest committee not to adhere to the two hours time limit. 'If it is lodged promptly after the facts are known, this is sufficient good reason for a protest committee to extend the normal time limit[1].'

That quotation came from a case where a scoring issue was not known about until after the event. But when a boat requests redress over an incident she claims affected her series score because of its effect on the score in a single race, the time limit for making the request is the time limit for the race, rather than the time limit based on the posting of the series results. In ISAF 102, *Scruples* requested redress at the end of an eight-race series over an incident that had occurred three weeks earlier in race 5 of the series. Her request was found to be out of time. She appealed, on the basis that rule 62 refers to redress being possible for a worsened series score, and she could not know the actual effect of the race 5 incident until the final series results were posted. Her appeal was dismissed. The incident affected her score in the series only through its effect on the score in race 5, and, therefore, the relevant time limit for requesting redress was the time limit that applied to that race.

The rule speaks of 'two hours after the incident'. What is 'the incident'? It is easily identified when requesting redress for an improper action or omission of the race committee (rule 62.1(a)), or after having given help (rule 62.1(c)). When there is a related protest, and redress is asked for on the same protest form because of injury or physical damage (rule 62.1(b)) or unfair sailing or gross misconduct (rule 62.1(d), then the request for redress will be in time if the protest is in time.

Suppose however that the protest form makes no mention of redress, the protest (probably under a rule of Part 2) is heard after the end of the time limit and is upheld, and the facts now found would support a claim for redress, based on injury, physical damage, unfair sailing or gross misconduct – yet the protest committee does not decide on its own initiative to award redress. Can the protestor now ask for redress for the first time, based on the 'incident' being the protest committee's announcement of the facts? This is not clear, but if the announcement is not an incident, there would nevertheless seem to be a good reason for the protest time limit to be extended, and a conscientious protest committee should in any case consider a possible unrequested redress entitlement during the protest hearing, or act separately under rule 60.3(b) in the affected boat's favour. Rule 62.2 speaks of a time limit only in connection with a 'request', and rule 62.1 distinguishes between a competitor's' request for redress' and a protest committee's 'decision to consider redress'. Therefore, there does not appear to be any time limit on a protest committee deciding to consider redress based on the facts arising from a protest hearing.

Section B - Hearings and Decisions

Rule 63
HEARINGS

63.1
Requirement for a Hearing
A boat or competitor shall not be penalised without a protest hearing, except as provided in rules 30.2, 30.3, 67, 69, A5 and P2. A decision on redress shall not be made without a hearing. The protest committee shall hear all *protests* and requests for redress that have been delivered to the race office unless it allows a *protest* or request to be withdrawn.

---

[1] RYA 1989/9. However the RYA has also confirmed as invalid a request concerning the handicap used in the posted results that requester did not read during the time limit, for lack of reading glasses: he knew from others that there was an issue, he could have asked them for details, and he had time to fetch his glasses.

The explicit exceptions to the general principle of 'no penalty without a protest hearing' are:
- Rules 30.2 and 30.3 – DSQ and DNE decided by the race committee under the Black Flag Rule
- Rule 67 – DNE by the protest committee under rule 42, Propulsion, but only when the sailing instructions allow
- Rule 69 – there must be a hearing, but it is not a protest hearing
- Rule P2 – various penalties imposed by the protest committee under rule 42, but only when the sailing instructions allow

That leaves the stated exception of A5, Scores Determined by the Race Committee. Rule A5 specifies explicit no-hearing penalties under rule 30 (duplicating the list in rule 63.1) and a voluntary scoring penalty accepted by a boat under rule 44.3(a) (which is not referred to in rule 63.1). It also specifies DNS, DNC, OCS, DNF and RAF as issues that can be 'scored by the race committee without a hearing'. This is confusing, as the link from rule 63.1 implies that all of DNS, DNC, OCS, DNF and RAF can be regarded as penalties, as well as scores. DNF (and possibly RAF) will sometimes be penalties if a rule required a boat to retire, for instance under rule 44.1(b) when serious damage was caused, but there is a difference between being penalised (done by the protest committee) and taking a penalty (done by a boat), which is presumably why Rule A5 refers to a scoring penalty accepted by a boat, while rule 63.1 does not. DNS, DNC and OCS are simply statements of fact with scoring consequences.

To confuse scoring with penalties is not helpful, even if the numerical value of a DSQ and a DNF are the same. RYA cases[1] are pains to distinguish between a penalty and a score, especially between DSQ and DNF when a boat that finishes as defined is seen by the race committee not to sail the course – the first requires a hearing, the second is never valid[2].

When none of the exceptions apply, a protest hearing is needed if a boat is to be penalised. This rule can be changed by sailing instructions, and, as discussed under rule 28.1, it is quite legitimate for this to be done to allow a race committee to disqualify a boat without a hearing when she is seen not to sail the course. If the boat is unhappy, she can request redress. Such a sailing instruction should say that rules 63.1 and A5 are changed.

Otherwise, penalisation without a hearing can be contested by requesting redress. If it is a protest committee that has disqualified a boat without a hearing, requesting redress is possible under rule 62.1(a) despite its second clause, since the boat was not previously a party to any hearing. Whether it is the protest committee or the race committee that has purported to penalise, the proper outcome of a redress hearing should be reinstatement, since it is the disqualification that is the incident, not the circumstances that gave rise to the disqualification. The scope of the hearing is not to be expanded beyond consideration of the incident[3]. So if the complaint is justified, reinstatement is the appropriate redress, and, if the time limit for protests has expired, there is no good reason for the protest committee to extend the time limit to allow a late written protest to be lodged over the same alleged facts, if a protest in writing could have been lodged within the time limit.

A protest must be heard even if a protestor has already been penalised for an earlier incident in, or has retired from, the race in question. 'When a boat continues to race after an alleged breach of a rule, her rights and obligations under the rules do not change[4].' That would seem to include a boat that is already disqualified in that race under rule 30.3, Black Flag Rule, and a boat already scored OCS.

The same would not seem to be true of a request for redress by a boat that has already been penalised for an earlier incident in the same race. A request for redress assumes that the protest committee may be able to adjust a boat's score, but a DSQ, OCS or DNF in respect of a different incident cannot be changed by a redress hearing concerning some other issue. The rule does say that all requests for redress are to be heard, but if a hearing is opened, it is likely to be closed fairly quickly once it is clear that the conditions precedent for a request for redress have not been met.

---

[1] e.g. RYA 1989/8, RYA 2006/8
[2] ISAF 80
[3] ISAF 80, RYA 1989/7, RYA 1989/8, RYA 1999/3, RYA 2001/12
[4] ISAF 1, US 1

Another reason why a protest or request for redress hearing will not get past 'first base' is that it is invalid. Validity is decided within the hearing, not before the hearing, and so there is nothing inconsistent with rule 63.1's requirement to hear all protests and requests for redress, and the protest committee's duty under rule 63.5 to close a hearing if it is then found to be invalid.

Neither the rules nor Appendix M, Recommendations for Protest Committees, give any guidance on allowing a protest to be withdrawn. The ISAF Judges' Manual suggests that permission should not be given if foul play is suspected, which might be a suspicion that some sort of inducement has been offered to get the protest dropped. If there was a collision, it is almost certain that a rule has been broken[1], and protestor that belatedly realises that she herself has broken a rule should retire. If she does not, withdrawal would seem to be inappropriate.

There does not appear to be any good reason why any request for redress cannot be withdrawn, except, perhaps, a suspicion of undue pressure by the race committee or organizing authority when the request alleges that one of those acted improperly.

63.2   **Time and Place of the Hearing; Time for Parties to Prepare**
All *parties* to the hearing shall be notified of the time and place of the hearing, the protest or redress information shall be made available to them, and they shall be allowed reasonable time to prepare for the hearing.

In essence, a protest committee must comply with the formalities, but a boat will not escape penalisation on a technicality.

Issues are usually avoided at major events with a procedure specified in the sailing instructions to the effect that a notice will be posted within a given time after the end of protest time, listing the details of protests and requests, the order in which they will be held and the approximate time of the hearing (this last usually becoming a work of fiction for later-scheduled hearings). The notice may also list witnesses mentioned in the protest form, and it will state that the notice is the notification required by rule 63.2. When it appears likely that two or more protests relate to the same incident, or to closely-related incidents, it is advisable to begin a single hearing in relation to all the protests, with the initial task of deciding whether it is the same incident, requiring only one hearing, or separate incidents, requiring separate hearings[2]. If the incidents are separate, each incident will require its own valid protest[3].

Making available the information to the parties is complied with in a protest by allowing a protestee a copy of the protest on request, or, if there is no copier on the premises, sight of the protest form. There is no requirement to give the protestee an unrequested copy or sight of the protest form[4], although my experience is that protestees often first ask to see the form at the start of the hearing, which can delay the proceedings – so if possible it is often better to try to get a copy of the form to the protestee as soon as possible. In the case of a request for redress against an alleged improper act or omission by the race committee or organizing authority, it is advisable for the protest committee to get a copy of the protest form to the race committee as soon as possible, if for no other reason than to ensure that the appropriate officials will be available for the hearing. (In a regatta, it is also recommended to give priority to cases involving the race committee, to allow its members recovery time before running the next day's racing.)

---

[1] RYA 2008/4
[2] ISAF 49, RYA 2003/3, CYA 66
[3] CYA 101, US 46
[4] US 8

In ISAF 48, the appellant's case seemed at first to be plausible. 'I was not aware that the protest was being held until I was told to attend it. I was not allowed to read the protest outside the protest room. I had to read it in the protest room while the protest was underway. I was not given a reasonable time to prepare a defence.' 'Not so,' said the protest committee. 'The time of the hearing was posted on the official notice board. The protest form was in the race office and available for reading for well over an hour. The appellant knew his boat was being protested. He made no attempt to prepare a defence, indeed he had to be summoned from the club's dining room when the protest committee, the protestor and the witnesses were assembled.'

Siding with the protest committee, the appeals committee said that the protestee's representative knew that his boat was being protested, and it was his duty to protect himself by acting reasonably, which included seeking out the protest form, reading it, and using the ample time available to prepare a defence. 'Part 5 of the racing rules aims to protect a boat from miscarriage of justice, not to provide loopholes for protestees.'

In RYA 1968/15, *Sylphide* appealed on similar grounds. The protest committee responded that the protest had been read out three times and had been available for inspection. *Sylphide* had made no complaint at the hearing, nor did she ask for an extension of the time limit to prepare a defence. The RYA dismissed the appeal, noting that a boat that claims she has not been allowed reasonable time to prepare her defence must raise this objection at the hearing of the protest against her if she wishes to rely on this in an appeal.

A protest committee has to be doubly careful when it is also the protestor, as for instance under rules 60.3(a)(1) or (2). In RYA 2001/15, a boat-v-boat protest alleged serious damage. The protestee did not attend the hearing, and the protest committee decided to continue with the hearing under rule 63.3(b). It found that the protest was invalid, and decided to bring its own protest under rule 60.3(a)1. It did not pause, but proceeded immediately, disqualifying the absent protestee. Her appeal was upheld, since the protest committee must 'lodge a fresh protest against her, and she is entitled to a new notification of the new hearing, even if she was the protestee in the invalid protest and had been properly notified of the original hearing but had not been present.'

Likewise, when a protest committee decides, on the evidence in a valid protest, to bring its own protest against a boat that is not a party to that protest under rule 60.3(a)(2), it must comply with rule 61.1(c), which embodies the same principles as in rule 63.2[1].

63.3 Right to Be Present

(a) The *parties* to the hearing, or a representative of each, have the right to be present throughout the hearing of all the evidence. When a *protest* claims a breach of a rule of Part 2, 3 or 4, the representatives of boats shall have been on board at the time of the incident, unless there is good reason for the protest committee to rule otherwise. Any witness, other than a member of the protest committee, shall be excluded except when giving evidence.

(b) If a *party* to the hearing of a *protest* or request for redress does not come to the hearing, the protest committee may nevertheless decide the *protest* or request. If the *party* was unavoidably absent, the committee may reopen the hearing.

A hearing is about to start, and the procedure is governed by the rest of rule 63. This is amplified in Appendix M, Recommendations for Protest Committees, which may be open on the table during the hearing as an aide-memoire to the members of the protest committee, to ensure that the proceedings meet all requirements. The parties entitled to be present at a protest are defined as the protestor and protestee, and at a request for redress they are the requester and, if applicable, a representative of the race committee or the organizing authority. The rule speaks of 'the *parties*…or a representative of each.' The word 'or' is unhelpful, since everything is done in the name of the boat, and anyone speaking for a boat will be a representative of it[2]. Only one person should speak for each boat[3].

---

[1] See also RYA 1981/14
[2] The situation is different for hearings under rule 69, where the party is a named individual.
[3] Appendix M

Although appeals over procedural errors of the protest committee are unlikely to succeed unless an objection is raised and rejected at the time of the original hearing, the right to be present appears to be sufficiently fundamental to give rise to a valid appeal when this is not complied with, a probable outcome being a direction to rehear the protest[1].

The effect of the requirement for the representative to have been on boat in protests concerning Parts 2, 3 and 4 is to preclude legal representation for most incidents, but that cannot be excluded for an alleged breach of a fundamental rule (for not giving help under rule 1, for instance, or sailing unfairly under rule 2 if no Part 2 rule is also involved). For a protest under Part 6's rule 78 for failure to comply with class rules while racing, it is quite possible that the owner may not have been on board, but he or she is the best person to represent the boat, especially if a failure by the owner is alleged.

When protests involve young children, a parent may ask to represent the boat, with those on board called only as witnesses. My view is that this is to be resisted. Learning about protests is just one part of learning to race. The protest committee must go out of its way not to be intimidatory when one or more of the parties is a junior – sitting round a table may be better than the usual cross-table confrontational layout, blazers are to be avoided, language must be gentle, and explanations need to be given for many things, especially over the procedure to be followed. Allowing a parent or guardian to be present as an observer is recommended, as a reassurance to the junior party and to enable the adult to see that if the child loses a protest, it was not for lack of fair play by the protest committee.

Indeed, observers should in principle always be admitted. The procedure is that an observer says nothing, and sits behind the party, with no eye-contact possible, in view of the protest committee. It must be made clear at the outset to observers that they are now precluded from being witnesses, so if it is possible that they might be able to give useful information, they should withdraw and wait to be called. As well as a parent, a typical observer might be a coach, or someone interested in learning more about protest hearings. It is reasonable to ask the parties if they have any objections to an observer being present: indeed, the protest committee might be nervous of being observed; and it is never wrong to decide not to admit observers. With a confident protest committee, holding a protest in open session can be a useful training exercise if the parties are willing, even asking observers to feed back after the decision is made, but the primary objective must always be the proper decision of the protest or request.

Witnesses are summoned when needed, and leave the room after giving evidence, subject to responding to questions from the parties and protest committee about their evidence (as stated in rule 63.6). It is not sufficient for witnesses to be allowed to sit at the back of the protest room, even if they cannot make out what is being said at the front[2].

The exception is when a member of the protest committee gives evidence, whether in a protest brought by a boat, by the race committee or by the protest committee, or in a request for redress. That member is entitled both to give evidence and to take part in deciding the issue, remaining present throughout. If it is known that a member of the protest committee will give evidence, and if the protest committee has the luxury of having sufficient other members available, some protest committees would exclude that member from the protest committee hearing the case, to enter and appear only when asked as with any other witness. Others take the view that this devalues the status of a member of a protest committee. When the protest committee is an international jury of five people, it normally needs all five to be present throughout the hearing for the right of appeal to be denied in the absence of illness or emergency[3], but rule N3.2, with conditions, permits fewer to decide a protest 'when it is considered desirable the some members not participate', which would allow a similar format change. When it is decided that a member giving evidence will remain as part of the committee or jury, then, as a slight procedural concession, that member might move round to the parties' side of the table to give the evidence and be questioned.

---

[1] US 8, RYA 1987/1: US appeals appear to be slightly more sympathetic towards other procedural defects, uncontested at the time, as grounds for upholding an appeal, compared with RYA appeals.
[2] US 62
[3] N1.5

There is one situation where it is appropriate to suspend the normal procedures concerning witnesses, namely a request for redress over an alleged mistake by the protest committee that may have affected several boats. A typical situation is a dispute over the course to be sailed. In deciding any suitable redress, the protest committee has to 'make as fair an arrangement as possible for all boats affected, whether or not they asked for redress[1]'. If the hearing involves only the evidence of the requester and the race committee, it frequently happens that a decision to award redress or the nature of the redress awarded is objected to by other boats, which in turn bring their own requests for redress to seek to reverse or change what has been decided. At a regatta, this can extend over two or more days, it can raise tempers, it takes time, and it can make the protest committee look foolish. The better option can be to encourage all those potentially affected to be present throughout as if they were parties, and to give evidence (or express their views on evidence given), in the hope that an outcome fair to all boats can be arrived at[2].

When the hearing has been properly advertised, it is normal for the protest committee to proceed with the hearing if the protestee does not appear, on the understanding advised to the protestor that if a good reason emerges for the protestee not to have been present, the hearing will be reopened. The usual consequence in a regatta is that the protestee comes to the protest committee next day, having been scored DSQ, complaining that he or she was not aware of the protest. When the fact of the protest and the time and place of the hearing has been properly notified as stated in the sailing instructions, most protest committees will not be sympathetic – a boat's representative should always check the protest hearings notice (or get someone else to do so) at the time that is stated or can be deduced from the end of protest time, even if no protest against the boat is known of.

On more than one occasion I have been a member of a protest committee that has decided to proceed with a hearing in the absence of the protestee, only to penalise the protestor based on her evidence alone.

Occasionally, it will be a protestor that will not appear. Rule 63.3(b) leaves it open for the protest committee to proceed with the hearing. Some will not do so, closing the hearing on the grounds that no evidence is presented. This may not be strictly correct, since what is alleged in the protest form is 'evidence', and it presents a case to answer – so other protest committees will continue with hearing the evidence of the protestee and relevant witnesses, and then decide the protest. Naturally, the dismissal of the protest is more likely in the absence of the protestor.

In RYA 1981/10, the race committee protested a boat, which was penalised. She appealed on the grounds that that the protest committee had treated the race committee's representative as if just a witness, giving evidence and then leaving, rather than being present for all the hearing, to hear the evidence of the protestee. The appeal was dismissed, as no rule required the protestor to be present throughout.

**63.4**

Interested Party
A member of a protest committee who is an *interested party* shall not take any further part in the hearing but may appear as a witness. Protest committee members must declare any possible self-interest as soon as they are aware of it. A *party* to the hearing who believes a member of the protest committee is an *interested party* shall object as soon as possible.

---

[1] Rule 64.2
[2] Sometimes, the other boats can be made parties by the protest committee acting under rule 60.3(b) to call a hearing to consider redress for them, to be heard jointly with the original request, but only where redress might be due to more than just the original requester. Where it is clear that only the requester(s) will be entitled to any redress, only they can be parties. See rule 64.2. The absence of a basic right to be present for a boat that may later need to bring her own request for redress became a legal issue for US Sailing concerning a request for redress that affected selection for the 2008 Olympics, and it does not appear to have been fully remedied by the 2010 change to the definition Party.

An interested party is defined as a person who may gain or lose as a result of a protest committee's decision, or who has a close personal interest in the decision. So any competitor in the same race, even in the same series, will be an interested party[1]. So too will be a member of the same family or a business associate where one can influence the other[2]. There is a positive duty on a protest committee member to consider whether a prejudicial interest exists, regardless of whether any party objects, and it is not sufficient just to declare the interest – the interested party must withdraw. It is not appropriate for a member of the race committee to be a member of the protest committee when redress under rule 62.1(a) over an alleged improper action or omission of the race committee is being considered[3].

It can be difficult for a club to comply with this when its best rules experts are also competitors in the same race or series as the party. In RYA 1984/2, the chairman of the protest committee that refused redress had taken part in the race (which presumably was also part of a series), and the requester's appeal on the substance of the refusal was upheld on its merits. The RYA went on to comment: 'It is accepted that sometimes, unavoidably, fellow competitors sit on a protest committee, but it is nevertheless undesirable…The chairman of the protest committee would have been well advised to refrain from serving on it. An interested party does not cease to be such because a party to the hearing is willing to accept him as a member of the protest committee.'

Personally, I would rather appear as a party before someone with rules expertise, even if an interested party, rather than be heard by a disinterested but less capable protest committee, and that would appear to be possible. If the party realises that a member of the protest committee is an interested party, but does not object, the RYA at least is unlikely to uphold an appeal on the grounds of the interest alone. In RYA 2007/1, at a regional championship, The protest of *Miss Elainey Us* against *Blue Tack* was dismissed. The protestor was a visiting boat and the protestee was a member of the host club. The protest committee that heard the protest included a member who had a close relative who had sailed aboard *Blue Tack* in the race concerned. That fact was not disclosed to *Miss Elainey Us*'s representative at the hearing.

When the protestor pursued this after the hearing, the chairman of the protest committee acknowledged that a mistake had been made, apologised and offered a rehearing, which was accepted by the protestor.

The organizing authority club then revoked this offer, and no new hearing was convened. *Miss Elainey Us* appealed. Her appeal was upheld. The decision of the protest committee to rehear the protest was confirmed, for a hearing by a new protest committee.

> An organizing authority has no power to override a decision of a protest committee, including a decision to reopen a hearing.
>
> While that is reason sufficient to uphold the appeal, the RYA notes that the protest committee was correct to decide to reopen the hearing. Rule 63.4 states that a member of a protest committee who is an interested party shall not take any further part in the hearing, and that protest committee members must declared any possible self-interest as soon as they are aware of it. The correct procedure is for the chairman of a protest committee to establish before a hearing starts that that no member is an interested party. See Appendix M, section 2. The proceedings of the protest committee were contrary to these requirements, and the original decision was improper, as the protest committee chairman then realised. This is not to cast any aspersion on the integrity of any member of the protest committee.
>
> The duty of the protest committee chairman to make sure that no member of the protest committee is an interested party is additional to the entitlement of a party to object to any member of the protest committee at the start of the hearing. It is sometimes the case that an interested party will serve on a protest committee with the knowledge and consent of the parties. When that happens, a party forfeits the right to appeal on that ground alone, since the party has not complied with the final sentence of rule 63.4. It is not clear in this case whether the parties were asked at the start of the hearing if they objected to any member of the protest committee, but it is clear that the appellant was unaware of facts that were known to members of the protest committee, and the RYA sees no reason to doubt his statement that 'if I had been told that there was a connection I would have objected to this person being a member of the panel.'

---

[1] However, a competitor who retires from a series ceases to be interested party: CYA 57
[2] I suppose one could exclude a co-worker when the club is part of a business's sports and social activities, for employees only.
[3] US 39, and see Appendix M, section 2.

The RYA cases admit of the possibility of an appeal over an interested party failing, because no objection was made at the time of the hearing, and, even when objection is made, the outcome may be the ordering of a proper hearing of the protest by a new disinterested committee unless the appeal can be upheld immediately on other substantive grounds. The abstract of US 22 appears to take a tougher line, in stating without qualification that the participation in the protest committee of a competitor in the same race or series as is the subject of the protest or request for redress makes the hearing invalid. However, examination of the facts of the case indicates that an objection to the composition of the protest committee was made (and presumably overruled) at the original hearing. Nevertheless, the appeal decision was the reinstatement of the disqualified competitor rather than a fresh hearing, even though the facts of the case indicated the *prima facie* breach of a rule.

Although the rule does not require it, it is wise, as recommended by Appendix M, section 2, to open a hearing by introducing the members of the protest committee and asking whether the parties have any objection on the grounds of interest to any member. Likewise, the protest committee members should be reminded of their obligations by asking them if they have any interest to declare. When the protest committee is an international jury, issues of nationality are no grounds for objection.

63.5

Validity of the Protest or Request for Redress

At the beginning of the hearing the protest committee shall take any evidence it considers necessary to decide whether all requirements for the *protest* or request for redress have been met. If they have been met, the *protest* or request is valid and the hearing shall be continued. If not, the committee shall declare the *protest* or request invalid and close the hearing. If the *protest* has been made under rule 60.3(a)(1), the committee shall also determine whether or not injury or serious damage resulted from the incident in question. If not, the hearing shall be closed.

Appendix M 3.1 summarises the validity checks to be made, as already discussed under the rules concerned. The related tick-boxes in up-to-date protest forms are another useful guide. Throughout this verification, a protestee should be given the opportunity to object. If there is any doubt over these issues, the parties should be asked to 'wait outside' while the protest committee discusses and decides the validity[1].

- Are the contents adequate (rule 61.2 or 62.1[2])?
- Was it delivered in time? If not, is there good reason to extend the time limit (rule 61.3 or 62.2)?
- When required, was the protestor involved in or a witness to the incident (rule 60.1(a))?
- When necessary, was 'Protest' hailed and, if required, a red flag displayed correctly (rule 61.1(a))?
- When the flag or hail was not necessary, was the protestee informed?
- Decide whether the *protest* or request for redress is valid (rule 63.5).
- Once the validity of the *protest* or request has been determined, do not let the subject be introduced again unless truly new evidence is available.

When a protest is then found to be valid, a protestee who, when asked, has made no objection to its validity cannot then raise validity as an issue in an appeal[3].

In addition, when the protest is brought by the protest committee under rule 60.3(a)(1) on suspicion of injury or serious damage, the next duty is to verify that there was indeed such injury or damage – if not, the hearing stops right there.

---

[1] RYA 1981/5
[2] As discussed, the contents of the protest or request can be very skimpy, as long as an incident is identified, and the misidentification by a protestor of the rule thought to be broken is not material, see ISAF 22.
[3] RYA 1981/5

All of these checks must be made within a hearing. A protest committee cannot refuse to open a protest hearing, for instance because the protest form was lodged outside the protest time limit. The protestor must be given the opportunity, within the hearing, to make out a good case for an extension of the time limit[1]. If no good case is forthcoming, only then can the protest be ruled invalid and the hearing closed.

63.6 Taking Evidence and Finding Facts

The protest committee shall take the evidence of the *parties* to the hearing and of their witnesses and other evidence it considers necessary. A member of the protest committee who saw the incident may give evidence. A *party* to the hearing may question any person who gives evidence. The committee shall then find the facts and base its decision on them.

Once again, Appendix M gives concise advice, here in section 3.2, to which are added further suggestions from this writer. Ask the protestor and then the protestee to tell their stories. Then allow them to question one another. In a redress matter, ask the *party* to state the request.

- *Have the parties sit apart from each other, with a chair between them set aside for a witness.*
- *The protest committee chairman may intervene to get immediate clarification of unclear points when they are made.*
- *The use of model boat shapes is recommended. Kits of models are available from the RYA or via ISAF, and ideally there should be sufficient models for each party to build up the sequence of what happened, resulting in something resembling one of the diagrams in this book. My experience, given four numbered models of the same colour for each party's boat, is that it is easiest to ask each of the parties to start with models nos 3 to represent the closest point of approach between the boats, and then to work back with models nos 2 then 1 to show how the incident developed, followed by models nos 4 to show what happened next. Each will thereby produce a separate 'diagram' of what is asserted to have happened, and once each party is satisfied with his or her own diagram, it must not then be touched, except as allowed by the protest committee. So at the end of the parties' evidence, there will be two diagrams on the protest room table.*
- *Many parties find it difficult to ask questions, and instead start making or repeating assertions. This must be gently deterred, or amended to the form 'Would you agree that…?'*

Invite questions from protest committee members.

- *Inconsistencies can often be identified from the model diagrams.*
- *When there are a number of protests to be heard, rotate the order in which the protest committee members ask their questions, so that each one will have the opportunity to ask the 'killer question'.*

Make sure you know what facts each party is alleging before calling any witnesses. Their stories may be different.

Allow anyone, including a boat's crew, to give evidence. It is the party who normally decides which witnesses to call, although the protest committee may also call witnesses (rule 63.6). The question asked by a *party* 'Would you like to hear N?' is best answered by 'It is your choice.'

- *There may be no witnesses, in which case the protest committee has to decide from evidence of the parties what happened[2]. There is a primary onus of proof on the protestor to show that a rule has been broken[3].*
- *The responsibility for having a witness ready to be called lies with the party wishing to introduce that witness's evidence. The fact that the schedule of protest hearings may identify named on the protest form witnesses does not put any obligation either on the witness to attend, or on the protest committee to secure the attendance[4].*
- *Parties are often reluctant to call witnesses from their boat, and assume that the protest committee will assume that the evidence will be the result of collusion. My experience is that witnesses are just as likely to tell a story slightly or considerably different from the party's, and this often sheds a useful light on what happened. Sometimes, the witness's evidence will torpedo the related party's case.*

---

[1] US 69: likewise, officious race office staff must be deterred from refusing to accept apparently out-of-time protest forms – the protest committee may find a good reason to extend the protest time limit
[2] RYA 1992/7
[3] RYA 1990/3
[4] RYA 1984/14

- *A party cannot be prevented from calling a witness but there comes a point when repetition of the same assertions will not add anything, a fact that the protest committee is entitled to draw to the attention of the party concerned.*

Call each *party's* witnesses (and the protest committee's if any) one by one. Limit *parties* to questioning the witness(es) (they may wander into general statements).

- *Do not allow the party to leave the room to find the witness. Instead send out a member of the protest committee, to avoid any possibility or suspicion of a quick conference before the witness appears.*
- *If the parties' model diagrams are on the table, cover them with paper, and get the witness to make a similar diagram with fresh models. You may end up with three or four diagrams on the table.*

Invite the protestee to question the protestor's witness first (and vice versa). This prevents the protestor from leading his witness from the beginning.

Allow a member of the protest committee who saw the incident to give evidence (rule 63.6) but only in the presence of the *parties*. The member may be questioned and may remain in the room (rule 63.3(a)).

Try to prevent leading questions or hearsay evidence, but if that is impossible discount the evidence so obtained.

Accept written evidence from a witness who is not available to be questioned only if all *parties* agree. In doing so they forego their rights to question that witness (rule 63.6)[1].

Ask one member of the committee to note down evidence, particularly times, distances, speeds, etc.

Invite first the protestor and then the protestee to make a final statement of her case, particularly on any application or interpretation of the *rules*.

The protest committee must now find the facts. Appendix M advises:

Write down the facts; resolve doubts one way or the other.

Call back *parties* for more questions if necessary.

When appropriate, draw a diagram of the incident using the facts you have found.

Easily said, but often difficult to do. The evidence will often conflict, with the story of each party being perfectly plausible were it not for the equally plausible case of the other party[2]. But the protest committee must arrive at a single set of facts[3]. If there was contact in a boat-versus-boat incident, that almost always obliges facts to be found leading to a finding that one or both boats, or another boat broke a rule[4]. In RYA 2008/4, *A Boen* was clear astern of *X Factor* and then became overlapped to leeward. There was contact resulting in minor damage. There was no change of course by *X Factor*. The protest committee found that *A Boen* could have avoided the contact, but decided that it had insufficient evidence to disqualify either boat as the evidence was conflicting, the damage was minimal and it had not been proven that a boat had broken a rule. It referred its decision to the RYA under rule 70.2. Correcting the decision of the protest committee (and penalizing *A Boen* under rules 14 and 15), the RYA said:

When there is an incident and one of the boats decides to protest, all boats involved are at risk of penalisation if they do not retire or (as was possible at this event) take an available penalty. It is of the essence of protests that the parties disagree as to what happened. The protest committee must decide facts regarding what they believe happened, and those facts need not coincide with what any one party alleged. It may be that the facts found differ from what happened, but that can only be demonstrated if new evidence gives rise to a reopening.

---

[1] US 63 disagrees, in upholding an appeal because written evidence was accepted, despite there being no reference to any objection to this at the hearing by the appellant

[2] This is written just after returning from the jury at a European dinghy championship where S the protestor said that P tacked so close and late that S had to tack off to avoid contact. Nonsense, said P, we never came within 7 metres. A witness from another boat supported the story of the protestor, perhaps too glibly. We came to finding a distance apart close enough to support a conclusion that S could not sail her course without needing to take avoiding action. P was disqualified, and was upset. It was with some relief that after the hearing a sequence of photographs from the event photographer was produced, showing almost exactly what the protestor had claimed. Had it been otherwise, we would of course have reopened.

[3] CYA 75

[4] But see ISAF 77, RYA 1999/5 and rule 22

Even if the facts are in dispute and there was no contact, that alone should not lead a protest committee to find facts that would not result in penalisation. However, when there is contact in an incident away from any mark or obstruction, then, except in a limited number of special cases (none of which apply in this protest), a right-of-way rule in Section A of Part 2 will already have been broken by one of the boats before the contact.

A protest committee is therefore required to make its best judgement as to what happened, in terms that will enable it to decide which rule or rules, if any, were broken by which boat. The protest committee may feel uncomfortable to do so, but the parties have, as stated above, consented to the risk of an unfavourable decision being made on facts with which they do not agree. Those facts will stand on appeal or reference, unless they are inadequate or perverse having regards to the evidence, in which case the national authority would require a fresh hearing.

I see many protest forms in the appeals decided by the RYA, and the commonest failing of protest committees is to arrive at conclusions without stating the facts leading to those conclusions[1]. To find that *Iris* did not keep clear of *Daffodil* is a conclusion, not a fact, to be derived from facts such as *Iris* on starboard tack ran into the stern of *Daffodil* on the same tack. The boundary between facts and conclusions is in fact somewhat blurred. As Mary Pera pointed out, to state that a boat is close-hauled on starboard tack may seem like a fact, but it is in fact a conclusion derived from the wind direction relative to her heading and to the setting of her sails. Ready-made conclusions of this sort are acceptable as facts, otherwise protest decisions would be needlessly elaborate.

Descriptions of damage are often on or over the borderline of fact and conclusion. To state that *Iris* was seriously damaged in a collision is a conclusion derived from facts that must be stated, such as that *Daffodil*'s bow struck *Iris* on her port side two metres from the stern, resulting in a hole 50 cm x 20 cm at its widest extent that broke a rib, admitted water and which was estimated to cost £4,000 to repair. Such facts are non-judgmental, even though the conclusion to be drawn may be obvious. ISAF 104 examines the fuzzy boundary between facts and conclusions in more detail.

> …the two concepts can overlap…a 'fact' is an action or condition that a protest committee 'finds' occurred or existed. A 'conclusion' is derived by reasoning from something else, and can be purely factual. For example, if the facts are that there were three classes in a race and five boats in each class, it is both a conclusion and a fact that there were 15 boat in the race. A conclusion can also be partially non-factual, as when a judgment is made that includes non-factual elements. An example is the statement 'Boat A displayed her protest flag at the first reasonable opportunity after the incident', which is based on a combination of the facts about an incident and an interpretation of the phrase 'first reasonable opportunity' in rule 61.1(a)[2].

There may be less to this ISAF case than meets the eye, at least as concerns distinguishing fact from conclusion. A less intellectual approach is to ask oneself 'Could a person with little knowledge of the club, the class and the conditions understand what happened from the 'facts found'? Could that person construct a diagram or picture what happened from what is written?' If not, it may be that a protest committee diagram would show the facts more clearly – indeed, a diagram is as much a finding of facts as the related words[3].

The task of the protest committee in boat-versus-boat right-of-way protest is more difficult when there was no contact. The facts found must be relevant to the rules applying to the situation, which is in part a putting of the cart before the horse. If is a question as to whether one boat kept clear of the other, the decision will be made by applying the definition Keep Clear to the facts, which will be a combination of the courses and speeds of the boats, of the conditions, and of communication between the boats. If the issue is whether room was given as required, the elements of the definition Room must be established as facts – the space given or available, the description of the existing conditions, and, if applicable the speed and description of the boat's manoeuvre. The conclusion will then be a judgement as to whether the space given was adequate in those existing conditions for a manoeuvre that was prompt and seamanlike.

---

[1] The distinction is important, since under rule 70.1 facts found by the protest committee have to accepted by the national authority unless they appear perverse, whereas the conclusions drawn from those facts are appealable.
[2] Even the words 'displayed her protest flag' are a semi-conclusion. The full facts might be 'broke out a red flag 20 cm x 15 cm from her backstay'.
[3] ISAF 104: diagrams are rarely produced by protest committees, if only because there is no longer any space on the standard protest form for one, but if an appeal is likely, the early production of a protest committee diagram while the case is fresh in the mind will assist the appeal process.

As a reality check, if the facts found include terms like 'did (or did not) keep clear / give room / avoid / interfere', there is a danger that this is a conclusion. If the facts supporting the conclusion are also stated, it is not a major crime for the conclusion to appear under 'facts found'. But if there are no facts, only conclusions, then the protest committee has not properly explained the reasons for its decision. In the exceptional circumstance that the case goes to appeal, this will be detected and corrected. If, as is usual, it does not, then one or both parties may be left with a feeling of dissatisfaction over the decision, and the protest committee may have unwittingly made an incorrect decision. A protest committee will not go far wrong in stating facts as bullet points, written on the assumption that the decision may go to appeal and so will need to be self-explanatory.

A similar approach is needed with requests for redress. What happened, the boat's score and whether a penalty has been imposed under rule 2 or there has been disciplinary action under rule 69.1(b) are all facts. 'Fault', 'significantly worse', 'improper', 'omission', 'injury', 'physical damage', 'breaking a rule of Part 2', 'not racing', 'required to keep clear', 'giving help' and 'in compliance with rule 1.1' are all conclusions – what are the facts relevant to such conclusions?

63.7

Conflict between the Notice of Race and the Sailing Instructions

If there is a conflict between a rule in the notice of race and one in the sailing instructions that must be resolved before the protest committee can decide a *protest* or request for redress, the committee shall apply the rule that it believes will provide the fairest result for all boats affected.

This rule should really be in rule 64, Decisions. It is getting ahead of itself in rule 63. This is the only racing rule that establishes a precedence between conflicting provisions. ISAF 98 says that otherwise there is no inherent precedence between a provision of the notice of race and a sailing instruction.

RYA 2002/8 would seek to qualify this.

Question
If the sailing instructions say that a sailing instruction prevails when there is a conflict between the notice of race and a sailing instruction, is that binding?
Answer
A statement in the sailing instructions that they are to prevail over the notice of race is not binding. Any such provision should be in the notice of race itself, and should refer to rule 63.7 as being changed.

The (unexplained) logic behind this is that the notice of race is produced by the organizing authority, which is also tasked with appointing the race committee, which is the body that produces the sailing instructions. The race committee therefore has only the powers granted to it by the rules and by the notice of race. No rule allows it to override the notice of race, over which it has no control, and so only the organizing authority can grant the race committee the power to create obligations that conflict with the notice of race. However, that is a very technical argument, and competitors cannot be expected to realise that a statement in the sailing instructions that says that the sailing instructions prevail over the notice of race in the event of conflict may be of dubious validity – added to which ISAF 98 does not appear to support such an interpretation.

The more important point arising from RYA 2002/8 is that when a sailing instruction purports to give precedence to the sailing instructions when there is a conflict, this will be ineffective unless the last sentence of rule 86.1(b) is complied with, and the sailing instruction explicitly says that rule 63.7 is changed.

Not that the word 'rule' in rule 63.7 is used twice without italics. This limits the rules concerned to conflicting clauses of the notice of race and the sailing instructions. Rule 63.7 does not extend to resolving differences between a clause in one of those documents and some other *rule* that is called up by the notice of race or the sailing instructions, for instance in a typical SI 1 which says that the event will be governed by the Racing Rules of Sailing. Apparent conflicts between a racing rule that governs the event and a clause of the notice of race or sailing instructions are to be resolved by deciding whether rule 86.1(b) has been properly applied. If not, the racing rule will prevail.

Conflicts between the notice of race and sailing instructions are not uncommon, particularly as they may have been produced by different people at different times.

For instance, the notice of race may say that two races may be discarded, and this might result in a boat deciding not to sail the two races scheduled for the first day, and making other arrangements for that day – only to arrive at the event to find that the sailing instructions say that only one race result may be excluded. When the boat asks for redress, and if the protest committee agrees that redress is due, it must apply the fairest (or, in this case, fairer) rule for all boats affected. If she is the only boat affected, the protest committee might decide as redress to allow her the two discards (as per the notice of race), or it might keep her to a single discard (as per the sailing instructions) but then award her average points for one of the day-one races missed.

Protests Between Boats in Different Races

A *protest* between boats sailing in different races conducted by different organizing authorities shall be heard by a protest committee acceptable to those authorities.

The rule is self-explanatory, and no issues have arisen in cases.

DECISIONS

Penalties and Exoneration

(a) When the protest committee decides that a boat that is a *party* to a protest hearing has broken a *rule*, it shall disqualify her unless some other penalty applies. A penalty shall be imposed whether or not the applicable *rule* was mentioned in the *protest*.

Once upon a time, if you broke a rule, you either retired or risked a protest and a disqualification. If you were to reinvent the sport of sailing, would you choose disqualification as the default penalty? Whatever your view, there has been a proliferation of penalties. These divide into those that a boat can take or her own volition, as we shall see under rule 64.1(b), those that a race committee can impose without a hearing (ZPF under rule 30.2, BFD and DNE under 30.3), those that a protest committee can impose without a hearing (DNE under rule 67 or Two Turns, DSQ, DNE and DNE all races under Appendix P), and, under this rule, those that a protest committee can give when there is a hearing[1].

When there is a hearing, as well as disqualification (DSQ), there is the harsher non-excludable disqualification (DNE) under rule 2, Fair Sailing. When, through Appendix G, Identification on Sails, rule 77 is broken, the protest committee has the option of penalisation (i.e., disqualification) or a warning provided she then complies. When rule 80, Advertising is broken (via ISAF regulation 20), the regulation provides a range of options from a warning to DSQ in one or more races, with the back-up of rule 69.1. When rule 64.3, Decision on Measurement Protests, applies, minor deviations caused by wear or damage may result in no penalty, while a measurement disqualification in respect of a deviation not then corrected and not reversed by any appeal will result in retrospective automatic disqualification from all subsequent races as well.

---

[1] In addition, there is the warning and wide range of penalties available under rule 69, Allegations of Gross Misconduct, which is a process separate from protest hearings.

Sailing instructions can and do change penalties. In events where the competitors are heavily sponsored, the tendency is not to use disqualification, and time penalties are usually used instead, for all but the most severe infringements. Often there is a tariff of time penalties depending on the nature of the infringement, and there may be an element of discretion given to the protest committee as to the 'length of the sentence'.

The RYA recommends the use of an exoneration penalty, being a 20% place penalty, as part of its Rules Disputes Procedure, which seeks to augment (and substantially replace) the protest system with one or both of an informal 'advisory hearing' and an arbitration hearing of a lodged protest by a single arbitrator for breaches of rules of Part 2 and of rule 31. The objective is to encourage issues to result in a hearing rather than just be ignored, to dispose of issues more quickly than by a protest hearing, and to allow a penalty of less than disqualification to be accepted as an incentive for compliance with the Basic Principle, Sportsmanship and the Rules[1].

Only a party to a protest hearing can be penalised[2]. When a protest committee believes from the evidence in a valid protest hearing that a boat that is not a party to that hearing was involved and broke a rule, and wishes to protest her, it must stop, notify the boat of a protest, and start again with her as an additional party[3]. When it realises while hearing a request for redress that a boat broke a rule, it cannot penalise her in that hearing[4], nor can it use that knowledge to protest and then penalise her unless injury or serious damage is suspected[5].

Just as a protest cannot be refused because the protest form quotes the wrong rule in relation to the incident[6], penalisation will follow even when the protest committee finds that the rule that was broken was any mentioned by the protestor on the protest form.

It may be that it is the protestor that is found to have broken a rule, and is to be disqualified[7], while the protestee can have the protest against her dismissed because she has not broken a rule, or she can be exonerated because the protestor compelled her to break a rule.

When a protest committee decides to penalise a boat, the race committee must implement the decision via the scoring system[8].

Unless a boat is compelled to break a rule by another boat, the protest committee must impose the appropriate penalty – disqualification, unless some other penalty applies. There is no standard provision for giving a lesser penalty because the infringement was trivial, or was partly the responsibility of another boat[9]. It is for this reason that sailing instructions often provide for penalties less severe than disqualification for infringements involving tallying, trash or wearing personal flotation devices. Because the rule accepts that sailing instructions can provide for a different penalty, it is not necessary, when stating a different penalty in the sailing instructions, to say that rule 64.1(a) is changed.

64.1(b)

(b) If a boat has taken an applicable penalty, rule 64.1(a) does not apply to her unless the penalty for a *rule* she broke is a disqualification that is not excludable from her series score.

---

[1] Full details are to be found on the RYA website.
[2] RYA 2004/1
[3] Rules 60.3(a)(2) and 61.1(c).
[4] RYA 2001/12
[5] Rule 60.3(a)
[6] ISAF 22
[7] RYA 2004/1
[8] ISAF 66
[9] RYA 2006/6

When a boat breaks a rule of Part 2, and takes a two-turns penalty, her turns (or retirement) will insure her against penalisation in any protest – likewise if she took a one-turn penalty (or retired) for touching a mark – because rule 44.1(b) says so. However, if she is nevertheless protested, and the protest committee decides that she broke rule 2, Fair Sailing, as well, for which the penalty is a non-excludable penalty (DNE), her turns will not prevent her penalisation under that rule. Likewise, if sailing instructions say that the penalty for breaking a specific sailing instruction is a DNE, and a boat retires having broken the sailing instruction, no rule prevents the boat being protested, and no rule says that retirement will preclude her further penalisation[1].

 **64.1(c)**

(c)   When as a consequence of breaking a *rule* a boat has compelled another boat to break a *rule*, rule 64.1(a) does not apply to the other boat and she shall be exonerated.

Iris touches a mark. She protests *Daffodil* for not giving her room at the mark. If the protest is upheld, and if the protest committee is satisfied that *Iris* was compelled to touch the mark because of *Daffodil*'s rule breach, *Daffodil* will be penalised, and *Iris* will be exonerated for her breach of rule 31.

Another example is when *Iris* touches a mark, does not take a penalty, and is protested by *Vindictive*. She shows that she touched the mark because *Daffodil* was required to give her mark-room and did not do so, thus compelling her to break rule 31. She is therefore to be exonerated. It is not necessary for *Daffodil* to be protested in order that she can be found to have broken a rule, although a protest committee might want to hear from *Daffodil* before agreeing that *Iris* was forced to break a rule, in which case it should act under rule 60.3(a)(2) and 61.1(c), to restart proceedings with *Daffodil* as a protested party, so that either *Daffodil* will be penalised under rule 18, in which case Iris will be exonerated: or *Iris* will be disqualified if *Daffodil* is not shown to have compelled *Iris* to touch the mark[2].

The situation is simpler if *Daffodil* can be shown to have taken a two-turns penalty at the time. Provided that the protest committee is satisfied that it was taken for not giving room (a turns acknowledgement form, if used at the event, may give sufficient information), the exoneration of *Iris* will be a simpler matter. Likewise, in both ISAF 3 and ISAF 10, the boat that caused the incident retired and was not protested (although she could have been protested but not penalised), but that did not prevent the retirer from being found to have compelled the protestee to have broken a rule.

ISAF 3 makes the further point that a right-of-way boat or one entitled to room is not required to anticipate that the other boat will not keep clear or give room, and may be able to play the 'compulsion' card even if the infringement was predictable.

In ISAF 51, there were multiple protests. *Daffodil* did not keep clear of *Iris* to leeward of her. Why? Because *Thetis* was overlapped to windward of *Daffodil*, and did not keep clear. Why? Because *Intrepid* was overlapped to windward of *Thetis* and did not keep clear when she bore away to try to avoid being OCS. So *Intrepid* was penalised for breaking rule 11, and *Thetis* and *Daffodil* were exonerated on appeal for breaking rule 11 because they were in turn compelled to do so by *Intrepid*. So the compulsion may be indirect. For a boat to be exonerated, there must be a causal link between her breach and the breach of the other boat. *Daffodil* may have been wrongly forced by *Iris* onto the course side of the starting line so as to be OCS at her starting signal, and she may win her protest against *Iris*, but that does not relieve of the obligation to return and start, since nothing prevented her from doing so[3]. Likewise, if *Daffodil* is wrongly denied room at a mark and is forced to pass it on the wrong side, she must return and pass it correctly to comply with rule 28. If *Iris* tacks in the zone at a windward mark so as to require *Daffodil* to luff above close-hauled to keep clear, *Daffodil* must luff if she can. If not, she breaks rule 11, even though *Iris* has broken rule 18.3. Two wrongs, unless intimately linked, do not make a right.

---

[1] RYA 2005/5

[2] US 84 says that no rule precludes a protest committee from deciding, based on the facts, that any boat in the incident has broken a rule, and, in that case, although the boat responsible for the situation was not a party to the hearing, the protest committee was able to find sufficient facts to decide that she broke a rule, leading to exonerate for the boat that was a party to the protest. My experience is that boats in *Daffodil*'s position will often not appear at hearing, despite having been called as a witness, which is perhaps understandable given a fear of self-incrimination

[3] RYA 2003/6

ISAF 3 and US 2 both look at a situation where the boat seeking to be exonerated had a choice as to what she could do.

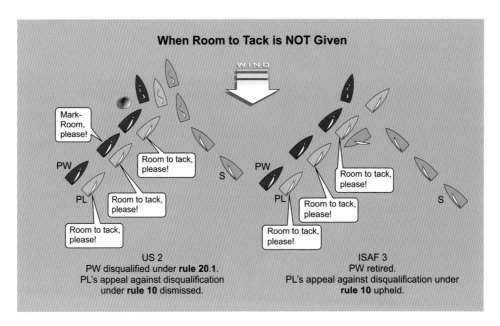

When Room to Tack is NOT Given

US 2
PW disqualified under **rule 20.1**.
PL's appeal against disqualification
under **rule 10** dismissed.

ISAF 3
PW retired.
PL's appeal against disqualification under
rule 10 upheld.

In each case, PL hailed PW for room to tack and clear S, an obstruction, and in each case PW did not respond, preventing PL from keeping clear and obliging S to take action to avoid contact (by bearing away in ISAF 3, by luffing in US 2).

In US 2, PL was not exonerated for breaking rule 10, because she was said not to have been compelled to break the rule, since she could have gone astern of S when PW did not respond. ISAF 3 says however that PW was not obliged to anticipate PW's failure to comply with rule 19. The difference appears to be that in US 2, when PW did not respond to the hail, PL still had the opportunity of passing astern of S and it was not clear that PW would not respond to the hail until she actually failed to do so; whereas in ISAF 3, by the time PW had failed to respond to PL's hail (her third), the diagram suggests that bearing away was no longer an option for PL, who could only stand on and hope that S would take avoiding action. But since ISAF 3's PL could have borne away astern of S when her first and second hails were unsuccessful, she had a way out at those points, and so became compelled to infringe only because she chose to stand on and hail again. These cases have stood for years[1], but it is not clear whether they are compatible. If not, ISAF 3 must prevail[2].

'Meat in the sandwich' situations are a regular source of cases related to compulsion. In US 78, *Daffodil* was the leeward of three overlapped port-tack close-hauled boats. She tacked to starboard, as did *Iris* to windward of her, but *Iris* was not able to give *Thetis*, to windward of her and still on port tack, room to keep clear. *Iris* was disqualified by the protest committee for not giving room to *Thetis*. On appeal, *Iris* was exonerated, since she was compelled to infringe because *Daffodil* had not given her room under rule 15. *Daffodil* was disqualified.

---

[1] 1940, 1962
[2] US 19's facts – a hail not responded to - and decision – the exoneration of PL -are similar to ISAF 3.

Exoneration will also be available to a boat compelled to break a sailing instruction. However, the wording of the sailing instruction may unexpectedly prevent exoneration. In RYA 2005/8, *Habanero* collided with a moored vessel, causing it to move into the path of *Jump the Gun!*, which touched the moored vessel. *Jump the Gun!* was protested by *Heartbeat 2* for breaking a sailing instruction that said that 'an entered boat that collides with or fends off a moored or anchored vessel at any time shall retire and report the collision to the race office.' *Jump the Gun!* had reported the collision, but had not retired. The protest committee noted that *Habanero* had retired, and exonerated *Jump the Gun!*, by implication because *Jump the Gun!* was compelled to break the sailing instruction because of an infringement by *Habanero*. *Heartbeat 2* appealed. The appeal was upheld, and *Jump the Gun!* was disqualified.

> The sailing instruction does not say 'a boat shall not collide with or fend off a moored or anchored vessel'. Rather it imposes an obligation on a boat when a collision occurs, namely to retire and report the incident. The collision itself is not prohibited. Nothing that *Habanero* did prevented *Jump the Gun!* from complying with the requirement in the sailing instruction to retire, and so exoneration under rule 64.1(b) is not appropriate. She failed to retire, thus breaking the sailing instruction, and is therefore disqualified for not retiring, by virtue of rule 64.1(a). Nor does any part of rule 62, Redress, allow any compensation.

> For the same reason, it should be noted that *Habenero* did not break the sailing instruction. Indeed, she complied with it by retiring.

> *Jump the Gun!* refers to several cases in support of her exoneration. These were all situations where a boat was compelled to break a 'shall not' rule.

In summary, a boat is to be exonerated only when compelled by another boat's infringement to fail to comply with what the rule concerned obliges her to do or not do.

(d) If a boat has broken a *rule* when not *racing*, her penalty shall apply to the race sailed nearest in time to that of the incident.

With one exception, if a boat breaks a rule of Part 2 before or after she is racing, she cannot be penalised, because the preamble to Part 2 says so. Therefore, this rule does not apply to her. The exception is rule 23.1, Interfering with Another Boat, which is aimed directly at a boat not racing, and where the same preamble allows for penalisation – which is therefore applied to the race before or after, whichever is nearest in time.

A common example of a rule that can be broken while a boat is not racing is a sailing instruction that says that competitors shall wear personal flotation devices at all times when afloat. This means what it says. Sometimes, a non-racing prohibition may not have been intended. A sailing instruction will often say that a boat shall not pass between the committee boat and an inner mark of the starting line 'at any time'. That too means what it says, although when I come across it before an event, I ask the race committee if a total ban was intended. Often the answer is 'no', and an amendment is put in to make it apply only while racing.

Decisions on Redress

When the protest committee decides that a boat is entitled to redress under rule 62, it shall make as fair an arrangement as possible for all boats affected, whether or not they asked for redress. This may be to adjust the scoring (see rule A10 for some examples) or finishing times of boats, to *abandon* the race, to let the results stand or to make some other arrangement. When in doubt about the facts or probable results of any arrangement for the race or series, especially before *abandoning* the race, the protest committee shall take evidence from appropriate sources.

Most decisions to award redress will flow naturally from the balance of the evidence in the hearing. However, when a boat is contesting a decision of the race committee, especially an OCS score, it is the competitor that has to prove that the race committee made a mistake, and, in effect, beyond a reasonable doubt. The race officer is the best person to 'call the line', and when he can show that the race committee procedures for recording OCS boats was reliable, that will usually prevail over even the most plausible contention from the boat that she was on the pre-course side of the starting line at all material times[1]. The competitor's task may be a little easier when the boat admits to having been OCS, but claims that she realised this, returned and started. It is possible that the race committee will not have seen her return because of other boats obscuring its view, and she may be able to convince the protest committee that she did return[2].

On the other hand, when redress is sought because of an alleged ambiguity in the sailing instructions[3] or in the display of the course[4], or when inadequate race committee equipment results in a loss of places by a competitor[5], the competitor is entitled to any benefit of the doubt.

When a protest committee decides that redress is due, it has a wide range of options from which to choose the most appropriate redress. The primary task is to compensate the requester for her worsened score, but the redress must also be as fair as possible for all boats affected. Other boats can be affected in two ways. They may be boats which were affected by the same issue as affected the requester, but they may not have asked for redress, and now find themselves the recipients of a pleasant unrequested surprise. On the other hand, they may be boats that were unaffected by the issue giving rise to redress, and that now find that the redress given to one or more boat has worsened their own positions relative to those boats. Sometimes, the redress that is as fair as possible for all boats affected may not be particularly favourable for the requester[6].

Despite this, many redress issues that are in effect the correction of mistakes will not in fact require the impact on other boats to be considered. For example, *Daffodil* is scored OCS. She did not return when a recall signal was made. She asks for redress, makes out a convincing case that she was not OCS, and is therefore simply reinstated into her finishing position. *Iris* is scored DNF because the race committee thinks she did not sail the course. She asks for redress because she DID finish as defined, and has not been protested for not sailing the course (which she would in any case deny). Again, she is reinstated into her finishing position. *Thetis* is caught on the course side of the starting line in the last minute of a Black Flag start that is then recalled. The race committee, by mistake, does not display her sail number, but, as she then sailed in the restart of the race, it scores her DNE. The fact that she broke rule 30.3 is not contested (or is not sustained if it is contested), and so redress corrects her score to the one that would have applied had her sail number been displayed and she had not taken part in the restart, namely a 'vanilla' BFD[7].

That last example is a reminder that redress is not intended to be a reward for the competitor or a punishment for the race committee. It is compensation: it is, as far as possible, the putting of the boat into the position that would have applied if the incident giving rise to redress had not happened. With a wrongful OCS or DNF, that is easily determined. But when *Daffodil* IS OCS, and does not return, and the race committee then removes flag X too early, the question in any subsequent request for redress by Daffodil against an OCS score is what Daffodil would have done if the X flag had not been removed early. RYA 2006/2 considers this:

> If the protest committee is satisfied that the boat would have returned if flag X had been displayed for longer, it should award redress. Appropriate redress would be to reinstate her in the race and add to her finishing time the estimated time for the boat to sail back to the start line and then return to the point at which she turned back, which, in this case, is unlikely to be less than two minutes. Reinstating the boat in her actual finishing position will be wrong as it will not be equitable to all boats, as required by rule 64.2. If the protest committee is not satisfied that the boat would have turned back if flag X had been displayed for longer, redress should be refused.

---

[1] RYA 1994/8
[2] CYA 97
[3] RYA 1984/2
[4] RYA 2008/2
[5] RYA 1989/10: surplus anchor line floated free, and a boat caught it, dragging the mark onto her.
[6] RYA 1994/3
[7] ISAF 96

This follows ISAF 31, which adds that no redress is due when the boat knew she was OCS – indeed by not returning and starting she breaks rule 2 and has not complied with the Basic Principle, Sportsmanship and the Rules.

When redress is due to a boat for having gone to help another boat, then it may be possible simply to deduct the time taken in giving help from her finishing time, if both can be established. In practice, given the short duration of most races, the helper might not be able to resume the race and finish in the time limit, or times might not be recorded, and the position of the helper in the race before she gave the help might be a better guide.

Redress for giving help in oceanic races can be difficult, even if all the relevant times are known. *Daffodil* responds to an emergency call from *Iris*, which is some miles away at a right angle to *Daffodil*'s course. She takes 20 hours to go to *Iris* and to help her. She then resumes her course towards the next mark or finishing line. Is it just a question of deducting 20 hours from *Daffodil*'s finishing time? Usually not. In going to help, in being delayed and in sailing the rest of the race in a different part of the ocean, she may have been affected by wind and weather conditions that she would not have encountered on her original course. A benefit of 20 hours might move her up or down many places compared with her expected finishing position. Fortunately, the positions of all boats in such races are plotted at frequent intervals, and redress can be calculated by reference to her charted position in the race relative to others when she departs her course to give help. But when boats are spread across the ocean, so there is no reliable reference boat to establish what might have happened if *Daffodil* had not gone to help, even this can be difficult. However, it is now possible to run 'what if' simulations, if the race committee has access to such software.

This adjustment of finishing times is specifically contemplated in rule 64.2. The places will follow from the redress granted. If however the data for granting a time benefit as redress is not available, and it is decided to adjust the scoring, that means in effect the awarding of points for a particular finishing place, as given as an example in rule A10(c). A scoring redress based on a position may be appropriate to redress under any clause of rule 62.1. The question then arises what to do about the scores of other boats – if *Daffodil* stops racing to give help when in 10th position, which is awarded to her as redress, are those whose race scores before redress was granted was 10th or lower to be moved down one place? If the redress arises from an incident so close to the finishing line, or when the boats were so widely spread, that her finishing in 10th place was a near certainty had not the incident occurred, then to move down the others might be appropriate. However, where such certainty is not possible, the usual procedure would be not to change the results of other boats, so that the race scores would include a 9th, two boats tied on 10th, then an 11th, 12th etc. The decision has to be an explicit one, since ties resulting from redress are not covered by rule A7, Race Ties (and so the outcome would not be to rescore two 10ths as 10.5 points each). In the 2008-2009 Vendée Globe round the world race, a boat in third place at two-thirds distance gave help, but in the process damaged herself and had to retire. The jury awarded redress of third equal place, based on her position at the time of the incident. Later, the boat lying second retired, and so the redressed boat was now equal third with a boat that had been many miles astern at the time of the incident. She did not seek any adjustment, perhaps because the international jury might have found that, given that only eleven of the thirty starters finished the race, she could quite likely have herself turned out to be a DNF had the incident not happened, and so the redress first awarded would have stood. A bird in the hand…

If one of the other two 'average points' options marked for consideration in rule A10 are considered, then there is no need to change the positions of other boats since the value of those average points will fall where they will, and the resulting scores for the race will follow automatically. Average points for all the other races in the series (A10(a)) is better when the incident occurs early in the series[1], but its value will fluctuate race by race as the series progresses. When the incident occurs later in the series, so that there already a good track record from which to calculate the average, the average of races before the race in question (A10(b)) gives the boat in question and her competitors the certainty of knowing what that redress score is for the remaining races.

---

[1] On the day I write this, I am asked for advice by a competitor who wishes to question redress given to another boat entitled to redress because damage on the first day prevented her from sailing any of the three races on the second day. Redress was granted based on rule A10(b), being the average results from three races on the first day. The second day's racing was difficult, and, of the top nine boats at the end of the second day, apart from the boat awarded redress, the results for seven of them were markedly worse. I recommended a request for redress seeking to establish the redress as 'improper', as not being fair to all boats affected, seeking that the redress be changed to an average of more races in the 11-race series, possibly using rule A10(a).

Abandonment should be the last resort, not the first, and, as with abandonment under rule 32.1 by the race committee after at least one boat has finished, rule 64.2 asks the protest committee 'Are you sure?' In RYA 1988/4, ten Merlin Rockets started the race in question. Five retired, four of them shortly after beginning the second round because the wind was dying and there was a long leg against the tide. The fifth retired rather further on but without passing the last two marks of the course. Returning, she crossed the finishing line, apparently from the direction from the last course mark, was given a finishing signal and recorded as first. The other boats that sailed the course and finished were given positions behind the erroneously recorded 'winner'.

The five other boats that finished correctly requested redress. The protest committee's decision was to abandon the race. Two of the five boats appealed on the grounds that five competitors had sailed the course correctly and should not be deprived of their results merely because the race officer had made an error in giving a finishing place to a boat that had in fact retired. The protest committee stated in its observations that when the race started the warning flag had not been lowered with the starting signal, thus leading to confusion, in which some boats started late, and that therefore the race should be abandoned. The appeals were upheld, the abandonment of the race was annulled and the race was reinstated.

> The five boats that completed the two-round course are to be scored for finishing positions in the sequence in which they finished. The boats that retired (including the erroneously recorded 'winner') are to be scored DNF. The protest committee acted correctly in inquiring into the occurrences before and at the start. However, there was no recall signal and no boats were recorded as OCS; no boat lodged any request for redress on the grounds that the start was unfair or that any finishing positions were prejudiced by the time differences when starting. When boats are entitled to redress, and the nature of the appropriate redress is clear, a protest committee cannot instead abandon the race, citing an error made by the race officer earlier in the race about which no boat has requested redress and the race committee has taken no action[1].

Sometimes, there is no alternative to abandonment. In RYA 1999/6, in a youth event on a reservoir with 259 boats, parking and launching arrangements were difficult. The Topper fleet of 111 boats had a single start, (warning signal scheduled for 1130), and on the first day found their launching delayed. A sailing instruction prohibited launching until a black ball signal was lowered. The signal was still displayed at 1100.

Just after 1100, a race official, realising that the black ball signal should have been removed, but unable to get this done promptly, told several competitors that they could now launch, and some did so. The black ball was lowered at 1105. The race officer started the race five minutes before the scheduled time. As a result, many boats were unable to reach the starting area in time for a reasonable start and requested redress.

The protest committee found that they had been affected by the race committee errors, and granted redress by abandoning the race. *Walsdos* and other Toppers requested redress in their turn, asking for the race to be reinstated with individual boats getting some other form of redress. This was refused and *Walsdos* appealed. In her appeal she suggested that the sailing instruction prohibiting launching before the signal was lowered had been overruled by the action of the race official. The appeal was dismissed.

> While it is to be avoided when more equitable arrangements are available, abandonment may, very occasionally, be the least unfair option. In this case, the launching problems were considerably aggravated by the start being made early and the effects of the race committee's errors on the fleet (not just on the boats seeking redress) are unquantifiable. The RYA sees no grounds for overturning the protest committee's decision at the time in favour of some other imperfect arrangement. The applicant is not correct when he says that the black ball signal had been overruled by the race officer. This could be effected only by a change to sailing instructions. Any earlier launching broke this sailing instruction, and any boat that decided not to launch until the signal was lowered was correct to wait.

---

[1] The principle is correct, although the case is questionable as concerns the automatic scoring as DNF of the erroneously recorded winner. As the cases on rule 28.1 indicate, that boat should have been protested. But by whom? And when?

Granting redress by letting the results stand is not the same thing as refusing redress. Rather, it is recognition that the protest committee does not have a plaster for every sore. Consider a 12-race regatta where *Daffodil* is hit and damaged beyond repair in the first race when lying first. She wins her protest, and asks for redress. Is she to be awarded the event? If not, should she be given average points redress if is after three races that she can no longer compete? After six races? After nine races? Does the decision depend on whether she was in a podium position in the series when damaged? There is no clear guidance[1].

Letting the results stand as the least worst option may result in rule breaches being accepted as unavoidable. In RYA 1993/1, the sailing instructions were badly drafted, so as to make it impossible to sail the course.

> All boats broke rule 28.1. This resulted from the act of the race committee in setting a course that could neither be started nor finished, and in which the only way rule 28 could be complied with…was neither as it must have been intended, nor as any boat might have reasonably expected. All boats, including the appellant, appear to have made a reasonable attempt to extract a sailable course from the instructions given.

> No boat was at fault, and so all boats are entitled to redress from their technical liability to disqualification. The appellant does not allege that the slightly greater distance she sailed compared with the protested boats affected her finishing position.

> The most equitable redress is for the appellant to be reinstated in her actual finishing position, and for the resulting positions to constitute the result of the race[2].

The history of ISAF 45 makes an important point. In that case, a sailing instruction specified a hook finish, contrary to the definition Finish. Some boats complied with this invalid instruction, hooked round a finishing mark before crossing the line and were given a finishing position: others ignored the sailing instruction, crossed the finishing line in the direction of the course from the last mark and were scored DNF. In the resulting requests for redress, the protest committee decided that the most equitable arrangement was to grant redress by letting the results stand in the order that boats had crossed the finishing line, regardless of the direction of finish, and one boat that had complied with the definition appealed. The case upholds the protest committee.

> Because the sailing instruction that conflicted with the definition Finish was invalid, issuing it was an improper action of the race committee that qualified…boats for redress…None of the boats racing gained or lost as a result of the race committee error, so the redress awarded was appropriate.

Consistent – but it is in fact history rewritten. For many years, the case's original decision said that all the boats might be entitled to redress, but those which finished in line with the definition should all be scored better than those that finished in accordance with the sailing instruction. In a rare reconsideration of an actual decision, it was more recently felt that to rank the boats in this way was wrong. To be entitled to redress, a boat must be without fault. If, as in this case, no boat was at fault, then it would be inappropriate to grant redress in a way that implied fault[3]. So if a protest committee finds itself in a situation where it feels a need to rank the redress it is to give, perhaps it should ask itself whether in fact one or more boat was at fault, and therefore not entitled to redress at all[4].

---

[1] My own decision would be not to give redress leading to a major prize when the boat has completed less than half the races, and not to hand over outright first place in the series in the event as redress whenever the incident occurred. I guess I would award first equal or second place to a boat unable to race again when in a clear first place after completing more than half the series.
[2] This case was an appeal against disqualification. It would have been an appropriate decision to have been taken at the original hearing.
[3] Usually, if an ISAF case is decided no longer to be correct (as can happen – but not in this case – because of a rule change), then the case is either edited or withdrawn. To edit it so as to change the substance of the decision is unusual, but it was felt that the corrected decision was important, and the national authority that had originally submitted the case gave its approval.
[4] Again, the benefit of the doubt may be relevant.

When redress for a misleading course is due, it may not always be possible just to let the finishing results stand, since some boats may have sailed a considerably longer distance that others. A protest committee can 'make some other arrangement', in the shape of identifying which boat sailed which course and treating these as races within a race. If, in a ten-boat race, seven boats sailed an 'improper' course intended by the race committee, but three sailed a shorter course that is found by the protest committee to be valid, then the race might scored with two firsts, two seconds, two thirds, then fourth to seventh[1].

The need for the protest committee to be aware of all possible consequences of the redress that is contemplated justifies the widening of a hearing to hear from all boats that may be affected by potentially controversial redress granted to only one or some of them, as discussed under rule 63.3.

64.3

Decisions on Measurement Protests

(a) When the protest committee finds that deviations in excess of tolerances specified in the class rules were caused by damage or normal wear and do not improve the performance of the boat, it shall not penalise her. However, the boat shall not *race* again until the deviations have been corrected, except when the protest committee decides there is or has been no reasonable opportunity to do so.

(b) When the protest committee is in doubt about the meaning of a measurement rule, it shall refer its questions, together with the relevant facts, to an authority responsible for interpreting the rule. In making its decision, the committee shall be bound by the reply of the authority.

(c) When a boat disqualified under a measurement rule states in writing that she intends to appeal, she may compete in subsequent races without changes to the boat, but shall be disqualified if she fails to appeal or the appeal is decided against her.

(d) Measurement costs arising from a *protest* involving a measurement rule shall be paid by the unsuccessful *party* unless the protest committee decides otherwise.

Rule 64.3 deals with particular issues arising from measurement. When none of clauses (a) and (c) apply, a boat that is found not to comply with her class rules will be penalised. The unanswered question is in which races is she to be penalised? Logically, if a boat is shown to have been in breach of her class rules in the first six races of the event, then she should be disqualified from all those races provided that the protest is not framed in such a way to restrict the 'incident' – and therefore the protest committee's jurisdiction[2] - to only one or a few races. However, I have sat on protest committees that have sought to restrict the disqualification to a single race only, where there was no evidence of advantage or cheating[3].

The other side of rule 64.3)(a)'s coin is that when excess deviations are **not** caused by damage or normal wear, then the boat is to be penalised, and that, if the boat does not protect her position under rule 64.3(c) and races again before correcting the defect, she will be open to further protest – not only under the class rule but possibly under rule 2, Fair Sailing, added to which a hearing under rule 69.1, Allegations of Gross Misconduct, is possible. It also follows that excess deviations, even if caused by damage or normal wear, will result in penalisation if they improve the performance of the boat, although it will be difficult to establish where the boundary lies.

---

[1] This does not extend to situations where a boat found a shorter way to sail a valid course, usually because what was intended to be a rounding mark was not suitably identified, and so did not have to be approached while racing. No redress is due to the others, except possibly the abandonment of the race. See under rule 28.1.

[2] ISAF 80

[3] Perhaps it can be argued that infringements in previous races are now outside the protest time limit. I think that is a case where there is a good reason for the protest time limit to be extended.

Protest committees are sometimes hesitant when faced with a measurement protest. There is usually no need to be. A ruling from 'an authority responsible for interpreting the rule' has to be called for only when the protest committee is in doubt about the meaning of a measurement rule. When there is no doubt, the protest committee can make up its own mind, and nothing stops a protest committee from seeking other expert evidence. In RYA 1992/2, *Samba* was protested by another boat for being 'out of class' in respect of several specific class measurement rules. The protest committee referred the matter to a class association measurer who was present at the championship. After receiving his report it disqualified her for not complying with class rules. She appealed on the grounds, among others, that the class measurer had competed in the regatta. Her appeal was dismissed.

> The protest committee misdirected itself when it took a class measurer who happened to be present as the 'authority responsible for interpreting the rule' referred to in rule 64.3(b). This is so only when that authority has previously specifically appointed such a person for the event. In the case of the class concerned, the class rules state that the authority for deciding questions of deviation from the design is the class committee. The protest committee was, however, correct to seek evidence from anyone it believed could contribute to resolving the case, including a class measurer, despite the fact that he was a competitor.

> Having received that evidence, the protest committee should then first have decided whether it was in doubt about the meaning of the class rules. If there was no doubt, it was able to decide the case. If there was doubt, it was then that the matter would have had to be referred for a binding interpretation to the 'responsible authority' - the class committee.

> In this case, the evidence before the protest committee proved beyond doubt that that *Samba* broke the class measurement rules, and she was rightly penalised without the need to refer the matter to the class association.

When an issue is referred under rule 64.3(b) to a relevant authority for a ruling, not only is the protest committee bound by the reply, but also when a boat is penalised as a result, a race committee that thinks that this is unfair has no option other than implement the decision by changing the event scores[1].

When a boat exercises her rights under rule 64.3(c), the rule does not identify the races under which the boat is to be disqualified if he fails to appeal or loses the appeal, a general issue already referred to. Should she also be disqualified from the 'subsequent races' as well? I think this is implied, and no further hearing is needed. It is in effect initially a suspended sentence.

When a measurement protest requires a large boat to be taken out of the water to be inspected, the cost implication for the unsuccessful party is a significant factor when deciding to protest. This risk applies equally to a race committee that decides to protest a boat, but if it is compulsorily protesting a boat because of a report under rule 78.3 from an equipment inspector or a measurer that a boat does not comply with class rules, there is the reassurance that the official has already decided that the boat or equipment is non-compliant, so there should be no need to lift the boat unless the protestee asks for this, at the protestee's risk.

 **Rule 65** INFORMING THE PARTIES AND OTHERS

 **65.1** After making its decision, the protest committee shall promptly inform the *parties* to the hearing of the facts found, the applicable *rules*, the decision, the reasons for it, and any penalties imposed or redress given.

65.2 A *party* to the hearing is entitled to receive the above information in writing, provided she asks for it in writing from the protest committee no later than seven days after being informed of the decision. The committee shall then promptly provide the information, including, when relevant, a diagram of the incident prepared or endorsed by the committee.

 **65.3** When the protest committee penalises a boat under a measurement rule, it shall send the above information to the relevant measurement authorities.

---

[1] ISAF 66

Appendix M 3.5, says that if time is pressing, announce the decision and give the reasons later. Neither the rule nor Appendix M remind the protest committee to tell the scorers of the decision as soon as possible if will change the results.

Rule 65.3 is sometimes overlooked by protest committees.

When A10(a) or A10(b) redress is given, I recommend referring specifically to the relevant rule in the redress decision. Just writing 'average points' is not specific enough. I then try to check the scorers' calculations when the results are posted. If it is done manually, mistakes can be made, and incorrect or inappropriate methods used. When A10(a) is used, resulting in a potential change to the value of a redress score, a further check after further races is sensible[1].

Rule 66 — REOPENING A HEARING

The protest committee may reopen a hearing when it decides that it may have made a significant error, or when significant new evidence becomes available within a reasonable time. It shall reopen a hearing when required by the national authority under rule F5. A *party* to the hearing may ask for a reopening no later than 24 hours after being informed of the decision. When a hearing is reopened, a majority of the members of the protest committee shall, if possible, be members of the original protest committee.

Only a party to a hearing can ask for a reopening. When a boat is aggrieved over the redress given to another boat in a hearing to which the aggrieved boat was not a party, she has no right to ask for a reopening. All she can do is to request redress herself[2]. The procedure is that when a reopening has been asked for by a party, the boat's representative will be called before the protest committee to explain the reason for asking for a reopening. No other party to the hearing is present. The protest committee decides whether the evidence is new, or if it may have made a mistake. If either applies, the hearing is reopened.

In CYA 99, *Daffodil* did not attend the hearing of a protest against her, despite the fact of the protest and the time and place of the hearing having been posted on the official notice board. She was disqualified, and, learning of this several days later, she requested a reopening, her 'new' evidence being that she disagreed with the facts found and the diagram, and that she had a different story to tell. The CYA upheld the protest committee's decision not to reopen. 'The new evidence was nothing more than *Daffodil*'s version of the facts. This is, presumably, the evidence she would have given if she had attended the hearing, and is therefore not considered to be new.' It follows that if a boat has a good reason for not having attended a protest hearing, the protest committee should be more sympathetic to a reopening if a different story will be told.

Appendix M 4 advises the protest committee then to 'hear the *party* making the request, look at any video, etc., and decide whether there is any material new evidence that might lead you to change your decision. Decide whether your interpretation of the *rules* may have been wrong; be open-minded as to whether you have made a mistake. If none of these applies refuse to reopen; otherwise schedule a hearing.'

In RYA 2008/3, the protest committee decided to reopen without either circumstance applying. When it then heard evidence that had in fact been available at the time of its original hearing, it realised it had made a mistake, and changed its decision. When it referred the whole process to the RYA for confirmation, the revised decision, although now correct, was held to be invalid. However, the RYA corrected the original valid (but incorrect) decision in line with the later invalid (but correct) decision.

---

[1] See the General Guidance to Scoring under Appendix A, at the end of this book. Computer scoring programs have been known to be wrong.
[2] RYA 1994/3: the converse is that a boat unhappy about redress granted in a hearing to which she is a party cannot use redress as a means of contesting it because of rule 62.1(a): her only option is to ask for a reopening under rule 66.

RYA 2008/5 gives comprehensive advice on reopening.

Question 1

Rule 66 begins: 'The protest committee may reopen a hearing...' Does the use of the word 'may' mean that a protest committee is entitled not to reopen in the circumstances stated in the rule?

Answer 1

Normally, as recommended in Appendix M4, a protest committee should reopen when it decides that it may have made a significant error, or when significant new evidence becomes available within reasonable time. However, it need not reopen if its error, if corrected, would not result in a changed decision, or if there are genuine time pressures to finalise the results for an event, and a change of decision would either not change the event results, or would have an effect only on minor placings.

Question 2

Is it necessary for there to be a request to reopen before the protest committee can consider reopening?

Answer 2

No. The rule does not require this. The protest committee may become aware of the need to consider reopening even if a party has not asked for it.

Question 3

In asking for a reopening, does a party to the hearing have to give a reason?

Answer 3

Yes. The party must identify a possible mistake, or describe the source and nature of the new evidence, and the protest committee may then question the requester in the absence of any other party to decide whether it may have been a mistake, or whether the evidence, if presented, will be 'new' as described in Answer 5.

Question 4

If the protest committee decides to reopen to hear further evidence, and a party to the original hearing believes that it should not do so, does a party have to raise an objection to the reopening at the start of the reopened hearing?

Answer 4

Yes, if it is wished to reserve the right to appeal against the fact of the reopening as well as against any subsequent change in the decision. It is possible that when evidence that is not 'new' as described in Answer 5 is heard, an appeal against the improper reopening may be upheld, regardless of the merits of the further evidence, but only when the party objected to the hearing of the further evidence at the beginning of the reopened hearing. The protest committee must consider an objection to its reopening before deciding whether to proceed with the reopened hearing. If the protest committee is an international jury, no appeal is possible.

Question 5

When a party asks for a reopening asserting that significant new evidence is available, how is the protest committee to decide whether it is 'new'? What degree of diligence is required of a party in seeking witnesses for the original protest hearing?

Answer 5

If it was reasonable for the evidence (or its provider) to have been discovered and brought to the original hearing, it is not 'new'. However, if it relates to issues not raised on the original protest form and becoming material only during the hearing, it may be 'new'.

Question 6

When at the original protest hearing a party states that a witness is being sought but cannot be produced in time for the hearing, how should the protest committee proceed? Does the answer depend on the nature of the event?

Answer 6

If the protest committee is satisfied that the statement is genuine, that no opportunity to find the witness was missed, and when a reopening based on this evidence is then asked for, it should reopen if the evidence might change the decision. The nature of the event is not directly relevant.

Question 7

When a hearing is reopened because one party is able to offer significant new evidence, is it open to other parties to call new witnesses or offer other evidence not heard at the original hearing? Is it relevant that the other parties' 'new' evidence may have been available at the time of the original hearing but not offered at the time?

Answer 7

Other parties are entitled to present new evidence relating to the evidence which was the basis for the reopening. This may include witnesses not originally called.

RULE 42 AND HEARING REQUIREMENT

When so stated in the sailing instructions, the protest committee may penalise without a hearing a boat that has broken rule 42, provided that a member of the committee or its designated observer has seen the incident, and a disqualification under this rule shall not be excluded from the boat's series score. A boat so penalised shall be informed by notification in the race results.

It is curious that this rule survives. It has largely been superseded by the 'yellow flag' procedures of Appendix P[1], (Note that Appendix P is quite separate from rule 67. Both Appendix P and rule 67 apply only when the sailing instructions say so, but to say that rule 67 applies does NOT make Appendix P apply). It is not as fair as Appendix P, since the harsh DNE penalty applies to a first offence, and when several races are sailed back-to-back, a penalty in the first race of the day will not be learned of until the results are published – so there is no opportunity either to modify behaviour in later races or to change tactics because of a known penalty.

DAMAGES

The question of damages arising from a breach of any *rule* shall be governed by the prescriptions, if any, of the national authority.

The current prescription of the RYA is that a claim for damages arising from an incident while a boat is bound by the Racing Rules of Sailing shall be subject to the jurisdiction of the courts and not considered by a protest committee[2], and a boat that takes a penalty or retires does not thereby admit liability for damages or that she has broken a rule. US Sailing's prescription is similar, but then goes further: 'By participating in an event governed by the rules, a boat agrees that responsibility for damages arising from any breach of the rules shall be based on fault as determined by application of the rules...', which would appear to be an optimistic attempt to get the courts to apply only the racing rules of sailing to claims for damages[3].

---

[1] Indeed, ISAF has agreed that it will disappear in 2013.
[2] France, the USA and many other national authorities have a similar prescription.
[3] See under rule 3

Section C – Gross Misconduct

Rule 69 **ALLEGATIONS OF GROSS MISCONDUCT**

69.1 **Action by a Protest Committee**

(a) When a protest committee, from its own observation or a report received from any source, believes that a competitor may have committed a gross breach of a *rule*, good manners or sportsmanship, or may have brought the sport into disrepute, it may call a hearing. The protest committee shall promptly inform the competitor in writing of the alleged misconduct and of the time and place of the hearing. If the competitor provides good reason for being unable to attend the hearing, the protest committee shall reschedule it.

(b) A protest committee of at least three members shall conduct the hearing, following the procedures in rules 63.2, 63.3(a), 63.4 and 63.6. If it decides that the competitor committed the alleged misconduct it shall either

    (1) warn the competitor or

    (2) impose a penalty by excluding the competitor and, when appropriate, disqualifying a boat, from a race or the remaining races or all races of the series, or by taking other action within its jurisdiction. A disqualification under this rule shall not be excluded from the boat's series score.

(c) The protest committee shall promptly report a penalty, but not a warning, to the national authorities of the venue, of the competitor and of the boat owner. If the protest committee is an international jury appointed by the ISAF under rule 89.2(b), it shall send a copy of the report to the ISAF.

(d) If the competitor does not provide good reason for being unable to attend the hearing and does not come to it, the protest committee may conduct it without the competitor present. If the committee does so and penalises the competitor, it shall include in the report it makes under rule 69.1(c) the facts found, the decision and the reasons for it.

(e) If the protest committee chooses not to conduct the hearing without the competitor present or if the hearing cannot be scheduled for a time and place when it would be reasonable for the competitor to attend, the protest committee shall collect all available information and, if the allegation seems justified, make a report to the relevant national authorities. If the protest committee is an international jury appointed by the ISAF under rule 89.2(b), it shall send a copy of the report to the ISAF.

(f) When the protest committee has left the event and a report alleging misconduct is received, the race committee or organizing authority may appoint a new protest committee to proceed under this rule.

The differences, similarities and interaction of rule 2 and rule 69.1 have been discussed under rule 2.

- Rule 69.1 is for action against a named competitor. It is not available for action against non-competitors such as coaches, parents or abusive bystanders, in respect of which the only option under the racing rules is a report to the national authority or to ISAF. Clubs and classes may also have their own sanctions against such people, via internal disciplinary powers.
- Only a protest committee can call a hearing under rule 69. If a race committee or organizing authority wants an action under rule 69.1 to be considered, and there is no preappointed protest committee to consider the matter, the first job is to appoint a protest committee for the purpose and send it a report and request for action, with which the protest committee may or may not agree.

- Rule 69.1 is not a vehicle for penalizing a boat or a competitor as a direct outcome of a protest hearing. Nor can a normal protest hearing seamlessly become a rule 69.1 hearing. If facts or allegations justifying a rule 69.1 hearing emerge during the hearing of a 'normal' protest or a request for redress, the protest committee must act in the same way as starting a hearing after receiving a report, namely to decide that a hearing is needed, and to inform the competitor in writing of the alleged misconduct and of the time and place of the hearing, giving the competitor time to prepare.
- If the allegation made in as part of a 'normal' protest involving breaking a race rule, the protest should be heard first, arising from which the boat may be disqualified, possibly non-excludibly (DNE) also under rule 2. This will generate facts that will accelerate any subsequent rule 69.1 hearing.
- The written allegation must be specific, not general. If bad language is alleged, the words alleged to have been used should be quoted, distasteful as that might be. If bad behaviour is alleged, it must be described in as much detail as is known or asserted. The written allegation must also say whether it is a gross breach of a rule, or a gross breach of good manners, or a gross breach of sportsmanship, or a bringing of the sport into disrepute that is alleged, and more than one of them if appropriate.
- The question sometimes has to be asked whether what is alleged is sufficiently closely associated with the event to come within the scope of a rule 69.1 hearing. There is no issue when misbehaviour occurs during a race, or at a regatta site during an event. The further in distance from the club or regatta site and the further in time before or after the event, the less likely this will be. If a complaint has been received from neighbours or from officialdom, the fact that the complainant associates the person complained of with the event tends to answer that question. In practice, the complainant is usually unable to identify the miscreant by name, and there may be a group of competitors, generally but not individually identifiable as being associated with an event, who have been making a nuisance of themselves. The protest committee may need to investigate further before a hearing is called to try to find who may have been involved, and it might have to initiate a hearing against a considerable number of competitors in order to discover more exactly during the hearing who was, and who was not, involved.
- If there is no suitable club member to chair the protest committee, or if perception of the independence of the process will be helped by having an outside person to chair the hearing, the national authority may be able to recommend a suitable judge.
- The protest committee must have at least three members[1].
- If the alleged incident occurred during a regatta, it is important for the hearing to take place as soon as possible during the regatta.
- If the alleged incident occurred in connection with normal club racing, it may take some juggling of diaries to get all concerned to hearing as soon as conveniently possible for those who need to be present.
- It is appropriate for the competitor to be legally represented in serious cases.
- There is no explicit time limit on the calling of a rule 69.1 hearing. The circumstances justifying a hearing may not emerge for some time after the end of an event, for instance when information emerges about a possible deliberate infringements of class rules. In this case, a new protest committee will almost certainly have to be set up to decide whether the allegation warrants a hearing, and it might be appropriate for it to consider whether there has been any undue delay in the information being made available: if that has been unjustifiably delayed, that might be a reason for a protest committee to exercise its discretion and not call a hearing.
- If the competitor is a junior, a parent or guardian must be informed of what is proposed, and the junior must have an adult to hand during the hearing, either as a representative or as an adviser.
- The protest committee may allow an observer to be present throughout the hearing, as long the observer does not interact with the process and sits out of eye contact with the competitor. Before allowing an observer to be present, the protest committee should consider any objection to this by the competitor.
- A transcription or a fair summary of the proceedings and the evidence should be kept.
- The only party to the hearing is the competitor, and so only the competitor has a right to be present throughout the hearing. Whoever is making the allegation, whether the race committee or another competitor, that person remains in the hearing, as a witness, only long enough to give evidence and answer questions.
- The protest committee and the competitor can ask questions of any witness. A witness cannot ask questions of the competitor.

---

[1] It is unhelpful that something that is absolutely NOT a protest is to be heard by a 'protest' committee.

- First, all witnesses supporting the allegation are heard and questioned by the competitor and by the protest committee. The competitor then makes a response and the protest committee will then ask questions.
- The competitor may call witnesses in support. The protest committee may question them.
- If the competitor concedes that what is alleged is completely true, at any stage of the proceedings, it will not be necessary to hear further witnesses
- Any early statement of regret by the competitor is to be welcomed
- When there is no more evidence, the competitor and any representative, adviser or observer are to withdraw, and the protest committee then finds the facts and decides whether it is indeed the type of misconduct described in the original allegation. While protests between boats are usually decided on the 'balance or probabilities', it is generally accepted that a higher standard of proof is needed in a rule 69.1 hearing, similar to the test in a criminal court of 'beyond reasonable doubt'.
- Once the protest committee has decided what happened, then, unless the allegation is to be dismissed, the competitor can be recalled, to hear those facts, and be invited to make any observation as to whether the protest committee should warn or impose a penalty. The protest committee can ask whether the competitor has been the object of any rule 69.1 hearing in the last few years, and, if so, what the outcome was, since this may be the only way that the protest committee will get to hear of any previous warning[1]. If there has been a previous warning, this is likely to steer the protest committee towards a penalty rather than a further warning. (The rule does not explain the nature or implication of a rule 69.1 warning: presumably, it is a warning that any future bad behaviour within a reasonably long period will result in a penalty.)
- Protest committees should not shy away from penalizing if that is justified by the facts. While the national authority reserves the right to take further action, I believe that this would be done in only the most serious cases (when a warning would never have been sufficient in the first place), otherwise, after being reviewed (assuming also that a file check reveals no previous penalties against the same person that might also justify national authority action), they are noted and filed, and the competitor advised accordingly.
- The primary penalty available is the exclusion of a competitor, which is the individual, not the boat. The rule is not clear, but I believe 'exclusion' to be a ban on a competitor taking part in a race. The competitor cannot be excluded from the race in which the misconduct occurred – it has already happened: not can the competitor normally be excluded from all the races of the series – some of them will have happened. If so, it follows that exclusion can only be from the remaining races of an event or series, and on a larger boat it is possible that, within any crew limitations in the event, a replacement could be found, and the boat could continue to compete. Going further and disqualifying the boat on which the competitor was sailing must be 'appropriate', which it would be if the misconduct took place during a race, and was by the person in charge of the boat, or was condoned by that person. I think disqualification would also be appropriate if the limitations on excluding a competitor precluded that from being a meaningful penalty, as for instance if the hearing does not take place until the event or series has finished.
- If disqualification is appropriate, it is non-excludable. The rule appears to permit disqualification from races that have not yet taken place, but does not explicitly prohibit a boat from taking part in them. Exclusion might have had that effect, but it also might not[2].
- What are the 'other actions' that are within a protest committee's jurisdiction? We are not told. I believe that a protest committee is within its rights to send a report of the hearing to a competitor's club, regardless of whether a penalty was imposed. If the misconduct takes place at the competitor's club, the club might consider empowering the protest committee to exercise any penalties available under the club's disciplinary rules: otherwise, some fresh hearing might be needed by some different body in order for club discipline to be imposed.
- The RYA suggests in its own guidance to rule 69 that there is an inherent power of the protest committee to penalise with additional non-excludable points. If selected, that would not preclude a boat from competing, but could be at such a penal level that the boat could never prosper in the series.

---

[1] This is one of the weaknesses of the rule: in theory, a competitor on an 'open' or international circuit could get into trouble at a series of events, and accumulate a number of warnings, each new protest committee being unaware of previous warnings.

[2] A boat intending to appeal against such a penalty might well want to continue to race. Rule P2.3, when applicable, also provides for disqualification from all races of a regatta, without explaining the consequences.

When a penalty (including exclusion) is imposed, it must be reported – to as many as three national authorities, and also to ISAF when the protest committee is an international jury which ISAF appointed[1]. The question of any further action by any of those bodies under rule 69.2 (and, if so, by which) is not one with which the protest committee need concern itself.

All the foregoing assumes that there is no difficulty in calling a hearing. At a regatta, the competitors can be assumed to be available at any time that a normal protest hearing would take place. When there is alleged misconduct within a club's normal programme, a hearing is more likely to be at a later date, and scheduling issues can arise. When a hearing **is** scheduled, and the competitor does not attend, offering no good reason, the the protest committee has two options: to proceed with the hearing, and, if necessary, to penalise, under rule 69.1(d); or, under rule 69.1(e), to collect all possible information and report to the relevant national authorities. That, in effect, is initially the same process, since evidence will have to be heard. I think that a protest committee has to decide, before it begins, which of these alternatives is its chosen route.

When a competitor has a good reason not to attend, and no rescheduling is possible, then the only option is to collect information and report it. This is most likely to happen over an incident towards the end a regatta when the competitor has a flight home booked immediately after the last race. In a very serious incident, the police may already be involved, and a prompt hearing may be impossible because the competitor is under investigation, in which case it would also be appropriate not to call any hearing until it is clear that there will not be any criminal proceedings, or until criminal proceedings have been concluded. If a competitor has been fined or imprisoned, that is no reason for a hearing under rule 69.1 not to be held later, or for a report to the authorities not be made as soon as possible.

It may be that it is the protest committee that is unavailable, all or some of its members having left a regatta at the prize-giving, only for one or more competitors to hit the town afterwards, causing annoyance and even damage. In this case (rule 69.1(f)), a new committee can be appointed, which in turn will have to decide whether there is a case to answer, and, if so, whether it can practically call a hearing.

69.2   **Action by a National Authority or Initial Action by the ISAF**

(a) When a national authority or the ISAF receives a report alleging a gross breach of a *rule*, good manners or sportsmanship, or a report alleging conduct that has brought the sport into disrepute, or a report required by rule 69.1(c) or 69.1(e), it may conduct an investigation and, when appropriate, shall conduct a hearing. It may then take any disciplinary action within its jurisdiction it considers appropriate against the competitor or boat, or other person involved, including suspending eligibility, permanently or for a specified period of time, to compete in any event held within its jurisdiction, and suspending ISAF eligibility under ISAF Regulation 19.

(b) The national authority of a competitor shall also suspend the ISAF eligibility of the competitor as required in ISAF Regulation 19.

(c) The national authority shall promptly report a suspension of eligibility under rule 69.2(a) to the ISAF, and to the national authorities of the person or the owner of the boat suspended if they are not members of the suspending national authority.

---

[1] An international jury appointed by the organizing authority – the more common situation – is not required (or even allowed) to report the outcome to ISAF.

A report under rule 69.2 has to be made under rule 69.1(c) after a competitor, and possibly a boat, has been penalised; and under rule 69(1(e) when it has not been possible to call a hearing concerning an allegation. Anyone can send a report at any time to a national authority: for instance, a competitor may be overheard in circumstances outside any event to admit having modified a boat with an intention to cheat. ISAF may now be involved – the national authority can be bypassed, and a report of this nature can be sent directly to ISAF. What ISAF will do in such circumstances is yet to be seen – probably referring the matter to a relevant national authority would be the first option. But it has the clear right to call its own hearing. It is also entitled to take further action when it receives a report of a penalty imposed by an international jury that it appointed[1], in which case it would presumably have to liaise with the national authorities concerned before deciding which body (if any) was to act.

Section D - Appeals

 **APPEALS AND REQUESTS TO A NATIONAL AUTHORITY**

70.1 Provided that the right of appeal has not been denied under rule 70.5, a *party* to a hearing may appeal a protest committee's decision or its procedures, but not the facts found.

70.2 A protest committee may request confirmation or correction of its decision.

 **70.3** An appeal under rule 70.1 or a request by a protest committee under rule 70.2 shall be sent to the national authority with which the organizing authority is associated under rule 89.1. However, if boats will pass through the waters of more than one national authority while racing, the sailing instructions shall identify the national authority to which appeals or requests may be sent.

 **70.4** A club or other organization affiliated to a national authority may request an interpretation of the *rules*, provided that no *protest* or request for redress that may be appealed is involved. The interpretation shall not be used for changing a previous protest committee decision.

 **70.5** There shall be no appeal from the decisions of an international jury constituted in compliance with Appendix N. Furthermore, if the notice of race and the sailing instructions so state, the right of appeal may be denied provided that

(a) it is essential to determine promptly the result of a race that will qualify a boat to compete in a later stage of an event or a subsequent event (a national authority may prescribe that its approval is required for such a procedure);

(b) a national authority so approves for a particular event open only to entrants under its own jurisdiction; or

(c) a national authority after consultation with the ISAF so approves for a particular event, provided the protest committee is constituted as required by Appendix N, except that only two members of the protest committee need be International Judges.

 **70.6** Appeals and requests shall conform to Appendix F.

---

[1] This is complicated by the title of the rule, which refers to 'Initial Action by the ISAF'. In this case, ISAF's action would not be 'initial', since its international jury has taken the initial action: but the title of a rule is not part of the rule, see definition Rule.

The decision of a protest committee can be changed either by an appeal under rule 70.1 or by a protest committee requesting confirmation or correction of its decision under rule 70.2. Protest committees will sometimes adopt the rule 70.2 route when an intention to appeal is known, in order to show that the protest committee is as interested as the party in knowing whether the decision was right. The process and the possible outcomes are essentially the same under rules 70.1 and 70.2. One difference, however, is that it is the right of **appeal** that can be denied under rule 70.5. Nothing stops a protest committee that cannot be appealed against from requesting confirmation or correction of a decision[1]. In theory, that could include an international jury, which is a protest committee sub-species, although I am not aware of it ever happening. If a decision is referred under rule 70.2, the whole of the decision is open to review, not just an issue over which the protest committee may have doubts[2].

There is a right to an official interpretation under rule 70.4. Published cases in a question and answer format usually originate from such questions. Only clubs and organizations affiliated to the national authority can ask such questions, and the rule makes clear that these are academic questions only[3].

Some appeals, references and questions raise no significant issues, but many do. The capacity of the racing rules to reveal unexpected wrinkles never fails to surprise and intrigue. The cases referred to and quoted in this book are derived from cases selected for publication by the national authorities concerned.

Suppose that a British club organizes a race to France, with a return race back to the south coast. There is an incident in the outward race, resulting in a protest which is heard in France during the stop-over, and the protest committee is provided by a French club. Where should any appeal be sent? To the RYA? To the FFV? Rule 70.3 now requires this problem to be considered from the outset[4]. In most situations however, the appropriate national authority is self-evident[5].

It is only a party to the hearing that can appeal a decision in that hearing. If a non-party is aggrieved (usually because redress granted to a party is deemed over-generous or inappropriate), her only option is to request redress, showing both that the decision was improper and that it significantly affected her score. Specifically, redress granted to *Daffodil* that may make *Iris*'s finishing position worse does not make *Iris* a penalised boat[6]. If further redress is then refused, a boat may then appeal the decision of that hearing if she remains unsatisfied[7].

The facts found cannot be appealed. However, if they can be shown to be perverse or inadequate, the national authority can, under rule 71.2, order a fresh hearing or a reopening of the original hearing. The 'decision' can be appealed. The decision is the conclusion derived from the facts found, and the application of the rules to the facts and conclusion. As discussed under rule 63.6, ISAF 104 admits that the distinction between a fact and a conclusion is often imprecise, and that a national authority is able to change on appeal any finding that is not exclusively factual in nature. In addition, the national authority may apply logic to derive additional facts from the protest committee's facts and diagram (the diagram being 'facts found', having equal status with the written facts, and requiring clarification when the diagram and written facts are in conflict).

---

[1] RYA 2005/2, concerning a decision related to the prompt identification of the team to proceed to the next round of a team race. The decision of the protest committee was upheld, on corrected grounds: had it been reversed, it would have been academic, as the event had long since finished, and I do not think the RYA could or would have sought to declare the event result invalid.
[2] RYA 2005/6
[3] The RYA offers an informal Racing Rules Advisory Service to individuals, details on the RYA website. Answers are from a team of experts but are non-authoritative. The questions can (and usually do) relate to live issues, and answers are given in days, sometimes in hours, as opposed to the weeks or months involved in answering questions under rule 70.4. ISAF officials and authorities also have access to an ISAF Question and Answer service, via the ISAF website.
[4] See also rule 88.1 as concerns applicable prescriptions in foreign waters. Both these rules attempt to ensure prior clarification on questions of jurisdiction in the further issue of an event from (say) Germany that will pass through Dutch and Belgian waters before arriving in the UK, particularly if there are stop-overs.
[5] Except perhaps in Northern Ireland, where some clubs have cross-border affiliations.
[6] RYA 1995/3
[7] ISAF 55, RYA 1974/1, CYA 44

The procedures of a protest committee can be appealed, but appeals on technicalities or on issues of validity are unlikely to be upheld unless the appellant party made an overruled objection at the time[1], or was not aware of circumstances that would have justified an objection[2].

Rule 86.1 says that rule 70 cannot be changed, and rule 70 places strict limits on the denial of the right of appeal. So a sailing instruction that says that 'the decisions of the protest committee will be final' is invalid[3], as is a sailing instruction that says that, when a decision is appealed, the results of an event will not be changed by the appeal decision – it has the same purported effect as denying the right of appeal[4].

For an appellant to be a party to a hearing, this presupposes that there was a hearing. From time to time, 'appeals' are received from boats that were denied any hearing of a properly lodged protest or request for redress, and when this was improper, the RYA does not hesitate to require a hearing to take place.

Denial of the right of appeal is automatic when an international jury is appointed for the event. It is routine under rule 70.5(a) in team racing, match racing and in other events which proceed through heats to finals[5]. The denial under rule 70.5(a) must be explicit in the notice of race and the sailing instructions, and to omit it from either or both may result in there being a right of appeal. The denial of the right of appeal because there is an international jury must also be stated in the notice of race (J1.2(12)) and the sailing instructions (J2.2(31)), but if that is not done, it will not affect the fact that the international jury is non-appealable unless it has not been properly constituted[6].

Approval of the denial of the right of appeal under rule 70.5(b) is available only when the entrants are under the national authority's jurisdiction (which the RYA's prescription to this rule defines as when 'The event is open only to boats entered by an organization affiliated to the RYA, a member of such an organization or a personal member of the RYA[7].') Denial under rule 70.5(c) is rare, and the RYA will not allow this clause to be used by an event that wants the certainty of the denial of appeal but does not want to bear the cost of a full international jury.

Rule 70.6 requires appeals and requests to conform to Appendix F[8].

This book does not examine Appendix N, International Juries, in detail, but the following observations can be made. Major events may require enough jury members for two panels or more panels to be appointed (therefore 10 or 15 members, more than two of whom may be from the same national authority, as long as no more than than two from the same national authority sit on the same panel)[9], and medium-sized events can benefit from upgrading from five to six members to enable hearings to be disposed of by two panels of three members from different national authorities, two of which must be international judges, subject to a right to a rehearing before a full jury or a 5-person panel[10].

---

[1] RYA 1981/5
[2] RYA 2007/1
[3] US 22
[4] ISAF 61, US 56
[5] The RYA policy is a 'light touch', and unlike other national authorities it does not require any prior approval of an international jury, nor does it prescribe that its approval is required under rule 70.5(a).
[6] N1.7
[7] The RYA prescription also requires a 'good reason' for approving such a request, and that would have to be a situation where it would not be reasonable for an international jury to be appointed, and where rule 70.5(a) did not apply).
[8] The RYA and US Sailing both prescribe a process that is slightly different from Appendix F.
[9] N1.4(a): for 'two', read 'three' in some geographical groups.
[10] N1.4(b)

The minimum requirement for an international jury is five persons, of whom no more than two members shall be from the same national authority[1]. This can be a considerable cost burden for a smaller event. Travel expenses have benefited from the growth of low cost airlines, and in parts of Europe some jury members can be acquired free of any travel costs falling on the event[2], but jury members still have to be housed and fed at the event. It is disappointing that ISAF does not place sufficient trust in its own officials to allow this to be changed to a minimum of three members (perhaps all from different countries, of whom two might be required to be international judges). The rule already allows for as few as three members in the event or illness or emergency, and there is no evidence when this happens that the standard of judging is any the worse[3]. Obviously, problems could arise when one of only two of three are then unavailable through illness or emergency, but that does not mean that a satisfactory work-round could not be devised.

Rule 71 — **NATIONAL AUTHORITY DECISIONS**

71.1 No *interested party* or member of the protest committee shall take any part in the discussion or decision on an appeal or a request for confirmation or correction.

71.2 The national authority may uphold, change or reverse the protest committee's decision; declare the *protest* or request for redress invalid; or return the *protest* or request for the hearing to be reopened, or for a new hearing and decision by the same or a different protest committee.

71.3 When from the facts found by the protest committee the national authority decides that a boat that was a *party* to a protest hearing broke a *rule*, it shall penalise her, whether or not that boat or that *rule* was mentioned in the protest committee's decision.

71.4 The decision of the national authority shall be final. The national authority shall send its decision in writing to all *parties* to the hearing and the protest committee, who shall be bound by the decision.

Some national authorities have a Racing Rules Committee and a separate Appeals Committee. The RYA's Racing Rules Committee performs both functions, meeting up to 10 times a year, and dealing typically with up to 30 appeals, references and questions a year as well as its other business related to education, prescriptions, submissions, the casebook, and *ad hoc* issues. Once the appeal package has been assembled, it goes electronically to committee members, who discuss it by email prior to the meeting, at which the issues that have become apparent are debated, and a decision is made. Sometimes, the decision is issued forthwith, but usually, because of the importance of precise drafting, the exact wording of the decision is put in the minutes, and confirmed or corrected at the next meeting, for issue soon afterwards. Any need to revert to the protest committee for further information can delay this process. It is therefore not unusual for an RYA decision to take at least three months to emerge after the original protest committee decision, and it appears that this is more prompt than many other national authorities can manage.

---

[1] N1.2, N1.3: for 'two', read 'three' in some geographical groups.

[2] Under the EUROSAF race officials exchange programme, jury members are requested by an event and are nominated by their national authority, on the basis that they travel on their own bottoms or have their travel costs met by their national authority.

[3] Another reason sometimes given against international juries of three is that it might reduce the opportunity to bring in members who are not (yet) international judges in order to gain suitable experience. That is true, but smaller juries might reduce the need for new officials, and should the competitors expect their entry fees to subsidise the training of race officials?

Some issues may be of long standing, but have no previous casebook authority, and ruling is long overdue. For instance, is a right-of-way boat required to keep a good lookout? Yes, it was decided by the RYA in 2004[1], as part of the process of complying with rule 14, Avoiding Contact, and a resulting warning hail is 'an act to avoid contact' under that rule. Others arise directly from a rule change, such as the move in 2005 from a '360° penalty' to a 'one-turn penalty' for touching a mark, resulting in a RYA case in that year which expanded the ways the penalty could be taken[2]. The decisions in both cases are now authoritative interpretations via their ISAF status, but that did not mean that there were not valid different views being considered by protest committees and sailors, and then debated in the hearing of the appeal, reference or question.

In carrying out its responsibilities under rule 71.2, the RYA normally:
- Will not declare a protest or request for redress invalid unless this is an issue that is raised by the appellant or the referrer, and was either the subject of an objection by the appellant at the original hearing, or where the reasons for the invalidity were not known by or disclosed to the appellant at the original hearing.
- Will not decide redress if it is now due, but will return the case to the protest committee to decide redress
- Will often require any new hearing by a different protest committee to be chaired by a national or an international judge
- Will reverse the penalisation by the protest committee of a boat that the appeal discloses was not a party to the hearing, even if it not that boat that has appealed[3].

It follows from rule 71.4 that the decision, if changed or reversed, must be implemented by, as appropriate, the organizing authority, the race committee and the protest committee[4].

Part 6 - Entry and Qualification

 **Rule 75**

ENTERING A RACE

75.1

To enter a race, a boat shall comply with the requirements of the organizing authority of the race. She shall be entered by
(a) a member of a club or other organization affiliated to an ISAF member national authority,
(b) such a club or organization, or
(c) a member of an ISAF member national authority.

75.2

Competitors shall comply with ISAF Regulation 19, Eligibility Code.

ISAF has a world monopoly over the organizing of formal racing. There is no law or treaty that grants this right. ISAF's power derives from its recognition by the Olympic movement as being the only International Sports Federation for sailing, from its control and copyright of the racing rules of sailing, and from its firm policy regarding anyone who would want to organize or take part in racing not authorised by ISAF.

---

[1] And rapidly submitted to and accepted by ISAF, as ISAF 107.
[2] Now ISAF 108
[3] RYA 2004/1
[4] ISAF 61

Control over competitors is exercised in part through rule 75.2. In outline, everyone has ISAF eligibility unless it is taken away 'after proper enquiry', either under rule 69.2, or after failing a doping control under rule 5, or for competing within the previous two years in an event that the competitor knew or should have known was a prohibited event. ISAF Regulation 19.4.1 defines a 'prohibited event' as:

- One that permits or requires advertising beyond that permitted by the ISAF Advertising Code: this could be a risk when the class association of a Category A class wrongly seeks via the notice of race and sailing instructions that competitors are to carry advertising of a class sponsor who is not the event sponsor.
- An event with big-money prizes that is a national event not approved by the national authority or an international event not approved by ISAF.
- An event that should pay an event fee to ISAF but has not done so
- An event not otherwise approved by ISAF that does not conform to the requirements of rule 89.1, which means when the organizing authority is not one of those listed in that rule: this could be a class that wants to run an event 'off the beach' without doing so in conjunction with an affiliated club, or a 'commercial event' either run without being in conjunction with an affiliated club, or, even then, if run without ISAF and national authority permission.

The first and last of these are risks into which the average competitor could unwittingly stray, and could risk loss of eligibility if caught in the backwash of attempts to stop or punish the breach by the organizing authority.

EXCLUSION OF BOATS OR COMPETITORS

The organizing authority or the race committee may reject or cancel the entry of a boat or exclude a competitor, subject to rule 76.2, provided it does so before the start of the first race and states the reason for doing so. However, the organizing authority or the race committee shall not reject or cancel the entry of a boat or exclude a competitor because of advertising, provided the boat or competitor complies with ISAF Regulation 20, Advertising Code.

At world and continental championships no entry within stated quotas shall be rejected or cancelled without first obtaining the approval of the relevant international class association (or the Offshore Racing Council) or the ISAF.

This rule can be an issue when there is some sort of 'history' between a competitor and a club – perhaps the competitor left the club under some sort of a cloud, and now wishes to enter an open meeting. As the rule says, the cancellation cannot be retrospective, but must happen before the start of the first race[1]. Does a reason have to be 'reasonable'? US Sailing's prescription to rule 76 says that 'an organizing authority or race committee shall not reject or cancel the entry of a boat or exclude a competitor eligible under the notice of race and sailing instructions for an arbitrary or capricious reason or for reason of race, color, religion, national origin, gender, sexual orientation, or age.' Similarly, but less specifically, the RYA prescribes that 'an organizing authority or race committee shall not reject or cancel the entry of a boat or exclude a competitor on unreasonable grounds. When asked to do so, the organizing authority or race committee shall promptly provide its reasons in writing. The boat may request redress if she considers the action improper.' In US 53, however, a boat was excluded from an event for 'offshore' boats because she was not what the organizing authority believed to be an offshore boat. Her appeal failed, since, outside the specific circumstances of US Sailing's prescription, it was held incorrect to assert that a reason must be 'legitimate', which is not the same as 'not arbitrary or capricious'; and 'rule 76.1 does not state or imply any qualitative tests for the acceptability of the reason…A race committee has broad authority to make such judgements as it considers to be necessary to ensure that a race or regatta is conducted so as to follow the intentions of the organizing authority, as well as the rules governing the event.' It is not clear that US Sailing and the RYA are saying the same thing. Where does 'unreasonable' rank compared with 'arbitrary' and 'capricious'?

---

[1] RYA 1999/3

Rule 76.1 makes a specific provision with regard to advertising. When the event sponsor is Adam's Ales, whose name will appear on a small area of the hull, it is not permitted to refuse an entry from a boat carrying conspicuous advertising for Brian's Beer, the name that will be seen in the press when the boat is pictured crossing the finishing line under a very 'promotional' spinnaker.

The rule provides both for excluding a boat and for excluding an individual competitor. Where an historic issue leading to a decision to exclude relates to a particular person, it should be only that named competitor who is excluded, even if the boat is a single-hander. It is then for the competitor (or owner or person in charge) to decide what to do about the boat continuing to take part.

 **IDENTIFICATION ON SAILS**

A boat shall comply with the requirements of Appendix G governing class insignia, national letters and numbers on sails.

Appendix G gives detailed requirements for ISAF international classes and ISAF recognised classes, as concerns the display on one or more sails of the class insignia, the national letters (at international events) and her sail number. Other boats have to comply with the requirements of their national authority or class association. The penalty is either a warning and time to rectify the mistake or omission, or disqualification.

The rule is commonly broken without enforcement. Boats arrive at major events without national letters, or with a new sail without numbers (other perhaps than a single digit), or with a spinnaker borrowed from a friend whose sail number is defaced, and with the boat's sail number hand-drawn and so hardly legible. Race committees give permission, and protest committees rarely want to make an issue of this if the race committee does not want to. When issues arise, protest committees will often fall back on rule G4, which permit it to choose between disqualification and a warning and time to comply for breaking Appendix G. This is less of a panacaea than it appears: Appendix G's requirements concerning identification on sails applies directly only ISAF international classes and ISAF recognised classes. However, rule G2 says that other boats shall comply with the rules of their national authority or class association. There does not appear to be any mechanism for a non-ISAF class to allow a penalty other than disqualification for breach of class rules concerning identification on sails, and so only a sailing instruction putting the protest committee in the same position concerning both ISAF and non-ISAF classes will allow for disqualification to be avoided.

Added to this, sailing instructions cannot directly change class rules, as stated in rule 87, unless this is provided for in the class rules, or the class has given written permission. So when a class rule concerning sails, even for an ISAF class, does not concern identification, no penalty other than disqualification is available to a protest committee unless the sailing instructions say so, varying rule 64.1(a) for breaches of class rules or rule 78. A example might be sail measurement and stamping requirements.

Rule 78 COMPLIANCE WITH CLASS RULES; CERTIFICATES

78.1 A boat's owner and any other person in charge shall ensure that the boat is maintained to comply with her class rules and that her measurement or rating certificate, if any, remains valid.

78.2 When a *rule* requires a certificate to be produced before a boat *races*, and it is not produced, the boat may *race* provided that the race committee receives a statement signed by the person in charge that a valid certificate exists and that it will be given to the race committee before the end of the event. If the certificate is not received in time, the boat shall be disqualified from all races of the event.

78.3 When an equipment inspector or a measurer for an event decides that a boat or personal equipment does not comply with the class rules, he shall report the matter in writing to the race committee.

When a valid measurement certificate has been presented in good faith, and the race or series has been completed, ISAF 57 says that the final results must stand, even though at a later date the certificate is withdrawn for defects or errors that must have been present during the event. RYA 2005/7 says that the protection of ISAF 57 does not extend to someone who knows, or should know, that a boat does not comply with her class rules. In ISAF 57, the error was made by the rating authority in translating measurements into a handicap. In RYA 2005/7, boats sailed by sailmakers used a sailcloth not permitted by class rules, as they must have known. ISAF 57 itself says that its principle applies only when an owner has complied with rule 78.1, which was clearly not the case in RYA 2005/7.

Unless the notice of race requires the production of a measurement or rating certificate at entry (as possibly extended by rule 78.2), it may be that boats do not have valid certificates when racing in class races, but it is not the duty of the race committee to be officious. In ISAF 39, a boat, whose own protest against another for sailing three-up in a boat restricted to two in the class rules, appealed on the grounds that the race committee ought, on its own initiative, to have protested that boat. The appeal was dismissed. 'To uphold this appeal would amount to a conclusion that a race committee ought to know the class rules of each class, and that it then has an obligation to enforce them when members of the class fail to do so. No such obligation is placed on a race committee, and, furthermore, rule 60.2(a) is clearly discretionary. The responsibility for protesting primarily rests with the competitors.' The case does not concern rule 78 directly, since no issue of construction or certification arises, but the principle must hold good for all class rules.

Rule 78.3's obligation to report non-compliance with class rules to the race committee (and the corresponding duty of the race committee to protest as required by rule 60.2) applies only to an equipment inspector or a measurer formally appointed for the event. ISAF 57 says that when a failure to comply is learned from an outside body, such as a rating office, rule 60.2 does not apply.

In practice, reporting under rule 78.3 is a last resort when there is pre-race inspection at an event: normally, a boat will be given some time to put right a measurement failure. However, when a breach of class rules is discovered in a mid-competition check, the measurer has little option but to report it[1].

Ultimately, the policing of class rules will depend on the nature of an event. A class championship is likely to impose strict inspection requirements, and confine competition to class members. A club, in its normal programme, is more concerned with getting as many boats on the water as possible, and clubs tend to put class rule issues in the 'too difficult' box.

---

[1] For many years, I have been a member of the international jury for the annual Solitaire du Figaro event for single-handed sailing in the Figaro class. Most of the protests are from the race committee, arising from boats that have broken lead and wire seals on specified equipment whose movement during the race could break rule 51, Movable Ballast or (in the case of the propeller shaft) rule 42, Propulsion. All seals on all boats are examined at the end of the three or four legs of the event, failures are reported and protested, resulting in time penalties when upheld. These mechanical protests are at least enlivened by the variety of reasons and excuses given by the competitors for breaking a seal.

 **CLASSIFICATION**

If the notice of race or class rules state that some or all competitors must satisfy classification requirements, the classification shall be carried out as described in ISAF Regulation 22, Sailor Classification Code.

Many events such as Cork Week[1], the Commodores' Cup and the Tour de France à la Voile want to give the amateurs a fighting chance against the professionals, and use the ISAF Sailor Classification code to limit the number or the functions on board of people who are paid to sail, or whose job in a marine industry gives them an additional insight into what makes boats go faster. A facility on the ISAF website allows all competitors to get a classification and to seek a review of that classification. The Code then provides a procedure for vetting crew composition and for protesting. It is the only method allowed for competitor classification as concerns work and skills. It is unrelated to the ability of organizing authorities to restrict entry by reference to age, sex, nationality or previous success in competitions on their own judgement, and those criteria may apply simultaneously with the ISAF Sailing Classification Code in the same event.

 **ADVERTISING**

A boat and her crew shall comply with ISAF Regulation 20, Advertising Code.

The new ISAF Advertising Code, Regulation 20, to be found on the ISAF website, says that advertisements, when permitted, and anything advertised, shall meet generally accepted moral and ethical standards, and that advertising of a political, religious or racial nature is not allowed. There is enough in these few words to keep lawyers busy for years should an issue arise. Are these supposedly 'generally accepted standards' universal? Or should allowance be made for local sensitivities? Many things deemed unremarkable in some parts of the world are unacceptable in others, sometimes criminally so. Many charities are known to operate in the political arena. Would the display of the just the name of a campaigning charity be allowed? If so, would it be different if a strapline like 'fighting for womens' rights' were added? The Code recognises the non-uniformity of our world – 'Attention is also drawn to the laws of our individual nations which may restrict Advertising within their territory or territorial waters[2].'

The details of the Adcode are beyond the scope of this book, but an RYA guidance note on the RYA website summarises the revised position as follows:

What are the main advertising rules now?

The basic position is now, **in order of precedence**:

- Particular rules can apply for events with Olympic Classes, Club Events, Invitational Events and Special Events. Most importantly:

  - if you are running an event for an Olympic Class, you cannot restrict their right to advertise without permission from ISAF; and

  - if you are running a Club or Invitational Event, you can ask the RYA for permission to restrict the right to advertise.

- ISAF Classes/Rating Systems have the right to prohibit or limit advertising and to adopt "global" sponsorship subject to certain rules.

- Organising Authorities have the right to make use of certain areas on the boats, boards and supplied equipment.

- Boats have the right to advertise on their hulls, spars and sails.

- Competitors have the right to advertise on their clothing and personal equipment, subject to permission from the person in charge. You can never require a competitor to wear advertising on a bib.

---

[1] Whose 2008 notice of race, which excludes paid professionals from most of its races, includes the following comment: 'The Organizers of Cork Week have continually asked our competitors if they wish us to retain our ISAF Sailor Classification requirements. The overwhelming response has been positive and we are happy to do so.'
[2] Regulation 20.2.2

RESCHEDULED RACES

When a race has been rescheduled, all boats entered in the original race shall be notified. New entries that meet the entry requirements of the original race may be accepted at the discretion of the race committee.

I think that a 'rescheduled race' is a race for which a new time for the warning signal is announced that is significantly later than the time of, and often the date of, the warning signal in the sailing instructions. The original race may have been postponed before the warning signal, postponed after the warning signal, abandoned either before or after the starting signal, or subject to a general recall after the starting signal. The term is used only in rule 81, for the purposes of notifying original entrants and accepting new entries.

In RYA 1999/9, the notice of race and sailing instructions for a 10-race series, with two discards, did not require an entry to be made in writing, and Flying Fifteens on their moorings were deemed to be entrants, scoring points for DNS when they did not take part.

After a race sailed in June, *Bones Jones* requested redress, and as a result the protest committee abandoned the race and ordered a resail. The race was rescheduled for 29th August, the last practical date in the season. *Bones Jones* then suffered damage and was unable to take part. The rescheduling was arranged by the owner of ff2278 who was the sailing secretary of the club. ff2278 had not taken part in the abandoned race, but competed in seven of the other nine races in the series.

After the resailed race, *Bones Jones* again requested redress, this time on the grounds that ff2278, which had not sailed the original race, had been allowed to sail in the rescheduled race, and because the resail date had been impossible for herself (*Bones Jones*) because of boat damage. The protest committee held the resailed race to be invalid for the reasons asserted by *Bones Jones* and abandoned it. It then gave redress of average points to those boats that raced in the first race, in which ff2278 had not started. The race committee's appeal was upheld.

The results of the race held on 29th August are to stand, including the result of ff2278. The decision by the protest committee to resail the first race is not the subject of this appeal and is therefore to be accepted.

In deciding the claim for redress by *Bones Jones,* the protest committee made an error when it decided that ff2278 was not entitled to take part in the resail. ff2278 was an entrant (albeit not a starter) in the race in question and therefore entitled to sail in the rescheduled race in accordance with rule 81.

When the date is chosen for a race to be resailed, it often follows that a boat that sailed the abandoned race is unable to take part in the resail. Provided that all boats that entered the first race are notified of the resail date, and that the date is chosen fairly, there is no error by the race committee and no boats are entitled to redress on the grounds of the rescheduled date.

The sailing secretary made every effort to ensure that the resail date suited as many people as possible. She cannot be held responsible, due to circumstances outside her control, for a competitor not being able to start. The fact that the appellant was unable to race on the day chosen for the rescheduled race was unfortunate, but not an improper action of the race committee.

Part 7 - Race Organization

GOVERNING RULES

The organizing authority, race committee and protest committee shall be governed by the *rules* in the conduct and judging of races.

The question is what happens when this rule is not followed. In ISAF 66, the question was whether a race committee could change or decide not to implement the decisions of a protest committee. The background was that the race committee judged that the disqualification of a number of boats was unfair, following a measurement protest in which the class association, having been asked for a ruling as the appropriate authority, had confirmed that they had broken a class rule. The question was however worded more generally.

The answer was in the negative. 'Rule 85 says that the race committee shall be governed by the rules. A race committee has no jurisdiction over a protest committee, and is not entitled to change or refuse to implement any decision that the protest committee may have made. Rule 64.1(a) provides that a protest committee's decision to penalise must be implemented[1].'

So who may take what action? 'In this case, the race committee and each boat protested by it are the parties to the hearing. Under rule 66 a party may ask that the hearing be reopened on the grounds that the protest committee made a significant error or that significant new evidence has become available. Also, under rule 70.1, a party may appeal the protest committee's decision or its procedures.'

Rule 86

86.1

CHANGES TO THE RACING RULES

A racing rule shall not be changed unless permitted in the rule itself or as follows:
(a) Prescriptions of a national authority may change a racing rule, but not the Definitions; a rule in the Introduction; Sportsmanship and the Rules; Part 1, 2 or 7; rule 42, 43, 69, 70, 71, 75, 76.2, 79 or 80; a rule of an appendix that changes one of these rules; Appendix H or N; or ISAF Regulation 19, 20, 21 or 22.
(b) Sailing instructions may change a racing rule but not rule 76.1, Appendix F, or a rule listed in rule 86.1(a). However, the sailing instructions may change to 'two' or 'four' the number of hull lengths determining the *zone* around *marks*, provided that the number is the same for all *marks* and all boats using those *marks*. If the sailing instructions change a rule or that definition, they shall refer specifically to the rule or definition and state the change.
(c) Class rules may change only racing rules 42, 49, 50, 51, 52, 53 and 54. Such changes shall refer specifically to the rule and state the change.
Note: The second sentence of this rule takes effect on 1 January 2011.

86.2

In exception to rule 86.1, the ISAF may in limited circumstances (see ISAF Regulation 31.1.3) authorize changes to the racing rules for a specific international event. The authorization shall be stated in a letter of approval to the event organizing authority and in the notice of race and sailing instructions, and the letter shall be posted on the event's official notice board.

86.3

If a national authority so prescribes, the restrictions in rule 86.1 do not apply if rules are changed to develop or test proposed rules. The national authority may prescribe that its approval is required for such changes.

The important question is usually whether sailing instructions can change a rule. The answer is reached in two hops. First, rule 86.1(a) lists the rules that a national authority cannot change by prescription. Then rule 86.1(b) says that sailing instructions cannot change those same rules either, with the exception of the definition Zone if two or four lengths are preferred, subject to the conditions stated, and with the addition that rule 76.1, Exclusion of Boats or Competitors, and Appendix F, Appeal Procedures cannot be changed either. Note that sailing instructions cannot change rule 42, Propulsion, but class rules can.

---

[1] Thus in RYA 2007/1 it was held that an organizing authority has no power to revoke a decision of the protest committee to rehear a protest.

A 'change' to a rule includes an addition to it, or a deletion of all or part of it[1]. If in doubt as to whether a sailing instruction is adding to a rule, it is safest to assume that it is, and the relevant sailing instruction will contain words to the effect of 'This changes / affects / adds to rule xx', as appropriate.

When those magic words are not used, the intended change will be ineffective if challenged. The commonest situation is, as previously discussed, rule 35's principle that all boats get a finishing time when one boat finishes within the time limit. This rule is nearly always changed in some way. Unless the sailing instruction says that rule 35 is changed, a boat scored for being out of time may be able to ask for and get redress in the form of a finishing place[2]. Another example is a sailing instruction that unsuccessfully purported to allow a course to be displayed after the warning signal[3].

Some rules themselves allow for different provisions to be made. If a sailing instruction specifies the use of the Scoring Penalty or some other penalty, this does not change rule 44.1, Penalties at the Time of an Incident, because the rule provides for it. Likewise, if a sailing instruction allows the protest committee to apply a penalty not provided for in the racing rules, this does not change rule 64.1, Decisions: Penalties and Exoneration, because the rule refers to some other penalty applying. So in each of these cases, it is not necessary for the sailing instructions to say that rules 44.1 or 64.1 are changed – because they are not.

To the limited extent that class rules are allowed to change racing rules, they too now have to refer specifically to the rule and state the change, with two years to bring the class rules into line.

Rule 86.2 and 86.3 are rarely used. However, the RYA has recently given a time-limited permission to a gennaker class to test a rule giving right of way to boats with gennakers set over those that are not, to try to deal with issues of poor downwind visibility and high downwind speeds.

Rule 87

CHANGES TO CLASS RULES

The sailing instructions may change a class rule only when the class rules permit the change, or when written permission of the class association for the change is displayed on the official notice board.

The relationship between class rules and sailing instructions is now clear in the rules themselves, confirming previous cases[4], despite which there were grey areas. This means that classes will have to address any topics where there is no objection to changes being made, and amend the class rules accordingly. Since that takes time, perhaps the second option of a letter for the official notice board could be a general one indicating now all the changes that the class wants to allow in the class rules.

Specific issues that will need to be addressed include:
- Whether sailing instructions can require VHF radios, mobile phones or other electronic aids to be carried for reasons of safety or for communicating courses and course changes when these are not allowed in the class rules
- Whether cushions and other items prone to mildew in damp conditions can be left ashore, particularly in winter
- Whether sailing instructions can change a class rule that says that, to be in class, the owner must be a member of the class association
- Whether class rules that set out event specifications, often called 'championship rules', can be varied.
- Whether class rules concerning sail limitations and sail numbering and lettering can be varied by sailing instructions in classes that are not international or ISAF-recognised classes

---

[1] See Introduction
[2] RYA 1998/2
[3] RYA 1997/2
[4] ISAF 98, RYA 2004/5

NATIONAL PRESCRIPTIONS

The prescriptions that apply to an event are the prescriptions of the national authority with which the organizing authority is associated under rule 89.1. However, if boats will pass through the waters of more than one national authority while *racing*, the sailing instructions shall identify any other prescriptions that will apply and when they will apply.

88.2

The sailing instructions may change a prescription. However, a national authority may restrict changes to its prescriptions with a prescription to this rule, provided the ISAF approves its application to do so. The restricted prescriptions shall not be changed by the sailing instructions.

The relationship of prescriptions to the rest of the racing rules has been another grey area. It was often wrongly thought that all prescriptions could be made not to apply in world and continental championships. The situation is now clearer. It is easiest to start with the explicit statement in rule 88.2, that the sailing instructions CAN change a prescription, unless ISAF approves an application from a national authority to make specific prescriptions non-changeable. Only a national authority can make such an application. By the time these rules are in force, national authorities should have republished their prescriptions, to include a prescription to rule 88.2 stating which prescriptions cannot be changed, and (preferably) confirming that ISAF approval for this has been received. In the UK, prescriptions cannot be changed, but a reduced set applies at an event with an international jury[1].

In choosing which prescriptions need not apply, a coastal national authority should take note of rule 88.1, to avoid needlessly imposing domestic restrictions on 'passing trade'. The term 'pass through' is unclear. Does it apply only to situations where boats race from country A to C, and in the process sail through the waters of country B? Or does it also include (as it should) a race just from country A to country B (usually followed by a return race from B to A)?

When national prescriptions apply, it does not need a sailing instruction to say so – they will apply because the event is governed by the rules, as defined, which includes the national prescriptions.

ORGANIZING AUTHORITY; NOTICE OF RACE; APPOINTMENT OF RACE OFFICIALS

89.1

Organizing Authority
Races shall be organized by an organizing authority, which shall be
(a) the ISAF;
(b) a member national authority of the ISAF;
(c) a club or other organization affiliated to a national authority;
(d) a class association, either with the approval of a national authority or in conjunction with an affiliated club;
(e) an unaffiliated body in conjunction with an affiliated club where the body is owned and controlled by the club. The national authority of the club may prescribe that its approval is required for such an event; or
(f) if approved by the ISAF and the national authority of the club, an unaffiliated body in conjunction with an affiliated club where the body is not owned and controlled by the club.

Notice of Race; Appointment of Race Officials
(a) The organizing authority shall publish a notice of race that conforms to rule J1. The notice of race may be changed provided adequate notice is given.
(b) The organizing authority shall appoint a race committee and, when appropriate, appoint a protest committee and umpires. However, the race committee, an international jury and umpires may be appointed by the ISAF as provided in the ISAF regulations.

---

[1] The RYA prescription to rule 88.2 is curently: 'Notices of race and sailing instructions shall not change a prescription of the RYA. However, when an international jury has been appointed for an event, only the prescriptions to rules 5, 68, 86.3 and 88.2 shall apply.' The RYA prescriptions are a relatively light burden.

Clauses (a), (b) and (d) are self-explanatory. It has been suggested that an 'other organization affiliated to a national authority' in (c) could include a class association, thus allowing it to organize races on its own. But that would be contrary to the intention of (d), which is that class associations are not to organize races on their own. A 2008 RYA submission to ISAF seeking greater clarity was deferred by ISAF to allow the problem to be debated further.

Clause (e) is aimed at situations where the organizing authority is a company with limited liability, owned by the club where the event is held, this being done to protect club members against what can be unlimited personal liability if the club were successfully sued.

Clause (f) makes possible large 'commercial' races such as the Volvo, the Solitaire du Figaro, the Tour de France à la Voile and the Vendée Globe.

Rule 90 — RACE COMMITTEE; SAILING INSTRUCTIONS; SCORING

90.1 Race Committee
The race committee shall conduct races as directed by the organizing authority and as required by the *rules*.

90.2 Sailing Instructions
(a) The race committee shall publish written sailing instructions that conform to rule J2.
(b) When appropriate, for an event where entries from other countries are expected, the sailing instructions shall include, in English, the applicable national prescriptions.
(c) Changes to the sailing instructions shall be in writing and posted on the official notice board before the time stated in the sailing instructions or, on the water, communicated to each boat before her warning signal. Oral changes may be given only on the water, and only if the procedure is stated in the sailing instructions.

90.3 Scoring
(a) The race committee shall score a race or series as provided in Appendix A using the Low Point System, unless the sailing instructions specify the Bonus Point System or some other system. A race shall be scored if it is not *abandoned* and if one boat sails the course in compliance with rule 28.1 and *finishes* within the time limit, if any, even if she retires after *finishing* or is disqualified.
(b) When a scoring system provides for excluding one or more race scores from a boat's series score, the score for disqualification under rule 2; rule 30.3's last sentence; rule 42 if rule 67, P2.2 or P2.3 applies; or rule 69.1(b)(2) shall not be excluded. The next-worse score shall be excluded instead.

Rule 91 — PROTEST COMMITTEE
A protest committee shall be
(a) a committee appointed by the organizing authority or race committee, or
(b) an international jury appointed by the organizing authority or as prescribed in the ISAF regulations and meeting the requirements of Appendix N. A national authority may prescribe that its approval is required for the appointment of international juries for races within its jurisdiction, except ISAF events or when international juries are appointed by the ISAF under rule 89.2(b).

Matching the structure in rules 90 and 91 (and in rule 89.2) to what actually happens at club level is sometimes not obvious, especially when some people wear more than one hat. The club itself may be the organizing authority, but most likely it will delegate some or all of the duties to a sailing or racing committee. The committee devises the club programme for the season, which is published in the club handbook. This is the notice of race, even though it may not describe itself as such, and my experience is that many of the relevant items referred to in J1.1 and J1.2 are often not explicitly covered. Rule 89.2 says that the organizing authority appoints the race committee. One of the duties of the race committee is to publish sailing instructions, but this is often done by the same committee as published the notice of race. The race team that actually runs a day's racing is the race committee for the purposes of the racing rules[1], but it is quite possible that none of the officials in action on the day will be members of the club's racing/sailing committee. While rule 89.2 says it is the organizing authority that appoints the protest committee 'when appropriate', it is often not appropriate, and the protest committee may in fact be an ad-hoc assembly of members gathered by the race officer when a protest materialises, in effect a race committee appointment as contemplated in rule 91(a)[2]. If you ask the average club member to identify the organizing authority and the race committee of the club, you may not get a sensible answer. Nevertheless, life goes on, and racing happens.

The requirement in rule 90.2(b) to post the applicable prescriptions in English used to apply to an 'international event'. But what is an international event? Many events are open to foreign entries but none is forthcoming. The rule now takes a more pragmatic approach – are overseas entries expected? Rule J1.2(4) also requires publication in the notice of race of any national prescription where compliance by an entrant from another country needs prior notice.

By rule 90.3, Appendix A, Low Point, is the default scoring system if no other system is mentioned in the sailing instructions, and Rule A2 says that the default is then one discard[3], unless more, or a number that changes with number of races completed, or none is specified. The fact that one discard is automatic unless it is modified is often not realised. When the sailing instructions simply repeat the fact that there is to be one discard, there is no problem. But when it is intended that there will be no discard, for instance in a two-or three-race series, the need to say so explicitly in the sailing instructions is sometimes forgotten. (If it is to be a no-discard event, I think that fact should be in the notice of race, as it may affect a decision to enter if it is possible that the boat will not be able to sail in every race of the event).

A race is to be scored if (a) it is not abandoned, and if (b) one boat sails the course and finishes within the time limit, even if she retires after finishing or is disqualified. If the only boat that finishes inside the time limit is then disqualified for not sailing the course, Rule 90.3(a) fills the gap in rule 35 – there is then no race to score, since no boat both sailed the course and finished inside the time limit. However, if rule 35 is modified so that boats finishing outside the time limit will be scored DNF, and if the only boat to finish inside the time limit is then disqualified under any rule other than rule 28, Sailing the Course, then rule A2 says the that race will have been 'completed' even though no boat will have received a finishing result in it, since the race has been scored. So if that was rule 6, the next race will be race 7, and the scores from race 6 are prime candidates for discarding.

Rule 90.3(b) states the obvious – a non-excludable score cannot be excluded! And so (slightly less obviously) it will be the next-worse score that will be excluded / discarded / thrown out.

---

[1] See under Terminology

[2] Rule 91(a) says that a protest committee may be a committee appointed by the organizing authority or race committee, but, while rule 89.2(b) gives the organizing quthority power where appropriate to appoint a protest committee, no such specific power is afforded to the race committee in rule 90.1

[3] The rules refer to races whose results are 'excluded', while the term 'discarded' and 'thrown out' are commonly employed on either side of the Atlantic.

APPENDIX A

Here is the text, together with guidance notes, as published by the RYA.

A1 NUMBER OF RACES

The number of races scheduled and the number required to be completed to constitute a series shall be stated in the sailing instructions.

A2 SERIES SCORES

Each boat's series score shall be the total of her race scores excluding her worst score. (The sailing instructions may make a different arrangement by providing, for example, that no score will be excluded, that two or more scores will be excluded, or that a specified number of scores will be excluded if a specified number of races are completed.) A race is completed if scored; see rule 89.3(a). If a boat has two or more equal worst scores, the score(s) for the race(s) sailed earliest in the series shall be excluded. The boat with the lowest series score wins and others shall be ranked accordingly.

> Rule 90.3(a) states that a race shall be scored if it not *abandoned* and if one boat sails the course in compliance with rule 28.1 and *finishes* within the time limit, if any, even if she retires after *finishing* or is disqualified. Therefore circumstances can theoretically arise when no boat receives a score for a finishing place, but the race is nevertheless 'completed' for the purposes of constituting a series – see rule A1. An abandoned race is not scored and therefore not completed. Normally, if race 5 (for instance) of a 10-race regatta is abandoned, the next race to be sailed will still be race 5 (and as a result race 10 may never be sailed). Care is needed over describing race prizes – is it a prize for race number x, or a prize for a race on a stated day?

A3 STARTING TIMES AND FINISHING PLACES

The time of a boat's starting signal shall be her starting time, and the order in which boats *finish* a race shall determine their finishing places. However, when a handicap system is used a boat's corrected time shall determine her finishing place.

> The rule no longer tells you to round corrected times (after applying the handicap). The rounding of corrected times is a matter for the handicap or rating system to specify. IRC and Portsmouth Yardstick, for example, have a time-rounding rule. If you need to decide a rounding policy for your own handicap system, consider whether a decimal of a second of corrected time, as in the following example, is meaningful when it derives from elapsed times taken at the finishing line at best to the nearer second.
>
> **Example:** Boat A is corrected to 1200.499 (etc) seconds, Boat B is corrected to 1199.5011 (etc) seconds. Without rounding, B gets the better place. If your handicap system states that corrected times are to be rounded to the nearer whole second, rounding 0.5 to the larger number, each time rounds to 1200 seconds, and the boats are tied for a place. Apply A7 to calculate their points for the tied place in that race. Rounding might be fairer, though it slightly increases the probability of a tie for a place.

A4 LOW POINT AND BONUS POINT SYSTEMS

Most series are scored using either the Low Point System or the Bonus Point System. The Low Point System uses a boat's finishing place as her race score. The Bonus Point System benefits the first six finishers because of the greater difficulty in advancing from fourth place to third, for example, than from fourteenth place to thirteenth. The Low Point System will apply unless the sailing instructions specify another system; see rule 89.3(a). If the Bonus Point system is chosen it can be made to apply by stating in the sailing instructions that 'The Bonus Point System of Appendix A will apply.'

> When the sailing instructions are silent, the default is that the series will be scored by the Low Point System (see rule 90.3(a)), with one discard (see rule A2). If all races are to count, using Appendix A scoring, this requires a sailing instruction to that effect.

A4.1 Each boat *starting* and *finishing* and not thereafter retiring, being penalised or given redress shall be scored points as follows:

Finishing place	Low Point System	Bonus Point System
First	1	0
Second	2	3
Third	3	5.7
Fourth	4	8
Fifth	5	10
Sixth	6	11.7
Seventh	7	13
Each place thereafter	Add 1 point	Add 1 point

A4.2 A boat that did not *start*, did not *finish*, retired after *finishing* or was disqualified shall be scored points for the finishing place one more than the number of boats entered in the series. A boat that is penalised under rule 30.2 or that takes a penalty under rule 44.3(a) shall be scored points as provided in rule 44.3(c).

> **Example 1**: 23 boats entered the series. Boat A finishes 3rd in the race but is ZFP. The penalty is 20% of 23 = 4.6 places, rounded to 5 places so she receives points for the place equal to her finishing place of 3rd plus 5 penalty places - 8th place. Under the Low Point System, 8th place receives 8 points so points for the race are: 1, 2, 4, 5, 6, 7, 8, 8, 9, 10 ... 23. (The boxed number is A's score.) The two boats scoring 8 points will share any race prize for 7th place; the boat scoring 9 points will receive any race prize for 9th place. Remember that under rule 44.3 (and therefore under rule 30.2) a boat shall not receive a score that is worse than DNF would receive. A DNF score in this race would be 24 (23 series entrants, plus 1), which would be the penalty for a ZFP boat with a finishing position of 20th or worse.

> Scoring penalties under rules 30.2 and/or 44.3 are cumulative but are calculated individually. For example, if a boat breaks rule 30.2 and the race is recalled and she again breaks rule 30.2 in the restart, she will have two 20% penalties. Similarly, if she breaks 30.2 and also takes a Scoring Penalty under rule 44.3 (SCP) she will have two 20% penalties (assuming the sailing instructions do not specify that the Scoring Penalty will be other than 20%).
>
> **Example 2**: Same as **Example 1** above except that boat A also takes a 20% SCP under rule 44.3. She receives two penalties of 5 places each for a total of 10 places (not a 40% penalty of 9.2 places rounded to 9 places). Her score would be the score for 13th place, namely her finishing place of 3rd plus 10 penalty places. Points for the race are: 1, 2, 4, 5, 6, 7, 8, 9, 10, 11, 12, 13, 13, 14, 15...

> The score of a boat receiving a scoring penalty may be affected by the disqualification of a boat whose finishing place is ahead of her.
>
> **Example 3**: Same as **Example 1** above except that the boat that finished second is disqualified (and receives 24 points). All boats with a finishing place after the disqualified boat move up one place (see rule A6(1)). Boat A receives points for 7th place, namely her adjusted finishing place of 2nd (as a result of the disqualification) plus 5 penalty places, leaving that ' 2 point slot' vacant . Points for that race would be: 1, 3, 4, 5, 6, 7, 7, 8, 9, ... 22, 24.
>
> **Example 4**: Same as **Example 3** above except that the boat that is disqualified finished sixth (not second). All boats with a finishing place after the disqualified boat move up one place (see rule A6(1)). Boat A receives points for 8th place, namely her finishing place of 3rd (not changed as the result of the disqualification of a boat whose finishing place is after her) plus 5 penalty places. The '3 point slot' remains vacant. Points for that race would be: 1, 2, 4, 5, 6, 7, 8, 8, 9, ... 22, 24.

A5 SCORES DETERMINED BY THE RACE COMMITTEE

A boat that did not *start*, comply with rule 30.2 or 30.3, or *finish*, or that takes a penalty under rule 44.3(a) or retires after *finishing*, shall be scored accordingly by the race committee without a hearing. Only the protest committee may take other scoring actions that worsen a boat's score.

DNC, DNS, OCS, ZFP, BFD and DNF are race committee scores. DSQ, DNE, DGM and RDG are protest committee scores. SCP and RAF are scores accepted by a boat, notified to and implemented by the race committee. See A11.

A6 CHANGES IN PLACES AND SCORES OF OTHER BOATS

A6.1 If a boat is disqualified from a race or retires after *finishing*, each boat that *finished* after her shall be moved up one place.

A6.2 If the protest committee decides to give redress by adjusting a boat's score, the scores of other boats shall not be changed unless the protest committee decides otherwise.

A7 RACE TIES

If boats are tied at the finishing line or if a handicap or rating system is used and boats have equal corrected times, the points for the place for which the boats have tied and for the place(s) immediately below shall be added together and divided equally. Boats tied for a race prize shall share it or be given equal prizes.

Example: Two boats have the same corrected time for third place. Under the Low Point System they would each score 3.5 points [(3+4)/2], and there is no change to the scores of any other boats. Points for the race are: 1, 2, 3.5, 3.5, 5... Note: As provided in rules A6(1) and 44.3(c), the 'split the points' principle of the first sentence of A7 does not apply when the tie in race scores results from a grant of redress or the application of a scoring penalty. (See A4.2, above).

A8 SERIES TIES

A8.1 If there is a series score tie between two or more boats, each boat's race scores shall be listed in order of best to worst, and at the first point(s) where there is a difference the tie shall be broken in favour of the boat(s) with the best score(s). No excluded scores shall be used.

Example: Scoring: Low Point – one score excluded

Race No:	1	2	3	4	5	6	TOTAL	REORDERED COUNTING SCORES	SCORES NOT USED
Boat A	3	4	1	6	2	7	**16**	1 2 3 4 6	7
Boat B	4	3	2	1	6	6	**16**	1 2 3 4 6	6
Boat C	1	2	7	3	3	14	**16**	1 2 3 3 7	14

Rule A8.1 is sometimes known as 'most firsts, etc.' It breaks the tie between C and the two other boats in C's favour. It does not break the tie between A and B. Rule A8.2 must now be applied to break that tie (in favour of B, for her better last race score).

A8.2 If a tie still remains between two or more boats, they shall be ranked in order of their scores in the last race. Any remaining ties shall be broken by using the tied boats' scores in the next-to-last race and so on until all ties are broken. These scores shall be used even if some of them are excluded scores.

Example: Scoring: Low Point – one score excluded.

Race No:	1	2	3	4	TOTAL
Boat A	3	4	5	~~10~~	**12**
Boat B	~~11~~	3	4	5	**12**
Boat C	5	~~15~~	3	4	**12**
Boat D	4	5	~~6~~	3	**12**

A8.1 does not break any tie, as they each have scores of 3, 4, 5 that count.

A8.2 applies, and the tie is broken in the order of D, C, B, A, the order of their last race scores. Note that A's race 4 result was her discard, but it is still used to break the tie.

Ties in A8.1 and A8.2 are broken on scores, not finishing places. If this had been a 40-boat entry, and A had been second in race 4, only to receive a 20% (8-place) ZFP, the outcome of the tie-break is the same. Normally, the last race will resolve most ties. The next-to-last race (and so on) will need to be used only if two boats have the same score in the last race, which might result from a ZFP, from a tie on the water or on handicap, or from both receiving non-finishing points resulting from DNC, DNS, OCS, BFD, DNF, RAF, DSQ, DNE or DGM.

The policy behind rule A8.2 is to add a little extra importance to the last race, particularly if this would result in a boat leading the series before the last race finding herself at risk of losing the series if she does not compete in the last race. That is very much a 'regatta-oriented' rule, and typical club 'long series' scoring sometimes disapplies rule A8.2 and specifies instead a different final tie-breaker, such as best discard, which incentivises participation in all races.

A9   RACE SCORES IN A SERIES LONGER THAN A REGATTA

For a series that is held over a period of time longer than a regatta, a boat that came to the starting area but did not *start*, did not *finish*, retired after *finishing* or was disqualified shall be scored points for the finishing place one more than the number of boats that came to the starting area. A boat that did not come to the starting area shall be scored points for the finishing place one more than the number of boats entered in the series.

A10   GUIDANCE ON REDRESS

If the protest committee decides to give redress by adjusting a boat's score for a race, it is advised to consider scoring her

(a) points equal to the average, to the nearest tenth of a point (0.05 to be rounded upward), of her points in all the races in the series except the race in question;

(b) points equal to the average, to the nearest tenth of a point (0.05 to be rounded upward), of her points in all the races before the race in question; or

(c) points based on the position of the boat in the race at the time of the incident that justified redress.

Example: average points of 2.85 rounds to 2.9. 'Upward' means to a larger number (and therefore worse score).

A11   SCORING ABBREVIATIONS

These scoring abbreviations shall be used for recording the circumstances described:

DNC   Did not *start*; did not come to the starting area

DNS   Did not *start* (other than DNC and OCS)

OCS   Did not *start*; on the course side of the starting line at her starting signal and failed to start, or broke rule 30.1

ZFP   20% penalty under rule 30.2

BFD   Disqualification under rule 30.3

SCP   Took a Scoring Penalty under rule 44.3(a)

DNF   Did not *finish*

RAF   Retired after *finishing*

DSQ   Disqualification

DNE   Disqualification (other than DGM) not excludable under rule 88.3(b)

DGM   Disqualification for gross misconduct not excludable under rule 90.3(b)

RDG   Redress given

DNF (like DNC and OCS) is a statement of fact – a boat has not finished, for whatever reason, whether as a result of gear failure, boredom, or because she was required to retire by rule 31.2, 44.1 or P2.2. There is no separate designation (such as RET) reserved for voluntary or required retirement during a race, but that could be specified and used when the sailing instructions call for retirement declarations.

A race committee will know which boats finished, but may not know, in a large regatta fleet, whether those that entered but did not finish are DNC, DNS or DNF. Since the score for these are the same, it would be appropriate for the convenience of scoring for a sailing instruction to say that any boat that enters but does not *finish* as defined will be scored DNF whether or not she came to the starting area or started. However, tallying or having the sail number acknowledged by the committee boat before starting will identify DNC boats.

How to score using Appendix A – General Guidance

1. Choose the appropriate wording to appear in the notice of race – see K13, Notice of Race Guide – and in the sailing instructions – see L17, Sailing Instructions Guide. If the series is to be scored by the Low Point System, Appendix A, with one discard, then the sailing instructions do not need to specify the scoring system, since this is the default (see rules 90.3 and A2). However, it does no harm to state the scoring system. State races to count. Some clubs like a different tariff of scores for non-finishing places, in particular scoring DNC more heavily to encourage participation.

2. The score for non-finishing places can change during a series if new boats can enter during the series (see rules A4.2 and A9); this is common in long club series (A9), affecting DNC scores. To avoid the need to recalculate, the sailing instructions can say that *'The last sentence of rule A9 is replaced with: "A boat that did not come to the starting area shall be scored points decided by the race committee".'* The race committee can then decide a value for this at the start of the series, being a number larger than the maximum expected series entry. Alternatively, give a fixed (but possibly heavier –see 1 above) value to DNC as with other non finishing scores by saying: *'The last sentence of rule A9 is replaced with: "A boat that did not come to the starting area shall be scored as if she did not start [+ n points]."*

3. If scoring manually, apply rules A3, A4 and A5 to the results, in tabular form. The sequence is:
- Take order of finish (non-handicap races) or elapsed times (handicap races)
- Correct elapsed times using handicap or rating factor (handicap or rating races only). Apply rounding if specified
- Identify and score for DNC, DNS, OCS, BFD, RAF and DNF (which includes those not finishing within a time limit if so provided in the sailing instructions[1]). Use A4.2 for short series, A9 for long series ('Longer than a regatta')
- Rank remaining boats for their preliminary finishing places by:
  - Corrected times (handicap races only), otherwise
  - Finishing order
- Assign points to preliminary finishing places based on the specified scoring system, breaking race ties (rule A7[2])
- Identify and add penalty places to the preliminary finishing places for boats scored SCP or ZFP (do not change the scores of other boats - see rule A4.2)
- If appropriate, post preliminary results for the race and series (stated to be 'subject to changes resulting from protests and requests for redress')
- Remove the finishing place and change the score of boats that the protest committee instructs should be scored DSQ, DNE or DGM. The finishing places, and thus the scores, of boats with finishing places after the boat to be scored DSQ, DNE or DGM will also change - see rule A6.1. When a boat in that race has been scored SCP or ZFP it is important to remember that her score, which is her finishing place plus penalty places, will change only if her original finishing place was after that of the DSQ, etc, boat before it was removed – see rule A4.2 example.
- Change the score of any boat granted redress (mark RDG against the revised score) when instructed by the protest committee. (The final value of RDG under A10(a) will vary until the end of the series; do not change the finishing places or scores of other boats unless the protest committee decides otherwise - see rule A6.2). If the redress score is the same as another boat's place score, do not treat it as a tie to be broken. If the protest committee's decision is stated to be simply 'average points redress', seek clarification as to whether it is A10(a), A10(b) or some other method that is to be applied[3].

---

[1] In the absence of a sailing instruction to the contrary, a race committee must give a finishing place to any boat that starts and finishes as defined. If a boat is believed not to have sailed the right course before she finishes, as defined, a protest is required for her score to be changed. Under the last sentence of rule A5 the race committee cannot disqualify her without a hearing nor score her DNF.

[2] When races comprise the fleet split into two or more flights or groups, the results of which are then combined, there will be initially at least two boats with the same score for every place. These do not rank as ties to be broken.

[3] Make sure your scoring system implements average-points redress (rule A10(a) and A10(b)) correctly. In standard format, the average is taken of all relevant race scores, including scores that will later be discarded. It has been detected that some scoring programs still default to an earlier (and normally over-generous) version of A10(a) which allowed an ultimately discardable score to be excluded from the race scores to be averaged. In a regatta, the redress score should reflect the full spectrum of the boat's other results, good and bad. The same worst score will still then drop out as a discard, **after** it has been used to find the average. However, the principle of that older system may still be appropriate for a protest committee to specify in its decision - to exclude from the races to be averaged not only the race in question but also any race before the race in question if the boat to be redressed did not compete in it (for instance, in a long club series). Where there is a separate qualifying series and final series (for example, with separate 'Gold' and 'Silver' fleets) the protest committee must be careful to specify exactly which races to include in the 'average points' calculation.

- Post final results for the race and update the series results, applying the discard(s) appropriate at that stage.
- At the end of the series:
  - Exclude the appropriate number of discards of 'worst scores' as required by scoring system or sailing instructions (exclude the earliest of two or more equal worst scores - see rule A2: however, due to previous changes to rule A8, no error occurs if it is not the earliest of two equal scores that is excluded)
  - Break any ties in series scores as provided by rule A8
  - Post the series results

Definitions

A term used as stated below is shown in italic type or, in preambles, in **bold italic** type

Abandon   A race that a race committee or protest committee *abandons* is void but may be resailed.

Clear Astern and Clear Ahead; Overlap   One boat is *clear astern* of another when her hull and equipment in normal position are behind a line abeam from the aftermost point of the other boat's hull and equipment in normal position. The other boat is *clear ahead*. They *overlap* when neither is *clear astern*. However, they also *overlap* when a boat between them *overlaps* both. These terms always apply to boats on the same *tack*. They do not apply to boats on opposite *tacks* unless rule 18 applies or both boats are sailing more than ninety degrees from the true wind.

Fetching   A boat is *fetching* a *mark* when she is in a position to pass to windward of it and leave it on the required side without changing *tack*.

Finish   A boat *finishes* when any part of her hull, or crew or equipment in normal position, crosses the finishing line in the direction of the course from the last *mark*, either for the first time or after taking a penalty under rule 44.2 or, after correcting an error made at the finishing line, under rule 28.1.

Interested Party   A person who may gain or lose as a result of a protest committee's decision, or who has a close personal interest in the decision.

Keep Clear   One boat *keeps clear* of another if the other can sail her course with no need to take avoiding action and, when the boats are *overlapped* on the same *tack*, if the *leeward* boat can change course in both directions without immediately making contact with the *windward* boat.

Leeward and Windward   A boat's *leeward* side is the side that is or, when she is head to wind, was away from the wind. However, when sailing by the lee or directly downwind, her *leeward* side is the side on which her mainsail lies. The other side is her *windward* side. When two boats on the same tack overlap, the one on the leeward side of the other is the *leeward* boat. The other is the *windward* boat.

Mark   An object the sailing instructions require a boat to leave on a specified side, and a race committee boat surrounded by navigable water from which the starting or finishing line extends. An anchor line or an object attached temporarily or accidentally to a *mark* is not part of it.

Mark-Room   *Room* for a boat to sail to the *mark*, and then *room* to sail her *proper course* while at the *mark*. However, *mark-room* does not include *room* to tack unless the boat is *overlapped* to *windward* and on the inside of the boat required to give *mark-room*.

Obstruction   An object that a boat could not pass without changing course substantially, if she were sailing directly towards it and one of her hull lengths from it. An object that can be safely passed on only one side and an area so designated by the sailing instructions are also *obstructions*. However, a boat racing is not an obstruction to other boats unless they are required to *keep clear* of her or, if rule 22 applies, avoid her. A vessel under way, including a boat racing, is never a continuing *obstruction*.

Overlap   See **Clear Astern** and **Clear Ahead; Overlap**.

Party   A *party* to a hearing: a protestor; a protestee; a boat requesting redress or for which redress is requested by the race committee or considered by the protest committee under rule 60.3(b); a race committee acting under rule 60.2(b); a boat or competitor that may be penalised under rule 69.1; a race committee or organizing authority in a hearing under rule 62.1(a).

Postpone   A *postponed* race is delayed before its scheduled start but may be started or *abandoned* later.

Proper Course   A course a boat would sail to *finish* as soon as possible in the absence of the other boats referred to in the rule using the term. A boat has no *proper course* before her starting signal.

Protest   An allegation made under rule 61.2 by a boat, a race committee or a protest committee that a boat has broken a *rule*.

Racing   A boat is *racing* from her preparatory signal until she *finishes* and clears the finishing line and *marks* or retires, or until the race committee signals a general recall, *postponement* or *abandonment*.

Room   The space a boat needs in the existing conditions while manoeuvring promptly in a seamanlike way.

Rule   (a)   The rules in this book, including the Definitions, Race Signals, Introduction, preambles and the rules of relevant appendices, but not titles;

     (b)   ISAF Regulation 19, Eligibility Code; Regulation 20, Advertising Code; and Regulation 21, Anti-Doping Code; and Regulation 22, Sailor Classification Code;

     (c)   the prescriptions of the national authority, unless they are changed by the sailing instructions in compliance with the national authority's prescription, if any, to rule 88;

     (d)   the class rules (for a boat racing under a handicap or rating system, the rules of that system are 'class rules');

     (e)   the notice of race;

     (f)   the sailing instructions; and

     (g)   any other documents that govern the event.

Start   A boat *starts* when, having been entirely on the pre-start side of the starting line at or after her starting signal, and having complied with rule 30.1 if it applies, any part of her hull, crew or equipment crosses the starting line in the direction of the first *mark*.

Tack, Starboard or Port   A boat is on the *tack*, *starboard* or *port*, corresponding to her *windward* side.

Windward   See **Leeward** and **Windward**.

Zone   The area around a *mark* within a distance of three hull lengths of the boat nearer to it. A boat is in the *zone* when any part of her hull is in the *zone*.

RACE SIGNALS

The meanings of visual and sound signals are stated below. An arrow pointing up or down (⬆ ⬇) means that a visual signal is displayed or removed. A dot (●) means a sound; five short dashes (▬ ▬ ▬ ▬ ▬) mean repetitive sounds. A long dash (▬▬) means a long sound. When a visual signal is displayed over a class flag, the signal applies only to that class.

POSTPONEMENT SIGNALS

AP

Races not started are *postponed*. The warning signal will be made 1 minute after removal unless at that time the race is *postponed* again or *abandoned*.

AP over H

Races not started are *postponed*. Further signals ashore.

AP over A

Races not started are *postponed*. No more racing today.

AP over a numeral pennant

Hours *postponement* from the scheduled starting time.

ABANDONMENT SIGNALS

N

All races that have started are *abandoned*. Return to the starting area. The warning signal will be made 1 minute after removal unless at that time the race is *abandoned* again or *postponed*.

N over H

All races are *abandoned*. Further signals ashore.

N over A

All races are *abandoned*. No more racing today.

PREPARATORY SIGNALS

↑ ● ↓ —

P
Preparatory
signal.

↑ ● ↓ —

I Rule 30.1
is in effect.

↑ ● ↓ —

Z Rule 30.2
is in effect.

↑ ● ↓ —

Black flag.
Rule 30.3 is
in effect.

RECALL SIGNALS

SHORTENED COURSE

↑ ●

X Individual recall.

↑ ● ● ● ↓

First Substitute
General recall.
The warning signal will be
made 1 minute after removal.

↑ ● ●

S The course has
been shortened Rule
32.2 is in effect.

CHANGING THE NEXT LEG

– – – – –

C The position of
the next *mark* has
been changed:

to starboard;

to port;

to decrease
the length of
the leg;

to increase
the length
of the leg.

OTHER SIGNALS

↑ ●

L
Ashore:
A notice to
competitors has
been posted.

Afloat: Come
within hail or
follow this boat.

– – – – –

M
The object
displaying this
signal replaces
a missing
mark.

↑ ●

Y
Wear a
personal
flotation
device.

(no sound)

Blue flag
or shape.
This race
committee boat
is in position
at the
finishing line.

Glossary

References are to rule numbers (for example, 27.3), appendices and their rule numbers (for example, C or E3.10), and sections of the Racing Rules of Sailing (for example, Introduction, Race Signals). Defined terms appear in *italics*. Appendices K, L and M are not indexed except for their titles.

Index

Page numbers in *italics* refer to illustrations.